To the memory of
Almamy Malik Yattara

LOUIS BRENNER

Controlling Knowledge

Religion, Power and Schooling in a West African Muslim Society

INDIANA UNIVERSITY PRESS
BLOOMINGTON AND INDIANAPOLIS

This book is a publication of

Indiana University Press
601 North Morton Street
Bloomington, IN 47404-3797 USA

http://iupress.indiana.edu

Telephone orders 800-842-6796
Fax orders   812-855-7931
Orders by e-mail iuporder@indiana.edu

Manufactured in India

Library of Congress Cataloging-in-Publication Data

Brenner, Louis.
    Controlling knowledge: religion, power, and schooling in a West African
Muslim society / Louis Brenner.
            p.   cm.
    Includes bibliographical references and index.
    ISBN 0-253-33917-0 (cl : alk. paper)
    1. Islam—Mali. 2. Islam and state—Mali. 3. Islam and politics—Mali. 4.
Islamic education—Mali. 5. Mali—Politics and government. 6. Islam—Africa,
West—History. I. Title

BP64.M29 B73 2001
297'.096623—dc21

                                                              00-063464

1 2 3 4 5 06 05 04 03 02 01

CONTENTS

v

MAPS

TABLES

ACKNOWLEDGMENTS

This book draws upon research conducted in Mali for over twenty years, but most intensively in 1987-92, when I was one of four coordinators of a collaborative research project on 'Islam in Modern Africa'. This project, funded by a grant from the Leverhulme Trust and administered by the British Academy, was co-directed by Murray Last (at University College, London), and by Donal Cruise O'Brien, David Parkin and myself (at the School of Oriental and African Studies, University of London). Research in the project was conducted in Kenya, Nigeria and Mali on several comparative themes, all designed to explore the changing nature of Muslim societies and Muslim institutions in the twentieth century. Several of these themes form the focus of the present book: the contemporary evolution of Islamic education, the emergence of Muslim voluntary associations, and the sociological and political import of urban Muslim youth.

This project was collaborative both in London and in Africa where local research groups were established to work on specific themes. A total of fifteen African colleagues were associated with the project in the three different countries, as well as additional local students and research assistants. By 1992 over thirty publications had been produced by participants in the project, and many more have appeared since.

This book is very much a product of the 'Islam in Modern Africa' research project. Not only was the research itself made possible by the generosity of the Leverhulme Trust and the British Academy, but the years of close collaboration with many colleagues provided a rich environment for a very fruitful exchange of ideas, which still continues. In addition to my co-directors, already mentioned above, I would also like to mention Elizabeth Hodgkin, Said Boumedouha, Stefan Reichmuth and John Edgar, whose untimely death in 1992 was much regretted by all of us associated with the project. All these persons made valuable contributions to the project, and also helped to generate the atmosphere of intellectual stimulation that was produced in our regular seminars.

I was joined in the Malian research group by Bintou Sanankoua, Shaka Bagayogo and Mamadou Lamine Troaré, who conducted research in their own right and also directed the research activities of the local research group which included a number of younger scholars. Soumaila Coulibaly, Kader Maiga, Tacko dite Oumou Maiga, Hamadoun Tolo, and Boukary Traoré managed to produce some excellent results in often very difficult circumstances, especially in 1991 during and following the events which led to the removal from power of Moussa Traoré and the birth of the Malian Third Republic. The reader will find evidence of their work throughout this book; their contributions to the completion of the project, and to my own reflections, have been invaluable. It is also gratifying to note that after the termination of the 'Islam in Modern Africa' project, Shaka Bagayogo organized a new research group, including most of the persons named above, and attracted funding for the support of further research on the theme of '*Jeunes et société au Mali*'.

I would also like to thank the many Malians who made this book possible by their continued cooperation during our various research activities in the field by giving generously of their time to talk with me and with other researchers. I cannot name all of them here, but I would like especially to mention and to thank Saada Oumar Touré, 'Abd al-Aziz Yattabary and Thierno Hadi Thiam, with whom I spent many hours and whose insights and observations as founders and directors of médersas provided essential guidance in my research. I would also like to mention the late Almamy Malik Yattara, colleague, companion and friend, to whose memory this book is dedicated. Almamy worked with me from the time of my first research visit to Mali in 1977, and although he did not accompany me so regularly during this research project as he had done in earlier years, we spent much time together and I always valued his insight and advice.

I also thank the Nuffield Foundation, the Jordan Foundation Bequest, the SOAS Research Committee, and the Leverhulme Trust for additional financial support between 1986 and 1992 which allowed me to make repeated field research visits to Mali.

The long delay in the appearance of this book can be attributed primarily to the necessity of my assuming administrative responsibilities as Head of the Department of African Languages and Cultures at SOAS from 1992-6. But this delay may have been fortuitous in allowing me the time to rethink some of the issues raised by my research, and especially to present and discuss them with various colleagues. In this regard I would particularly like to mention Jean-Louis Triaud and David Robinson, both of whom have provided me with the benefits of their own knowledge and insight over the years and also encouraged me in my work. In the last several years, their jointly directed project on Islam in colonial French West Africa has provided a stimulating forum for the formulation of many of my own ideas.

I am most grateful to David Robinson, Donal Cruise O'Brien and Jean-Loup Amselle for reading and offering their very helpful comments on an earlier version of the manuscript. I have attempted to incorporate their suggestions, but I must add, as is customary and appropriate, that only I am responsible for what appears in the book.

And finally, I would like to express my gratitude to all my friends and family, including my grandchildren, who over the years have tolerated my work habits, especially in the farmhouse in the south of France to which we retreat every summer. They have allowed me to retire into my room, close the door and get on with my work, when they would have much preferred that I be relaxing and playing with them. Perhaps from now on I will!

London   L. B.
January 2000

ABBREVIATIONS

AEEM	Association des Elèves et Etudiants au Mali
AIDC	Association Islamique pour le Développement et la Concorde
AMI	Archives du Ministère de l'Intérieur du Mali
AMJM	Association Malienne des Jeunes Musulmans
AMRAD	Association Malienne de Recherche-Action pour le Développement
AMUPI	Association Malienne pour l'Unité et le Progrès de l'Islam
ANM	Archives Nationales du Mali
ANS	Archives Nationales du Sénégal
APE	Association des Parents d'Elèves
CAOM	Centre des Archives d'Outre-Mer, Aix-en-Provence, France
CFA	Communauté Financière Africaine
CHEAM	Centre des Hautes Etudes Administratives sur l'Afrique et l'Asie Modernes, Paris
CODESRIA	Conseil pour le Développement de la Recherche Economique et Sociale en Afrique
CPLA	Centre pour la Promotion de la Langue Arabe, MEN
CTSP	Comité de Transition pour le Salut du Peuple
DCASM	Division du Contrôle et de l'Animation du Système des Médersas
DEF	Diplôme d'enseignement fondamental
DNAFLA	Direction Nationale de l'Alphabétisation Fonctionnelle et de la Linguistique Appliquée
ENA	Ecole Nationale d'Administration, Bamako
ENSup	Ecole Normale Supérieure, Bamako
FAEF	Fonds d'Appui à l'Enseignement Fondamental
IMRAD	Institut Malien de Recherches Appliquées au Développement
IPEG	Instituts Pédagogiques d'Enseignement Général
IPN	Institut Pédagogique National
ISASS	*Islam et sociétés au sud du Sahara*
MEN	Ministère de l'Education Nationale

PAI	Parti Africain de l'Indépendance
PSP	Parti Soudanais du Progrès
REMMM	*Revue du Monde Musulman et de la Méditerranée*
UCM	Union Culturelle Musulmane
UDPM	Union Démocratique du Peuple Malien
UNDP	United Nations Development Programme
UNEEM	Union Nationale des Etudiants et Elèves du Mali
UNJM	Union Nationale des Jeunes du Mali
USAID	United States Agency for International Development (abbreviated to AID)
US-RDA	Union Soudanaise-Rassemblement Démocratique Africain

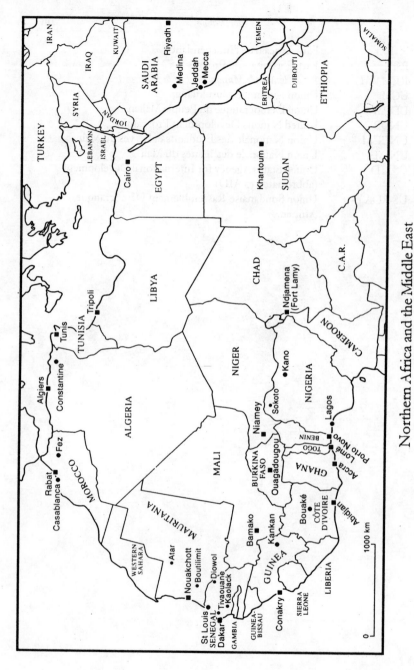

Northern Africa and the Middle East

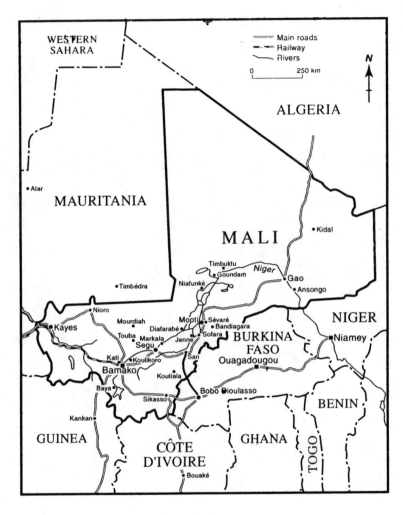

Mali

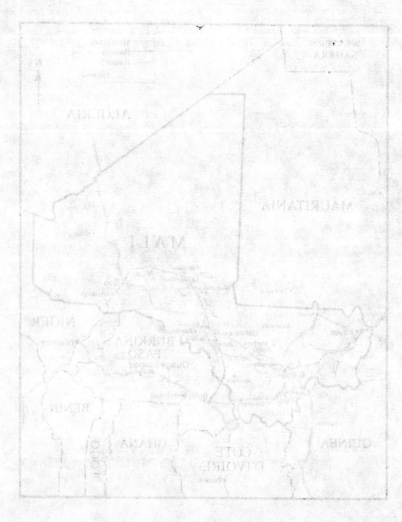

Mali

INTRODUCTION
DEFINING THE TERMS OF ANALYSIS

This book explores the history of a West African Muslim society in the twentieth century with specific reference to the recent evolution of Islamic schooling. A detailed history of Muslim schools is carefully documented in what follows, but this specific theme is intended to serve as a kind of 'focal point' around which to arrange the complex array of social and political factors which have informed the broader history of the society. A major aim has been to tease out, identify and analyze this complexity in order to rethink our understanding of contemporary Muslim history, but also with an eye to rethinking Muslim history in the *longue durée*. The analytical approach which has been adopted for this (overly) ambitious project is multi-disciplinary, and this chapter is intended to familiarize readers with the conceptual frameworks and some of the terms of analysis which are employed in the book.

The Muslim society referred to in the title of the book is the Republic of Mali, formerly the French colony of Soudan Français; chronologically, the study extends from the early colonial period to the early 1990s. Although Muslims did not constitute a majority of the population in this region at the beginning of the twentieth century, recent estimates of the Muslim population of Mali range from 70 per cent upwards. In fact, no reliable statistics on religious affiliation exist, but most informed observers suspect that the proportion of Muslims is continually rising, and that Islamization is continuing to make significant headway in the rural areas; urban centres have been predominantly Muslim since early in the century. Among the non-Muslim population a tiny proportion of persons (1-2 per cent) are Christian and the remainder participate in various forms of local, endogenous religious practices.

The history of Islam and of relations between Muslims and non-Muslims in this region is usually presented as a gradual but persistent spread of Islam, albeit in the face of considerable resistance. Such an approach is not completely without justification, especially when one focuses on the series of *jihads* that quickened the pace of Islamization in the nineteenth century. But these processes have always been much more complex than many analyses would suggest. The most rapid advances of Islam occurred during the colonial period, despite (and perhaps because of) the fact that French policy was explicitly, and often aggressively, anti-Islamic. During the first three decades of independence, the material presence of Islam became even more evident. The network of Islamic *médersas* (modernized Muslim schools) expanded at a very rapid rate, and from the 1970s, numerous imposing new mosques and other Muslim institutions, such as community and cultural centres, clinics and even pharmacies have been constructed which identify much of public space in Mali's cities, towns and even many villages, as Islamic. The adoption of Islam by formerly non-Muslim populations during the twentieth century has been entirely voluntary. And recent research has suggested that the mutual influence and the exchange of ideas between Muslims and non-Muslims during the pre-colonial period were much more extensive than previously thought.[1]

A Muslim versus non-Muslim problematic is not absent from the present analysis, but neither is it privileged. Rather more emphasis is placed on the religious pluralism of Muslim societies. For example, even if the Malian population were one hundred per cent Muslim, it would still be analytically appropriate to treat Malian society as religiously pluralistic since Malian Muslims divide themselves into various groups whose separate and distinct Muslim identities are often energetically projected and sometimes hotly contested. In addition, a small, but disproportionately powerful body of secularist opinion also exists in Mali; indeed, the Malian constitution proclaims Mali to be a secular state. But secularism can have no significance as a political position in a society where religion itself is not perceived as politically relevant. Most of Mali's secularists are themselves Muslims, and in fact their view that 'religion' can be separated from 'governance' in Muslim societies is not a twentieth-century innovation in this region.[2] Therefore, describing Mali as a Muslim society is not intended to imply that it is a homogeneous society, either religiously, politically or socially, but that people's perceptions of Islam inform in a significant manner the internal social and political dynamics of that society.

It follows from this discussion that the 'religion' referred to in the title of the book is the Islamic religion, although it is important to emphasize from the outset that this is not a study of 'Islam', but of the social and political dynamics of a Muslim society in which the Islamic religion is but one, albeit powerfully defining, element. Some readers may object to this assertion, for example, those Muslims who claim that all of life, including public law and forms of governance, should be subsumed to Islamic principles. Such an ideal is certainly embraced by many Muslims, but the fact is that Muslims often disagree among themselves about how to interpret the prescriptions of Islam. For example, as suggested above, some Muslims (such as Malian secularists) are fully prepared to live in social and political contexts which fall far short of what other Muslims purport to constitute an ideal Islamic society; in the past, some West African Muslims have sought to establish theocratic polities

---

[1] See, for example, Bréhima Kassibo, 'La géomancie ouest-africaine. Formes endogènes et emprunts extérieurs', *Cahiers d'études africaines*, XXXII (4), no. 128 (1992), pp. 541-96.

[2] For example, this distinction between the secular and the religious in Muslim society has been explored by J.O. Hunwick in 'Secular Power and Religious Authority in Muslim Society: The Case of Songhay', *Journal of African History*, 37 (1996), pp. 175-94.

governed by scholarly elites charged with interpreting and enforcing Islamic law, whereas other scholars have sought to avoid all political associations, arguing that the exercise of political power is inherently *anti*-Islamic.

The analytical framework adopted in this study is intended to highlight such disparate Muslim views and therefore places great emphasis on the social and political locus of Muslim expression. Muslims have been present in West Africa for centuries where they have occupied many different social roles, such as merchants, religious clerics, healers, diviners, scholars, rulers, warriors, etc. Available historical evidence demonstrates clearly that both among (and within) these social categories there have been a wide range of differing forms of expression and understandings of Islam. To take one very obvious example, the content of Muslim (like any other) political discourse is likely to vary considerably depending upon whether a protagonist is opposing or defending incumbent power and, if that incumbent power claims to be Muslim, upon whether it is seen as *legitimately* Muslim or not. If Muslims who have lived under the political authority of those they consider non-Muslims have not always felt called upon by their religion to challenge that authority, there has probably been no Islamic polity in West Africa, including those established by the *jihads* of the eighteenth and nineteenth centuries, which has not at some point been challenged by other Muslims with doctrinal arguments which question its legitimacy.

This analysis will therefore attempt to avoid any reliance upon normative notions of Islam, which seems to be the only tenable position from which to analyze how Muslims contest among themselves about the nature of Islam itself. Paradoxically, such conflict is as healthy as it is inevitable, since it is a direct result of the fact that Islam is a living religion that is constantly being reinterpreted and re-understood by those who adhere to its doctrines. Over the centuries, the tension between a committed belief in the eternal immutability of God's word on the one hand, and the diverse pressures and demands of ordinary life on the other, has produced many varied 'Islamic' solutions to social and political problems, without eliminating Islam. As one scholar has said, in writing about a very different socio-political context, '... a tradition is a process: it lives only while it changes'.[3]

This is the kind of change that will be explored in this study. During the course of the twentieth century, many Muslims have coped in various ways with the question of how to reinterpret the precepts of their religion, as they understood them, to conform with the rapidly changing conditions that they have experienced: subjugation by imperial powers, the economic effects of world capitalism, the political transformation into putative nation-states, and the many social dislocations associated with these processes, to name but a few. Only a few decades ago, many well-informed observers were predicting that the rise of secularist political regimes would relegate Islam to the private

---

[3] Jan Vansina, *Paths in the Rainforest: Toward a History of Political Tradition in Equatorial Africa* (Madison: University of Wisconsin Press, 1990), p. 251.

domain. The subsequent political resurgence of Islam in the form of what is often called 'fundamentalism' has proved these predictions to be, at best, premature. Of course, the contemporary rise of fundamentalist religious thinking is not limited to Muslims, which is an important point to emphasize. Some Muslims may be in the forefront of this trend, but they represent only one part of a broader social and political phenomenon that is present across the globe in many different religious contexts. The pertinent questions for any investigation of fundamentalist trends are about the conditions that have made possible their emergence.

This book does not pretend to address this kind of issue on a global scale, but it will explore similar questions on a local and regional level in West Africa. Fundamentalist ideologies, although they have their advocates in Mali, remain somewhat marginal. Nonetheless, during the course of the century Muslims have experimented in many ways with inserting an 'Islamic voice' into the dominant political discourse; or conversely, to appropriate concepts from elsewhere for application in an Islam-focused discourse. To take a very recent Malian example, following the granting of freedom of association by the government which replaced Moussa Traoré in 1991, there was an explosion of new organizations in the country, a significant minority of which identified themselves as specifically Islamic. The goals of many of these Muslim associations were religious in the narrowest sense. But some embraced much broader objectives and stated them in a language that borrowed directly from the current dominant political discourse, for example, from the ideology of 'development'. The Association Malienne des Jeunes Musulmans (AMJM) aims to 'unify the youth of Mali in Islam for a just and developed society'.[4] The Association Islamique pour le Développement et la Concorde (AIDC) states among its goals the aim of supporting, economically and financially, Mali's national development programs, and of 'promoting the Islamic path of development'.[5] 'Progress' is also a word that appears frequently in the names and objectives of these organizations. The concepts of progress and development were not part of the Muslim discourse (nor, indeed, of the French colonial discourse) at the beginning of the century, and their usage should not be dismissed as a mere play on words. The promotion of an 'Islamic path of development' suggests that the founders of AIDC have attempted both to address the issues of Mali's national development from a specifically Islamic perspective and at the same time to absorb the debate about development into an Islamic framework. Leaving aside any assessment of the viability of their proposals, their initiative says much about how Muslim perceptions of what is Islamic, or of the role which 'Islam' should play in society, are modified by social circumstances.

Another example of such change can be seen in the area of education. At the time of the French conquest, elementary Muslim education in the region

[4] *Journal Officiel*, 15 July 1991.
[5] *Journal Officiel*, 30 June 1991.

was provided exclusively by Qur'anic schools, and advanced religious studies by a form of personalized tuition (referred to locally as the *majlis*) in which students studied specific texts from one or several qualified teachers. By the end of the century these venerable educational institutions still existed, but tens of thousands of Muslim children were also attending Muslim schools, known in Malian French as médersas (from the Arabic, *madrasah*), in which religious studies were being taught alongside secular subjects in accordance with the same pedagogical principles employed in the state schools. This innovative transformation in Muslim schooling, in the face of considerable hostility, is a focal theme of this book, which will trace in some detail the early history and subsequent evolution of the médersa network of schools. Opposed on every side, both by conservative Muslims wedded to their received methods of teaching and by French colonial officials (and later Malian bureaucrats) who feared the political implications of these new-style schools, the pioneers of the médersa movement nonetheless managed to construct an extensive system of médersa schools. This achievement might justifiably be described as an 'Islamic path of development', although as we shall see, various political factors ensured that for a long time it was not publicly recognized as such.

In fact, the Islamic médersas were not formally and officially recognized as schools until the 1980s; the Qur'anic and *majlis* schools have never been so recognized. Generically, of course, all these are 'schools', that is, educational institutions which formally teach a specific body of skills and knowledge. Recognition has been withheld for both political and allegedly pedagogical reasons. The Qur'anic and *majlis* schools were much disdained by the French, and still are disparaged by many contemporary educationists, in spite of the numerous highly gifted and prolific scholars that they produced in the past. The recent recognition accorded to the médersas is based on a compromise requiring their curriculum to conform with that of the French-language state schools, which can only be accomplished by drastically reducing the number of hours devoted to religious subjects. At stake here, among other things, are competing perceptions of what constitutes a school and the possible purposes of its existence, issues with many ramifications. For example, the French may have disparaged the Qur'anic school and *majlis*, but they did not doubt their significance as the educators of men (almost exclusively men) who might use the knowledge gained in them to subvert French interests, which is one reason why they decided to set up their own 'Muslim' schools, the French médersas. On the other hand, when the first Islamic médersas appeared in the 1940s, they were opposed not only by the French, but by many Muslims as well who objected that the methods employed in these schools were not appropriate for the teaching of religious subjects.

This book is more an analysis of the changing role and concept of 'school' than a history of Muslim education as such. Analysis focuses more on how interested parties talk about schools and schooling (policies and criticisms, hopes, expectations, and disappointments) than on what actually happens in schools (curriculum and pedagogy). The gap between expectations and actual results, or between public rhetoric and reality, is often enormous. It is through a study of the discourse about schooling, and the social and political context which fashioned it, that one can gain some understanding of the conditions which made possible, perhaps even inevitable, the appearance of the Islamic médersa.

The 'knowledge' referred to in the title of this book is also a complex concept which takes its analytical point of departure from the work of Michel Foucault. Foucault's ideas about different 'levels' of knowledge, and how they will be interpreted for the purposes of this study, can be briefly introduced here with reference to the discursive environment in which schooling developed in Soudan Français and Mali during this century. There is firstly the level of discourse which includes all schooling-specific knowledge: the substantive subject-matter transmitted to students in school, the knowledge of teachers of their subject and of their craft (their pedagogical skills), combined with the technical and business know-how required to administer a school. Following Foucault, this level of knowledge can be referred to by the French term *connaissance*; *connaissance* links specific individuals to a more or less specific body of knowledge intended to serve a specific purpose. For example, when the first founders of the Islamic médersas began to launch their projects in the 1940s, they called upon specific bodies of knowledge about curriculum content, pedagogy, financial resources, etc. This kind of specificity is characteristic of *connaissance*. The second level of knowledge, or *savoir*, is much broader and non-specific. If *connaissance* is the knowledge employed by persons actually involved in schooling, *savoir* is the knowledge expressed by persons *talking about* schooling. *Savoir* is a knowledge that is constituted through broader discursive exchange, and it was in the formative context of such discourses that the project of creating the Islamic médersas first emerged and subsequently developed.[6]

Foucault also proposed the existence of yet a third level of knowledge, the *episteme* that exercises an even more fundamental influence on shaping the body of discourse:

The *episteme* may be suspected of being something like a world-view, a slice of history common to all branches of knowledge, which imposes on each one the same norms and postulates, a general stage of reason, a certain structure of thought that the men of a particular period cannot escape - a great body of legislation written once and for all by some anonymous hand.[7]

---

[6] For *connaissance* and *savoir* see Michel Foucault, *The Archaeology of Knowledge*, translated from the French by A.M. Sheridan Smith (London: Tavistock, 1986), pp. 15, note 2, and 181ff. Although the object of analysis in this book is quite different from that of Foucault, which was to trace the historical development of the sciences, his reflections are very pertinent to the problematic which informs this book, as will be explained below.

[7] *Ibid.*, p. 191.

The *episteme* is implicit; Foucault describes it as a set of relations which unites the discursive practices of a particular period. During the course of the twentieth century, the *episteme* underlying the Islamic discourse in West Africa has begun to shift as a result of both the European presence and the opening up of communications with the wider Muslim world. This shift is clearly evident when one compares the kinds of knowledge (both *savoir* and *connaissance*) which are associated with Muslim schooling, that is, the broader discourses and specific knowledges which are associated with Qur'anic schools on the one hand, and with the médersas on the other. Although both institutions are intended to fulfill a similar purpose in transmitting Islamic religious knowledge, they do so in ways which reflect very different 'structures of thought' concerning the nature of Islamic knowledge itself, and how and to whom it should be transmitted.

This shift can be described as a movement from an esoteric to a rationalistic *episteme*, the broad contours of which can be sketched here with relationship to concepts about the nature of Islamic knowledge (*'ilm*) and the conditions of its transmission. Within the context of an esoteric *episteme*, Islamic knowledge is perceived as hierarchical. For example, religious knowledge is seen to be superior to 'secular' knowledge, but hierarchical distinctions are also made among kinds of Islamic knowledge, for example between 'legal' knowledge that can be acquired simply through the intellect, and 'spiritual' knowledge that is acquired directly and without mediation of the intellect. Distinctions are also made between 'public' and 'secret' knowledge; all knowledge is not meant to be available to all persons. This hierarchy of knowledge is intimately related to the initiatic nature of its transmission. Islamic knowledge can be legitimately acquired only through personal transmission from persons who are qualified, and have been authorized, to transmit it; similarly, and significantly, 'spiritual' knowledge can be transmitted from deceased holy persons or even from the Prophet through dreams and visions, on the model of the revelation of the Qur'an to the Prophet. The acquisition of Islamic knowledge is also intimately related to devotional praxis; the very process of acquiring knowledge is intended to transform its possessor. Conversely, personal 'spiritual' transformation prepares one for access to the higher levels of 'spiritual' knowledge and to acquire ever more secret or hidden bodies of knowledge. Possession of and access to secret or esoteric knowledge is therefore closely associated with one's religious persona and ultimately with one's social status and possible political influence. This hierarchical structuring of knowledge and the initiatic form of its transmission tends to restrict the dissemination of Islamic knowledge to a very few specialists who occupy its higher and more 'spiritual' levels; the hierarchy of knowledge is therefore replicated in a hierarchy of religious specialists. Finally, reflection and explication which are informed by an esoteric *episteme* are deeply imbued with analogical and metaphorical forms of thought. This feature is particularly evident in the many esoteric healing sciences practiced by Muslims in which the words of the

Qur'an (the words of God) are manipulated in order to affect the lives of living human beings. Such analogical thought and their related applications derive from fundamental notions about the unity of God's creation and the power of His word; access to this power by a human being, and the ability to use it, is an excellent example of the kinds of knowledges and practices which are produced by an esoteric *episteme*.[8]

For Muslims operating within a rationalistic *episteme*, religious revelation and divine law are retained while accepting rationalist concepts of knowledge and its transmission. In this paradigm knowledge is theoretically available equally to everyone. Reflection and explication are based on principles of rational exposition as derived from divine revelation. Religious devotion becomes separated from the process of learning, and the individual's intellectual development is no longer associated with divine intervention. Qur'anic revelation is the ultimate guide to human behaviour, but humans are not seen to have access to further revelations. Of course, access to and control of Islamic knowledge continue to affect social status and possible political influence, but these qualities become detached from expressions of personal 'spiritual' development and religiosity.

As will be seen in the chapters which follow, these analytical distinctions are never so clear cut in practice as in theory; however, one of the hypotheses to be explored is that a fundamental epistemic shift has been taking place in Mali, driven by social and political change, which has profoundly affected the way in which Muslims see themselves and their religion.

Which brings us to a consideration of the word 'controlling' in the title of this book. The phrase 'controlling knowledge' can be understood in two ways, firstly, as a verbal phrase in which 'knowledge' becomes the object of the action of control by a purposeful agent who is consciously seeking to achieve a particular purpose by manipulating the content of a given body of knowledge (*connaissance*), for example in the development of school curricula. Virtually all the schooling initiatives and policies discussed in this book, Muslim and secular, were driven by the conviction that social behavior could be controlled through the knowledge transmitted in school, and one focus of our analysis will be the tensions and confrontations generated by conflicting efforts to control knowledge through schooling.

But the word 'controlling' in the phrase 'controlling knowledge' can also act grammatically as an adjective modifying the word 'knowledge', a reading which is intended to suggest that some knowledges are imbued with determining attributes of which individuals may not be consciously aware. The focus of this line of analysis will be on the broader social and discursive

---

[8] Further discussion of aspects of the esoteric *episteme* can be found in L. Brenner, 'The Esoteric Sciences in West African Islam' in B.M. Du Toit and I. Abdalla (eds), *African Healing Strategies* (Buffalo, NY: Trado-Medic Books, 1985); *Réflexions sur le savoir islamique en Afrique de l'Ouest* (Centre d'Etude d'Afrique Noire, University of Bordeaux I, 1985); and 'Sufism in Africa' in J. Olupona (ed.), *African Spirituality* (New York: Crossroad Press, forthcoming).

context of schooling and on the process of socialization effected by schooling. At this level of discourse knowledges are non-specific (*savoir*) and cannot be reduced to a subject in the curriculum but nonetheless produce the most significant socializing results of the schooling process. For example, the médersas and the Qur'anic schools may teach precisely the same Islamic subject matter, but they are located in very different social and discursive environments and socialize their students in very different ways. For example, successful médersa students are adapted to the modernized political economy in a way that Qur'anic school students are not; some of them have even entered government service. The controlling influence of *savoir* is therefore both empowering and constraining.

The ambiguity communicated by the word 'controlling' in the title is intentional. Knowledges can control and can be controlled, although the extent to which knowledges can in fact be *effectively* controlled by a conscious agent may well be questioned. This book certainly explores the dynamic produced by persons who persistently acted as if they thought it was possible to control knowledge. On one level this process was pedagogical, but it was also political, which brings us to a discussion of the remaining term in the book's title, 'power'.

The juxtaposition of the words 'power' and 'knowledge' in the title again suggest an influence from the works of Foucault. However, it is important to emphasize that the present work, although drawing upon Foucault's ideas for aid in conceptualizing its analytical problematic, is designed neither to test Foucault's theories nor rigorously to apply his method to a new body of evidence. For one thing, Foucault drew a sharp distinction between his own studies in the archaeology of knowledge and the history of ideas. The archaeology of knowledge focuses on discursive practices and *savoir*, a level of analysis in which specific individuals and agents do not appear; the history of ideas focuses on a study of *connaissance*, knowledge which is consciously expressed by specific individual actors. The present study is much more a historical than an archaeological analysis.

Secondly, Foucault's archaeological studies have been focused primarily on the internal dynamic of European culture, society and institutions from a perspective which analyses these as more or less self-contained entities free from external influences. However, a study of Muslim society in West Africa in the twentieth century presents a very different scenario in which local Muslim discursive fields are suddenly and peremptorily confronted by the knowledges and associated discourses of a non-Muslim imperial power. And the matter is even further complicated by the existence of other endogenous[9] knowledges,

---

[9] This term is used in the sense suggested by P.J. Hountondji in *Les Savoirs endogènes. Pistes pour une recherche* (Dakar: CODESRIA, 1994), p. 15: ' "Endogenous knowledge" [is] ... a knowledge which is lived by a society as an integral part of its heritage, as opposed to exogenous knowledges which are still perceived, at least at this stage, as elements of a different system of values'. Hountondji rejects the use of the term 'indigenous' as con-

which, although not the primary focus of this book, are nonetheless significant in the complex political equation that evolves. Imperial power, imposed in the first instance through the exercise of superior force, is not the object of Foucault's analysis; his conceptualization of power, as sets of relationships and strategies, does not seem even to allow for the existence of such a phenomenon, although an assessment of it is unavoidable in the present study.

Nonetheless, Foucault's ideas about power relations have much to offer the historian because they raise many provocative questions and open to examination many subtleties of social and political process that might otherwise be overlooked. There is no intention here to assess Foucault's work on the relationships between power and knowledge (*pouvoir/ savoir*), which he saw as inextricably linked, but only to highlight a. few relevant points. Firstly, the form of knowledge that Foucault explores in the power/knowledge relationship is *savoir*, the body of collective and anonymous discursive practices. Further, Foucault's approach to the study of power departs from most received notions, which he criticizes as based on a presupposition that power exists without actually exploring how it is constructed.[10] Many examples exist of analyses of the power of the state which imply, without questioning the underlying assumptions of such a position, that power is an inherent attribute of the state, rather like breathing is an attribute of the living human being. Power in this sense, according to Foucault, does not exist; 'power exists only when it is put into action.'[11] He provides the following description of power:

It is a total structure of actions brought to bear upon possible actions; it incites, it induces, it seduces, it makes easier or more difficult; in the extreme it constrains or forbids absolutely; it is nevertheless always a way of acting upon an acting subject or acting subjects by virtue of their acting or being capable of action. A set of actions upon other actions.[12]

This acting upon the actions of others is effected through what Foucault calls technologies of power; his questions are about the 'how' of power, how it is exercised in the specific circumstances of a whole range of power relations on all levels of society. The relevance of this approach to the present study can be illustrated by a simple example. The imposition of French colonial rule in West Africa can be adequately explained in terms of normally accepted notions of a state power which is manifested through the exercise of superior force. However, the appearance and subsequent success of the Islamic médersas, and the inability of the colonial authorities to control them, cannot be comfortably

---

noting something viewed from outside and classified as exotic, local, and without more general relevance.

[10] This discussion is based primarily on M. Foucault, 'The Subject and Power', in H.L. Dreyfus and P. Rabinow, *Michel Foucault: Beyond Structuralism and Hermeneutics* (London: Harvester Wheatsheaf, 1982), pp. 208-26.

[11] *Ibid.*, p. 219.

[12] *Ibid.*, p. 220.

explained by the same notion of power as equivalent to violence. One requires an analytical approach which can account for the intriguing fact that the Islamic médersas, while on the one hand resisting colonial authority, on the other hand were absorbing various pedagogical and organizational concepts and practices which were imported by the French. In reality, the médersas emerged in a complex field of power relations in which colonial preoccupations about control and asserting their own authority interacted with many other factors, including the agendas of the educational entrepreneurs who founded the first médersas, the motivations of their supporters and the families of their first students, the vested interests of the incumbent religious establishment who often opposed this new experiment, the relationship of the médersas to state-supported schooling, and so forth. The interactions among these elements constitute power relations in that each actor in the process was mobilizing a set of actions designed to affect the actions of others.

It is in this context of power relations that the relationship between power and knowledge is significant. Strategies and technologies of power are inextricably linked with knowledges, intimately intertwined and embedded in one another. The médersas have evolved in the context of a complex web of power relations and discursive practices, about politics, Islam, pedagogy, money etc. As this new institution emerged, it took on a particular form which was both the product of this power/knowledge equation, as well as a contributor to it, and which deeply affected the persons associated with the médersas, and many others as well. The schooling which takes place in the médersa consists of much more than the transmission of religious knowledge in a 'modernized' format; it draws participants into a discursive environment and an institutional ethos, consisting of particular practices, which are radically different from those produced by the Qur'anic/*majlis* environment. These are some of the factors that have produced an epistemic shift.

An analysis from this perspective suggests that the new understandings of Islam and the new perceptions of self as Muslim which are being produced in the médersa environment (and more widely in Mali) are the product of more than shifts in doctrinal interpretation, although these can sometimes be very significant. A new kind of Muslim 'subject' is being produced, in the ambivalent sense which Foucault gave to the word, that is 'subject to someone else by control and dependence', and 'subject' in the sense of being 'tied to [one's] own identity by a conscience [consciousness?] or self-knowledge'.[13] Such an analysis also suggests that the formation of this 'new kind of Muslim' is beyond the direct control of the educational entrepreneurs in the médersas, despite their many stated ambitions to that effect. For example, it is not uncommon (although it is also not universal) for the directors of médersas to disparage what they label as 'Western' forms of reasoning, analysis, and even forms of knowledge. 'Western' in this sense refers to what some Muslims

---

[13] *Ibid.*, p. 212. The French word *conscience* can be translate! into English as either conscience or consciousness; the latter would seem to be more appropriate in this context.

consider to be culturally loaded ideas and practices which for them are associated with European and American domination; the social sciences are often condemned with these kinds of accusations. Other forms of knowledge, for example medicine, the pure sciences and mathematics, are deemed culturally neutral. However, when the classical religious studies curriculum is broken down into separate subjects that are taught in a structured curriculum alongside science and math using contemporary pedagogical methods in classrooms of upwards of fifty pupils, the discursive and practical environment cannot fail to affect how religious knowledge is presented, transmitted and received, and one of the effects is to transmit it in a form which is conceptually compatible with other forms of non-religious knowledge. This process is deeply affecting for everyone caught up in it. It is here, too, that an epistemic shift is induced, operating largely outside the consciousness of those involved in it, including the teachers and directors of the médersas.

The knowledges that circulate in the médersa environment therefore create and control 'subjects' in both senses in which Foucault uses the word. Foucault's interest in schooling was evoked in his discussions about discipline and surveillance which focus on how the functioning of modern institutions like the school, the factory, the army, the hospital and the prison were informed by political technologies that created visible subjects who could be observed, classified and controlled.[14] It is precisely these technologies, developed at the micro-level of such institutions, which, Foucault argues, are subsequently amassed at the state level and which have made possible modern forms of totalizing governance.

His discussion of the school examination is particularly illuminating in this regard. The examination is accepted as an integral and necessary part of modern education by most participants in the schooling process; its ultimate aim is to distinguish among students: '... to define the aptitude of each individual, situate his level and his abilities, indicate the possible use that might be made of them'.[15] Viewed from a strictly pedagogical perspective, this process may seem relatively innocuous, but Foucault places the examination into a broader context of political technologies.

The examination that places individuals in a field of surveillance also situates them in a network of writing; it engages them in a whole mass of documents that capture and fix them. The procedures of examination were accompanied at the same time by a system of intense registration and of documentary accumulation. A 'power of writing' was constituted as an essential part in the mechanisms of discipline.

The examination, and the system of schooling of which it is a part, is therefore a locus of the expression of power because it transforms students into subjects (in Foucault's ambiguous sense of the term) and then classifies them

---

[14] See M. Foucault, *Discipline and Punish: The Birth of the Prison* (London: Penguin Books, 1991), especially the passages on schooling in the section entitled 'The means of correct training', pp. 170ff.

[15] *Ibid.*, p. 189.

according to success or failure. But the 'power of writing' and its associated 'mechanisms of discipline' are also learned in school and are also empowering, because they become valuable assets in other contexts of political relations, and are indeed indispensable for those who would aspire to a career in the state bureaucracy, the seat of political domination in a county like Mali where the vast majority of the population remains illiterate. In a recent study of schooling in Mali, Etienne Gérard has argued that literacy and knowledge of the French language, skills that have been transmitted by both colonial and postcolonial schools, are transformed into instruments of social control and political domination in the context of governance. One could cite many examples of how the bureaucratic state uses the 'power of writing', in the form of registers and official documents, to classify and control its 'subjects'; Gérard refers primarily to legal codes, enforced by the law courts and the police, and interpreted to the non-literate masses by bureaucrats or highly trained legal experts.[16]

Perhaps the most profoundly provocative of Foucault's ideas is that power and power relations are inherent to social relations, and not something imposed upon some idyllic, egalitarian social formation from above or from outside. This approach posits a kind of constant tension in society, on all levels and in all contexts, between a will to power whose aim is to create and dominate subjects, and a will to freedom, a refusal to submit. Power and freedom are inextricably entwined and dependent upon one another; expressions of power are evoked by expressions of freedom or resistance to domination, and power is constantly being challenged and (re)created on all levels of society, in family, community, institution, government, etc.[17] These ideas have exerted considerable influence on the work of some political scientists in recent years, to which we will refer in the later chapters of this book which are devoted to the postcolonial period in Mali.[18]

Schooling has been one of the most significant locations for the exercise of power relations in both Soudan Français and Mali. Whereas much of the 'subjectification' which transpires in schools may be relatively subtle, one fact seems undeniable. The bureaucratic bourgeoisie who inherited the mantle of state power and authority when Mali achieved its independence belonged to an educated social class that had been invented during the colonial period primarily through the process of Western schooling. Western schooling was therefore a valuable cultural resource; indeed, it was indispensable for anyone wishing to gain access to the perquisites and benefits offered by participation

---

[16] Etienne Gérard, 'L'Ecole déclassé. Une étude anthropo-sociologique de la scolarisation au Mali. Cas des sociétés malinkés', doctoral thesis (Nouveau Régime), Université Paul Valéry, 1992), pp. 8 and 44. A revised version of the thesis was published as *La tentation du savoir en Afrique. Politiques, mythes et stratégies d'éducation au Mali* (Paris: Karthala and ORSTOM, 1997).

[17] See Foucault, 'The Subject and Power', pp. 216ff.

[18] See, for example, the works of Jean-François Bayart and Achille Mbembe.

in the apparatus of governance and administration. It was also, and remains, a very scarce resource; even by the 1990s the literacy rate in Mali was still less than 20 per cent. These facts have led some observers to claim that the greatest impact of Western schooling in many parts of sub-Saharan Africa has been the creation of new forms of social inequality and new techniques of political domination, facts that are persistently ignored by those who advocate education as a neutral prerequisite for 'development'.

Whether or not one wishes to embrace such a radical view, the point does raise some profound questions. For example, the French clearly viewed the schooling they introduced into colonial Africa as a key institution for supporting their objectives of political domination; it was widely accepted among them that French-language schooling would create loyal subjects. Perhaps it did, but it also created a highly politicized group of critics who eventually led the struggle for independence. Once in power, the leaders of the independence movement in Mali sought to reform and 'de-colonize' this same educational system in order to 'liberate' the Malian people. By the 1990s, the results had been anything but liberating, except for the very few; the system was wasteful and ineffective, and the small percentage of students who actually succeeded in obtaining academic qualifications, at whatever level, found themselves socially marginalized primarily because they could not find jobs which conformed to their educational background.

These examples suggest that power relations, and their related technologies of power, often function outside the consciousness and intention of those involved in the schooling process and almost inevitably produce unanticipated results, except possibly in the narrowest pedagogical sense. The actual social product of the school seems to be beyond the control, and certainly the competence, of teachers and administrators.

The Islamic médersa emerged and evolved in the same social environment as French-language schooling, and like the French-language school, it has been a significant locus for the creation and exercise of power relations. The persons, discourses and practices associated with the médersas manifest all the tensions and ambiguities which Foucault ascribes to power relations: both a will to power (to create a new kind of subject) and a refusal to submit (to the successive hegemonic ambitions of both French administrators and Malian bureaucrats). The first move in this complex dialectic was made early in the century by the French with the introduction of an educational policy which was explicitly designed to 'domesticate' (*apprivoiser*) their new African subjects. The establishment of the French médersa of Djenné in 1906, which was later moved to Timbuktu, was similarly part of a policy explicitly designed to control Islam. It was not until the 1940s that a formal Muslim educational response to the French presence appeared in the form of the first Muslim médersas, from the beginning an amalgam of Middle Eastern and European pedagogical models, leavened by the imposed necessity of conforming to French administrative regulations about 'schools'. But as already mentioned, the French never formally recognized these institutions as 'schools', nor indeed did successive Malian governments, until the 1980s when the régime of Moussa Traoré, after almost twenty years of malign neglect, decided to integrate the médersas (now teaching nearly 60,000 primary school children) into the Ministry of National Education. This act of 'domestication' was undertaken in the same spirit as the French initiatives at the beginning of the century. The Malians were more discreet; they did not refer openly to their policy as domestication (*apprivoisement*), but close study of how these measures were effected, and the manner in which they addressed and referred to the médersa constituencies, make clear that many of the bureaucrats responsible for the implementation of these measures were intent upon 'creating subjects whom they could dominate', to paraphrase Foucault. This was, after all, the period when the Traoré régime was at the height of its power, and just before it entered its rapid decline.

From this perspective, the médersas represent a 'will to freedom', a search to escape, or at least avoid, the impositions of state power. That 'Islam', or in this case, Muslim schooling, should become a referent for such a political stance is by no means new in the history of the region. But the médersas were new, an innovative institution providing a new kind of religious training in a context and manner quite explicitly different from that provided by Qur'anic and *majlis* schools. For one thing, they employed Arabic as the language of instruction and began to teach it from year one; and from the 1960s, they began to offer secular subjects and French language as well, something which was never allowed by the French before independence. The aim was to provide a Muslim religious education to children while at the same time to prepare them to be integrated into newly emergent sectors of the changing political economy. Whatever the achievements or failures in this regard, the break with the past was in many ways profound and significant. It is best reflected in the nature of the médersas themselves: these are private, fee-paying schools, most of which in Mali have been founded by educational entrepreneurs who invested in them in part in the expectation that they would get a return on their money.

These few observations demonstrate once again that the significance of the médersas is not limited to the fact that they are 'denominational' schools, nor indeed to the particular doctrinal interpretations which they propagate, which in fact vary widely. Their more profound significance resides in their contribution to, and their association with, the creation of new kinds of Muslim 'subjectivities' in the context of evolving forms of power relations in post-colonial Mali.

The first chapter in this book presents an overview of relationships between power and knowledge in pre-colonial Muslim societies in West Africa in an attempt to establish a baseline for the historical analysis that follows. Qur'anic schools, of course, also exercised 'mechanisms of discipline' and produced their own kinds of 'subjects'. However, as already suggested above, the underlyng *episteme*, as well as the knowledges and practices which gave rise to the Qur'anic school, were fundamentally different to those which are associated with more modern forms of schooling, both secular and médersa. These two types of schooling (Qur'anic and 'modernized') produce very different kinds of 'subjects' who are subjected to, and inculcated with, very different technologies of power. If this process is neither conscious nor intentional, it is nonetheless not without significant effect. A person educated in the Qur'anic and *majlis* system is by no means excluded from participation in the contemporary political process, but neither is it possible to cite an example of such a person working in the state bureaucracy. By contrast, quite a number of médersa graduates are employed by the state, most of whom are, of course, also literate in French. If such employment is the aim of many students who are successful in their médersa studies, an aim endorsed by many médersa directors, few of them are prepared to admit an interest in 'politics', and even fewer are aware that they are engaged in a process of 'power relations' which constitutes a kind of political action 'from below'.

1

KNOWLEDGE AND POWER IN PRE-COLONIAL MUSLIM SOCIETIES

Muslim schooling and the esoteric episteme

The central focus of this study is the changing contours of Muslim schooling and of Muslim society in Mali during the twentieth century. The increasingly rapid shift during the latter half of this century from Qur'anic and *majlis* forms of Islamic schooling to those offered by the 'modernized' médersa provides clear and visible evidence of the kinds of transformations which have been taking place. These institutional changes in forms of schooling are but one manifestation of more profound and less visible shifts in the nature of power relations and, it will be argued here, of *episteme*.

A single example of how social and political change has initiated an epistemic shift in Muslim thought in West Africa will indicate the nature of the process which will be explored in this book. If during the pre-colonial period Qur'anic and *majlis* schools produced the 'organic intellectuals' of Muslim societies, persons educated in these schools today have been relegated to the role of 'traditional intellectuals' who might still enjoy sometimes considerable influence over persons in power, but who for the most part are marginalized from the institutions of political power.[1] The 'organic intellectuals' of late twentieth-century Mali have been produced predominantly by French-language secular schools, even though the overwhelming majority of them are Muslims. They are, however, the bearers of new forms of Muslim subjectivity in terms of how they understand their Islam, and of how they present and represent themselves as Muslims. The existence of *grands marabouts* who allegedly minister to the private and political needs of presidents and ministers, and indeed of ordinary persons, rather than negate the evidence that this epistemic shift is taking place, illustrates the tentative and gradual nature of the process. By contrast, the existence of the Islamic médersas provides tangible evidence that such an epistemic shift is indeed advancing. Despite the fact that the French language state schools and the Islamic médersas represent

---

[1] For 'traditional intellectuals' in Africa, see S. Feierman, *Peasant Intellectuals: Anthropology and History in Tanzania* (Madison: University of Wisconsin Press, 1990), pp. 20-1; see also his 'Struggles for Control: The Social Roots of Health and Healing in Modern Africa', *African Studies Review*, vol. 28, no. 2/3, 1985, pp. 73-147, especially Part III: 'The Healing Occupations and their Uses', pp. 105-31.

very different approaches to the curriculum content of schooling, the two institutions are closely related in many ways, particularly in that they have emerged in the same socio-political environment. One of the arguments to be developed in this book is that the discursive practices and forms of power relations which gave birth to the secular schools also made possible the emergence of the médersas. The médersa as an innovative teaching institution is therefore both the product of changing social and political forces and a potent vector for reinforcing the epistemic shift which is taking place and contributing to the production of new forms of Muslim subjectivity.

We can begin to understand how an esoteric *episteme* has exerted a formative influence on Muslim thought in West Africa in the past through an exploration of relationships between knowledge, power and schooling in pre-colonial Muslim societies. As indicated in the preceding chapter, an *episteme* is a kind of implicit world view or structure of thought which orders relationships among discursive practices; because the *episteme* is implicit, its structures can be implied only from an examination of social praxis and discursive practice.

Considerable evidence can be elicited to justify the claim that in the past Qur'anic and *majlis* forms of schooling in West Africa were informed by an esoteric *episteme*.[2] Much has been written about the structure and pedagogy of Qur'anic and *majlis* schools, which it is unnecessary to survey in detail here; what is important for our purposes is to understand more clearly the features of the esoteric *episteme*, and its implications for power relations. The reader will recall that among the defining features of an esoteric *episteme* is a hierarchical conceptualization of knowledge, the highest 'levels' of which are made available to only relatively few specialists. Knowledge is transmitted in an initiatic form and is closely related to devotional praxis. The acquisition of knowledge is progressively transformative: one must be properly prepared to receive any particular form of knowledge, the acquisition of which can provide the basis for a subsequent stage of personal transformation. Such transformative stages are explicitly expressed in the spiritual hierarchies of the Sufi orders, but they provide the basic framework for the transmission of all religious knowledge within an esoteric *episteme*.

All these features can be identified in the structures and methods of Qur'anic and *majlis* schooling, including the teaching of the Qur'an. The Qur'an, of course, is both the highest form of knowledge which God has revealed to

---

[2] The following analysis draws upon various previous publications, including L. Brenner, 'Concepts of Tariqa in West Africa: the Case of the Qadiriyya' in D. Cruise O'Brien and C. Coulon (eds), *Charisma and Brotherhood in African Islam* (Oxford: Clarendon Press, 1988); 'The Esoteric Sciences in West African Islam' in B.M. Du Toit and I. Abdalla (eds), *African Healing Strategies* (Buffalo, NY: Trado-Medic Books, 1985); 'Muslim Thought in Eighteenth-Century West Africa: the Case of Shaikh 'Uthman b. Fudi' in N. Levtzion and J. Voll (eds), *Eighteenth Century Renewal and Reform Movements in Islam* (Syracuse UniversityPress, 1987); *Réflexions sur le savoir islamique en Afrique de l'Ouest* (Centre d'Etude d'Afrique Noire, University of Bordeaux I, 1985); 'Three Fulbe Scholars in Borno', *Maghreb Review*, X, no. 4-6 (1985), pp. 107-17.

mankind and the first body of knowledge which is taught to young children. At first glance, this arrangement seems paradoxical, if not contradictory. However, the pedagogical methods employed are fully consonant with the principles of an esoteric *episteme* in which layers of meaning are revealed gradually as an individual progresses through successive stages of learning. Young children learn to recite the sacred text of the Qur'an by rote and without being taught its meaning. The ultimate aim of the Qur'anic school, although most children will not achieve it, is to commit the entire text to memory, in effect to make it one's own.[3] The pedagogical methods associated with this task are also intended to imbue the child with a wide range of appropriately submissive postures of respect (both internal and external) toward the Holy Word and its great powers.[4] The disciplinary régime of the Qur'anic school, about which much has been written, can be understood as integral to the aim of schooling at this early stage, which is to fuse the Holy Word into the very being of the child.[5] The Qur'anic school is therefore a first essential phase in the creation of a Muslim subjectivity which is achieved by nurturing both specific postures of submissiveness and a specific form of consciousness.

The meaning of the Qur'an is taught only at a later stage; translation, interpretation, and commentary (*tafsir*) are part of the advanced curriculum in the *majlis*. The curriculum of the *majlis* is structured around the study of individual 'books', texts from the various religious studies disciplines such as jurisprudence, *hadith*, and eventually *tafsir*, which the student will read under the individual supervision of a specialized teacher who will explain and comment upon them. As in the Qur'anic school, the acquisition of knowledge continues to be intimately associated with the religious or 'spiritual' transformation of the learner, with the religious *persona* of the individual. But as adults, advanced students are no longer subjected to the physical discipline so prevalent among the children of the Qur'anic schools but are expected to conduct themselves in a manner which indicates that they are worthy of receiving 'higher' forms of knowledge.

[3] Dale F. Eickelman in *Knowledge and Power in Morocco: The Education of a Twentieth-Century Notable* (Princeton University Press, 1985), defined Islamic knowledge as 'fixed and memorizable truths' (p, 167), and his study demonstrated the high value that Moroccan Muslims place on what they refer to as the 'mnemonic possession' of religious knowledge (p. 57). For purposes of the present study, these mnemonic practices and their associated values are treated as integral to an esoteric *episteme* which is being challenged by other concepts and practices of knowledge.

[4] G. Mommersteeg, 'L'éducation coranique au Mali. Le pouvoir des mots sacrés' in Sanankoua et Brenner (eds), *L'enseignement islamique au Mali* (Bamako: Editions Jamana, 1991).

[5] A classic literary and oft-quoted description of the disciplinary régime of the Qur'anic school opens Cheikh Hamidou Kane's *Ambiguous Adventure* (New York: Walker and Co., 1963). See also Lamin Sanneh, *The Crown and the Turban: Muslims and West African Pluralism* (Boulder, CO: Westview Press, 1997), ch. 6. For a parallel example of how African children were similarly 'subjected' in Christian mission schools, see V.Y. Mudimbe, *The Idea of Africa* (Bloomington: Indiana University Press, 1994), pp. 114-23, on the Tactics and Strategies of Domestication.

Because much of this description is reminiscent of Sufism, it is important to emphasize that the structures and practices of Sufism were derivative of the esoteric *episteme* and not vice-versa. Muslim hagiography is replete with stories of holy men and miracle workers in the past who made no claim to being Sufis. More fundamental than Sufism was the close relationship which was thought to exist between access to knowledge on the one hand, and devotional practices as a means of effecting 'spiritual' transformation on the other. Visible expressions of piety and the possession of religious knowledge were intimately associated with one another, as were piety, knowledge and certain forms of power, such as the performance of 'miracles' or the power to bless or to curse. Qur'anic and *majlis* schooling therefore produced particular kinds of 'subjects' in the form of a hierarchy of more and less learned (and more or less 'powerful') persons who, by employing their skills, knowledge, or power might be in a position possibly to influence the actions of others. This class of persons (almost entirely male) represented only a tiny proportion of the total Muslim population.

Over the centuries, this system of schooling produced many astute and highly prolific scholars whose scholarly expertise lay in subject areas that could hardly be described as substantively 'esoteric', such as grammar, rhetoric and law. Many engaged in closely argued legal and doctrinal debates. The existence of an esoteric *episteme* does not therefore eliminate more 'rationalistic' forms of discourse. However, when one examines how religious knowledge was transmitted and deployed in the broader context of power relations, especially the fact that the possessors of religious knowledge and of the appropriate religious *persona* were also viewed as having access to various kinds of religious power, the profound significance of the esoteric *episteme* becomes patently clear.

Even more so when one compares the qualities expected in, and attributed to, médersa-trained Muslim clerics in the late twentieth century, who have been schooled in accordance with pedagogical principles which derive from a more 'rationalistic' *episteme*. Religious commitment, and maybe even a certain form of religiosity, may be nurtured in such persons, but gone is any notion that they have access to special powers or to 'secret' knowledge; the pedagogical notions which prevail in the médersas are intended to make religious knowledge easily available to all Muslims equally.

Finally, it is important to note that the determining influence of the esoteric *episteme* was not limited to Muslim thought, but was characteristic of all pre-colonial societies in sub-Saharan Africa, as is evidenced by non-Muslim religious thought and practice throughout the continent. We cannot here explore how the esoteric *episteme* affected knowledge/power relations in non-Muslim societies, but its predominance among non-Muslims helped to reinforce its influence among Muslims, for example in the popularity among both Muslims and non-Muslims of Muslim healing practices based on the esoteric sciences. The social and political changes which were put in train during the twentieth century would begin to undermine this influence, and the esoteric *episteme* would begin to be displaced by more 'rationalistic' modes of thought.

Legitimacy, knowledge and power[6]

The following discussion presents an historical overview of how the esoteric *episteme* informed relationships between knowledge and power in precolonial Muslim West Africa. The discussion focuses on several specific aspects of Muslim social and political history in West Africa, especially on the complex interrelationship of legitimacy, knowledge and power in the various forms of Islamic socio-political organization which have appeared in the region in the past. For purposes of this analysis, an Islamic socio-political organization will be defined as a polity or social formation which is legitimized with reference to allegedly Islamic principles. The word 'allegedly' is inserted here because, as explained in the Introduction, certain of these principles are often the subject of contestation. At the same time, Islamically-based claims to legitimacy inevitably refer to certain fundamental Islamic principles, such as protection and enforcement of the *shari'a* (Muslim law), which claims in turn are based on scholarly access to, and interpretation of, the classical Islamic sources, such as Qur'an, *hadith*, legal texts, etc. But this is only part of the story. If claims to legitimacy rest in part on a demonstrable command of Islamic knowledge, they also rest on local social and political practices, and indeed on varying social and political strategies, thus producing a wide range of different forms of Islamic socio-political organization. Among these, one can identify a number of analytically distinct forms which have been historically significant in West Africa.

Firstly, there existed what might be described as descent-based forms of Islamic socio-political organization, for example, the *zwaaya* in southern Mauritania, the *mory* among Jula-speaking peoples further south, or the *toorodbe* of the Senegambia region. Descent-based social formations have been and are widespread throughout Muslim Africa; for example, scholarship and teaching have often been associated with certain families or lineages. But the descent-based groups, or 'Muslim lineages', referred to here are of special interest to this analysis because of the manner in which they employed Islam as a factor of social and political distinction in a regional political economy which was informed by genealogical or lineage ideologies and structured on the basis of inherited occupation groups and social status.

A second form of Islamic socio-political organization was the Sufi *tariqa* which was first developed as a self-conscious corporate group in the region

[6] The following discussion is based in part upon an earlier article, L. Brenner, 'Representations of Power and Powerlessness in West African Islam' in J.-P. Chrétien, *et al.* (eds), *L'invention religieuse en Afrique. Histoire et religion en Afrique noire* (Paris: Karthala, 1993), pp. 213-34.

during the eighteenth century by Sidi al-Mukhtar al-Kunti and which rapidly spread under the influence of his successors. The Sufi *turuq* became widespread and extremely influential in West Africa during the nineteenth century.

There was also the Muslim state, which appeared in West Africa in at least two analytically distinct forms: the first was represented by the early states (empires) of Kanem-Borno, Mali and Songhay, to which might be added such examples as the later emirates of the Western Sahara, in which political authority was retained by 'rulers' who were distinct from the Muslim scholars (*'ulama*) who advised them and legitimated their rule in Islamic terms.

And there were also the Muslim states, usually established as a result of *jihads*, in which the *'ulama* themselves assumed positions of political authority and became the rulers. The earliest attempt to form such a state in West Africa is usually attributed to Nasir al-Din in seventeenth-century Mauritania, but during the following two centuries a number of *jihadi* states were established across West Africa from the Senegal valley to Hausaland in the central Sudan.

Finally, mention should also be made of a phenomenon that might be described as the autonomous Islamic community. This category includes the small, self-contained Muslim communities which have appeared across time and space in West Africa in which Muslim leaders have attempted to establish a kind of utopian Muslim order isolated from mundane influences and temporal political interference. During this century, such communities have existed in Medina Gonasse in Senegal, and in Dar al-Salaam, near Gao in Mali.[7] Closely related to this form of polity is the Muslim 'free city' in which an urban Muslim leadership has sought to maintain the political autonomy of the city, of which Timbuktu is a prominent example.[8] The basic (and important) difference between these two kinds of autonomous communities is that the first seeks to isolate itself completely from the surrounding social and political environment, whereas the latter was often deeply involved in economic and other forms of exchanges with other communities.

These examples clearly demonstrate that West African Muslims have not in the past endorsed either practically, doctrinally or ideologically any one particular form of socio-political organization, but have experimented with several, depending upon the conditions and circumstances in which they have lived. What all these examples share is the fact that each form of polity was defended as 'Islamic' on the basis of 'knowledge claims' by either scholars (*'ulama*) trained in classical religious studies, or by 'mystics' whose access to hidden knowledge did not necessarily require such study, or (as was often the case in West Africa) by single individuals who possessed both these

---

[7] See Ronald W. Niezen, 'The "Community of Helpers of the Sunna": Islamic Reform among the Songhay of Gao (Mali)', *Africa*, 60 (3), 1990, pp. 399-423, and his 'Diverse Styles of Islamic Reform among the Songhay of Eastern Mali', unpubl. Ph.D. thesis, Cambridge University, 1987.

[8] See Elias N. Saad, *Social History of Timbuktu: The Role of Muslim Scholars and Notables, 1400-1900* (Cambridge University Press, 1983).

qualities. 'Islam' has therefore legitimized widely divergent forms of socio-political organization, and it is this variation which interests us here.

The concepts of legitimate Muslim authority which have informed these various polities are themselves complex and variable. Muslim authority could be vested in certain families or lineages and legitimately transmitted through inheritance, as evidenced by the existence of numerous Muslim ruling dynasties; and principles of inherited authority and blood relationship were of course crucial to the organization of descent-based Muslim communities. Muslim authority could also be accepted voluntarily through the willing submission of one individual or group to another; such voluntarist concepts of Muslim authority and social organization were most fully expressed in the Sufi *turuq* and perhaps in some autonomous Muslim communities, but the principle of an individual freely associating himself or herself with Islam, and of consciously submitting oneself to the will of God, derives from the very core of the Islamic message. And Muslim authority could also be imposed and maintained through the use or threat of force, a practice which was also legitimized with reference to the *sunna* of the Prophet and which was most often associated with the structures of the Muslim state.

Our aim is not to explore these concepts of authority as ideal types, but to employ them as points of reference in a broad analysis of the variations that have appeared in Muslim political thought and practice in West Africa. The discussion will focus on a prevailing tension in the West African Muslim political discourse between imposed versus voluntary and inherited forms of authority. This tension can be readily illustrated by, on the one hand, those Muslims who have advocated the position that because of its fundamentally theocratic nature, the fullest realization of Islam can only be found in the establishment of theocratic polities, often in the form of centralized states. Many such states have come into existence through the use of force, as evidenced by the series of *jihads* that have punctuated the history of West Africa. But even in those cases where ruling groups have gradually become Islamized, state power was expressed through tangible forms of domination, such as the levying of taxes, often backed up by the threat of force as the ultimate basis of the state's exercise of authority over constituent populations. In such situations, Islam became associated with the imposition of power. An alternative line of political reflection, however, has sought to distance Islam from those who wield power through force and even to present Islam as a refuge for the powerless. This kind of thinking is, justifiably, most often associated with the Sufi orders, but in fact ideas which seek to separate Islam, and Muslims, from the imposition of power by force have much deeper historical roots in West Africa than the Sufi *turuq*.

For example, the descent-based Islamic communities mentioned above, which may well be one of the oldest forms of Muslim social organization in West Africa, consistently distinguished themselves socially and ideologically from 'warrior or governing lineages'. The *zwaaya* Muslim lineages of southern

Mauritania distinguished themselves in this manner from the *hassan* 'warrior' lineages, as did the *toorodbe* from the *sebbe* in the Senegal River valley, and the *mory* from the *tun tigi* among Jula speakers. Various internal and external explanations have been preferred for these social distinctions. These include the subjugation of Muslim lineages as a result of defeat in warfare (the *zwaaya* in Mauritania),[9] the propagation of specific doctrinal arguments which proposed that a correct understanding of Islam required Muslim lineages to isolate themselves from politics (the Suwarian tradition among the Jula),[10] and the claim that Muslim lineages were established as a part of the founding social charter of certain polities (northern Ghana).[11]

The precise historical origins of such 'Muslim lineages' are still the subject of research, although it does seem clear that they emerged in socio-political contexts which were deeply informed by lineage ideologies which emphasized principles of inherited status, and where the regional political economy was organized as a collection of various hereditary occupation groups.[12] Among these occupation groups were those which claimed inherited rights to political power; male members of these lineages were warriors who bore arms and whose métier was warfare and governance (*hassan, sebbe, tun tigi*). The predominant (or at least the culturally defining) métier of the males in the Muslim lineages was scholarship and related religious occupations. From this perspective, 'Islam' was perceived as a kind of craft, the expert practitioners of which provided certain religious services (prayer, divination, healing, teaching, etc.) to both Muslims and non-Muslims alike. The Muslim lineages, *zwaaya, toorodbe,* and *mory,* therefore occupied specific socio-economic niches in regional lineage systems; their economic production was based upon a combination of commercial and/or agricultural activities with the provision of religious services. Like other hereditary occupation groups, the Muslim lineages constituted semi-autonomous polities with their own social structures, systems of production and reproduction, and ideologies, while occupying a specific niche in the wider political economy.

[9] See C.C. Stewart, with E.K. Stewart, *Islam and Social Order in Mauritania: A Case Study from the Nineteenth Century* (Oxford: Clarendon Press, 1968); A.W. Ould Cheikh, *Nomadisme, islam et pouvoir.*

[10] Robert Launay, *Beyond the Stream: Islam and Society in a West African Town* (Berkeley: University of California Press, 1992); Lamin Sanneh, *The Jakhanke Muslim Clerics: A Religious and Historical Study of Islam in Senegambia* (University Press of America, 1989); Ivor Wilks, 'The Transmission of Islamic Learning in the Western Sudan' in J.R. Goody (ed.), *Literacy in Traditional Societies* (Cambridge University Press, 1968), pp. 162-97.

[11] N. Levtzion, *Muslims and Chiefs in West Africa* (Oxford: Clarendon Press, 1968).

[12] For a discussion of this aspect of West African social history, with special reference to the history of casted occupation groups, see Tal Tamari, 'The Development of Caste Systems in West Africa', *Journal of African History*, 32 (1991), pp. 221-50, and her thèse de doctorat d'Etat, 'Les castes au Soudan occidental: étude anthropologique et historique' (University of Paris X - Nanterre, 1987), subsequently published in revised form as *Les castes de l'Afrique occidentale. Artisans et musiciens endogames* (Nanterre: Société d'Ethnologie, 1997).

Lamin Sanneh, in his historical study of the Jakhanke, demonstrates the central role played by classical Islamic scholarship and teaching in such Muslim lineage groups.[13] He also demonstrates that the 'craft' of Islam was widely associated with the efficacy of the Muslim esoteric sciences which offered clients access to supernatural protection, healing and divination.[14] The reasons why African Muslims developed these particular sciences and skills were several. Firstly, much religious practice in the region was addressed to the healing of both individuals and communities and to protecting them from misfortunes. The development of the Muslim esoteric sciences therefore responded to a pervasive religious and social demand. Secondly, the effective exercise of political power was also closely associated with control of sacred and secret powers designed to sustain both ruler and community and protect them from misfortune. Both Muslim and non-Muslim rulers sought the healing and protective powers of Muslim clerics. Indeed, Muslim protective, healing, and predictive practices gained considerable renown among all social strata, and ranged from the resolution of individual problems to the protection of armies from defeat in warfare. And finally, these religious activities were commercially profitable; Muslim practitioners, like others, charged for their services.

The contours of Muslim thought which evolved within the descent-based system were therefore the product of numerous influences, both internal and external to Islam. Islamic referents informed the self-image and the organization of these Muslim communities, but Muslims also responded to what others, often non-Muslims, wanted or expected from them. Much of this complex dialectic must have consisted of reflections or comparisons of allegedly Muslim versus allegedly non-Muslim attributes, qualities and characteristics.

If one of the favorable representations of Muslims to emerge from this context was as providers of religious (and social and health) services, there were also more ambiguous characterizations. For example, the hard-fighting and sometimes hard-drinking warriors, who took great pride in their exploits on the battlefield and who saw themselves as the only persons who could legitimately govern, often disparaged the Muslims as weak. Some Muslims, for their part, reinforced this idea with their own reflections on how association with political power was incompatible with true religion; they nurtured a kind of 'politically passive' form of religiosity, which nonetheless did not eliminate the possibility of pursuing political aims by other means.

Some insight into the content of this discourse which represented Muslim lineages as a-political, or as politically weak, can be derived from the existing literature. For example, John Ralph Willis has argued that the early history of the *toorodbe* lineages was as a socially marginal group, composed of a 'mass of rootless peoples who perceived in Islam a source of cultural identity'.[15] He

[13] L. Sanneh, *The Jakhanke Muslim Clerics.*
[14] See also, L. Brenner, 'The Esoteric Sciences in West African Islam'.
[15] John Ralph Willis, 'Reflections on the Diffusion of Islam in West Africa' in J.R. Willis

suggests that this identity was constructed not only through adherence to Islam as a religion, and the practice of the 'craft' of Islam, but also through the widespread derision of *toorodbe* by non-*toorodbe* as low-class beggars and former slaves. He traces the possible origins of the term *toorodbe* from the Fulfulde *torade* meaning 'to implore Allah' or 'to ask Allah for a favour'. Whether this etymology is valid or not, local proverbs collected by Henri Gaden, which Willis cites, provide examples of how the *toorodbe* were demeaned in the local discourse:

> *The Torodo is a beggar.*
> *The Torodo is the son of the calabash (the begging bowl).*
> *If the calabash did not exist, the Torodo would not survive.*
> *A Torodo is a slave.*
> *A slave need only pursue learning in order to be considered a Torodo.*[16]

These proverbs, recorded in Fulfulde (or Halpulaar), originated among the non-*toorodbe* Fulbe, members of *sebbe* (sing. *ceddo*) warrior and ruling lineages who, through their derision, emphasized their own dominant free status as rightful rulers. Willis cites a Pullo *satigui* who abused the Imam of Bundu with the words: 'You are nothing more than a Torodo; you have been created for nothing more than misery and servitude'.[17]

The Jula case provides an interesting contrast. Although all Jula considered themselves Muslim, the *tun tigi* carried their Islam very lightly, giving little more than lip service to their religious obligations. They drank heavily and participated in inititation ceremonies that differed little from those of non-Muslim religious associations in the region. According to Robert Launay, *mory* Islam in northern Ivory Coast was profoundly, and consciously, a-political, in the sense that the *mory* avoided participation in the politics of governance and consistently supported the incumbent political leadership.[18] Among Jula, this a-political interpretation of Islam was elaborated and doctrinally justified on the authority of a fifteenth-century scholar, al-Hajj Salim Suware. Launay and others[19] refer to a Suwarian tradition that not only counselled that Muslim scholars should distance themselves from 'politics', but explicitly opposed the imposition of Islam by force. Some *mory* scholars even opposed proselytization in any form, seeing Islam as the rightful heritage only of the *mory* lineages. Launay argues, however, that these religious views must be understood also in relationship to their socio-economic context. The Jula were not particularly keen on proselytizing Islam, he suggests, because they wanted to protect their

---

(ed.), *Introduction to Studies in West African Islamic History*, vol. 1: *The Cultivators of Islam* (London: Frank Cass 1979), p. 21.

[16] *Ibid.* See also David Robinson, *Chiefs and Clerics: The History of Abdul Bokar Kan and Futa Toro, 1853-1891* (Oxford: Clarendon Press, 1975), p. 13.

[17] *Ibid.*, p. 22, cited from A. Arcin, *Histoire de la Guinée Française, Rivières du Sud, Fouta-Dialo, Région sud du Soudan*, 1911, p. 69.

[18] R. Launay, *Beyond the Stream*.

monopoly on trade and cloth production. Similarly, that the *mory* scholars embraced the Suwarian tradition of the separation of religion from politics as a 'deep-seated principle' is not surprising, given their minority position within the population.[20]

Jula groups for the most part remained loyal to the Suwarian tradition, and to their status as Muslims by inheritance. They refused increasingly frequent calls to *jihad*, especially in the nineteenth century, which proposed to impose the authority of Islam by force, and only disappeared as a salient Muslim presence in the twentieth century when the general Islamization of northern Ivory Coast rendered their inherited Muslim status socially irrelevant. By contrast, Fulfulde-speaking Muslim lineages like the *toorodbe* became the preeminent leaders of the eighteenth- and nineteenth-century *jihads*, thereby actively and positively rejecting the idea that Islam should be restricted to a particular socio-economic group, or that Muslims could fulfill their Islam while living under the political authority of non-Muslims or of nominal and 'backsliding' Muslims.

A different pattern of historical development occurred in southern Mauritania. Abdel Wedoud Ould Cheikh, has explored the role played by Islamic principles in the transformation from a segmentary tribal society subdivided by status groups (warriors, clerics, artisans, griots, slaves etc), to the emergence of more permanent political structures in the form of emirates.[21] Ould Cheikh describes the emirates as 'embryos of centralised political power'[22] whose legitimacy was based upon an Islamic ideology. Significantly, Islamic doctrines and values provided a basis for both the tensions between *zwaaya* and *hassan*, as well as the means to mobilize these and other lineage-based loyalties in order to establish overarching political institutions.

Pierre Bonte has developed an alternative interpretation of the evolution of emiral authority, which he argues emerged not only without reference to the *zwaaya* but in opposition to Islamic values and as a result of the factional conflicts and struggles for hierarchical domination inherent to the 'tribal' politics of the Western Sahara.[23] In Bonte's view, it was these same conflicts which gave birth to the *zwaaya*, as certain tribes mobilized Islamic values in order to resist domination by the more powerful and politically successful *hassan*. The *zwaaya* tribes managed to use their Islamic expertise and esoteric

[19] I. Wilks, 'The Transmission of Islamic Learning', *op. cit.*; L. Sanneh, *The Jakhanke Muslim Clerics, op.cit.*

[20] Launay, *Beyond the Stream*, pp. 57-8.

[21] A.W. Ould Cheikh, *Nomadisme, islam et pouvoir.*

[22] A.W. Ould Cheikh, 'La tribu dans tous ses états', *al-Wasit* (Nouakchott), no. 1 (1987), p. 94. This article is the conclusion to his thesis.

[23] Pierre Bonte, 'L'émirat de l'Adrar. Histoire et anthropologie d'une société tribale du Sahara occidental' (thèse de doctorat d'Etat, Ecole des Hautes Etudes en Sciences Sociales, Paris, 1998). It is important to note that Bonte employs the concept of 'tribe' as both a descriptive and analytical concept, and that much of his thesis explores variations in the role of Islam and Muslim values in this specific socio-political context.

power to establish and then maintain their autonomy from the sphere of 'politics'.

However, for Bonte Muslim ideologies were often employed to obscure underlying political realities, as demonstrated by the groups known as *tiyyab*. The term *tiyyab* is derived from the Arabic *tawba* which connotes repentance and is associated with Sufi practice; *tawba* is the first step on the spiritual journey of a new disciple who renounces the material world in favour of the spiritual one. The *tiyyab* were former members of *hassan* lineages who, in the name of Islam, abandonned warrior codes and values. As repentant Muslims, they ceased carrying arms and surrendered their political and tributary rights over other subordinate groups and became the clients of the *zwaaya*. Bonte demonstrates that although the *tiyyab* explained their rejection of political power in the religious language of repentence and of renewed commitment to Islamic values, close study of their lineage histories reveals that transitions to *tiyyab* status were normally the result of a lengthy process of marginalization in local political struggles; in other words, the *tiyyab* were among those who had suffered defeat in the tribal politics of the Western Sahara.[24]

This example illustrates the role which Muslim ideology, and Muslim social formations, can play in responding to political adversity by providing an alternative route to social status in the face of political defeat; integration with a *zwaaya* tribe was a way to avoid political subordination to the *hassan*. This process also illustrates how 'Islam' could be deployed to engage in politics by other means, and in particular to compensate for political weakness. The fact that both *tiyyab* and *zwaaya* self-representations were based on a kind of 'politically passive' religiosity shows how certain forms of Islamic expression could become associated in popular consciousness with social marginality or political weakness. Similar themes have repeatedly appeared in West African Muslim discourse over the centuries.

The Mauritanian case is central to an understanding of subsequent Muslim history in the region and to the evolution of the Islamic political discourse. The distinction between *zwaaya* and *hassan* was not between Muslim and non-Muslim lineages. The *hassan* were Muslims, albeit not 'properly observant' Muslims, and both *hassan* and *zwaaya* agreed that the latter, as the retainers and guardians of religious knowledge and its transmission, should be charged with what Ould Cheikh has described as the 'management of the sacred'. This configuration suggests yet another permutation in the possible roles played by representations of Islam in the social and political landscape. If in a predominantly non-Muslim context one can speak of 'Muslim lineages' practicing the 'craft of Islam' by providing various religious services to Muslims and non-Muslims alike, in the context of a broader Muslim society, the former Muslim lineages become clerical or *maraboutic*[25] lineages; whose members act

[24] *Ibid.*, Ch. 9 'Pouvoir politique et mobilité statutaire La *tawba*', II, pp. 944ff.
[25] *Marabout* is local French usage for Muslim cleric.

as Muslim intellectuals. And it was these Muslim intellectuals, (primarily *zwaaya* and *toorodbe*), who in the eighteenth and nineteenth centuries would take the lead in some of West Africa's most significant social and political experiments: the emergence of the Sufi brotherhood as a self-conscious corporate group, and the series of *jihads* intended to establish Muslim states.

Both these developments represented efforts by Muslim intellectuals (*'ulama*) to organize society on the basis of Muslim principles under their own leadership, although their political orientations were quite different from one another. The new Muslim states were founded as the result of *jihads* that their leaders justified on the basis of their ultimate intention of instituting a political order based on Islamic law. By contrast, the brotherhoods were founded, at least ideologically, upon the voluntary association of followers, or disciples, to the religious Way (*tariqa*) of the *shaikh* or leader of the order. Of course, the appearance of corporate Sufism and the eruption of the *jihads* were not entirely independent of one another; the two movements were closely interrelated, and some of the most successful leaders of *jihads* were themselves Sufis.[26] But there were also fundamental differences between these two movements. Successful *jihads* resulted in the establishment of polities which had gained, and which maintained, their authority through the use or threat of force. Such states were legitimated with reference to Islamic texts, but ultimately their effective functioning relied on a monopoly of force. By contrast, no Muslim leader could build a polity founded upon the concept of a Sufi brotherhood through the use of force, because adherence to a *tariqa* was by definition voluntary. This is not to say that Sufi groups could not, and did not, defend their interests by force of arms; but Sufi disciples were not recruited by force.

Recognition of this fundamental difference in orientation is helpful in analysing and understanding the complex permutations of the Muslim political discourse as it evolved through the eighteenth and nineteenth centuries. Prior to the reorganization of the central Saharan branch of the Qadiriyya Sufi order in the eighteenth century by Sidi al-Mukhtar al-Kunti, adherence to a *tariqa* in the region was a highly personal matter which focussed on the private recitation of specific prayers authorized by an individual's Sufi superior.[27] Sidi al-Mukhtar transformed this predominantly personal and devotional form of Sufism into a self-conscious religious organization with rules for membership and a hierarchical leadership structure of defined statuses. The Qadiriyya-Mukhtariyya, as it came to be called, incorporated within itself commercial and

---

[26] Nor was this association between Sufism and and Islamic 'renewal' in this period limited to West Africa; see N. Levtzion and J. Voll (eds), *Eighteenth Century Renewal and Reform Movements in Islam* (Syracuse University Press, 1987).

[27] There were isolated Sufi communities in the region before the eighteenth century, but they did not survive for long, and their influence did not extend very far afield. See H.T. Norris, *Sufi Mystics of the Niger Desert: Sidi Mahmud and the Hermits of Aïr* (Oxford: Clarendon Press, 1990), and J.E. Lavers, 'Diversions on a Journey, or the Travels of Shaykh Ahmad al-Yamani (1630-1712) from Halfaya to Fez' in Y.F. Hasan and P. Doornbos (eds), *The Central Bilad al-Sudan, Tradition and Adaptation* (Khartoum, n.d.).

pedagogical networks as well as lineage ideologies (the Kunta held the highest positions in the brotherhood), and added to these a guarantee of salvation through the intercession and *baraka* of its founder and *shaikh*, Sidi al-Mukhtar. He established a set of 'spiritual' relationships (master/disciple) which were modeled on the kinship relationships of lineages, through which were transmitted both religious knowledge and *baraka*.

The success of the Qadiriyya-Mukhtariyya resulted in the extension of *zwaaya* hegemony over a large expanse of the Sahara, and eventually into Sudanic West Africa as well. Sidi al-Mukhtar's initiative was full of fascinating contradictions and tensions. On the one hand, he emphasized a voluntarist Islamic ideology which could transcend the lineage-based loyalties which predominated in the Sahara, while at the same time calling upon these same loyalties to unite the Kunta under his leadership. But perhaps more fundamentally, this was an experiment in establishing a political order that did not rely on enforcement through force of arms. At the centre of this Islamic polity was the saintly holy man who attracted followers to himself by his *baraka*. If this was not exactly an attempt to 'turn the tables' on the *hassan*, the qualities of the emergent Sufi community were certainly described as starkly contrasting to those of the warrior lineages of the region. Sidi al-Mukhtar described his brotherhood as the only 'pure' Muslim community of the age over which he did not impose his authority; rather people submitted to him by voluntary initiation into the brotherhood. He attempted to distance himself from all the 'warrior' symbols and acts of governance. He did not levy taxes; persons brought gifts which he redistributed in emulation of Muslim ideals of generosity and charity. He did not surround himself with pomp and panoply, but lived in simple, modest surroundings. He did not impose judgments, but mediated disputes. Nor did he take up arms, except (according to him) in extreme circumstances; rather, he used his curse to punish his enemies.[28]

The social and political organization of the Sufi order constructed by Sidi al-Mukhtar contrasted with that of the emirates, those 'embryos of centralised political power' analysed by Abdel Wedoud Ould Cheikh. Ould Cheikh's analysis of the career of Shaikh Sidiyya al-Kabir, the nineteenth-century disciple and protegée of the son and successor to Sidi al-Mukhtar, further illustrates how this Sufi approach to the organization of power and authority in Muslim polities was implemented.[29]

Shaikh Sidiyya returned from his lengthy sojourn among the Kunta as a widely recognized possessor of 'religious capital' in the form of his sanctity

[28] For an analysis of this innovation, see L. Brenner, 'Concepts of *Tariqa* in West Africa: the Case of the Qadiriyya', *op. cit.* See also A.A. Batran, 'An introductory note on the impact of Sidi al-Mukhtar al-Kunti (1729-1811) on West African Islam in the 18th and 19th centuries', *Journal of the Historical Society of Nigeria*, VI, 4 (1973), pp. 347-52.

[29] Abdel Wedoud Ould Cheikh, 'La tribu comme volonté et comme représentation : Le facteur religieux dans l'organisation d'une tribu maure, les Awlâd Abyayri' in P. Bonte *et al.*, *Al-Ansâb. La Quête des origines. Anthropologie historique de la société arabe* (Paris: Editions de la Maison des Sciences de l'Homme, 1991), pp. 201-38.

and his scholarship. The transformation of this 'religious capital' into 'political capital'[30] was accomplished by various means. Firstly there was the building of a local social base in southern Mauritania by creating a strong sense of unity within his own *zwaaya* tribe, the Awlad Abyayri. Such pleas for unity relied on a subtle balance between repeated references to the tribe as *jama'a*, a Muslim community based upon Islamic principles of law and legitimacy, and appeals to tribal values of lineage and genealogy. In fact, the concept of *jama'a* transcended lineage loyalties, as was evident in the kinds of relationships established between Shaikh Sidiyya and his many Sufi disciples. Initiation into the Qaidiriyya Sufi order, and the master-disciple relationships that this entailed, was a second aspect of Shaikh Sidiyya's strategy. Thirdly, he was able to employ with great efficacy his considerable skills as a mediator in local disputes. Ould Cheikh analyses a lengthy and complex case of compensation following some murders which Shaikh Sidiyya resolved and which was the single most important incident in securing his reputation in the region and within his own tribe.

Ould Cheikh highlights the paradoxical nature of this situation. Shaikh Sidiyya's status as a scholar and Sufi had been derived from his association with the Kunta, and was in no way derived from the Awlad Abyayri, although they were a *zwaaya* lineage or tribe. However, he could not have built up his power and influence in the manner he did without the social base provided by the Awlad Abyayri. Nor could he have done so except in a socio-political space that was devoid of centralized political power. 'He could not have played his role as mediator, pacifier, and protector of a sanctuary except in a space defined by the absence of a legitimate and recognized power'.[31] Indeed, Ould Cheikh cites a specific occasion in which Sidiyya argued against a proposal to appoint a politico-religious chief who would be empowered to impose the strict punishments of Islamic law.[32] Although he agreed with the claim of the petitioners that they were living in corrupt and lawless times, he argued that the empowerment of such a chief might well lead to increased anarchy and disorder and most certainly increase the suffering of the weakest members of society. It was not possible, he argued tautologically, to appoint a just sovereign in order to create a just society, because one was not living in a just society. But, as Ould Cheikh points out, such an argument was of course also self-serving; Shaikh Sidiyya's influence and political position were in part dependent precisely on the absence of centralized power. And, perhaps most significantly, Sidiyya's authority existed only insofar as it was voluntarily accepted. Neither his Sufi disciples nor his fellow Awlad Abyayri had the military means to enforce any of his decisions. Ultimately, Shaikh Sidiyya's success depended upon his religious *persona* as an accomplished Sufi, as a learned and holy man.

---

[30] Ould Cheikh refers often to theories and concepts developed by Pierre Bourdieu.
[31] Ould Cheikh, 'La tribu comme volonté ...', p. 236.
[32] Technically, the proposal was to appoint a ruler who would be empowered to impose *hisba*, the commanding of good and the forbidding of evil. *Ibid.*, p. 231.

It seems significant that the emergence of Sufi brotherhoods in West Africa was contemporary with the explosion of militant Islam in the region. Whereas both movements were part of an Islamic resurgence which affected the entire Muslim world in the eighteenth and nineteenth centuries,[33] one also needs to understand why local conditions made West African Muslims receptive to the new ideas which were being generated there and elsewhere. Clearly, some Muslims were beginning to reject the the constraints imposed or implied by a descent-based organization of society which in effect limited both the relevance of Islamic thought as a social and political charter and the scope of social and political roles open to Muslims.

The Sufi orders were not implicated in the early West African *jihads* in southern Mauritania and the Futas Bundu, Toro and Jallon. Indeed, it is arguable that many Muslims preferred the Sufi order as a model of reformed social organization to that of the state, which ideologically embraced the use of force in order to enforce Islamic prescriptions and to maintain political domination. During the nineteenth century, however, the orders became increasingly associated with *jihad* and the organization of Muslim ruling groups. This development reached its peak with al-Hajj 'Umar, who used the Tijaniyya order as a key element in organizing early support for his own *jihad*. Shaikh 'Uthman dan Fodio had employed his Qadiri affiliation in a much more subdued manner earlier in the century.[34] However, they both claimed to have received authorization for their *jihads* in visions; in other words, ultimate legitimacy for their actions came to them in an esoteric form, available only to persons of their own exceptional religious status.

Both men also played upon the classic distinction in the Muslim political discourse between power as exercised through force and power as exercised in accordance with the religious principles of Islam, a variation on the theme of voluntarist versus imposed authority. According to 'Umar, the Prophet Muhammad had appeared to him in a vision and proclaimed: 'Don't associate with rulers [*al-salatin*, the sultans], because association with them results in disloyalty to me.' 'Umar interpreted this message as one of the many signs which demonstrated his spiritual elevation to the status of *khalifa* of the Tijaniyya Sufi order in West Africa.[35] 'Umar's declared intention to avoid the sultans, those who allegedly exercised political power in a manner which was not consonant with Islamic principles, was an integral part of his effort to establish his own religious legitimacy. His project was based upon a particular blueprint of Islamic polity grounded in Tijani Sufism which presented himself as *khalifa* of the Tijaniyya order and as *amir al-mu'minin* of the Muslim community which he founded. For those who accepted his leadership, his authority came from God, the Prophet, and Ahmad al-Tijani, as evidenced by visions of the kind cited above.

---

[33] See Levtzion and Voll, *Eighteenth Century Renewal and Reform*.

[34] See L. Brenner, 'Muslim Thought in Eighteenth Century West Africa'.

[35] 'Umar b. Sa'id al-Futi, *Rimāḥ ḥizb al-raḥīm 'alā nuḥūr ḥizb al-rajīm*, I, 187, published in the margins of 'Ali Harazim, *Jawāhir al-ma'ānī* (Beirut, no date).

In the years immediately following his return to West Africa from the pilgrimage, 'Umar's successes in recruiting for the Tijaniyya were primarily among political dissidents (such as the deposed Saifawa in Borno and in the Gwandu areas of the Sokoto Caliphate) and among young, ambitious scholars (in Macina and in his own Futa Toro). His activities were never without opposition, but it was when he began his *jihad* that some Muslim leaders refused to join him on the principle that warfare, even holy warfare, was fundamentally a quest for worldly power. This opposition was hardened when later he declared the Muslim leaders of Hamdullahi to be apostates and attacked them. The suffering and destructiveness which accompanied many of 'Umar's military campaigns led to his being condemned by his enemies as an oppressive political tyrant.[36]

Consequently, 'Umar's legacy has varied in West Africa between those members of the Tijaniyya who have remained loyal to his religious reputation as a scholar and a holy man, and his detractors who have perceived him as an embodiment of oppressive political authority. In this connection, the emergence of the Hamawiyya movement is an illustrative example of how a particular Islamic ideology can be transformed to respresent specific social and political interests. The Hamawiyya was a branch of the Tijaniyya which was born in Nioro in the first decade of the twentieth century.[37] From a religious perspective, its adherents presented it as the 'true' Tijaniyya, the only legitimate line of succession from the founder, Ahmad al-Tijani. Politically, it was both anti-French and anti-Umarian, and it attracted anti-colonial dissidents and anti-Umarian Muslims, including many recently-converted Bambara in the region of Nioro itself. Mention of the Hamawiyya brings this discussion into the twentieth century, and it is appropriate to conclude this analysis with a brief discussion the fate of Muslim socio-political organizations during the colonial period.

If the late eighteenth and early nineteenth centuries witnessed a series of fundamental innovations in Muslim institutions, the imposition of European colonial power in the late nineteenth and early twentieth centuries brought further transformations in its train. Perhaps the most immediate and visible change was the reversal of fortunes for Muslim political authority; areas formerly ruled by Muslims were now under the political authority of non-Muslim administrations. This change affected Muslim state structures much more directly than it did the Sufi orders. In the French areas of West Africa, Sufi leaders were placed under political surveillance; some were even exiled, such as Amadu

---

[36] See David Robinson, *The Holy War of 'Umar Tal: The Western Sudan in the Mid-Nineteenth Century* (Oxford: Clarendon Press, 1985).

[37] For the Hamawiyya, see Benjmin F. Soares, 'The Spiritual Economy of Nioro du Sahel: Islamic Discourses and Practices in a Malian Religious Center' (unpubl. Ph.D., thesis Northwestern University, 1997); Alioune Traoré, *Cheikh Hamahoullah, homme de foi et résistant* (Paris: Maisonneuve et Larose, 1983), and L. Brenner, *West African Sufi: the Religious Heritage and Spiritual Search of Cerno Bokar Saalif Taal* (London: Hurst; Los Angeles: University of California Press, 1984).

Bamba, founder of the Mourides in Senegal, and Shaikh Hamallah, founder of the Hamawiyya. But these interventions, far from weakening their influence, served to strengthen the coherence of these respective movements and the resolve of their adherents, and the orders seemed to expand more rapidly than ever. In this situation, the leaders of the Mourides, the Hamawiyya, and the Ibrahimiyya (the Niasse branch of the Tijaniyya) took important new initiatives in organizing Muslim social space in a manner that often insulated Muslims from the direct impact of the decline in their political fortunes. They managed to maintain a relative political autonomy and eventually to develop working relationships with colonial (and postcolonial) political authorities, often acting as political mediators between them and the membership of the Sufi orders, while at the same time protecting their image as Sufi leaders whose authority rested upon the voluntary submission of their followers.[38]

The success of the Sufi orders in maintaining their relative autonomy in these changing political circumstances was reminiscent of the historical patterns we have been discussing. Their leaders managed to negotiate relationships with incumbent powers, based explicitly on the fact that they were Muslim communities, which allowed them a certain immunity from interference in their internal affairs. These relatively self-contained Muslim communities offered their adherents both political and economic security in this world and eternal salvation in the next.

Descent-based forms of socio-political organization also persisted into the twentieth century. Andrew Manley has argued that local colonial and postcolonial politics in Mali can best be analyzed in terms of inter-lineage conflict, and he has demonstrated how the Sosso and Haidara lineages in Segu reconstructed themselves as 'Muslim lineages' in the colonial period in their quest for political status and influence.[39] Jean Schmitz has developed a similar argument, demonstrating how lineage politics continues to exert a fundamental formatory influence on contemporary political conflict and competition in the late twentieth century.[40] The analytical comparisons he draws are not between warrior and religious lineages, as discussed above, but between territorial-based and clerical lineages. According to Schmitz, clerical lineages are founded on

---

[38] The political role of Sufi leaders has been explored in greatest depth in Senegal. See Donal Cruise O'Brien, *The Mourides of Senegal: The Political and Economic Organization of an Islamic Brotherhood* (Oxford: Clarendon Press, 1971); Christian Coulon, *Le marabout et le prince: Islam et pouvoir au Sénégal* (Paris: A. Pedone, 1981); and Leonardo A. Villalon, *Islamic Society and State Power in Senegal: Disciples and Citizens in Fatick* (Cambridge University Press, 1995).

[39] Andrew Manley, 'The Sosso and the Haidara: two Muslim lineages in Soudan français, 1890-1960' in D. Robinson and J.L. Triaud (eds), *Le Temps des marabouts. Itinéraires et stratégies islamiques en Afrique Occidentale Française, ca. 1880-1960* (Paris: Karthala, 1997), pp. 319-36.

[40] See especially 'Un politologue chez les marabouts', *Cahiers d'Etudes africaines*, 91, XXIII 3, 1983, pp. 329-51, which is a review article of Christian Coulon, *Le marabout et le prince, op. cit*; see also Schmitz, 'Autour d'al-Hajj Umar Taal, Guerre sainte et Tijaniyya en Afrique de l'Ouest', *Cahiers d'Etudes africaines*, 100, XXV-4, 1985, pp. 555-65; and 'L'Etat géomètre. Les leydi des Peul du Fuuta Tooro (Sénégal) et du Maasina (Mali)', *Cahiers d'Etudes africaines*, 103, XXVI-3, 1986, pp. 349-94.

pedagogical relationships between teacher and student and are reproduced through the recruitment of students and the exchange of daughters and sisters with the purpose of forming matrimonial alliances. These relationships are distributed geographically in networks which themselves are infinitely expandable, through the establishment of new schools or religious communities. Schmitz's work focuses on the reproduction of Muslim intellectuals as a clerical class, and he successfully illustrates the supple dynamism of the clerical lineages in organizing social and political space.

The French were very aware of the political significance of both the Sufi orders and of the Muslim educational networks in West Africa, but they were never able effectively to intervene directly in either. The Sufi orders seemed to thrive in response to the threat of political intervention, and the only direct attempt to address Muslim schooling was in the form of administrative regulations. By contrast, most local political leaders, whether Muslim or not, were systematically removed from authority, and the compass of their political influence was drastically reduced. Such influence did not completely disappear, but it was transformed and could no longer depend upon superior force of arms to enforce its will. Indeed, the tactics which Muslim leaders employed in these circumstances in order to cling to authority and influence further illustrates the themes under discussion here, as evidenced by the varied careers of certain members of the Tal family during the colonial period. Even before the arrival of the French, al-Hajj 'Umar's son Ahmadu encountered enormous difficulties in protecting his claims to the political succession of his father, but in this period, force of arms remained the ultimate deciding factor.[41] After the French had fully imposed their authority, Tal claims to leadership could no longer be imposed by force. The result was a kind of unpeeling of the layers of ideology to which Muslim leaders could turn to support their claims to leadership. Hashimi, another son of 'Umar who was now in Medina, came to be seen as the leading inheritor of 'Umar's Tijani Sufi heritage. Aguibou, his youngest son, tried to save his political authority by collaborating with the French and agreeing to be named King of Bandiagara, but he did not long retain this position and ended his political career in humiliation when the French abolished the post which they had created and to which they had appointed him. Seydou Nourou Tal, a grandson of 'Umar living in Senegal, assumed the mantle of a '*grand marabout*' who, on the basis of his reputation as a scholar and the influence of his name, acted on behalf of the French administration as a mediator of Muslim disputes and an assuager of Muslim discontent.[42] Muntaga, another grandson in Segu, managed in time to develop a firm

[41] See John H. Hanson, *Migration, Jihad, and Muslim Authority in West Africa: The Futanke Colonies in Karta* (Bloomington: Indiana University Press, 1996).
[42] See Sylvianne Garcia, 'Al-Hajj Seydou Nourou Tall, 'grand marabout' tijani: L'histoire d'une carrière (v. 1880-1980)' in Robinson and Triaud (eds), *Le Temps des marabouts*, pp. 247-75. For an excellent case study of the local rejuvenation of Tal family fortunes, see Soares, 'The Spiritual Economy of Nioro'.

political grip in that region, based upon his position within the Tal lineage and his status in the Tijaniyya Sufi order, but only because the French found his role to be useful to their own political purposes.

We can discern here the various elements which serve to make up the components of Muslim authority and leadership: scholarship, the *baraka* and religious *persona* which are central to the functioning of a Sufi order, the political and religious heritage of the lineage, especially as the defenders of Islam. But these elements which were formerly concentrated among the Tal, fragile as they may have been after the death of al-Hajj 'Umar in 1865, were now slowly being reformulated in response to the new social and political conditions which emerged in the colonial context.

The preceding overview illustrates the complex array of permutations that have evolved in West Africa between representations of Islam and expressions of political power and authority. Clearly, the voluntarist concept of political authority is no less 'political' than the concept of imposed authority; voluntarism expresses political aims in a non-political language! This statement, and the preceding discussion, may give the impression that the argument being developed here is to demonstrate how religious aims are consistently determined by social and political conditions. However, the reality seems to be much more complex, and can perhaps best be explored from the perspective of power relations.

The *tiyyab* renunciation of their *hassani* social and political status in favour of Islam might be interpreted in a manner that distinguishes analytically between religious and political domains, for example, that the *tiyyab* had recourse to religious ideology in order to escape the full impact of their political defeat. However, the preceding discussion has demonstrated that *tiyyab*, *hassan*, and *zwaaya* social identities were all produced within an historical context in which the religious and the political were constantly juxtaposed in relationship to one another. The *hassan* were defined as much by their Islamic laxity as by their status as 'warriors'; the *zwaaya* were the guardians of religious knowledge and authority, but they also tended to sanction incumbent *hassani* political authority. Inevitably in this situation, religious pronouncements had political implications, and political actions could not fail to have religious ramifications.

This intimate association between the political and the religious is also evidenced in the emergence of the Qadiriyya Sufi order under Sidi al-Mukhtar al-Kunti. The political (as well as economic and social) significance of the Qadiriyya is very evident by the early nineteenth century when the movement had reached the peak of its influence, but did this initiative on the part of Sidi al-Mukhtar begin as a 'political' project? We have virtually no detailed evidence about how Sidi al-Mukhtar began to attract his first followers nor precisely when or how his actvities were transformed into the grand project that it became. However, other examples indicate that there were at least two possibilities.

Firstly, that in a manner similar to Amadu Bamba, founder of the Mourides in Senegal, Sidi al-Mukhtar gradually built up a following of disciples and students who had come to him primarily for religious instruction and spiritual guidance which at some point reached a critical mass and was transformed into a significant social and political movement. Or, secondly, that his recognition as a Sufi leader as a young man had immediate local political implications so that those who flocked around him did so with political as well as religious intention, rather like the case of Shaikh Hamallah in Nioro. In either scenario, there is an inextricable relationship between religious and 'political' elements.

One perceives similar differences in the origins of jihadist movements. I have argued elsewhere that Shaikh 'Uthman began his career as a preacher who was gradually pressured over time to an increasingly militant position by the reactions of the political authorities to his activities. In other words, he did not begin his public career with the intention of launching a *jihad*.[43] The case of al-Hajj 'Umar appears to be somewhat different in that at a certain stage in his career, he began to plan a series of *jihad* campaigns against local non-Muslims.

Each of these separate and evolving situations and contexts evokes different Muslim discourses, and different representations of both Islam and Muslim authority, which also evolve in the context of shifting power relations. In some instances, a 'religious' initiative evokes a social response which can eventually assume a more salient political character; in other instances, political interventions evoke religious responses which are employed to mobilize social and political resources in reaction.

The variable elements which affect these permutations can be many and their interrelationships complex, but the study of such cases reveals how representations of Islam both produce and are produced by the dynamics of power relations in any given context. However, this is only one level of the analysis of power relations. The preceding discussion also illustrates the existence of a number of different 'kinds' of Muslims, or what might be called (following Foucault) 'Muslim subjectivities'. *Zwaaya* Muslims differentiate themselves from *hassani* Muslims, Sufis from non-Sufis, and so forth, and these varying representations of self as 'Muslim' are produced by social forces. The issue being posited for study is not about attributions of being 'good' or 'bad', 'proper' or 'improper' Muslims, as emerges so often from the discourse. The analytically demanding question is how society produces and reproduces *hassani*, *zwaaya*, Sufi, and other Muslim subjectivities. Or, to state the question more specifically, how is the 'Muslim subject' produced who willingly will submit himself to the authority of a Sufi master or a *jihadi* leader; or by contrast, the 'Muslim subject' who will vehemently oppose Sufism as a blameworthy innovation or reject *jihad* as 'un-Islamic'?

Among the many and varied social forces that contribute to the production of such subjectivities, schooling is among of the most significant, not only

[43] See L. Brenner, 'Muslim Thought in Eighteenth Century West Africa'.

in terms of the transmission of knowledge, but as a locus of power relations that creates Muslim subjects in the dual sense discussed in the Introduction: 'subject' as conscious self-identity, and 'subject' in the sense of being subjected to someone else's control. Islamic knowledge, who had access to it, how it was interpreted and how applied, was central to all the political permutations which have been discussed in this chapter. Social hierarchies and political relations were produced in consonance with an individual's or group's access to and control of such knowledge. Schooling produced both Muslim leaders (the *'ulama*) and Muslim followers. The attitude of complete obedience of student to teacher, or of Sufi disciple to *shaikh*, was one manifestation of this process; access to knowledge, and ultimately eternal salvation, was gained through humility, social submission, and even suffering. The ability of the *zwaaya* to resist the political domination of the *hassan* was based on the latter's acceptance of the former's claims to 'control the sacred' through their mastery of Islamic knowledge.

And informing this system of schooling, as well as all aspects of thought and social practice more generally, both Muslim and non-Muslim, were the precepts of the esoteric *episteme*. Islamic religious expertise, access to and control of certain forms of Islamic knowledge, were associated with access to esoteric powers. This social and religious environment was conducive to the elaboration of the Muslim healing and predictive practices, based on knowledge of the esoteric sciences. It was also conducive to notions about the powers of holy men and saints who could work miracles, protect rulers and soldiers, or alternatively use their powers to bring defeat or disaster to their enemies. The same social environment validated the efficacy of the devotional prayers of the Sufis and the intercessionary powers of Sufi *shaikhs*, and rendered both credible and acceptable the claims of leaders like Shaikh 'Uthman dan Fodio and al-Hajj 'Umar that the Prophet Muhammad had appeared to them in visions in order personally to authorize their religious and political projects.

During the twentieth century, following the arrival of the European colonial powers, much in this social and political context would begin to change. The grip of the esoteric *episteme* would begin to erode, challenged by the imposition of new power structures that ignored and denigrated esoteric claims to knowledge and power. The emergence of new forms of social and political dynamics would call for new institutions, among them new forms of schooling that would also distance themselves from the esoteric and begin to embrace the terms of a 'rationalistic' *episteme*. And these schools, both Muslim and secular, would contribute to the production of new 'subjects' and new Muslim 'subjectivities', possessors of new forms of knowledge which would become integral to a newly evolving form of power relations. It is this process which is the subject of this book.

2

MEDERSAS, FRENCH AND ISLAMIC

It would be difficult to exaggerate the emphasis placed on schools and schooling during the twentieth century by West African Muslims, French colonial administrators and postcolonial Malian governments. For Muslims, schools were the institutions through which essential religious knowledge was to be maintained and transmitted. For colonial administrators, French-language schools were meant to train a relatively small number of African auxiliaries who would assist in the smooth functioning of the administrative apparatus. But more importantly, the French were convinced that if future generations of African leaders (the children of chiefs and notables) were imbued with the values of French culture, and facility in the French language, then the future of their colonial project would be assured.[1] In postcolonial Mali, schooling was first seen as the institution that could 'decolonize' the African mind, and later as a panacea for the country's future development. Although each of these strands of thought and action could be explored separately, the purpose of the present analysis is to examine their various interactions and how each affected the other. The content and impact of policies and initiatives will therefore be exposed as the history of schooling in the region unfolds. We begin with early French efforts to intervene in Muslim schooling through the establishment of the French médersas.

Médersa is a French language form of the Arabic word *madrasa*, or school. The word médersa in Mali[2] has had two distinct historical meanings. The first schools to be designated as médersas in West Africa were established by the French in Jenne, Timbuktu, St Louis and several other communities. Although instruction in Arabic language and Islamic religious studies was offered, these

[1] For a general discussion of French schooling policies in colonial West Africa, see D. Bouche, 'L'enseignement dans les territoires français de l'Afrique occidentale de 1817 à 1920', thèse d'Etat, University of Paris I, 1975; David E. Gardinier, 'The French Impact on Education in Africa, 1817-1960' in G. Wesley Johnson (ed.), *Double Impact: France and Africa in the Age of Imperialism* (Westport, CT: Greenwood Press, 1985), pp. 333-44; and A.Y. Yansané, 'The Impact of France on Education in West Africa' in *ibid.*, pp. 345-62.

[2] The present Republic of Mali was administratively reorganised several times during the colonial period. In 1890 it was named Soudan Français, in 1902 Territoires de la Sénégambie-Niger, in 1904 Haut-Sénégal-Niger, in 1920 Soudan Français, in 1958 République Soudanaise, and from 1960 Mali. These changes in name were often accompanied by changes in territorial boundaries. In the present text the territory will be referred to as Soudan before 1960, and as Mali after.

schools were meant to serve the objectives of French colonial policy; they were a French invention which had been developed first in Algeria and were entirely dependent on the French administration.

From the mid-1940s a quite different form of médersa appeared, created through the initiative of African Muslims who wished to provide religious schooling to Muslim children employing reformed pedagogical methods. These schools were referred to by their founders in Arabic as *madaris* (pl. of *madrasa*), or as médersas in the French rendering, although the French resolutely refused to refer to them officially as such. For political reasons, the French consistently referred officially to the Islamic médersas as Qur'anic schools, although these two institutions differed from one another in many fundamental ways. Indeed, both the French and the Islamic médersas posed a serious and intentional challenge to time-honored local forms of Qur'anic and *majlis* schooling, although their objectives were profoundly different: the African Muslims saw themselves as nurturing Islam while the French were seeking to limit and control its influence. Although the adoption in this study of the respective French and Arabic terms of médersa and *madrasa* might effectively reflect the many significant differences which distinguish these two institutions, it might also lead to confusion since the French usage has permeated the French-language discourse in Soudan and Mali. The French form has therefore been retained and the differences between the two kinds of schools have been indicated by referring to them respectively as French and Islamic médersas.

The French médersas in Soudan never enrolled a significant number of students and were minor and somewhat peripheral colonial institutions whose historical influence is barely discernible. However, we begin our study with them because their early history clearly demonstrates how the French intended to employ allegedly Islamic schooling as a means of dominating their Muslim colonial subjects. Many official policies, as well as unofficial colonial attitudes, towards Muslims and Islam were formulated with reference to the French médersas, many of which persisted with only slight modification into the postcolonial period. Furthermore, whereas it would be an exaggeration to assert that the early founders of the Islamic médersas drew inspiration for their projects of educational reform from the French médersas, it is true that some of them were encouraged to think that the French might endorse their initiatives because of the existence and publicly stated objectives of the French médersas. Official endorsement of the Catholic mission schools in Soudan gave further cause to believe that similarly organized Muslim schools might be accepted as contributing to schooling in the colony.

This was not to be the case, however. After much political wrangling, the French found a bureaucratic loophole that enabled them to avoid granting the first Islamic médersas the same status as the Catholic schools. They refused to recognize the Islamic médersas as 'educational establishments' and classified them as Qur'anic schools, which under existing legislation were severely restricted in what they could teach. What the French wanted to avoid at all costs was the evolution of effective Islamic schooling under the direct and independent control of Muslim administrators and teachers.

The brief discussion of the French médersas that follows is intended to illustrate the evolution of official thinking about the relationship between Islam and schooling in the early colonial period that subsequently would inform the ways in which the administration responded to the appearance of the first Islamic médersas in the 1940s. We begin with a chronological presentation of policy statements.

The French médersas

The contours of French médersa policy. The first French médersa in West Africa was founded in Jenne in 1906; its aims were to 'develop higher Muslim education and train the teachers of Qur'anic schools', as well as 'to teach an élite of young Muslims how to speak and write in French and at the same time to give them proper views on the civilising role of France in Africa'.[3] The Governor General of French West Africa boldly asserted that the new médersa would be 'our most effective answer to Islamic propaganda'.[4] In 1910 his successor William Ponty, elaborated on the kind of thinking which was meant to justify this sanguine opinion:

Everyone knows that the study of French is the most effective cure one can employ against [religious] fanaticism, and experience teaches us that Muslims who know our language are less imbued with prejudice than those who know only Arabic.[5]

In 1908 a second médersa was opened in St Louis, in Senegal,[6] and in 1910 a third was opened in Timbuktu, in part because the one in Jenne had failed to attract an adequate number of students from the region, especially around Timbuktu.[7] On this occasion, Governor Clozel of Soudan expressed the administration's objectives for the médersas as follows:

(1) to exercise an indirect control over the activities of the indigenous educators of Timbuktu;
(2) to attract [*attirer*] to French culture the young persons of a milieu which is closed to the influence of France, using the lure (appât) of their own

[3] ANS, J 94, Arrêté, 4 July 1906, cited in Christopher Harrison, *France and Islam in West Africa, 1860-1960* (Cambridge University Press, 1988), p. 62. Harrison's book provides a useful overview of early médersa policy in French West Africa, but also see Bouche, 'L'enseignement', Ch. 17: 'Ecoles coraniques et médersas (1903-1920), and Alice L Conklin, *A Mission to Civilize: The Republican Idea of Empire in France and West Africa, 1895-1930* (Stanford University Press, 1997), pp. 130ff.
[4] ANSOM, Soudan I/11, Rapport politique AOF, 2ème trimestre, 1906, cited in Harrison, p. 62.
[5] 'Circulaire de William Ponty, du 30 août 1910', *L'Afrique Française. Bulletin du Comité de l'Afrique française et du Comité du Maroc*, 1910, p. 341.
[6] See Harrison, pp. 63-4, and Mamadou Ndiaye, *L'enseignement arabo-islamique au Sénégal* (Istanbul: Centre de Recherches sur l'Histoire, l'Art et la Culture Islamiques, 1985), ch. VI.
[7] A report shows 30 students in the Jenne médersa in 1907, but does not indicate their provenance. ANM, 1-G-114 FA: Ecoles coraniques Djenné, 1907.

traditional culture – that is, Muslim education;

(3) to domesticate [*apprivoiser*] these young people, and even the entire population, and to familiarise them with the institution of French education.[8]

The Timbuktu médersa opened early in 1911 with thirty students selected from the families of 'notables'. Before the beginning of classes, the new director, named in archival documents simply as Mohamed Ali, spent several months visiting local Qur'anic schools in order to become acquainted with the Muslim clerics in the city and to inform himself about their 'mentality and their personal disposition toward French policy'.[9] Within only a few months of opening the médersa, Mohamed Ali introduced a course in elementary French, an initiative that was apparently met with indifference from both parents and local clerics. In 1913 the Jenne médersa was closed,[10] and its director and twelve of its best students were transferred to the Timbuktu médersa that was now officially named the Sankoré Médersa in an effort to associate it with the renowned university mosque. The idea that the Timbuktu médersa was the legitimate heir to the intellectual heritage of the Sankoré mosque remained alive in the minds of some French administrators for many years. In 1914 instruction in the French language became an official part of the curriculum.

All of these developments were in accordance with the objectives outlined by Governor Clozel in 1910, which he himself described as uniquely political and not pedagogical,[11] and which he reiterated in 1912 in the following manner:

Our goal is not to raise the level of Arabic studies, which is rather low in our *maraboutic* schools, nor to finance Muslim religious education. We are simply proposing to control indirectly the activities of the indigenous educators of Timbuktu and to introduce a French influence into the intellectual formation of their young pupils.[12]

In 1921 the Inspector of Education for French West Africa summarized these policies in the following manner:

The médersas are Muslim educational establishments designed, in principle, to divert to the profit of French policy the influence that the *marabouts* exercise over the Muslim populations. The médersas are meant to dissipate the pretensions of the Muslim world against our civilisation. To this effect, they train interpreters,

[8] Letter no. 940/B of 12 Oct. 1910, cited in ANM, 1-G-72 FR: B. Fadiga, Rapport sur la Médersa de Tombouctou, Feb. 1935.

[9] ANM, 1-G-72 FR: B. Fadiga, Rapport sur la Médersa de Tombouctou, Feb. 1935.

[10] Harrison, p. 109, cites a report that claims the Jenne médersa was closed because it had failed to 'purify Islam' (ANS, 15 G 103, Rapport sur la politique musulmane suivie par le cercle de Djenné pendant l'année 1913). Bouche, 'L'enseignement', pp. 728-32, describes the Jenne médersa as a disastrous.failure in every respect.

[11] See Harrison, p. 102.

[12] ANM, 1-G-72 FR: Quoted in letter from the Director, Ecole Régionale de Tombouctou to the Gouvernor of Soudan Français, 25 Feb. 1936.

secretaries for the Muslim courts, etc. ... and they develop advanced Qur'anic studies while giving the students a proper view of the civilising rôle of France.[13]

The original policies which governed the French médersas were therefore intended to subvert indigenous Islamic education, to infuse a selected group of young people (especially the sons of chiefs and notables) with French ideology, and to train a bilingual Arabic/French-speaking cadre of junior administrative personnel. These policies would later be described as the provision of French education 'under the guise of studying Arabic'.[14] The question of their efficacy, however, was a matter of considerable disagreement. Some subsequent administrators argued that Clozel's policies had 'put the Qur'anic schools to sleep ... and dealt them a mortal blow'.[15] Others claimed that the médersa had itself 'been sleeping' for many years, and that the education service had fallen into the habit of ignoring its existence.[16] These observations were offered in the mid-1930s, when the role and even existence of the Timbuktu médersa became the object of serious debate.

This debate, which was at its height between 1935 and 1940, emerged from disagreements about how specifically to define, and then achieve, the political objectives of the Timbuktu médersa. The seeds of this dispute were actually planted in 1917, following a visit by Paul Marty to Timbuktu, when he recommended that the médersa should seek primarily to recruit children from the families of nomadic chiefs residing in regions neighboring on Timbuktu; Clozel's intention had been to attract the sedentary Songhay populations to the médersa. Marty was at this time Director of Muslim Affairs in Dakar; in his opinion, 'médersas were an error in black Africa'[17] because with few exceptions black Africans were only superficially Muslim and largely ignorant of their religion. No improvement in their knowledge of Islam could possibly work to the benefit of French interests, and their children should be oriented toward French-language secular schools. The true Muslims were 'white', and it was they who should be the target of a policy which would 'lure' them into an appreciation of French cultural values by means of a carefully planned and controlled curriculum of Arabic and Islamic religious studies.

Marty's views juxtaposed an analysis of Islam with what was a prevalent attitude among French administrators about the political import of ethnicity and race, and new policies were crystallized around the idea that 'black Islam' differed fundamentally from 'white Islam'. From 1917 'ethnic' and 'racial' considerations became an increasingly important aspect of recruitment policy for the Timbuktu médersa and of Islamic policy in general. Emphasis was to be placed on attracting to the médersa the children of aristocratic nomadic

---

[13] *Ibid.*

[14] ANM, 1-G-72 FR: April 1935 Bulletin d'inspection, Médersa de Tombouctou.

[15] ANM, 1-G-72 FR: Letter from *commandant de cercle* Bertrand to the Governor of Soudan, 10 Nov. 1937.

[16] ANM, 1-G-72 FR: Bulletin d'inspection, Jan. 1936.

[17] Cited by Harrison, p. 109: ANS J 94, P. Marty, La médersa de Djenné, 16 June 1917.

families who 'were destined to lead the nomadic populations'; courses in Tamashek and later Hassaniyya languages were introduced into the curriculum. A series of educational reforms instituted in 1924 authorized colonial governors to open new médersas to train literate Muslims for jobs in the colonial administration. The only new médersas to be opened under this decree were among the nomadic populations of Mauritania, the first in Boutilimit in 1930, the second in Timbédra in 1933, and a third in Atar in 1936. Enrolment was strictly limited to the sons of chiefs and notables with the intention of training them for what the French called the *commandement indigène*.[18]

The racialist ideas about Islam which were formulated during this period would persist for many decades in official circles as a means for understanding and manipulating subject populations, as will be illustrated in the chapters which follow. But it cannot be denied that racialist distinctions were alleged by the African populations themselves who resided in the region, so that the French were basing their policies on real social tensions. However, the French policies never seemed to work as planned.

For example, despite the new initiatives in the 1920s in recruitment targets, the Timbuktu médersa was never able to attract a significant percentage of students from either nomadic or aristocratic families; a report in 1935 records the following 'ethnic' breakdown of the 105 students then in attendance: 85 Songhay, 1 Bellah, 7 Peul, 8 Sharif, 3 Bérabish, 1 Kel-Arawan. Of these, only ten students came from 'nomadic' families and only eight were the sons of chiefs or notables.[19] In fact, the majority of these students were from families resident in Timbuktu, and the report observed that 'white' nomadic aristocrats refused to send their children to school in the city of Timbuktu because they did not want them mixing with 'black' children, thus reinforcing French racialist notions as well as alleged differences between 'white' and 'black' Islam.

The 1935 report was written by Bouillagui Fadiga, who was appointed director of the Timbuktu médersa in 1934, in another attempt to restructure it. According to this far-reaching and ambitious plan, developed by Frédéric Assomption, chief of the Soudan educational service, the médersa was renamed the Ecole Médersa des Fils de Chefs et Notables Indigènes du Soudan Français, reflecting its new orientation towards schooling the children of the 'Soudanese' aristocracy (the designation 'Soudanese' here being employed as a euphemism for 'black and sedentary'). All aspects of the operation of the médersa were subject to reform and Fadiga was instructed and empowered to effect these changes, which he set about doing in a ruthless and somewhat disdainful manner with the result that by 1936 he had been removed from his post in Timbuktu, literally chased from the town by certain of those who opposed both his presence and his policies.[20]

[18] Harrison, pp. 183-6.
[19] ANM, 1-G-72 FR: B. Fadiga, Rapport sur la Médersa de Tombouctou, Feb. 1935.
[20] This episode is discussed in somewhat greater detail in L. Brenner, 'Amadou Hampâté

This crisis arose for several reasons. First, Assomption's plan was designed to 'recapture' the médersa for purposes of French policy, which could not be achieved without serious disruption. The médersa had been virtually ignored by officialdom and left to its own devices for more than two decades. Both staff and students were largely of Timbuktu origin, as indicated in the enrolment figures cited above, and the médersa was seen by them and most of the local population as a local institution. In order to implement the new policies of recruiting 'Soudanese nobility', Fadiga was required to cancel local scholarships, since most of the students did not meet the new eligibility requirements; he also decided to dismiss staff for alleged incompetence. The impact of these disruptive interventions was no doubt exacerbated by his hostile and contemptuous attitudes towards both Islam and the people with whom he had to deal, which he openly expressed in his official reports. He was a confirmed advoacte of French policies:

The médersa is a mixed school [French and Arabic], a school for domestication [*apprivoisement*], and also a school for pacification [*apaisement*]. Its existence reassures and gives confidence to the population. Besides being a symbol of tolerance with regard to the most fanatical of religions, it is a charitable institution because instruction is given free of charge and assistance is offered in the form of scholarships. It sets in motion a process of education which, when well executed, can liberate young people from the mystique of life to which they have been consigned by indigenous society and which is the cause of so many errors, misunderstandings and disappointments.[21]

But Fadiga's 'absolute devotion' to the French cause, as Assomption put it,[22] may have been less offensive to his Timbuktu enemies than the fact that he was a 'Soudanese', a non-Muslim outsider seeking to intervene in local affairs. All these factors combined to defeat both Fadiga and the planned reforms.

His initiative having dismally failed, Assomption wrote a venomous report in 1936 recommending the definitive closure of the médersa because of its 'absolute uselessness' in achieving the goals of French policy.[23] The report emphasized the fact that of the 84 students now in the médersa, only ten had been recruited from elsewhere in Soudan; these had been offerred scholarships in accordance with the new 1934 policies, but all of them were either from families which were economically well-off or somehow associated with Fadiga himself. The remaining 74 were all Timbuktu residents who represented a wide variety of social classes. 'Should we continue to offer the

---

Bâ: Tijani francophone' in J. L. Triaud and D. Robinson (eds), *L'ascension d'une confrérie musulmane. La Tijaniyya en Afrique de l'Ouest et du Nord (XIXe-XXe siècles)*, forthcoming.

[21] ANM, 1-G-72 FR: B. Fadiga, Rapport sur la Médersa de Tombouctou, Feb. 1935.

[22] ANM, 1-G-72 FR: Bulletin d'Inspection, Ecole Médersa de Tombouctou, Jan. 1936.

[23] For other of Assomption's views on the medersas, see Harrison, pp. 184-5. It should also be noted that in 1935, a recommendation had been made to close the médersa and move it to Bamba, east of Timbuktu, in order to serve the local Tuareg populations; ANM 1-G-177 FR: Procès-verbaux. Médersa de Tombouctou, 1928-40; see also Harrison, p. 185.

sedentary population of this city a free Qur'anic education?' Assomption demanded. 'Do they possess special rights that they should receive such a favour and privilege?'[24]

The médersa was not closed, but following this incident it was the object of yet another reorganisation. The ten 'Soudanese' scholarship students were sent home, and all the 'sedentary' Timbuktu residents were transferred to the French '*école régionale*'. A new recruitment campaign was begun which allowed the médersa to reopen in October 1937 with five students, all sons of nomad chiefs and notables; a report from the *commandant de cercle* in April 1938 confidently predicted a total of 15 to 20 students by the end of the year. The same report offerred a 'racial/ethnic' explanation for the recent fiasco, for which it placed the blame squarely on Fadiga's appointment. The médersa had been unsuccessful in recruiting the sons of chiefs and notables since the 1934 reforms for the following reasons:

The newly appointed Director was a Soudanese schoolmaster and a foreigner to Timbuktu who, for various reasons, was opposed by the teachers of Arab origin, by the former students of the médersa and by the local notables. The principal teacher was dismissed, which discredited the médersa. In these circumstances, it was not possible to obtain the cooperation of the Maure or Tuareg chiefs, but since the departure of the Soudanese headmaster, and the appointment of a French specialist as Director, ... the *commandant de cercle* has obtained (in 1937) an undertaking from the chiefs which we are in the process of putting into effect.[25]

The new director of the médersa need not be an Algerian, the report continued, but in no case should he be a 'Soudanese'. A Frenchman would be preferable, and it was proposed that the present director of the *école régionale* might also assume the directorship of the médersa. Finally, it was suggested that the *commandant de cercle* should play a predominant and active role in the management of the médersa since the basic objectives of a school for the sons of chiefs were political in nature.

As we have noted, the major objective in educating the sons of chiefs and notables was to produce future generations of leaders who would be sympathetic to French interests; indeed, colonial educational policy was invariably formulated to serve political needs. The disposition of the nomadic desert populations posed a series of political problems which it was thought would be susceptible to amelioration, at least in part, through educational intervention in the médersas. The language used to describe this process was crude, but nonetheless descriptive: administrators spoke of *apprivoisement* and

---

[24] ANM, 1-G-72 FR: Bulletin d'Inspection, Ecole Médersa de Tombouctou, Jan. 1936.

[25] ANM, 1-G-72 FR: Letter from *commandant de cercle* Bertrand to the Governor of Soudan, 11 April 1938. The dismissed teacher was Mustafa Baba, who seems to have led the campaign against Fadiga: see Lansina Kaba, *The Wahhabiyya: Islamic Reform and Politics in French West Africa* (Evanston IL: Northwestern University Press, 1974), pp. 27-8. However, there seems little justification to support Kaba's speculation that Mustafa Baba's harsh criticisms were an early manifestation of West African 'Wahhabism'.

défrichement, words which connoted domestication, pacification and the rendering of persons more docile. Not surprisingly, the nomadic chiefs (like many other African leaders) resisted these efforts to 'domesticate' their children, and they offerred many excuses to keep them out of school. But it was the racial arguments which found most resonance within the French administration. The 'white' nomads did not want their children mixing with 'black' children; they did not even want them to be taught by 'black' teachers, no matter how expert in Islamic studies. Such indiscriminate social mixing (*promiscuité*) according to them might undermine their prestige.[26]

It was in this context that the Fadiga incident became the pretext to exclude local 'black' children from the Timbuktu médersa. After the dust had settled, the Governor of Soudan would write that 'the médersas had been created in Soudan in order to domesticate the nomads and not to respond to the aspirations of our black subjects who only seek French schooling'.[27] In any case, he asserted, Arabic language and culture are foreign to 'our Bambaras, Malinkés and Sarakollés'. In other words, in accordance with the precepts of 'black Islam', black African Muslims were only nominally Muslims and could be better 'domesticated' in French rather than médersa schools.

Not all the administration was taken in by this ideology, and in 1940 a new director of the Timbuktu médersa, A. Tebikha, put forward an imaginative proposal to reorganise it on the Algerian model into a higher school, an *école supérieure,* 'worthy of the title of médersa'.[28] With the exception of his agreement that the médersa should continue to serve French policies of 'domestication', Tebikha's thinking was so thoroughly innovative and profoundly contrary to accepted wisdom that its rapid and complete rejection might have been predicted. The great strength of his proposal was that it sought to redefine the role of the médersa, both educationally and politically, in very broad terms; its fatal weakness was that it completely contradicted current French thinking on both Islam and race, that is, the dominant administration ideology of 'black Islam'.

The proposed 'higher school' médersa would reassert its educational role. It would recruit students from about the age of fifteen years, the best products of both the *école régionale* and the indigenous Qur'anic schools. Rather than suppress the Qur'anic schools, *marabouts* should receive subventions in order to encourage them to send their best students on to the médersa. Students from the *école régionale* who received their certificate of primary studies but did not want to leave Timbuktu should be encouraged to enrol in the médersa in order to continue their schooling. The médersa would thus train persons to fill a wide range of tasks: Muslim judges, teachers, secretaries, inter-

[26] Issues of schooling and race had many complex ramifications in the region; see the discussion of Mohamed Ali Ag Ataher in Ch. 3, below.

[27] ANM, 1-G-134 FR: Letter from Governor of Soudan, 16 Sept. 1940.

[28] ANM, 1-G-176 FR: A. Tebikha, Rapport. Propositions en faveur de la médersa de Tombouctou, 27 July 1940.

preters, as well as *shaikhs, qa'ids* and chiefs. But Tebikha also suggested that the very best students be allowed to pursue futher studies in Bamako at the Lycée Terrasson de Fougères where they could be introduced to scientific subjects. The newly organised médersa would thus play a specific role in a redefined educational system that now would incorporate the indigenous Qur'anic schools, at least to the extent of furnishing promising students to the médersa.

Tebikha also argued forcefully that the médersa was fundamentally a Timbuktu institution, and that it was unwise to deny admission to the children of the local black population. Was it possible, he asked, to bar the door to the sons of the Imam, of the *commandant de cercle*'s interpreter, of the president of the local court, of his own predecessor, or to the grandson of the médersa's longest serving director, Yacouba Dupuis, simply because they were black?

Apparently it was; within two months every one of Tebikha's detailed recommendations had been rejected.[29] The reasons given for this decision were that an Algerian-style médersa could never be successful in Timbuktu because Arabic was not the mother tongue of the local populations; that from their origin the objective of the médersas had been to educate nomadic children for political reasons; and finally that 'blacks' preferred to attend the French schools. None of these assertions would resist close scrutiny. French was no more the mother tongue of Africans than Arabic; the founding policies of the médersas had not been formulated in order to respond to the political necessities of governing nomadic groups; and the overwhelming majority of students in the Timbuktu médersa had always been 'black'. And furthermore, the *école régionale* began offering Arabic language instruction in 1938 when the médersa had transferred its 'black' students there. But Tebikha was not given any opportunity to offer such rebuttals.

The 1938 reorganisation of the médersa has been described as a 'cataclysm' by one Timbuktu observer, 'the destruction of all the progress that had been achieved during twenty-seven years of effort and experimentation'.[30] But during the 1940s the school was resuscitated, not as an Arabic 'higher school' as advocated by Tebikha but in the form of a primary school in which the curriculum was the same as that in the colonial schools with the exception that Arabic was taught as a second language. The recruitment of students was opened to all social classes.[31] This modification laid the foundation for the network of schools that would eventually become known as the *écoles franco-arabes*, although even at the time of independence they were still being called médersas. The official change in designation was effected in order to avoid confusion with the expanding system of Islamic médersas. With the educational reform of

[29] ANM, 1-G-134 FR: Note on the Tebikha Report by Chef de Service de l'Enseignement, Assomption, 8 September 1940; and Letter from Governor of Soudan, 16 Sept. 1940.
[30] Baba Mama, 'La médersa de Tombouctou' in *Culture et Civilisation Islamiques. Le Mali* (Rabat: ISESCO, 1988), p. 147.
[31] *Ibid.*, pp. 147-8.

1962 introduced by the government of Modibo Keita, the *écoles franco-arabes* would be officially defined as 'Elementary schools in which the teaching of Arabic begins in the reception class'.[32] The Timbuktu médersa was transformed into the Lycée Franco-Arabe.

The médersa students. Most of the information about the students who attended the French médersas during this period comes from Fadiga's 1935 report on the Timbuktu médersa. At the time of his report, 306 young men had passed through the médersa, and 105 students were in attendance. Of the 306, 23 had subsequently become 'administrative employees': 6 scribes, 5 interpreters, 5 Arabic or French teachers, 1 agricultural monitor, 1 vaccinator, 1 weighman, and 4 Arabic editors. Seventy-four had set themselves up in commerce. The occupations of the remaining 209 were not enumerated. These had been 'reintegrated into family life', perhaps a euphemism for saying that they continued their lives as if they had never attended the médersa. Among them, a certain unspecified proportion (probably very low) were from local aristocratic families, but others worked as artisans: tailors, embroiderers, and leatherworkers. Not a single former student, contended Fadiga, could be considered a 'failure'. Three were counted among the city's leading religious dignitaries, one who had become Imam of the Grande Mosquée, and two who had performed the pilgrimage to Mecca.

Fadiga gives a brief history of recruitment in his report. The médersa opened in 1912 with 36 students, all of them sons of chiefs or notables of the sedentary populations of Timbuktu (Songhay or Maure); admission was also dependent upon their being able to read Arabic fluently. Scholarship payments were offerred ranging from 20 to 7.50 francs. In 1919 recruitment was extended to the entire colony, but the admissions requirements seem to have been slightly modified. Priority was now to be given to the children of chiefs and notables, and greater effort was made to recruit nomadic children. Until 1926 the number of students fluctuated but gradually increased to a high of 64. And then in 1927 enrolments jumped to 107, allegedly as a result of the introduction of Qur'anic studies. Enrolments dropped slightly again during the next few years, but from 1931 they remained well above 100. Fadiga observed that although recruitment had become much easier, the 'quality' of students had fallen; this allusion to quality seems to refer to social status, because the problem is attributed to competition from the *école régionale*, 'which justifiably also makes claim to its share of the sons of notables'.

Of the 105 students attending the médersa in 1935, 95 were from the city of Timbuktu, three from Timbuktu *cercle* and seven from each of five other *cercles*; the ethnic distribution was predominantly Songhay (as illustrated above). The majority of the students were between eight and twelve years of

[32] Oumar S. Touré, 'Etude sur des expériences en cours d'éxecution et sur l'état actuel de l'utilisation de l'alphabet arabe dans l'enseignement formel et non-formel au Mali', Rapport à l'UNESCO, 1985, p. 57.

age, and the occupations of their parents were as follows: 8 chiefs or notables, 21 merchants, 6 commercial employees, 5 butchers, 14 leatherworkers, 23 Tailors, 6 civil servants, 16 marabouts, 3 blacksmiths, 2 Jewellers, 1 domestic. One year later, following Fadiga's débacle, there were only 84 students, ten of whom were recruited from outside Timbuktu under the conditions of the 1934 reform; these came from Segu, Mopti, Koutiala, Niafunké, and San. The remaining 74 were from Timbuktu and were drawn from 'all social classes'.[33] By late 1937 there were about 60 children of Timbuktu residents in the médersa, mostly artisans but including a few sons of *qadis*, interpreters and teachers, and five sons of Maure chiefs.[34] In 1938, the decision was taken to send the Timbuktu residents to the *école régionale*, and enrolment plummeted to five students, all from nomad families. By 1940 enrolments had increased to 23 students, but it is not clear whether this number included what were known as the two '*classes marocaines*', created in 1938 in the médersa to serve the children of Moroccan and Syrian merchant parents who refused to send their sons to the *école régionale* because Arabic was not taught there.[35] In fact, following popular demand in 1938, it was decided to offer Arabic instruction in the *école régionale*; the *classes marocaines* were established because 'Arab' parents did not want their children to attend school with 'blacks'.

Limited as this information might be, it certainly suggests that the real appeal of the Timbuktu médersa was to be found among black Africans of non-aristocratic origin. Furthermore, this appeal increased dramatically with the introduction of Qur'anic studies in 1927.[36] Not surprisingly, administrative documents report absolutely nothing about why parents decided to send their children to the médersa; but they have a fair amount to say about parental resistance, particularly among the nomads. It should be noted that recruitment was never easy for the médersas, or for the French-language schools, either. One reason for this situation was that the target populations for schooling, chiefs and notables, did not want their children subjected to the influence of French propaganda; Africans were fully aware of the objectives of the schools and médersas, and the French were not beyond using pressure and even force to procure the entry of the children they wanted into these institutions.

The fact that the médersas were to offer a form of Arabic and Islamic religious studies made little difference to these parents. They were distrustful of French motives and did not respect the teachers, who for the most part were considered poorly qualified. In 1906 the Jenne médersa had great difficulty in recruiting its first thirty students; it was closed in 1913 because of the

[33] ANM, 1-G-72 FR: Bulletin d'Inspection, Ecole Médersa de Tombouctou, Jan. 1936.
[34] ANM, 1-G-72 FR: Letter from *commandant de cercle* Bertrand to the Governor of Soudan, 10 Nov. 1937.
[35] ANM, 1-G-72 FR: Letter from *commandant de cercle* Bertrand to the Governor of Soudan, 11 April 1938.
[36] This modification in the curriculum may have been part of the educational reforms of May 1924; see Harrison, p. 185.

continuing problem of attracting an adequate number of students. Its first teacher, a young Algerian, was shunned by the local populations who thought he was a Christian.[37] Each subsequent médersa experienced similar recruitment difficulties, and the problem became even more exacerbated when it was decided to target aristocratic nomadic children. A wide range of excuses was offered. The Maures who were targeted for recruitment in 1933 for the new médersa in Timbédra argued that they would be setting a bad example for others if they enrolled their children and only agreed to do so under threat of force; parents were so dissatisfied with the quality of Arabic teaching in this médersa that they preferred that their children be taught only French and to entrust Arabic and religious studies to their own *marabouts*.[38] Tuareg chiefs argued that warriors did not teach their children the Qur'an and that they were not the least bit interested in school, which was the affair of the *marabouts*.[39] One Tuareg chief claimed in 1940 that, given the present quality of instruction, the Timbuktu médersa was capable of producing only 'uprooted idlers and malcontents'.[40] And the opinion was becoming widespread that 'the whites pay children to come to their school so they can turn them into *fonctionnaires*' (civil servants);[41] this was a perceptive insight given the subsequent development of schooling in Mali.

This sustained resistance from nomadic parents should be juxtaposed against the modest success of the Timbuktu médersa in attracting local students; enrolments exceeded 100 students for six of the nine years between 1927 and 1935. The first significant increase in enrolments came in 1927 following the introduction of elementary Qur'anic studies into the médersa; until that date Qur'an had not been taught so as not to compete with local Qur'anic schools. Was there a relationship between these two events, as French observers suggested? Had parents begun to perceive a value in the pedagogical methods being used in the médersa, even if most of the teachers were not very skilled? Were parents attracted to the médersa because of the opportunities it might offer their children for social mobility? These questions cannot be answered from the information presently available.

The curriculum. As we have seen, the program of study in the French médersas was designed to serve the objectives of colonial policy. Although the curriculum was modified on numerous occasions, its basic aims and underlying philosophy remained one of 'domestication'. Schooling in the colony, both secular and religious, was to imbue children with French values with the intention of producing loyal and trustworthy colonial subjects; in the case of the médersas,

[37] Harrison, pp. 62-3.
[38] ANM, 1-G-175 FR: Ecole médersa de Timbédra.
[39] ANM, 1-G-174 FR: Médersa de Bamba, 1935.
[40] ANM, 1-G-176 FR: A. Tebikha, Rapport. Propositions en faveur de la médersa de Tombouctou, 27 July 1940.
[41] ANM, 1-G-134 FR: Note on the Tebikha Report by Chef de Service de l'Enseignement, Assomption, 8 Sept. 1940.

Arabic and Islamic studies were only a 'lure' (*appât*) to attract Muslim children into an institution where they could be 'domesticated'. The idea that Arabic and Islamic studies might be of educational value in themselves, as argued by Tebikha in 1940, was rarely expressed. J.M. de Coppet, who became Governor-General of French West Africa in 1937, was also of this opinion, and he favoured educational support for the 'maintenance of classical Arabic culture'.[42] But even he did not demur from the opinion that French-controlled education was the most effective means available for subverting the political potential of Islam. His own proposal to open an academically respectable médersa in Dakar was defended in just such political terms: maintaining the Muslims in a state of passive receptivity to colonial authority. This kind of thinking was completely compatible with the aims of the first médersas thirty years earlier: to insert a 'domesticating' influence into existing Qur'anic schools by training Qur'anic teachers.

Central to the entire educational package was the teaching of the French language, perceived as an essential and indispensable vehicle for the transmission of French values. Of course, students in the médersas, in theory, were being trained for positions in the *commandement indigène* or the lower echelons of the colonial administration, where knowledge of French was desirable if not indispensable. Consequently, médersa curricula usually included two academic 'cycles', one taught in French and the other in Arabic. There were exceptions; the Atar médersa opened in 1936 in Mauritania without French in the curriculum, although this situation was allowed to exist for only two years in order to allow the médersa to win local confidence before introducing French. And the 1938 reorganization of the Timbuktu médersa instituted a full Arabic program for the first time in its history; French would now be taught only on request.[43] De Coppet was directly responsible for establishing the all-Arabic program in Atar, although his influence on later developments in Timbuktu is not clear.

The language question was a complex and anomalous issue, about which it would be useful to have much more information. The trend in Timbuktu, until 1938, was steadily to increase the French part of the program; by 1934, the French 'cycle' was accorded more time per week than the Arabic. The elimination of French in 1938, as viewed from the perspective of local administrators, seems to have been more the result of efforts to mollify nomadic parents than any new-found respect for Islam of the sort which de Coppet advocated. But the French still don't seem to have got it right. The parents of the 'black' students expelled from the médersa in 1938, allegedly because blacks 'only wanted French schooling', demanded and obtained Arabic instruction once their children were enrolled in the *école régionale*. And in Timbédra in the same year, nomadic parents were complaining about the poor level of Arabic instruction and claiming that they only sent their children to the médersa to learn French

---

[42] For de Coppet's comparatively favourable approach to Islam, see Harrison, pp. 185ff.
[43] ANM, 1-G-72 FR: Arrêté no. 2/89/E 27 Sept. 1938.

anyway; a plan to make Arabic optional was under consideration.[44] So the French found themselves in the curious position of teaching French to those who preferred to learn Arabic, and Arabic to those who preferred to learn French!

In Fadiga's 1935 report on the Timbuktu médersa, he outlined four stages of curriculum development that were related to the various reforms to which the médersa was subjected. His discussion is not very detailed, and he does not describe the French 'cycle' at all. The subject matter of the Arabic 'cycle' included Arabic language and literature, Islamic law and theology. A better idea of the content of these cycles can be obtained by examining the program of the médersa in St. Louis, keeping in mind that the history of these two médersas differed and that their curricula evolved considerably over the years. In 1909, the French cycle in St. Louis included French language, arithmetic, history, geography, elements of physical and natural science, administrative organization of France and of Africa, and something called 'principles of colonial hygiene'. The Arabic cycle included the subjects taught in the Qur'anic and *majlis* schools: grammar, law, theology and exegesis, literature, prosody, rhetoric and logic.[45] However, although standard Maliki and Ash'ari texts were taught, these were carefully vetted to take into account what Fadiga referred to as 'their points of friction with French ethics and *civisme*'. Unfortunately, there is no information available on precisely how these texts were abridged and presented in class. Classical Arabic poetry was studied in literature classes, but students also read works which never appeared in Qur'anic school curricula, such as *The Thousand and One Nights*.

These innovations in religious instruction were intended to 'secularize Muslim education'.[46] The vetting of Muslim texts may have been the most objectionable and most clumsy aspect of this policy, but the gradual adoption of French pedagogical methods was of much more profound and lasting significance. Classical texts were taught in the classroom according to a fixed timetable extending over several years; there was also an effort to vulgarize Islamic letters and sciences by using texts which made these subjects more accessible to a wider public. Eventually, contemporary Arabic-language texts, with illustrations, were introduced into the Arabic cycle, as were practical courses in translation. This dilution of the religious content of the curriculum was therefore accompanied by a gradual desacralization of the Arabic language. To these developments were added a general inclination, despite several brief interludes, to increase the amount of time devoted in the program to French at the expense of Arabic. By 1949, when the Timbuktu médersa had become a primary school in which Arabic was taught as a subject, 24 hours per week

[44] ANM, 1-G-175 FR: Ecole Médersa de Timbédra.
[45] *Journal Officiel du Sénégal*, Oct. 1909, cited in Ndiaye, *L'enseignement arabo-islamique au Sénégal*, p. 116
[46] ANS, Série J 92, Médersa de St. Louis, cited in Ndiaye, *L'enseignement arabo-islamique au Sénégal*, p. 111.

were devoted to French instruction and only 6 hours to Arabic.[47] By now the French had dropped all pretension to teaching religious studies in the Timbuktu médersa.

But it was precisely when the French were beginning to eliminate their direct involvement in Muslim education that the first Islamic médersas appeared in Soudan. The transition was sudden and dramatic. Judging from available French documentation, no African Muslim opinion had been solicited about the presentation and teaching of the Islamic religious sciences in the French médersas since the founding of the Jenne médersa in 1906; certainly none was recorded. In 1945 and 1946 the Muslim silence was broken. Three separate initiatives in Kayes, Segu and Bamako set in motion a pedagogical revolution in Islamic education which has been accompanied by profound social and political ramifications. As we shall see, the influence of the checkered history of the French médersas was not absent from some of these initiatives.

The origins of the Islamic médersa movement

The first three Islamic médersas in Soudan were opened between 1946 and 1950 in Kayes, Segu and Bamako. These schools were intended by their founders to be very different from the prevailing forms of Muslim religious education in the region, as found in the Qur'anic schools. Although these new schools evolved in different ways and in different rhythms, they would eventually share many characteristics which distinguished them from Qur'anic schools. Curriculum, pedagogical methods, even physical structures of the schools would be profoundly modified; children would be taught in classrooms in graded groupings, religious knowledge would be subdivided into subjects to be taught in designated scheduled slots in the school day, and Arabic would be taught as a foreign language from the first year of school with the intention that it should become the language of instruction. To reinforce these differences with Qur'anic and *majlis* education, their founders often referred to their new schools by the Arabic term *madrasa*, or médersa in local French usage. By contrast, official French documentation consistently referred to them as Qur'anic schools, 'to avoid confusion with the official [French] médersas'.[48] There was certainly plenty of confusion about, not least because the new Islamic médersas, especially the one in Bamako, very much resembled the French médersas, with the very significant difference that the former would be under the direct control of African Muslims. However, it was not until the early 1950s that the colonial administration began to realize that French policy on Islamic education was in danger of being outflanked and that they were confronted with a series of Muslim initiatives which had developed in spite of extensive efforts at surveillance and even subversion. If French médersa policy had been intended in part to influence and control Muslim education, it had certainly failed.

[47] AMI, Soudan, Rapport Politique Annuel, 1949.
[48] AMI, Soudan, Rapport Politique, 3e trimestre, 1950.

There is some disagreement in Mali about who should receive the honors for initiating the very first Islamic médersa in the country. The details of this dispute are of little relevance to our purposes, although it is of interest to note some of the causes for the confusion, which reside in the distinction between taking the first steps to establish a médersa and its official authorization by the administration. Thus, a group known by the French as the Azharists, four young men who had recently returned from studies in Cairo at the University of al-Azhar, are reported to have made their first request to open a médersa in Bamako in 1945, although their first officially recorded request was in 1946; formal authorization was received in 1947 but the médersa did not actually open until 1950.[49] Saada Oumar Touré opened a school in Segu in 1946, in which he was experimenting with new methods in teaching a few young children and which was officially recognized by the administration in 1948.[50] But al-Hajj Mahmoud Ba opened his médersa in Kayes, with official authorization, in April 1946.[51] In fact, he had opened a school in his home village in Mauritania as early as 1941.

The precise chronological sequence of these events is less significant than the social and political context in which they occurred. These initiatives, and the Islamic médersa movement to which they ultimately gave rise, emerged as part of a regional and international network of personal contacts and exchange of ideas. The early founders were all young men in their thirties who had grown up in and been molded by the ambiguous and ambivalent realities of life in colonial West Africa which had introduced them to experiences and opportunities not available to their parents' generation. These experiences encouraged and prepared them to challenge both colonial policy and accepted forms of Islamic teaching and practice. The early history of the médersas in Bamako, Kayes and Segu reflects the different personal and academic itineraries of their various founders, which will be explored in the present chapter. The next chapter will analyse these events in the broader context of the transformative forces of which they were an expression.

Bamako. The Bamako médersa, known officially as the *Ecole Coranique Supérieure*, was founded under the leadership of four former students of al-Azhar who

[49] AMI, Soudan, Rapport Politique, 3e trimestre, 1950, states that the new school was inaugurated with a public ceremony on 22 July 1950 and classes began on the 24th. The same report says the school received its initial authorisation in 1947, and this date is confirmed by another document: AMI, Carnets de personnalité religieuse-musulmane, al-Hajj Kabiné Kaba. Lansiné Kaba, relying on information from its directors, says the school was authorised, and actually opened, in November 1949. A second and final authorisation may have been received in 1949, and the delay may be due to the negotiations that ensued which are discussed below. Archival documentation also suggests that the classrooms were actually constructed between November 1949 and June 1950. See Kaba, *The Wahhabiyya*, p. 139.

[50] Décision no. 590/APS/3 of 26 février 1948, cited in Seydou Cissé, *L'enseignement islamique en Afrique Noire* (Paris: L'Harmattan, 1992), p. 125. This was also reported in ANM, I-E-40 (II) FR: Revue du 1er trimestre, 1948.

[51] AMI, Kayes, Rapport Politique, 1er trimestre, 1954.

also founded one of the first modern Muslim cultural associations in West
Africa, the *Shubban al-muslimin*, or Muslim Youth.[52] Strictly speaking, the new
médersa was founded by the association, which was itself an innovation since
it was a novel way for Muslims in West Africa to organize themselves. The
four former students were al-Hajj Kabiné Kaba, al-Hajj Muhammad Fodé Keita,
al-Hajj Muhammad Sanusi Diabi and al-Hajj Mamadou Lamine Tounkara.
The latter two were from the Gambia. Kaba and Keita, about whom rather
more is known, were from Kankan in Guinée; they traveled to Mecca in 1937
and 1938 respectively and then enrolled in al-Azhar where they studied until
1944.[53] They returned together to Kankan in February 1945 and later the same
year went to Bamako where they requested permission to open a médersa. As
we have noted above, the opening of the school was delayed until 1950. The
reasons for this are discussed below.

Published accounts suggest that the Azharists returned to West Africa with
the conscious intention of executing pre-planned educational and cultural
projects. This interpretation no doubt contains some truth, but there are a
number of inconsistencies in the information available about these events
which suggest that the project of a médersa may have evolved rather more
slowly in response to the conditions which greeted Kaba and Keita in
Guinée. In an account strikingly reminiscent of the return of al-Hajj 'Umar
Tal from Cairo approximately one hundred years earlier, Kabiné Kaba claimed
that he and his colleagues were harassed and treated with profound suspicion
by colonial authorities throughout their overland journey home which took
them through Sudan, Chad, Cameroun, Dahomey, French Soudan, and finally to Dakar. However, the allegedly harsh and derisive treatment along their
route seems to contradict the solicitous official support they received in Cairo
where, following an interview and an offer of financial aid from the Egyptian
Prince Muhammad Ali Pasha, the French consulate issued them passports
and letters of recommendation along with a free pass from Cairo to Dakar
including a generous free baggage allowance and loans to help them settle their
affairs once they reached home. In Dakar, where they 'informed the Governor
General of their intentions', they were simply issued passes to return to their
home territory. And in Conakry, they were reportedly offered a position in the
local administration, which they declined 'on the basis of their inadequate
knowledge of French and their intention to be Qur'anic schoolteachers'.[54]

Given the information presently available, it is not easy to explain these
anomalies. But Kabiné Kaba's own testimony suggests that upon leaving Cairo
a special relationship existed between the Azharists and the French administration, and that Kaba and his colleagues anticipated some kind of support

---

[52] *Shubban al-muslimin* was founded in Bamako in January 1949. See CAOM, Affaires Politiques,
2256, dossier 4, Lettre du 7 juillet 1950 du Gouverneur-Général Dakar au Ministère de la
France d'Outre-Mer; see also, Kaba, *The Wahhabiyya*, p. 139.
[53] Kaba, *The Wahhabiyya*, ch. 3, gives a detailed account of student life in Cairo.
[54] *Ibid.*, pp. 83-5.

upon their arrival in Guinée. Precisely what kind of support remains unclear, but there is a tantalizing reference in the French documentation to the fact that, rather than having been offered work by the administration in Conakry and refused it, they had themselves sought work 'in accordance with their instruction and their diplomas' and had been denied it.[55] Some months later, they filed their petition to open a médersa in Bamako, but not before having made a similar request in Kankan which was summarily refused, presumably through the intervention of Shaikh Muhammad Sharif,[56] a religious leader of enormous prestige in West Africa and whose influence penetrated deeply into the French administration.[57]

Could the Azharists have left Cairo with the understanding that they would be integrated into the colonial administration on their return to West Africa? Although not based on any direct evidence, this idea is not so far-fetched as it might at first appear, since much of French Islamic policy was in any case based on co-opting Muslim leadership. Even as late as 1955, the French attempted to lure no less a figure than the renowned Salafi teacher and propagandist, Abdurrahman al-Ifriqi, then resident in Saudi Arabia, to take up a position in the French médersa at Boutilimit.[58] As for the Azharists themselves, why shouldn't they have aspired to an administrative post, or perhaps to become teachers in the French médersas, armed as they were with their diplomas from a prestigious university? Had not the French médersas been designed to prepare Arabic-speakers for such positions? Whatever their hopes (and certainly they would have been justified by any standards), they were dashed, not so much by the French it would seem, but by the intervention of Muhammad Sharif in Kankan.

[55] AMI, Carnets de personnalité religieuse-musulmane: al-Hajj Kabiné Kaba.

[56] Muhammad Sharif was known locally as Shaikh Fanta Mady and by the French as the *Grand Chérif de Kankan*.

[57] Marcel Cardaire, *L'Islam et le terroir africain* (Koulouba: Imprimerie du gouvernement, 1954), p. 117. Lansiné Kaba does not mention this effort to set up a médersa in Kankan and suggests that the Azharists would not have had the 'audacity' to confront a *grand marabout* like Muhammad Sharif; *The Wahhabiyya*, p. 91. However, Ali Diallo, a participant in many of the events described in this book, claimed that not only did Muhammad Sharif refuse permission to start a médersa in Kankan, he also began to work to ostracise the young Azharists; interview in Bamako, 24 March 1989. This view is supported by Muhammad Sharif's remarks in Bamako in May 1950, when he reportedly stated that when the Azharists had attempted to install themselves in Guinée, he had 'unmasked them and required them to leave the country'. CAOM, 19 G 11, Synthèse mensuelle des questions musulmanes, May 1950. On Shaikh Muhammad Sharif, see L. Kaba, 'Cheikh Mouhammad Chérif de Kankan: Le devoir d'obéissance et la colonisation (1923-1955)' in D. Robinson and J. L. Triaud (eds), *Le Temps des marabouts*, pp. 277-97.

[58] AMI, Rapport du Chef de Bataillon Amadou Fall, Commissaire du Gouverneur de l'AOF au Pèlerinage à la Mecque, 1955. An Institut des Hautes Etudes Islamiques had been opened in Boutilimit in 1953 to discourage local scholars from going abroad to study, AMI, Procès-verbal de la Conférence interterritoriale sur les problèmes musulmans, Fort Lamy 1956.

The plausibility of this interpretation is reinforced by the fact that in the ensuing years the Azharists engaged in a series of confrontations with Muhammad Sharif which culminated in their being forced to make a public apology to him in Bamako in June 1950 before being allowed to open their médersa the next month.[59] This incident had resulted from a mission by Muhammad Fodé Keita to Kankan several weeks earlier designed to announce their newly formed association, the *Shubban al-muslimin*, during which he had delivered an inflammatory public lecture critical of the established leadership. But if the Azharists were plagued by the opposition of Muhammad Sharif, they continued to work in close cooperation with the local administration in Bamako in order to realize their project of opening a médersa. It is true that the Governor of Soudan expressed some political misgivings in 1946, 'by virtue of the influences which the interested parties might have undergone in the course of their studies and the political connections they might have kept with Arab countries'.[60] But the Azharists were granted an initial authorization in 1947 to open a school, and they entered into extended negotiations with the administration that lasted for over two years about the specifics of their proposed curriculum.

These negotiations seem to have centered on the extent to which the Bamako médersa would resemble the French médersas. According to information provided by Kabiné Kaba,[61] the Azharists submitted a proposal that implies that they wanted to set up a private Muslim school on the model of a French médersa. The curriculum would have been divided into two sections, Arabic and religious studies directed by one of the al-Azhar graduates, and French, including secular subjects, directed by a French-educated teacher. Very significantly, the French segment of the program was not allowed, and the curriculum of the new school was almost entirely composed of religious subjects. Also, the French refused officially to refer to the school as a médersa, but only as an *Ecole Coranique Supérieure*. The legal distinction between these two designations was very significant. Under existing legislation, Qur'anic schools were not considered 'teaching establishments' and were not eligible for government subventions; they were permitted to teach reading and writing, but their major objective was defined as religious education.[62] Apparently the Azharists were attempting to create a private médersa, according to the French definition of the term, which would have qualified for financial assistance from the government. If so, it was a bold initiative and its failure may have been due in part to the fact that the French would not have been able to exert full control over the curriculum as it did in its own médersas.[63] But

[59] CAOM, 19 G 13, Synthèse mensuelle des questions musulmanes, Aug. 1950; AMI, Carnets de personnalité religieuse-musulmane: al-Hajj Kabiné Kaba.

[60] ANM, Gouverneur Louveau, RP, no. 6 (April 1946), cited in Kaba, *The Wahhabiyya*, p. 136.

[61] See Kaba, *The Wahhabiyya*, pp. 138-9.

[62] AMI, Arrêté no. 2549/A.P. du 21 août 1945, Gouverneur-Général de l'AOF.

[63] Kaba, *The Wahhabiyya*, p. 139, says the plan was rejected 'because such a school was not

official support for such a venture would have been a very radical departure from established policy; in the event, within only a few months of allowing the new school to open, the administration took the decision that it must squash this new initiative. This campaign of government opposition will be discussed below.

To summarize the preceding interpretation of events, it is suggested that the Azharists returned to West Africa with the expectation that they would receive employment and be attributed a social status which was commensurate with their education as university graduates. No doubt they were idealistic and ambitious young men, as their innovative projects attest, and they could be at times somewhat impetuous, witness the inflammatory speech by Fodé Keita in Kankan, but then, they were also among the best educated Africans in the region at the time, and their expectations were gradually being disappointed at every turn. Certainly there was nothing particularly rebellious in their behavior; not a single note of reprimand appears in the French records before 1950, with the exception of the vague suspicions expressed by the Governor of Soudan in 1946. Quite the contrary; they were negotiating with the French about launching a major new educational initiative in the colony. On the other hand, however, Muhammad Sharif was mounting an increasingly hostile campaign against their activities. Thus, in May 1950 in Bamako he warned local Muslims against supporting the médersa project by chastising its founders in the following manner:

... instead of following the sharifs and chiefs who founded this country, you have taken up with these self-styled *marabouts* who claim to have diplomas from Cairo, who follow the heretical doctrine of the Wahhabis and are against God, the Prophet and the most venerated *marabouts*.[64]

Muhammad Sharif's opposition was not without effect; not only was support for the new project blunted among some supporters in Bamako, but the Azharists found it necessary publicly to reaffirm their 'orthodoxy'.[65]

Whatever the behaviour of the Azharists, Muhammad Sharif was taking a lead in politicizing their actions and in castigating them as dangerous Wahhabis. The appearance of 'Wahhabism' and opposition to it will be discussed in subsequent chapters. Here it might be observed that the conflict between Muhammad Sharif and the Azharists can also be seen as a confrontation between the rising ambitions of youth and the power of established authority, and that, as the conflict deepened, the Azharists and others became increasingly radicalized.

In the meantime, the new médersa in Bamako was by all accounts experiencing considerable success. It opened in July 1950 with about 60 students,[66]

---

needed and would have competed both against traditional Quranic schools and Western education offered in public and mission schools'.

[64] CAOM, 19 G 11, Synthèse mensuelle des questions musulmanes, May 1950.
[65] CAOM, 19 G 13, Synthèse mensuelle des questions musulmanes, Aug. 1950.
[66] AMI, Soudan, Rapport Politique, 3e trimestre, 1950.

and when it was abruptly closed by the administration in December 1951, it had 400 students in attendance from Senegal, Guinée, Soudan and Ivory Coast.[67] The official justification for this closure, noted in the 1951 Annual Political Report for Soudan, was 'for contravening the general decree regulating Qur'anic education in French West Africa'; the same report implies that the program had exceeded the number of hours of Arabic instruction permitted in a Qur'anic school![68] A 1956 document offers a similar explanation, stating that the school was closed because 'their curriculum had exceeded the authorized limits imposed by the regulatory texts in force.'[69] These observations reveal an aspect of French intervention in Muslim schooling not hitherto discussed: attempts to control the curriculum in order to limit the levels of schooling which could be obtained in Qur'anic schools. The French had decreed that Qur'anic schools were not 'educational establishments', and they seem to have been determined to ensure that they did not become such!

Other explanations for the closure of the Bamako médersa were also offered in various contexts, although none of them appears in official documentation: that the administration feared the new school would draw students from other Qur'anic schools and from the French colonial schools, and that it was necessary to close the school in order to avoid possible violence.[70] This last explanation appears in a 1954 book by Marcel Cardaire,[71] chief of the *Bureau des Affaires musulmanes* in Soudan and coordinator in the 1950s of what came to be known as the 'counter-reform movement' which opposed the Islamic médersas. In 1949, Amadou Hampaté Ba and some like-minded colleagues had formed an association which they called *Saut al-din*[72] (Voice of Religion), which was intended to compete with the *Shubban al-muslimin*. In May 1951, *Saut al-din* opened their own school in Bamako, which they called *Radiyu 'l-'ilm* in the hope of attracting students away from the new médersa of the Azharists. As tensions increased between the constituencies of the two schools, there was certainly the possibility of a violent confrontation. But if this is so, why was the official reason for the closure of the médersa based on an alleged contravention of regulations governing the curriculum of Qur'anic schools, and why did Cardaire not mention this, particularly in light of the fact that in his book he presented a detailed analysis of the curricula in both the

[67] Cardaire, *L'Islam et le terroir africain*, p. 118.

[68] AMI, Soudan, Rapport Politique Annuel, 1951.

[69] AMI, Procès-verbal de la Conférence interterritoriale sur les problèmes musulmans, Fort Lamy 1956.

[70] Kaba, *The Wahhabiyya*, pp. 162-3.

[71] Cardaire, *L'Islam et le terroir africain*.

[72] The precise name of this association is unconfirmed, due to variations in the transcription of the name in different documents. Marcel Cardaire, *ibid.*, p. 119, writes '*Saoud-Ud-Dine*', which Kaba, *The Wahhabiyya*, p. 162, modifies to *Saud-Ud-Dine*. Hampaté Bâ, in a document dated 10 Jan. 1951, writes '*Sawtou-Dine*' (a copy of this document, headed *Avis* and announcing Hampaté Bâ's appointment as a *muqaddam* in the Tijaniyya Sufi order, is located in the private papers of Prof. Théodore Monod, Paris; see L. Brenner, 'Amadou Hampaté Bâ, Tijani francophone'). *Saut al-din* has been adopted pending confirmation.

new médersa and in *Radiyu 'l-'ilm?* And why wasn't *Radiyu 'l-'ilm* also closed? Indeed, in Cardaire's analysis, the curriculum of the Azharists was markedly superior to that of *Radiyu 'l-'ilm.*

Available evidence does not provide unambiguous answers to these questions, but one suspects that the official, legally justifiable reason for the closure of the Azharist médersa was found in the existing regulations controlling both private schooling and the practice of religion, whereas the publicly disseminated justification was the need to take measures to avert possible violence. The real reason, however, was political: the administration had come to view the Bamako médersa as a dangerously subversive institution. The entire incident was laced with contradictions, not least the policy implications of the relevant decrees themselves. These, originally promulgated in 1922,[73] read as follows:

Art. 3 [modified by the decree of 29 September 1938]: General education must be given in the French language; however, indigenous languages can be authorized in practical courses and in centres of native education. In addition, the Qur'anic schools and the 'catechism schools' are authorsied to give exclusively religious education in the local dialect. These schools are not considered to be educational establishments.

Art. 7: Only French, Latin and the indigenous languages spoken in the colony are authorized for use in the practice of religion.

Since Arabic was not considered by the administration to be an 'indigenous language' in Bamako, opponents of the médersa argued that its curriculum contravened these regulations and should be closed. That the médersa was ever allowed to open in the first place suggests that political opposition to this educational innovation took some time to organize effectively. However, the contradictory nature of these events becomes more evident when one compares the curriculum of the Azaharist médersa with that of *Radiyu 'l-'ilm.*[74]

The new médersa projected a full program of nine years, divided into a primary cycle of four years and a secondary cycle of five years. (When the school opened it offered places for the first two primary classes only, a pattern that would become prevalent for many new médersas which opened with one or two classes and then subsequently expanded by admitting a new first-year class in each subsequent year as the older classes advanced.) The emphasis during the first year was on Arabic language (14 hours a week) including writing and grammar. The sole text was the Qur'an, for which 7 hours, 30 minutes a week were set aside for specific study. The only other subject was arithmetic (3 hours a week). In the second year the hours were reduced for both Arabic (to 8 hours, 30 minutes) and for the Qur'an (to 4 hours, 30 minutes), and the religious sciences were introduced (theology, Islamic law and the biography

---

[73] Décret du 14 février 1922, règlementant l'enseignement privé et l'exercice de la propagande confessionnelle en AOF, in CAOM, Affaires Politiques, 2256, dossier 4.

[74] The curricula of the two institutions are described and compared in Cardaire, *L'Islam et le terroir africain*, pp. 117ff. and Annexes.

of the Prophet) for a total of 10 hours, 30 minutes a week. Arithmetic was also reduced to 2 hours.

The curriculum of *Radiyu 'l-'ilm*, although religious in stated intention, resembled much more the program of a French school. Here four classes were opened simultaneously. The first two years included approximately 11 hours a week of 'language' and 4 hours, 30 minutes of theology. The remainder of the program was devoted to mathematics (4 hours, 35 minutes), singing (50 minutes), physical education (2 hours, 30 minutes) and *morale* or civic education (5 hours). The basic change during the second two years was the addition of the study of Qur'an (5 hours a week). These hours were made available by reducing the time devoted to other subjects; language instruction was now allotted 9 hours a week. According to Cardaire, the original ambitions of the founders of *Radiyu 'l-'ilm* far exceeded the academic qualifications of their staff. Thus, they were unable to offer instruction in Islamic law and the biography of the Prophet, as well as other non-religious subjects such as literature. The result was a schedule that appeared to Cardaire to have been fleshed out with subjects such as physical education, singing and *morale*, because the teaching resources for the religious sciences were not available.

Of more specific interest, however, is the question of what precisely was being taught in *Radiyu 'l-'ilm* under the rubric of 'language': Arabic or French (or both)? If it was Arabic, then this school should have been closed along with the médersa. If it was French, then the inconsistency of policy was equally evident, since the Azharists had been forbidden to offer their proposed French curriculum. In fact, the fundamental objection seems to have been to the doctrinal content of the médersa curriculum, which by 1951 had become identified as 'Wahhabi'. Cardaire remarked:

> If the vast majority of black Muslims are ignorant of the sources of Maliki law, the students of the Ecole Supérieure in Bamako were expected to know the sources of Wahhabi law by the end of their second year.[75]

There is no discussion in the French documentation, nor by Cardaire, of the specific texts used in the médersa, but as early as 1950 the Azharists were being portrayed as 'Wahhabi heretics' by Muhammad Sharif. By 1951 the French seem to have become convinced that 'Wahhabism' was the new Muslim threat to their presence and policies in West Africa. In the annual political report of that year, the same that recorded the closure of the médersa, 'Wahhabism' was described as having been brought by pilgrims from Mecca in a corrupted form that manifested itself primarily in violent opposition to *marabouts* and to Sufi brotherhoods, and its alleged advocates were identified for close surveillance.[76]

---

[75] *Ibid.*, 118.

[76] AMI, Soudan, Rapport Politique Annuel, 1951; the earliest recorded mention of Wahhabism by the French was alleged to have been made in Mopti in 1941 with reference to one Abdou Samadou who was visiting from Abidjan (ANM, Surveillance des marabouts, Feb. 1941), cited in Alliman Mahamane, 'Le mouvement wahhabite à Bamako (origine et évolution)' (mémoire de fin d'études, l'ENSup, Bamako. 1985), p. 24.

The previous annual report in 1950, which recorded the opening of the médersa, had made no mention of 'Wahhabism'.

The emergence in Soudan of the 'Wahhabi' movement, and of its opponents, who came to be known as the 'traditionalists' or 'orthodox', is a central theme in the succeeding two chapters. In analyzing this process, a distinction will be made between 'Wahhabism' as a socio-political movement and the doctrine upon which it was allegedly based, that is, Salafi doctrine which was derived from the writings of such authors as Ibn Taimiyya (d. 1328CE) and Muhammad b. 'Abd al-Wahhab (d. 1787CE). An emphasis on this distinction is justified by the fact that the proponents of this doctrine often referred to it in Arabic as Salafi,[77] whereas the term 'Wahhabi', from the time of its introduction into the Soudanese discourse, was a pejorative denomination used almost exclusively by the enemies of the movement, be they French or African. This distinction will also help to clarify the specific contribution which doctrinal confrontation has made to the evolution of 'Wahhabism' as a socio-political movement.

As suggested above, the evidence points to Muhammad Sharif in Kankan as the principal Muslim organizer of the anti-'Wahhabi' resistance, as well as the chief opponent of the médersa project of the Azharists. He was certainly not alone in his opposition, having been joined, for example, by Abdullahi Ould Cheikh Sidiyya of Boutilimit in publicly endorsing the closing of the Bamako médersa in 1951.[78] But he seems to have been the person who originated the resistance to the médersa, since the very beginnings of that conflict can be traced to Guinée, even to Kankan itself, where the young Azharists were confronted with their first rebuffs. By the early 1950s the program of the Azharists was being conflated by its critics with the anti-'traditional' campaign of the 'Wahhabis'. However, it is not clear how significant doctrinal issues might have been for the Azharists at that time, because no contemporary record exists of precisely how they expressed or communicated their objectives.

The aims of the new médersa, as elaborated by two of its founders two decades later, suggest that their project had at least as much to do with preparing young Muslims for contemporary life as with doctrine. Of course, religious instruction was at the core of their curriculum; they believed that the essential function of education was to produce well-informed and committed Muslims, aware and proud of their identity. But in their view médersa education should also prepare students for an active and productive life and lead eventually to productive employment on the same basis as French schooling. These ambitions were nipped in the bud by the administration's refusal to accept the original proposal of the Azharists to include a French/scientific course of study in their program alongside the Arabic/religious

---

[77] See Jean-Louis Triaud, 'Abd al-Rahman l'Africain (1908-1957), pionnier et précurseur du wahhabisme au Mali' in O. Carré and P. Dumont (eds), *Radicalismes islamiques*, vol. II (Paris: L'Harmattan, 1986), pp. 162-80.
[78] Cardaire, *L'Islam et le terroir africain*, p. 119.

studies course. They also wanted the médersa students to be encouraged and assisted by the government to attain their full potential in their studies and to complete them abroad, if appropriate.[79]

Of course, the *Ecole Coranique Supérieure* of Bamako was not permitted to achieve these ambitions; but the few months of its existence convincingly demonstrated the soundness and potential of the project. In spite of growing resistance, and the fact that they had not been able to introduce the full academic program that they had proposed, the directors of the new médersa succeeded in attracting 400 fee-paying students within less than two years. Tuition was 500 francs registration fee and 200 francs per month, an amount that many families could not afford to pay.[80] The founders had attempted unsuccessfully to open the school under regulations allowing them to receive government subventions, and in the absence of such assistance, they were forced to charge fees. The matter of fees is important, because their payment was seen by some critics as leading to the commercializaton of Muslim education. Of course, Qur'anic education was also paid for, in gifts and in the labor of the students, but the economic base upon which this innovative form of pedagogy would be built would have to be quite different.

But the charging of fees was only one of the many innovations introduced by this venture. The Bamako médersa was meant to be a modern educational establishment. Following both Egyptian and local French precedents, Arabic was taught by contemporary pedagogical methods with the intention that it should become not only the language of instruction in the médersa but also provide confident access to the sources of Islamic religious knowledge. The school was housed in purpose-built classrooms and instruction was arranged according to a fixed time-table. Classes met daily, morning and afternoon, from Saturday through Thursday morning. And the teachers were well-trained and competent graduates of a Muslim university.

The most immediate political influence of the new médersa is to be seen in its rival institution, *Radiyu 'l-'ilm*, which was set up in reaction to it. Its directors had hoped to beat the Azharists at their own game, something they singularly failed to do. Cardaire observed that they avoided any direct discussion or debate with the Azharists on the subject of the religious sciences;[81] and a former student in *Radiyu 'l-'ilm* said 'the school took everyone unawares because neither the teachers nor the parents were prepared for this new kind of teaching'.[82] But in December 1951, *Radiyu 'l-'ilm* had attracted 90 students, which was not bad considering that the school had opened only seven months earlier. And in the same year, *Saut al-din* requested authorization to open another school in San where, Cardaire noted, there was no Azharist school at

---

[79] Kaba, *The Wahhabiyya*, pp.157-8.
[80] *Ibid.*, pp. 160-1.
[81] Cardaire, *L'Islam et le terroir africain*, p. 119.
[82] Quoted in Ibrahim Baba Touré, 'L'Islam dans ses manifestations actuelles à Bamako', Mémoire de fin d'études, ENSup, Bamako, 1989, p. 31.

all.[83] Indeed, even the reaction to the Azharist initiative would lead to the spread of the médersa movement. Cardaire even suggested that the médersa of Saada Oumar Touré in Segu was established as part of this 'traditionalist' reaction, but this is a contention that Saada himself would flatly deny. But before turning to Segu, let us look at developments in Kayes, which were more clearly independent of those in Bamako.

Kayes. The founder of the médersa in Kayes was al-Hajj Mahmoud Ba b. Umar al-Futi, born in 1905 in the village of Diowol (near Gorgol) on the left bank of the Senegal River. Like the Azharists, his educational experiences in the Middle East were the direct inspiration for his commitment to médersa education, although his subsequent career became much more specifically political in orientation. According to his own account,[84] Mahmoud Ba did not commence Qur'anic studies until 16 years of age when in only four years he memorized the Qur'an. He subsequently continued his studies in various centres in Mauritania, until in 1932 he departed on the lengthy and arduous overland journey toward the Holy Cities of the Middle East with the aim of performing the pilgrimage and further pursuing his education. In Mecca he first attended a primary school called *El Virabi* (or Vorabia – both variants are given in the interview transcript) and then *al-Sawlatiyya*, where he obtained a diploma of higher studies in law and *hadith*.[85] In 1940, he began his return journey to West Africa during which he encountered the official suspicion of numerous colonial authorities, especially in Niger, where he was detained for a year while confirmation was sought from Dakar that he was in fact a French colonial subject. Even then, he was allowed to continue his journey only under close police surveillance; in St Louis he and his companions were 'lodged' in a

[83] Cardaire, *L'Islam et le terroir africain*, p. 120.

[84] The biographical information which follows is taken from several sources, most importantly an interview with Mahmoud Ba published in *Chaab* (Mauritania) nos 281 and 293, 1 June and 15 June 1976, a copy of which was kindly furnished to me by the late Mouhamed Moustapha Kane. The fullest published account of Mahmoud Ba's career is Kane's, 'La vie et l'oeuvre d'el-Hadjj Mahmoud Ba Diowol (1905-78): Du pâtre au patron de la "Révolution al-Falah"', in D. Robinson and J. L. Triaud (eds), *Le Temps des marabouts*, pp. 431-65. See also Abu Bakr Khalid Bah, 'Risālat al-Islām wa dauruhā fī 'l-thaqāfat al-ifrīqiyya', in *Ifrīqiyā wa 'l-thaqāfat al-'arabiyyat al-islāmiyya* (Rabat: ISESCO, 1987), pp. 203-5; and 'Abd al-Qadir Sylla, Al-Muslimūn fī 'l-Sinighāl, ma'ālim al-hādir wa āfāq al-mustaqbal. [The Muslims of Senegal, Contemporary Characteristics and Future Horizons] (Qatar: al-Wahda, 1986), pp. 150-1.

[85] There is some uncertainty surrounding the names of the schools attended in Mecca. Abu Bakr Khalid Bah, 'Risālat al-Islām', p. 203, claims the primary school attended by Mahmoud Ba was called *Madrasat al-Falah*. The transcript of Ba's interview gives the two variants of *El Virabi* and Vorabia, perhaps simply a mistake in transcription. Similarly, in interview Ba said he also attended the 'University of Essoli', which presumably refers to another Meccan school, *al-Sawlatiyya*, which Bah names as *al-Sawlatiyya al-Hindiyya*. Both *al-Sawlatiyya* and *al-Falah* are mentioned in the entry on 'Makka' in the *Encyclopedia of Islam*, new edition, VI, pp. 173-4, the latter, along with a sister school in Jedda, having been founded in about 1912 and considered 'the best in the land' and of 'enormous influence through their graduates'.

prison. Having finally reached Kaedi in Mauritania, he was again confronted by the local French authorities and placed under the direct responsibility of the local *chef de canton* before being allowed to return to Diowol, where he immediately opened a school.

Suspicions were apparently aroused because Mahmoud Ba was accompanied by a considerable number of companions as well as 40 trunks filled with books. Such visible signs of wealth and prestige in a traveler would have attracted the official attentions of any political authority in West Africa, but the French were always concerned about such qualities in Africans, and perhaps especially in Muslims. And in the early 1940s, there were added concerns about security aroused by the war situation. Judging by his subsequent highly political profile, it is also possible that Mahmoud Ba was attracting attention to himself by making known his own views about the reform of Islamic education and Muslim society in general. Whatever the sources of official suspicion, the tensions generated by this situation would have affected Mahmoud Ba's attitudes toward the French authorities, of which he may already have been critical, while the administration would mark him as a man to be closely watched.

Mahmoud Ba's new school opened in Diowol in 1941 (Monday, 15 Sha'ban, 1360 AH), which he named after his school in Mecca. He described it in the following manner:

I set it up in a modern style: I organized boarding arrangements and students were forbidden to seek alms for their food. I requested that each student's father who could afford it give his son two milk cows. I told the parents that those who are learning the Holy Book should not live by begging. In this way the students lived in a respectable fashion, worthy of the knowledge which they were acquiring. The students also engaged in physical education regularly; and they had their own uniforms for their training exercises. At this time, some people compared them to the European armies during the First World War.

These innovations served both to confirm and deepen already existing suspicions among the French and also to create some enemies among local Muslims. In his interview, Ba alleged that reports sent to St. Louis claimed that he was an enemy of France who was providing military training to his students with the purpose of engaging in subversive activities. He described the contents of one such report as follows:

He claims to be a Qur'anic teacher, although his entire system of teaching differs from what is done here; in fact, everything he does is dangerous and it is necessary to move against him while there is still time.

The potential for confrontation was growing, as a 1945 report suggests:

To signal in Gorgol a teacher, of Peul origin, who studied in Mecca where he obtained a diploma and who appears to employ relatively modern teaching methods, and who might be of Wahhabi inclinations hostile to the [Sufi] brotherhoods.[86]

---

[86] CAOM, Affaires Politiques, 2256, dossier 4, 'Rapport sur l'enseignement musulman en AOF' 7 Mar. 1945.

Like the Azharists, Mahmoud Ba was not only introducing innovative forms of pedagogy, he was also possibly challenging the local religious establishment.

Perhaps as a result of the growing tensions, Mahmoud Ba decided in about 1944 or 1945, to move his school to Dakar; he claimed that about 150 students accompanied him there. In his interview, he represented this move as an act of defiance against the government by moving his educational experiment to the heart of French power. 'If you fear for your belongings, place them in the care of the thief', he explained, quoting an Arabic proverb. Abu Bakr Khalid Bah, in his brief biographical note, suggests that the move was made because the rural community of Diowol could not support the numbers of students who were coming to the school. Perhaps local opposition was also deepening, or indeed, Mahmoud Ba's ambitions were outgrowing the town. In any case, he does not seem to have remained in Dakar more than two years, possibly because he was never able to receive authorization to open his school there.

In April 1946 he opened a new school in Kayes that the government of Soudan Français authorized to operate as a Qur'anic school, although some official documents do occasionally refer to it as a '*médersa (école primaire)*' or a '*médersa libre*'. One report stated there were 300 students enrolled in 1948;[87] in rather stark contrast, Mahmoud Ba claimed that not long after it opened the school had 1,500 students from Mauritania, Soudan, Senegal and Guinée.[88] Official records reveal virtually nothing about the curriculum of the school;[89] one report states simply that it offered 'religious and general Arabic language instruction, utilizing very modern methods which are borrowed from Egypt'.[90] No local opposition to the school itself is recorded, although the French did find cause to close it in 1953.

However, Mahmoud Ba did arouse opposition through his other activities. In a further development from the first school in Diowol, the Kayes médersa was financed by what Mahmoud Ba referred to in his interview as *zakat* donations from the Muslim community. But this was more than a financial innovation; he transformed it into something of a political and doctrinal issue in a manner which undoubtedly fueled accusations that he was a Wahhabi:

Among the obstacles that I encountered] were false Shaikhs who saw me as undermining their interests. These false Shaikhs lived off the backs of their students and of the poor. One of the principal bones of contention between us was the *zakat* [*sic*] which they took from everyone. On my return [from the Middle East] I set myself against this distortion of the teachings of Islam. I was teaching that God intended the *zakat* for the poor and destitute and not for the rich and lazy, which is

---

[87] AMI, Kayes, Rapport Politique, 4e trimestre 1948.

[88] The school also attracted a significant number of recently converted Bambara and Khassonke, CAOM, Affaires Politiques, 2158, dossier 3, Rapport de Mission sur la situation de l'Islam in AOF (3 April-31 July 1952), J. Beyries.

[89] Kane, 'La vie', p. 465, presents a curriculum for Kayes médersa which was reconstructed from oral testimonies.

[90] CAOM, Affaires Politiques, 2256, dossier 4, 'Rapport sur l'Enseignement de l'Arabe en AOF à l'intention de M. Louis Massignon'.

what the Prophet taught in his message. I said to the people that two-thirds of the *zakat* must be set aside for the children of the poor so that these children do not have to live by begging, and the remaining third should be distributed among the poor. I also said to these Shaikhs that the task of defending Islam fell to them and that they must fulfill this responsibility instead of conspiring with colonialism against Islam. This position incited the hostility of these Shaikhs against me.[91]

It is not particularly surprising that such a confrontational attitude should have aroused hostility!

The archival record contains a tantalizing, albeit passing, reference to the 'collection of *zakat*' by Mahmoud Ba's students. Mahmoud Ba departed Kayes in 1951 in order to return to the Middle East, leaving one Diafaray Ly in charge of the school. Allegedly, groups of students would meet at Ly's home from time to time 'where their principal occupation is to seek charity from the inhabitants of Kayes in order to subsist'.[92] One must be cautious not to extrapolate too much from what is an unsympathetic reference, but there are two points to be made here. Firstly, Mahmoud Ba himself clearly stated that one of the basic principles of his educational reforms was to release his students from the indignities of begging by financing Islamic education through the contribution of *zakat*. We are not told how the students obtained the 'charity' upon which they relied, but it would appear that they were required to solicit it. Such solicitation might be described as begging in another form, which is arguably more dignified than individual students passing through the streets seeking leftovers from the evening meal. Moreover, Mahmoud Ba seems also to have been trying to engender the idea that the religious education of young persons was a communal rather than an individual responsibility; Mustapha Kane places great emphasis on this aspect of Ba's approach to Islamic schooling.

Which leads to the second point: how the donation, collection, and distribution of *zakat* was transformed into a political issue. The same report that refers to the collection of 'charity' by the Kayes students goes on to say:

... the propaganda of al-Hajj Mahmoud Ba in this city has found an echo among some Muslims who, in spite of an agreement between their spiritual guide [i.e. Mahmoud Ba] and the Imam of the Friday mosque, Tierno Mamadou Ibra Sall, refuse along with the Hamallists to participate with the other faithful in the Friday prayers. None of them presented themselves to us.[93]

Apparently Mahmoud Ba's plan for communally-supported religious education appealed to only a small segment of the Muslim community of Kayes, who publicly expressed their commitment to these new ideas in part by refusing to attend the Friday mosque, another tactic which would become

[91] *Chaab*, no. 293, 15 June 1976, p. 3. See also, Kane, 'La vie', pp. 442-3..
[92] CAOM, Affaires Politiques, 2158, dossier 3, Rapport de Mission sur la situation de l'Islam in AOF (3 April 31 July 1952), J. Beyries.
[93] *Ibid.* The last sentence of this excerpt seems to suggest that none of Mahmoud Ba's people agreed to speak with those who accompanied Beyries on his mission in 1952.

characteristic of those who came to be known locally as Wahhabis. Abu Bakr Khalid Bah claims that Mahmoud Ba had founded a religious organization upon his arrival in Kayes, *Jam'iyya tadris al-Qur'an wa-mabadi' al-din* (Association for the Teaching of the Qur'an and Religious Principles).[94] (It will be recalled that the médersa in Bamako was also founded by a new association, the *Shubban al-muslimin*.) Bah gives no details on the membership of this organization, except to say that it was composed of some 'notables' of the city, but he does say that it was this association, rather than Mahmoud Ba himself, who founded the médersa, which would certainly conform with Ba's notions of communally-based education. Colonial records do not mention *Jam'iyya tadris al-Qur'an*, but do refer to Ba's close association with a group of five or six al-Hajji's, described as 'influential members of an extremist political party', (the *Rassemblement Démocratique Africain* [RDA]).[95] It is therefore likely that these were youngish men whose commitment to changes in the social and political order were expressed in part through their views on Islam and Islamic religious practice. Although the *commandant de cercle* described Mahmoud Ba in one report as a 'zealot of reformist Islam', he also had the impression that it was Ba's companions who were pushing him into an open confrontation with the Imam. As early as 1948 there had been a conflict over the date of *Tabaski* (*'Id al-kabir*), although on this occasion the dissenters were forced by the *commandant de cercle* to conform to the Imam's position.

But, given the overall pattern of Mahmoud Ba's active life, it seems unlikely that he would have been easily influenced to contravene his own convictions. In the late 1940s the French seemed still to be puzzled by him; on one occasion he was described as 'rather mysterious'. He emerges from the French documentation as a very active, even restless individual. He does not seem to have spent much time in Kayes between 1946 and 1951, when he returned to the Middle East for several years. He travelled extensively in French West Africa during this period, conducting conversion campaigns among non-Muslims and advocating the expansion of Islamic education. In 1950 he was acting as a lecturer for *Fraternité Musulmane*.[96] In August of that

---

[94] Abu Bakr Khalid Bah, 'Risālat al-Islām', p. 203; see also Kane, 'La vie', p. 446, n. 52, in which he names several 'wealthy merchants' who contributed to the support of the médersas.

[95] Colonial accounts of Mahmoud Ba's political activities are found in the following documents: ANM, 1-E-21, FR, Rapports politiques et Rapports de tournées, Cercle de Kayes (1914-1958); AMI, Fiche de Renseignement, 1949; AMI, Rapport Politique Annuel (Soudan), 1949; AMI, Rapport Politique Annuel (Kayes), 1949 and 1950; AMI, 'Rapport du Capitaine Cardaire, Commissaire du Gouverneur de l'A.O.F. au Pèlerinage à la Mecke en 1952'; CAOM, 19 G 15, 'Rapport de M. Sankale sur le Pelerinage à la Mecque en 1953'; AMI, 'Rapport du Chef de Bataillon Amadou Fall, Commissaire du Gouverneur de l'A.O.F. pour le Pèlerinage de 1954;' and AMI, 'Rapport fin de mission, 2 septembre 1955, par Cardaire, Commissaire au pèlerinage aérien pour 1955'.

[96] According to Sylla, Al-Muslimūn fī 'l-Sinighāl, p. 156, the foremost aim of this organization, founded in 1936, was to return Islam to its original purity as practised by the Prophet.

year, he attracted an audience of some 2,000 to a lecture in Bamako where he spoke about the 'matrimonial alliance existing between French and Arabic instruction which was owed to the children [of French West Africa]' and he concluded the lecture by thanking France for their civilizing mission (small wonder the French were puzzled). The preceding June he had delivered a much more moralistic lecture in St. Louis decrying the shortcomings of youth who were more interested in drink and worldly pleasures than the practice of a proper religious life. He urged his audience to establish an *école coranique supérieure* in Senegal similar to his school in Kayes.[97]

Despite their early suspicions and their continued surveillance of Mahmoud Ba, the French authorities expressed only passing concern about his activities until he departed for the Middle East in 1951 in two trucks with 17 of his students in order to perform the pilgrimage.[98] The money to finance this journey had been donated as *zakat;* not only had Mahmoud Ba been raising money during his lecture tours, but he claimed that donations given to the school in Kayes had far exceeded its needs, creating a surplus of 1.5 million francs CFA. These funds would be used to finance both the pilgrimage and the enrolment of his students in al-Azhar in Cairo in order to pursue advanced studies. However, no authorization for further study had been given by the administration in West Africa, and the students were ordered by the authorities to return home. Ba ultimately agreed to this demand, 'in order to appease' the French, and early in 1953 he was in Cairo arranging for their return passage (although three of them refused to go).

It was only when they saw Mahmoud Ba in action in the Middle East that the French authorities began to understand the full impact of his activities. Of course, by the early 1950s, official concern about the dangers of pan-Islamism, Wahhabism, and other forms of Muslim activism had become intense. For four successive years, from 1952 to 1955, the government of French West Africa appointed a colonial official to accompany the pilgrims who traveled by sea and to oversee and report on their welfare. They were also charged with gathering intelligence on West Africans residing in the Middle East.[99]

Marcel Cardaire, who accompanied the 1952 pilgrimage, met and interviewed Mahmoud Ba in Jedda in that year. Cardaire portrays him as a major activist at the hub of an extensive personal and financial network designed to encourage greater contact among West Africans, as well as between them and Middle Eastern Muslims. Ba is attributed with personally initiating the

[97] CAOM, 19 G 11, Synthèses mensuelles des questions musulmanes, juin et août 1950; Ba is referred to here as a '*marabout tidjaniste*', no doubt adding to the puzzlement!
[98] This date is given by Cardaire in *L'Islam et le terroir africain*, p. 152.
[99] Reports of these missions are to be found in AMI, 'Rapport du Capitaine Cardaire, Commissaire du Gouverneur de l'A.O.F. au Pèlerinage à la Mecke en 1952'; CAOM, 19 G 15, 'Rapport de M. Sankale sur le Pelerinage à la Mecque en 1953'; AMI, 'Rapport du Chef de Bataillon Amadou Fall, Commissaire du Gouverneur de l'A.O.F. pour le Pèlerinage de 1954'; and AMI, 'Rapport fin de mission, 2 septembre 1955, par Cardaire, Commissaire au pèlerinage aérien pour 1955'.

first sustained contacts between Senegalese, Mauritanian and Soudanese Muslim students. In the Middle East, his network of influence extended through Egypt, Saudi Arabia and Sudan, where he worked in particular to ease entry and residence regulations for West Africans coming to the region. Two of the most common solutions to residency problems, according to Cardaire, were either to enroll in al-Azhar or to join the Saudi army. The network allegedly had access to funds from bank accounts in Jedda, Khartoum and even Kano. These activities were also funded by wealthy pilgrims.

In his 1952 report Cardaire was not particularly critical of Mahmoud Ba; he perceived him as a significant figure in the international network. And he tried to recruit him to the French cause, which seems still to have been the operative French policy with respect to influential Muslims. And this in spite of the fact that Ba had reportedly passed himself off as the Senegalese Director of Muslim Religious Instruction to both the Rector of al-Azhar University and the Egyptian Minister of Education, whom he encouraged to send an educational mission to Senegal.[100] In his 1955 report, when Cardaire was once again appointed to accompany the pilgrimage, he delivered a much harsher assessment. He now accused Ba of spreading religious propaganda favorable to eastern political interests, and even asserted that he had been implicated in slave trafficking.

This last accusation, which was never substantiated and for which no evidence was ever presented, was originally made by M. Sankale, pilgrimage officer in 1953. Sankale had a particularly hostile opinion of Mahmoud Ba, accusing him of being a 'veritable intelligence agent (not to say spy) in the pay of the Saudi government'. He perceived Ba as a very dangerous character full of cunning who, for example, presented himself before the French consulate in Khartoum as 'Director of the Ecole Coranique of Kayes who was travelling with the authorization of Captain Cardaire'. He was seeking a letter of introduction to the French authorities in Cairo, which he did not obtain! Sankale was of the view that Mahmoud Ba must be 'neutralized' by not allowing him to travel again after he returns to West Africa.

Mahmoud Ba returned to Kayes in May 1954, where he found the médersa had been closed since the previous October, due in part to his own extended absence. His colleagues and companions had interceded with the local authorities to keep it open, but they were refused and told they could make an application to reopen the school under a new director. An unsuccessful attempt was made

100 This idea had been in circulation for some time. Cardaire cites a report in the newspaper *Journal d'Egypte* in October 1947 to the effect that the Minister of Foreign Affairs wrote to the director of al-Azhar for his opinion on assisting the creation of a religious school in Senegal. Cardaire suggests that this might have referred to the Bamako médersa, but it could well have referred to Mahmoud Ba's own efforts to establish his school in Dakar. Another article in *Akhbar al-Yaum* in January 1948 reported that the King was interested in building a mosque and school in Senegal. By 1951, special scholarships for African students were being offerred by al-Azhar. AMI, 'Rapport du Capitaine Cardaire, Commissaire du Gouverneur de l'A.O.F. au Pèlerinage à la Mecke en 1952'.

to keep the médersa open secretly, but this plan was discovered and the perpetrator, Diafara Ly mentioned above, was fined. Early in 1955 Mahmoud Ba requested an authorisation to reopen the médersa under the patronage of the recently founded *Union Culturelle Musulmane* (UCM). Permission was not granted until 1956, and Ba was not allowed to resume the directorship. In the meantime, Cardaire (seemingly the only person in this entire episode to have traveled as much as Mahmoud Ba himself!) had visited Kayes to investigate the UCM, which he labelled as an 'extremist organization'. He also counseled the opening of a school by the counter-reform movement to compete with the reopened médersa; this development will be discussed in the next chapter.

Here ends the story of Mahmoud Ba's association with the Kayes médersa, but not the story of his influence. He claimed that students from Kayes later founded as many as fifty new schools modeled on his ideas. Although this number may be another of his exaggerations, there can be no doubt about his impact on the reform of Muslim education, and indeed of Muslim thought, in the region. The contemporary Falah Movement in Senegal traces its roots to his activities in Senegal and Kayes during the 1950s.[101] The Falah movement is a well-financed Muslim cultural and religious association with strong political overtones in its opposition to both Sufism and to secularism. Its membership, or at least its leadership, is drawn largely from merchants and well-educated professionals. All of these features resonate of the interests, activities and personal associations of Mahmoud Ba, which viewed from the perspective of the 1990s seem almost unremarkable, but which viewed in the context of the 1940s from within the Sufi heartlands of Futa Toro and Kayes must have been seen by many as the aberrant views of a distinct minority of persons.

In his biographical note, Abu Bakr Khalid Bah suggests that Mahmoud Ba first attracted local Muslim criticism because of both his educational innovations and particularly his non-affiliation with any Sufi order, which was the source of claims that he was a Wahhabi.[102] But Bah argues that this was a misunderstanding, and indeed, there is no clear record of Mahmoud Ba having embraced the doctrines of Wahhabism as such, in spite of his continued connections with Saudi Arabia and the Middle East. On the other hand, he had certainly returned from the Middle East with perceptions of Islam and of Islamic religious education which were not easily accepted in the West African milieu, and he pushed forward his ideas and his projects with untiring energy and enthusiasm. And there seems little question but that he became increasingly politicized during the 1950s, as did so many of his fellow Africans.

After his return to Kayes in 1954, Mahmoud Ba assumed a much more militant demeanor. By now the political situation had changed; the French

---

[101] For the Falah Movement, the contemporary name of which is *Harakat al-Falah li-'l-thaqafa al-Islamiyya al-Salafiyya*, see Sylla, *Al-Muslimūn fī 'l-Sinighāl*, pp. 164-6; and Muriel Gomez-Perez, 'Associations islamiques à Dakar', *ISASS*, no. 5 (1991), pp. 10-11.

[102] Abu Bakr Khalid Bah, 'Risālat al-Islām', p. 204;.

administration had reformulated their policies in an attempt to contain the threat of a renascent Islam. This shift in policy had already resulted in the closure of the Bamako and Kayes médersas, and the counter-reform movement, backed by the resources of the administration, had moved into high gear to oppose the new educational initiatives. Ba joined with the newly formed and very militant UCM to promote the cause of the médersa, which suggested to some his alliance with what came to be known as the Wahhabi camp. But in fact, his various alliances were too complex to be subsumed under any single classificatory category. Kane notes that unlike the 'Wahhabis' of Soudan and Guinée, who tended to be allied with the relatively moderate RDA, Mahmoud Ba was associated at times with members of the more radical *Parti Africain de l'Indépendance*, which was affiliated with the Communist Party of France.[103] Whereas such an orientation may seem more than unusual in a religious reformer, there is ample evidence to indicate that much of the appeal of Mahmoud Ba's far-flung activities was among socially marginalized constituencies, not only youth in general, but other social categories who found in his ideas and actions a means of turning to Islam to 'liberate' themselves from local religious and political hierarchies; Mustapha Kane places considerable emphasis on this reading of Mahmoud Ba's influence.

However, he does not seem to have engaged in a self-conscious and ideologically consistent program of social reform, and there are many seeming inconsistencies in his actions. For example, there was a curious twist of events in the 1950s, associated with his continuing conflict with Ibra Sall, Imam of the Friday mosque in Kayes, and which seems to contradict his role as a critic of Sufism and the religious hierarchy. He joined in alliance with one Abdoulaye Koné, a Qadiri *marabout* and preacher who was embarked on his own campaign to establish his prestige and influence.[104] In addition to his proselytizing campaigns among non-Muslims, and his efforts to expand his network of Sufi adherents, he joined with Mahmoud Ba in a provocative campaign against Sall. Together they built a mosque, for which they found an Imam with the aid of none other than Muhammad Sharif of Kankan! (Mahmoud Ba was disqualified from being Imam, according to the precepts of Islamic law, because he had lost the sight of one eye.)

This overview of events suggests that the founding of the Kayes médersa was but one part of a complex array of political and religious activities which combined within it a bewildering array of ideological orientations: a mixture of independence and Islamist politics, educational and social reform, challenges to the religious establishment, and any number of sparsely documented local conflicts. To this we must now add the very different story of the founding of the first médersa in Segu.

---

[103] Kane, 'La vie', p. 462.
[104] References to Koné appear regularly in the French documentation during 1954-6; see also M. Chailley, 'Aspects de l'Islam au Mali' in M. Chailley *et al.*, *Notes et études sur l'Islam en Afrique Noire*, Collection du CHEAM (Paris: Peyronet, 1962), pp. 12-13.

Segu. Although today in Mali it is generally accepted that the Segu médersa was founded by Saada Oumar Touré, the official authorization issued in February 1948 names three persons, Saada Touré along with Hashimi and Abu Bakr Thiam.[105] In contrast to the founders of the Bamako and Kayes médersas, these men had never been to the Middle East and were educated entirely within the local Muslim school network. Furthermore, they were Tijanis, descendants of the Tukolor companions of al-Hajj 'Umar who had conquered Segu during the nineteenth-century *jihad.* This Tijani heritage has remained extremely important to them, and they have been staunch opponents of all manifestations of the anti-Sufi 'Wahhabi' movement in Mali. But they also became deeply committed to the reform of Muslim education, and particularly to the teaching of Arabic as a living language, innovations that aroused fierce opposition from many quarters.

Another important distinction which belongs to the Segu médersa is that, despite opposition, it was never closed from the day Saada Oumar began experimenting with a new way of teaching in 1946 or 1947 with his own eldest child and several others.[106] The motivation for these experiments had come from Saada's own experience as a child in both Qur'anic and French schools. As a young child he had been placed in French school against the wishes of his parents, an incident which according to him profoundly affected the course of his adult life. Because his own words so eloquently evoke the significance for him of this experience, he is quoted here at length. We join the interview at the point when he is recounting his entry to Qur'anic school, when he was between six and eight years of age.[107]

It was, I believe, at the beginning of 1920 that [my father] placed me in the Qur'anic school of Muhammad al-Amin Thiam, a Tukolor here who had followed al-Hajj

---

[105] Décision no. 590/APAS/3, 26 février 1948; see ANM, 1-E-40 (II) FR: Rapports politiques et rapports de tournée, Cercle de Ségou (1940-1959), Revue du 1er trimestre 1948.

[106] The question of the precise date of creation of the school relates to the disputes discussed at the beginning of this chapter. For years, Saada Oumar claimed that he first began teaching in 1947; this date appears in several sources, and this is what he told me when I first interviewed him in 1977. However, in the mid-1980s, the date was changed to 1946. This modification occurred in the context of a formal interest from UNESCO in Arabic education in Mali. Saada's own son Oumar, at the time *Inspecteur-général d'arabe* in the Ministry of Education, was commissioned to write a report on the subject: Oumar S. Touré, 'Etude sur les expériences en cours d'éxecution et sur l'état actuel de l'utilisation de l'alphabet arabe dans l'enseignement formel et non-formel au Mali', Rapport à l'UNESCO, 1985. He also penned another document in the same year for UNESCO entitled 'Note explicative sur l'identité d'el-Hadj Saad Touré'. Is it possible that Saada Oumar became aware at this time that the Kayes médersa might have been opened before his own? In 1989, I viewed a *certificat de scolarité* from the medersa which included the statement, 'Created 3 January 1946'. For additional information on the history of the Segu médersa, see S. Cissé, *L'enseignement islamique,* pp. 125ff, and S. Cissé, 'Les médersas de Ségou' in *Culture et Civilisation Islamiques. Le Mali* (Rabat: ISESCO, 1988), pp. 149-50.

[107] Calculating from internal evidence in the interview, Saada would have been eight years old when he began Qur'anic school in 1920; but his son's 'Note explicative', cited above, gives his year of birth as 1914.

'Umar. I remained in the Qur'anic school for four years, by which time I had already finished the first quarter of the Qur'an. At this time our parents did not want us to go to French school. They said that the French had come and had fought a war against us, that they had destroyed our libraries and our way of life, and that they wanted to put an end to the Muslim religion. Therefore their children would not go to French school. My father was completely against it, and we were all brought up with this attitude so that I too was opposed to it. But at this time they took children by force, and I was taken by force. My family cried that day; even today the cries of my mother ring in my ears.... My family was crying. All the neighbours came, 'What is going on?' 'Our child has been taken by force to be placed in the French school'.

I remained there four years. When I reached the fifth year, they selected the ten best students to send to Bamako in the higher primary school. [Saada was not among those selected.] When I left the school my father was happy and so was I. But he wanted to put me back in Qur'anic school again, and I said, 'Father, excuse me. I have lived a certain experience that for me is a reality. Perhaps it is false, but for me it is a reality'. (Because you know that a child has not yet experienced very much.) I said, 'Here are four years of Qur'anic school and four years of French school. The four years of Qur'anic school have passed without result, because I understand absolutely nothing of what I read. Four years in the French school have borne fruit; I read and I understand what I read. Consequently, my father, I do not wish to return to a deaf teaching'.

'Are you mad? If you persist in your stubborness then from today you are no longer my son; you have abandoned me'.

I said, 'From now on, my father, I give up my projects for your project. I apologize in the name of God. I am at your service'. And he placed me in his own Qur'anic school.[108]

Much of significance has been encoded into this text: a criticism of local Qur'anic pedagogy, a profound ambivalence about the French presence and influence, and a generational conflict which is resolved by the culturally appropriate submission of son to father. But what most interests us here is Saada Oumar's insistence that these first eight years of his education, equally divided between Qur'anic and French schooling, constituted the formative and crucial experience which led directly to his experiments in médersa pedagogy. Saada reluctantly resumed his Qur'anic studies, but in later years he would become increasingly preoccupied with the question of why he had been able to learn French so rapidly but had had to struggle for many more years to acquire Arabic. His son would later write that these questions had led to an internal conflict between Saada's 'love for his religion with its sterile scholastic method and his training in the [French] school with its active and effective method'. He began to question himself in the following manner:

Why should a student like himself, having completed only four years of study in a French school, be able to express himself [in French], both orally and in writing, while students pursuing more than fifteen or even twenty years of Qur'anic study in

---

[108] Interview with Saada Oumar Touré, 13 October 1977, Segu. See also L. Brenner, 'Al-Hajj Sa'ad 'Umar Touré and Islamic Educational Reform in Mali' in E. Breitinger and R. Sander (eds), *Language and Education in Africa*, Bayreuth African Studies series, no. 5, 1986.

the Islamic schools of his city were still unable for the most part to speak or even write [in Arabic].

Why should one have to wait for so long, or be a member of certain learned families, in order to have access to the Arabic language?

Is it because, as the French delight in spreading about, that 'Islam and Arabic education contribute only to inactivity and backwardness'?

Or is it the fault of the methodology employed by the traditional alfas?[109]

Saada's conclusion, of course, was that the difference lay in methodology, which led eventually to his first teaching experiments.

This presentation of events proposes that the initiative for the Segu médersa was Saada's alone, which seems to contradict the fact that he received official authorization for it in 1948 jointly with Hashimi and Abu Bakr Thiam. The Thiam version of the story is that the idea of a médersa in Segu first came to Hashimi following a visit to Bamako where he observed the new teaching methods of Muhammad Fodé Keita.[110] Saada Oumar agrees that the Thiam brothers approached him with this idea, but claims that by then he was already teaching. He also relates that about six months after he began his private experiments, he was obliged by local demand to open his school to a wider public;[111] presumably this was the moment when Saada's experiments were transformed into a more clearly focussed project to open a médersa. When the new médersa officially opened in 1948 (classified yet again by the French as a Qur'anic school), its enrolments were so small (seventeen pupils) that it could employ only one teacher. It was agreed that Saada would take this first class, and that the others would begin teaching as new classes were added in subsequent years. For reasons that are much contested, this plan was not followed, resulting in a rupture between the Thiams and Saada Oumar.[112] This dispute is significant for the subsequent history of the médersas, because in the 1950s the Thiams would open their own school in direct competition with that of Saada as part of the counter-reform movement orchestrated by the French.

Saada Oumar's presentation of events therefore seeks to make a clear distinction between the genesis of his own médersa and those in Bamako and Kayes, where the founders drew their inspiration from their Middle Eastern experience. According to him, the idea for the Segu médersa had grown out of a uniquely West African experience. There is no reason to doubt the personal significance of his own schooling in the formulation of his experiments, but he was certainly not unaware of the médersa in Kayes, nor of the efforts of the Azharists to open another in Bamako. Indeed, there is the tantalizing

---

[109] Oumar J.Touré, 'Note explicative'.

[110] Although the Bamako médersa did not formally open until 1951, it is possible that the Azharists were experimenting with their new methods earlier, in the fashion of Saada Oumar himself.

[111] Interview with Saada Oumar Touré, 13 October 1977, Segu.

[112] The differing versions of these events were reported in interviews with Thierno Hadi Thiam, 7 January 1988, Bamako; and Saada Oumar Touré, 30 March 1989, Segu.

fact, perhaps only coincidence, that the Segu médersa was named *Sabil al-Falah al-Islamiyya*.

But there is a strong sense in Saada's account that his creation of a médersa was part of his personal destiny; he even recounts a dream in which the Prophet appeared to him predicting the many difficulties he would encounter when he opened his médersa.[113] But Saada was a reluctant student, and he had continued his Qur'anic studies only under pressure from his father. (It was during this period of conflict that he had his dream of the Prophet.) He wanted to leave school altogether and go to work, and finally he convinced his father to allow him to set up as a petty trader during the hours he was not in school. Then, in 1935, he left his formal studies and joined an aunt in Niamey where, until he was mobilized into the army by the French in 1939 and ordered to return Segu, he worked with her in the cattle trade to Nigeria. He was soon demobilized following the French defeat, and his father once again insisted he resume his studies, this time with the man Saada calls his '*maître*', Madani Tal, a great-grandson of al-Hajj 'Umar; he also took up work as a tailor.

By the time he left Segu in 1935, Saada could read Arabic, and his sojourn in Niamey saw his transformation into an autodidact. He read a great deal in both Arabic and French: 'I wasn't learning anything, but I was a great reader'. So, in addition to the many new experiences and ideas which he undoubtedly encountered in his travels, he was also opening himself to new ideas from the wider world through his reading. The evolution of this intellectual independence was extremely important to his personal development as a teacher; after all, he did not have the formal experience and training of either the Azharists or Mahmoud Ba. He began to focus his reading on the pedagogical questions which would lead to his experimental teaching and which would form the basis of his ideas when he began to organise and develop the curriculum of the new médersa.

Saada's efforts to develop his academic program in the médersa extended over many years, of course, and he had to rely on the assistance of many sympathetic persons; he took advice from anyone competent and willing to offer it. But this project was clearly his own, and to him should go the credit. He taught the basic texts in the Islamic sciences which were used in the local Qur'anic schools, but he was required in effect to invent the courses for teaching Arabic language, which he did by consulting a broad range of works published in the Arab world. He eventually wrote two grammar texts himself.[114] He also consulted pedagogical journals and books in both Arabic

---

[113] The text of this dream is recounted in L. Brenner, 'Al-Hajj Sa'ad 'Umar Touré and Islamic Educational Reform in Mali'. It is difficult to imagine a more provocative challenge to his anti-Sufi opponents than claiming that his médersa had been inspired by the Prophet appearing to him in a dream.

[114] *Al-Mubādi' al-ṣarfiyya*, 2 parts (Tunis, 1973, 4th printing); and *Al-Durūs al-naḥwiyya li 'l-madāris al-ibtidā'iyya*, 2 parts (Tunis, 1981). Saada Oumar has written numerous books, in both French and Arabic; see the bibliography.

and French, and he referred to the curriculum in the French schools for guidance in such subjects as mathematics, geography and natural science. Indeed, the entire program was inspired by French pedagogical methodology, because as Saada said, an 'Arabic methodology simply did not exist'.[115] It was a very ambitious project, the aim of which was nothing less than providing Muslim children with a religious and scientific education which would prepare them to function effectively in the twentieth century.

These innovations were not long in attracting local opposition. According to Saada, all the religious leaders of Segu, with the exception of Madani and Muntaga Tal, criticized the new school. The *Grand Imam*, Abdurrahman Jiré, wrote to the Governor to have him arrested as an agitator; Saada was accused of being against Islam, of introducing a subversive form of teaching in Segu. His was no longer a religious school but a French school; some even charged that Saada was no longer a Muslim. Eventually, he was summoned by the *commandant de cercle*:

The *Commandant* said to me, 'OK, you little scoundrel, since when have you been opposed to the Muslim religion, to the Muslim population, and to the *marabouts?*'

I responded, '*Mon Commandant*, it is completely the contrary.'

'Well, you teach arithmetic. Does that have anything to do with the Muslim religion?'

I asked him who told him that, and he responded, 'The religious chief, the Imam, the Grand Imam, of the city.'

I said, 'Well, either the Imam is ignorant or the Imam is an egoist.'

'Right, they told me that you abuse the dignitaries of the city, and now I am a witness. You have just insulted the Imam.'

I said, 'Never! I did not insult him. I simply said that an Imam who claims that arithmetic has nothing to do with the Muslim religion is either ignorant or an egoist. And I maintain this contention, *mon Commandant*, whatever the consequences. ... Permit me to ask you a question.'

'What?'

'Does the Qur'an form a part of the Muslim religion?'

'Saada, my child, of course!'

'Is there not, in the Qur'an, the distribution of inheritance?'

'Certainly!'

And so I said, '*Mon Commandant*, excuse me, but is one expected to divide up someone's millions with a knife?'

He stared at me; he was angry because I was being a bit rude, but he controlled himself and said, 'My child, one divides it by arithmetic.'

I continued, 'If one cannot divide up an inheritance without arithmetic, and if inheritance is part of the Qur'an, and if the Qur'an is the very basis of Islam, then a religious chief who says that arithmetic has nothing to do with the Muslim religion is either ignorant or an egoist.'

'Get out of here you little shit [*salaud*].'

'Thank you, *mon Commandant*, I'm going.'[116]

---

[115] Interview with Saada Oumar Touré, 5 Feb. 1978, Segu.
[116] Interview with Saada Oumar Touré, 13 Oct. 1977, Segu.

It is not clear precisely when this incident occurred, but it was probably in the early 1950s about the time when the counter-reform movement was gaining momentum. Of course, it was not possible to accuse Saada Oumar of being a 'Wahhabi', and it seems likely that his school survived all the pressure which was subsequently brought against it in part because of support by the Tijani leadership in Segu, and possibly in Senegal in the person of Seydou Nouru Tal. In this regard, it is important to note that Marcel Cardaire's analysis of the Muslim initiatives of the 1940s and '50s, which we will examine in detail in a subsequent chapter, was based upon a distinction between educational and doctrinal reform. In his view the Wahhabis placed their emphasis on doctrine and ritual practice, whereas the most worrying (for the French) element in the program of the educationists was the teaching of Arabic. The reform of Arabic pedagogy was at the heart of Saada Oumar's program, and by 1951 the French were officially expressing concern about its impact:

In effect, in spite of regulations limiting the number of hours which Arabic can be taught in the Qur'anic schools, this teaching develops each day. Thus, in one school in Ségou a *marabout* has been recommending that his students speak only Arabic among themselves.[117]

This statement appears in the same annual report which recorded the closure of the Bamako médersa for contravening the regulations governing Qur'anic education. But in 1954, Saada Oumar was also cautioned by the administration for having engaged someone to teach French, which similarly contravened the regulations governing Qur'anic schools.[118] (It will be recalled that the Azharists had been refused permission to introduce a French cycle of instruction into their curriculum.) This issue almost resulted in the closure of the médersa, and it was not until 1959 that official authorisation to teach French was obtained from the authorities of the newly independent République Soudanaise on the specific condition that the school could not apply for subventions from the state.[119] The realities of the academic program in the Segu médersa were such that they were stretching the official definition of a 'Qur'anic school', which according to the regulations in force was not an 'educational establishment' and therefore did not qualify for financial support from the state.

Once again, as in Bamako and Kayes, the economic question posed itself. Saada Oumar charged fees in his new médersa. As already mentioned, Qur'anic school teachers had always received compensation for their services in the form of gifts from parents and labour from their students, but these economic exchanges were embedded in a set of religious concepts that viewed teachers as providing their students with a religious 'education' in the full meaning of the term, including the transmission of moral and religious instruction as well as spiritual merit in the form of *baraka*. Even if not

[117] AMI, Rapport Politique Annuel (Soudan), 1951.
[118] ANM, I-E-40 (I)-Ségou: Revue trimestrielle, Oct.- Dec. 1954.
[119] Interview with Saada Oumar Touré, 5 Feb. 1978, Segu.

evident at first, it would eventually become clear that the médersas would not be able to reproduce this form of religious education. These new schools were destined to become commercial enterprises, fully consistent with the changing social and economic realities of the twentieth century. Religious education would no longer be personalized, transmitted from individual to individual; rather it would become a commodity.

Perhaps Saada Oumar welcomed this challenge, because it allowed him to combine his religious commitments with his keen interest in business and education. He recalled his own personal economic sacrifice in deciding to transform his little family school into a commercial venture. At the time, working as a tailor, he enjoyed a daily income of 1,500 francs. The school opened with seventeen pupils who paid 100 francs per month. 'Imagine', he said, 'giving up 1,500 francs per day for 1,700 francs per month'.[120] And he agreed to this reduction in income, he claims, because it was the fulfillment of his personal destiny as revealed to him by the Prophet in his dream twenty years earlier. Within a couple of years he was earning an adequate salary, and by 1954 enrolments had reached 200 pupils[121] resulting in a monthly income of 20,000 francs, assuming the fees had remained at the same level. Certainly the médersa had all the makings of a profitable business enterprise. This evident profitability brought resentment from some quarters, especially from those who found it difficult to pay, but also from many who felt that religious education should be 'free'.[122]

But Saada Oumar felt that the benefits to be derived from the commercialization of religious education outweighed the disadvantages:

I could see that if the Muslim religion was not very strong in our country, it was because those responsible for teaching Islam were poor; they received no salary. The marabouts were obliged to beg, and anyone who does that will not be able to speak the truth. … I wanted religious education to get out of this rut, so children would know that in studying Arabic and the Muslim religion they would not only be able to practice their religion but also earn their living. …

For example, I can refuse many things that others cannot. It is very difficult to speak the bitter truth to someone from whom you might expect money tomorrow. I have my salary; what I earn is adequate for my needs, and I speak the truth as I see fit. It was teachers of this kind that we wanted to train. … I wanted to change this situation. I always said to my father that I loved to work. I wanted to earn my living by what I did myself. That was why I said it was necessary to pay me [in the médersa]. Now many others, and not only students who have studied here, are earning their living by what they have learned. [123]

---

[120] Interview with Saada Oumar Touré, 13 October 1977, Segu. It would seem that in its early years the médersa also was financed by donations from the Muslims in Segu. Personal communication from Oumar S. Touré.

[121] ANM, I-E-40 (I)-Ségou: Rapport Politique Annuel 1954.

[122] There was a very public reaction to this issue in Bamako by a popular singer; see Kaba, *The Wahhabiyya*, pp. 160-2.

[123] Interview with Saada Oumar Touré, 5 February 1978, Segu.

These views are very similar to those expressed by Mahmoud Ba, and they touch on many issues and problems which emerged from the médersa movement in subsequent years: the ability of the médersas to prepare their students for productive work, and the relationship between médersa education and the evolution of a public Islamic discourse in which one feels free to speak the 'truth'.

During the 1950s and after, Saada Oumar's médersa would be exposed to increasing official opposition, but these events are best explored in the context of an analysis of the counter-reform movement.

Although the Segu médersa did not attract as many students in its early years as those in Bamako and Kayes, enrolments increased steadily during the 1950s, and by the middle of the decade the success of the school had already inspired the foundation of two médersas in Burkina Faso, the first in that country.[124] The Kayes médersa had been reopened in 1956 under the auspices of the *Union Culturelle Musulmane*, and although Mahmoud Ba had not been permitted to continue his directorship of that school, he applied his considerable energies elsewhere and was instrumental in the creation of additional médersas in both Mauritania and Senegal, in the Futa Toro region, in Kaolack and in the Casamance. By the end of the decade, there were approximately thirty new médersas in Senegal, for which much of the inspiration had come from the activities of Mahmoud Ba and the UCM.[125] The Azharist médersa was allowed to reopen in 1957, and by 1960 four other médersas were established in Bamako accounting for enrolments in all five schools of between 800 and 850 students.[126] Médersas had also been opened in Bouaké, Sikasso and even in Kankan.[127]

Within less than fifteen years, the pioneers of the médersa movement had laid the foundations of a new system of religious schooling which would profoundly modify the nature of Islamic education in the region and eventually pose a challenge to the French-language schools as well. Some French would continue to argue that children were sent to the new méderas only because adequate places did not exist in the state schools,[128] a hollow echo of the assertion twenty years earlier by the governor of Soudan, when justifying

---

[124] The two médersas were created by Ibrahim Diénopo in 1955-6 in Bobo-Dioulasso and by Sanogo Mahamoud in 1957. Sanogo Mahamoud had actually studied in the Segu médersa, but Ibrahim Diénopo had only received pedagogical advice. See Issa Cissé, 'Les médersas au Burkina. L'aide arabe et la croissance d'un système d'enseignement arabo-islamique', *ISASS*, no. 4 (1990), p. 59.

[125] Jean-Claude Froelich, *Les musulmans d'Afrique noire* (Paris: Editions de l'Orante, 1962), pp. 172 and 226. Kane, 'La vie', p. 462, claims that Mahmoud Ba was directly or indirectly responsible for the founding of 76 médersas in West and Central Africa.

[126] *Ibid.*, p. 227, note 3.

[127] *Ibid.*, p. 174, and Kaba, *The Wahhabiyya*, p. 163.

[128] Froelich, *Les musulmans d'Afrique noire*, p. 274.

the exclusion of 'blacks' from the Timbuktu médersa, that 'our Bambaras, Malinkes and Sarakollés' only want French schooling. One could still hear the same argument in the 1990s in Mali (that the success of the médersas was due primarily to the failure of the state schools) even though the médersas account for approximately 20 per cent of children enrolled in primary schools. Of course, there is a demonstrable relationship between assessments of the efficacy of the two systems by parents and where they enrol their children, but the idea that the médersas exist only because of the failure of the French system to expand more rapidly is a seriously flawed interpretation of the factors which have been at play in the evolution of the médersas.

In fact, by the 1950s French Islamic policy was under considerable strain; all efforts to contain the influence of Islam had come to nought, and one symptom of this reality was the rapid and unexpected success of the new network of Muslim schools. Marcel Cardaire recognized this fact as early as 1952 when he wrote that the government was unable to stop the momentum of the médersa movement, because no sooner did the administration close one school than another soon opened. Furthermore, he added, the proprietors of the new schools were able to convince parents that 'religion can be taught in a rational manner that does not require urban children to neglect either their material future or their general education'.[129] He concluded that the various decrees that regulated Qur'anic education were dead letters. It will be recalled that this legislation limited the program of study that could be taught in Qur'anic schools so that they could not be defined as educational establishments and could not qualify to receive financial assistance from the government. These regulations were used to control and limit the influence of the new médersas, which is precisely why the French insisted upon designating them officially as Qur'anic schools rather than médersas. The Azharists were not permitted to introduce a French cycle of study into their curriculum, and even after being allowed to open as a Qur'anic school, it was closed in 1951 for allegedly failing to conform to the regulations. Saada Oumar had been reprimanded for contravening the same regulations in 1951 for teaching too much Arabic, and in 1954 for introducing instruction in French, which he was not formally authorized to do until 1959, only after promising that he would not request any government assistance. It must be said that authorization to teach French was a significant concession on the part of the administration (now the République Soudanaise), but Saada Oumar had to fight hard to obtain it, and his médersa was almost shut down before the issue was resolved.

In spite of this sustained campaign by the colonial administration to retard the scholastic development of the new médersas, in 1962 J.C. Froelich could write:

Frequently the heads of Qur'anic schools solicited financial assistance, like the Catholic or Protestant schools; it was always difficult to make them understand that the missionary schools benefited from government subventions to the extent that they taught

[129] AMI, Cardaire, 'Rapport … Pèlerinage à la Mecke en 1952'.

secular subjects in conformity with the programs of the official schools, and that their religious activities were not financed. However, the heads of Muslim schools were unable to create schools that were comparable to the missionary establishments in which religious education is presented as an annex to the scholastic program. Several attempts of this sort by the reformists or the counter-reformists were not sustained and, little by little, these mixed schools disappeared or fell back to the level of traditional Qur'anic schools.[130]

One suspects that the heads of the 'Qur'anic schools' understood better than Froelich what was happening; any effort to conform with the existing legislation in order to receive subventions was consistently refused by the administration. But this sustained subversion of their efforts did not stop them trying. In 1957, a group of fifty-eight Muslims in Sikasso submitted the following petition for the creation of a new médersa:

Considering that it is the duty of every Muslim parent to provide a religious education for his children,

Recognizing that a rational knowledge of Arabic is the most effective means for combating the religious obscurantism which generates fanaticism,

Considering, also, that Africa must offer its moral contribution to the rest of humanity,

The Muslims of Sikasso request:

(1) the creation of a médersa, which already exists in embryo,

(2) the positive assistance of the Administration for the construction of the establishment in the public interest.[131]

In addition to its testimony about the gathering momentum of the médersa movement, this petition gives expression to an arresting ironic twist, because its authors contend that knowledge of the Arabic language is an effective antidote to religious fanaticism. One wonders if they were aware of the statement cited earlier in this chapter by Governor-General William Ponty who almost fifty years earlier had this to say about combating fanaticism:

Everyone knows that the study of French is the most effective cure one can employ against [religious] fanaticism, and experience teaches us that Muslims who know our language are less imbued with prejudice than those who know only Arabic.

Of course, the discourse about 'fanaticism' versus 'rationality' was not new, nor would it end here; nor would the political struggles surrounding language conclude with the move to Malian independence. But the apparent paradox of Muslims advocating the 'rational knowledge of Arabic' as a means for opposing 'fanaticism' is symptomatic of the patterns of change which were emerging. The appearance of the Islamic médersas might in part be interpreted as a reaction to the French presence and to French schooling, and perhaps in some degree to the French médersas. But more fundamentally this new institution emerged as a result of the movement of persons and ideas between West Africa and the Middle East, and also in response to changing conditions within West Africa brought by the new colonial situation.

[130] Froelich, *Les musulmans d'Afrique noire*, p. 169.
[131] AMI, Motion par la population musulmane de Sikasso, 18 Sept. 1957.

The first Islamic médersas were established by young men whose life experiences had to a greater or lesser extent dislodged them from local social and religious contexts and norms and caused them to reflect not only on the nature of their own religious practice, but also on how best to transmit Islamic knowledge to young Muslims in the constantly evolving colonial context. These educational pioneers were caught up in the contemporary flow of social change; most endorsed the political movement toward independence, and their initiatives were in no way designed to turn back the social, political, or indeed religious clock. And the médersas they founded were intended to promote such change, to produce educated Muslims who could function effectively as such in contemporary social, political and economic conditions. All these young men seem to have been conscious of these goals, although they might not have been so aware of other implications of their actions, for example that they were moving Muslim schooling into a public domain where it would become the object of external administrative regulation, or that their médersas would necessarily become integrated into a cash exchange economy in which religious education would risk becoming commoditized. Both these factors were evident from the initial appearance of the médersas, although the attention of the first directors was necessarily attracted primarily by the political opposition to their activities, to which we now turn.

3

REFORM AND COUNTER-REFORM: THE POLITICS OF MUSLIM SCHOOLING IN THE 1950s

The preceding chapter documented the origins of Muslim educational reform in Soudan Français. Here we will analyze the broader social and political context of these initiatives as well as the response to them in what came to be called the 'counter-reform' movement. The pioneers of the médersa movement had clearly and consciously broken with established forms of Muslim education. They also seem to have accepted both the challenges and the opportunities presented by the social, economic and political realities of post-war West Africa, and their initiatives were among the first steps toward enabling transformed Muslim institutions to respond to these new conditions. Among them, Mahmoud Ba seems from the first to have been the most conscious of the political implications of his actions, but over time all of these men, and their successors, would come to realize that in order for their new-style schools to succeed, they would have to engage with the structural underpinnings of the newly emerging political economy. The result was a dynamic interaction of contradictory religious, political and cultural influences from the Middle East, local African society and French colonial institutions. This process extended over a considerable period of time (and, indeed, still continues), sometimes comfortably and even imperceptibly, sometimes accompanied by the tensions of resistance and confrontation.

During the 1950s Muslims were not so much seeking an Islamic alternative to French hegemony as trying to reshape Muslim institutions to function effectively in the prevailing conditions. In fact, even these somewhat limited, if nonetheless ambitious, objectives may well have evolved rather slowly, and in the early stages the motivations of many of the médersa pioneers may well have been more pedestrian, such as acquiring a secure livelihood. But their own individual experiences, diverse as they were, inevitably influenced the manner in which they would teach and the futures that they would envisage for their students. Thus, Saada Oumar would experiment with French pedagogical methods in the teaching of Arabic, and Mahmoud Ba would accompany a group of his students to the Middle East in order to enrol them in al-Azhar. Similarly significant, and characteristic of this period of profound change, was the founding of new kinds of Muslim organisations, like *Shubban al-muslimin* and the *Union Culturelle Musulmane*, based on both Middle Eastern and western models of voluntary associations. These new departures, fuelled by either imposed or voluntary contact with the outside world, inevitably challenged local perceptions of Islam.

West African Muslims had never been completely isolated from contacts with North Africa or the Middle East, but the introduction of more convenient and less expensive methods of transport was offering the possibility of travel to many more people. African Muslims who traveled to the Middle East from the 1930s onwards, either to perform the pilgrimage or to study, were plunged into an Islamic milieu of intense political activity and intellectual ferment, ranging from the political radicalism of the Muslim Brothers to the religious radicalism proposed by the interpreters of Salafi doctrine.[1] All these various activities were expressions of an intense commitment on the part of certain Muslims to formulate Islamic interpretations and responses to contemporary problems and issues. Few Africans were unaffected by the energy and excitement of these movements, and some, like the Azharists and Mahmoud Ba, welcomed the opportunity to explore new ideas and ideologies.

The appearance of the médersas, therefore, was but one aspect of the broader evolution of social and political transformation which was taking place both within West Africa, in response to the stimulus of the French presence, and through the internationalization of personal experience and personal contacts. The Azharists and Mahmoud Ba returned from the Middle East in possession of all the ingredients for an Islamic ideological challenge to the domination of both the French and the local Muslim establishments. Even Saada Oumar, whose travel outside of Soudan was relatively limited, was in touch through his reading with contemporary developments on the international scene, particularly with respect to education. The experiences and the expectations of these young men were quite different from those of their parents' generation, and indeed from those of many of their contemporaries, and they began to explore and test new ideas of what it might mean to be a Muslim in the mid-twentieth century.

From this situation there emerged a complex religio-political contest about the nature of 'Islam' itself, of its substantive content, and about the form of its practice. Among the parties to this contest were elements of the French colonial administration (essentially the agents of the *Bureau des Affaires musulmanes*, which was under the administrative authority of the *Direction des Affaires politiques*) who usually allied themselves with those Muslims who came to be known as the 'traditionalists', among the most prominent of whom were such leaders as Muhammad Sharif of Kankan and Seydou Nourou Tal of Senegal, the *grands marabouts* of the colonial period. Ranged against them were those who were labelled the 'reformists' or the 'Wahhabis'; these two terms however are not synonymous, since for example, one of the earliest

---

[1] See both Kaba, *The Wahhabiyya*, and Cardaire, *L'Islam et le terroir africain*.

educational reformists, Saada Oumar Touré, was a committed Tijani and opponent of Wahhabism in all its manifestations.

The French were concerned about the internationalization of Islam and very anxious to resist any spread of the Arabic language in West Africa. The most fundamental innovation of the early médersas was the teaching of Arabic as a foreign language. For their part, and typically, the Muslim factions of all persuasions very soon began to debate the relevant issues in doctrinal terms. It matters little whether Muhammad Sharif labeled the Azharists 'Wahhabi fanatics' before or after they denounced the Muslim establishment; the tensions which led to these conflicts would have had inevitably to be stated in doctrinal terms for them to have had any purchase in a Muslim context. The critical year for the crystallization of this contest seems to have been 1950. That was when Muhammad Sharif confronted the Azharists in Bamako, and when local French administrators began to abandon their analysis of the dynamics of Muslim society on the basis of adherence to the different Sufi orders. Henceforth, their reports would refer to 'modernists', 'reformists', and eventually 'Wahhabis' whom they would contrast with 'traditionalists'.[2] More significantly, and perhaps the stimulus for the shift in analytical perspective, was a directive in January 1950 from the Ministère de la France d'Outre-mer to the Governors General of French West and French Equatorial Africa ordering the adoption of policies designed to check the spread of Islam into regions where it had not yet taken firm root. The language of this communication was unequivocal and extreme: it called for a policy of containment (*politique d'endiguement*) to dam up the flood of this 'fanatical and xenophobic' Islam, and for the appointment of only ...

... the best-informed administrators on Islamic matters, and definitely not those who are seduced by the external aspects of Islam or by the relative learning of certain black Africans or who are interested only in an aesthetic or intellectual satisfaction, but those who really perceive in Islam an eminent danger and are capable of denouncing and combating it.[3]

It was in the context of this new battle against the spread of Islam that Marcel Cardaire came to *Affaires musulmanes* in Soudan in early 1952. He was certainly well informed about Islam, but it is questionable that he fit well the profile of the kind of administrator the Minister was seeking. He endorsed and supported the counter-reform program, which was first proposed by Amadou Hampâté Bâ, at this time attached to the Bamako branch of the *Institut français*

---

[2] This change in perception can be traced in the monthly reports of 1950, where major entries are reserved for the different Sufi orders, and references to Wahhabis or 'tendances Jeune-Islam' appear under the heading 'Divers'. In subsequent years, very little official attention was given to the Sufi orders. See CAOM, 19 G 11, Synthèse mensuelles des questions musulmanes, 1950.

[3] CAOM, Affaires Politiques, 2158, dossier 4, quoted from J.-L. Triaud, 'Le Crépuscule des "Affaires Musulmanes" en A.O.F. (1950-1956)', in Robinson and Triaud (eds), *Le temps des marabouts*, p. 494.

d'Afrique noire (IFAN). The aim of the program was to demonstrate that children could learn to be good Muslims without the formal study of the Arabic language, and it was to be based on the teachings of Hampâté Bâ's spiritual guide and Sufi master, Cerno Bokar Salif Tal.[4] The plan was to provide Islamic religious instruction in local African languages either in purpose-built schools or as a supplement to the French school curriculum after normal school hours. Hampâté Bâ's views complemented those of the French; he opposed the introduction of Arabic language and culture into West Africa, which he felt would hasten the deterioration of the local cultural heritage whose richness and sophistication he wished to preserve. He was also a defender of his own version of 'black Islam' which in his view was both tolerant and ecumenical.

The reader will recall that almost half a century earlier, Paul Marty had also endorsed the notion of a 'black Islam', which he distinguished from 'white Islam'. In his view, since 'blacks' were only superficially Muslim they should not be offered a French médersa schooling that might improve their knowledge of Islam. These kinds of views still circulated in the 1950s, and not a few in the colonial administration viewed 'black Islam' as a submissive, unworldly and largely collaborative phenomenon which recognized the (natural?) superiority, authority and good will of the French. Such views were encouraged by Hampâté Bâ himself, although official support for his project of counter-reform was based more on hope than conviction. By the early 1950s, regardless of directives coming from Paris, local administrators (especially Cardaire) had already accepted that it was unlikely they would be able to turn the tide of reform. On the other hand, they felt they had nothing to lose by endorsing the counter-reform experiment that like the médersas drew its inspiration from a complex mix of influences and inspirations. The project did not succeed, but neither was it without impact during the 1950s.

The social and political context of reform

Only gradually during the latter half of the 1940s, did the administration in Soudan Français begin effectively to read the signs of the internationalization of Islam that was beginning to appear in West Africa. Authorization to open the Kayes médersa was given without any apparent hesitation; and suspicions about the Azharists in Bamako were mild until deepened by the intervention of Muhammad Sharif in Kankan. In the mid-1940s the French for the most part still perceived West Africa as a kind of self-contained enclave. Adherence to Islam was growing at what appeared to them to be an alarming rate,[5] but few in the local administration felt that they could stop this trend. In 1944 new

---

[4] See A.H. Bâ, *Vie et enseignement de Tierno Bokar. Le sage de Bandiagara* (Paris: Editions du Seuil, 1980) and A.H. Bâ and Marcel Cardaire, *Tierno Bokar. Le sage de Bandiagara* (Paris, 1957), and Brenner, *West African Sufi*.

[5] Census figures reported an increase in French West Africa from 3,875,000 Muslims in 1924 to 6,241,000 in 1936.

procedures were introduced designed to increase the surveillance of prominent religious figures (Muslim and non-Muslim alike), for whom official
support was to be reduced. A new and more thorough system of intelligence
records was adopted, and further assistance in tightening these controls was
requested from the officers of the *Affaires militaires musulmanes*, soon to become the *Bureau des Affaires musulmanes*.[6] In 1945 two decrees were promulgated
which regulated the functioning of both Qur'anic and 'catechism' schools;[7]
this was the legislation which the French would use in their attempts to
control and limit the evolution of the médersas as well as to support the
counter-reform schools.

The ultimate cause for closure of the médersas in Bamako and Kayes was
certainly the new 'policy of containment' declared from Paris, whatever reasons were circulated locally to justify these actions. Indeed, the fact that these
institutions were allowed to open in the first place was a sign of the kind of
alleged weakness in Islamic policy that the 1950 directive was intended to rectify.[8] But even if the French managed to close a few médersas, many officials
became increasingly aware over time that they could not effectively contain
the social forces which were gathering strength in post-war West Africa. During the period from 1945 to 1960, new patterns of regional and international
Muslim networks and organizations began to take shape, of which the appearance of the first médersas was but one symptom.

The Bamako médersa and its founders were located within the Malinké-
Jula regional network of Muslim merchants and young teachers.[9] The heartland
of this network was bounded by the cities of Kankan, Bamako, Sikasso and
Bouaké, but extended to the coast, for example in Conakry and Abidjan, and
into the sahel via Bobo Dioulasso and Mopti to the Niger bend. During the
twentieth century, many of these cities had been transformed from villages
into major commercial entrepôts along the now reorientated trade routes of
the region which for centuries had traversed the sahelian, savanna, forest and
coastal zones. The Muslim merchant communities which had dominated most
of this long-distance trade did not escape the impact of these transformations.

Groups which formerly had not engaged in trade were attracted to the
expanding commercial opportunities offered by the colonial economy; integration into their new métier was accompanied by their conversion to Islam.

---

[6] AMI, Circulaire du décembre 1944, signé par Cournarie, Chef de Bureau Politique
(AOF) et Texier, Chef du Cabinet.
[7] Arrêtés no. 2541 of 20 Aug. 1945 and no. 2549 of 21 Aug. 1945; see CAOM, Affaires
Politiques, 2256, dossier 4. See also AMI, Lettre du Gouverneur Soudan aux Commandants de Cercle du 26 septembre 1945, citing the two *arrêtés*.
[8] For a discussion of the development, and demise, of Islamic policy in the *Bureau des
Affaires musulmanes* during the 1950s, see Triaud, 'Le Crépuscule'.
[9] For the Malinké-Jula network, see Kaba, *The Wahhabiyya*; Cardaire, *L'Islam et le terroir
africain*; J.-L. Amselle, *Les négociants de la savane. Histoire et organisation sociale des Kooroko (Mali)*
(Paris: Anthropos, 1977); Robert Launay, *Traders without Trade: Responses to change in two Dyula
communities* (Cambridge University Press, 1982) and *Beyond the Stream*.

A well-documented example of this process can be found among those Kooroko of southwestern Mali who successfully entered the kola trade during the colonial period.[10] The same factors which were facilitating the movement of commercial goods, and which were attracting new competitors into commerce, also stimulated the resettlement of many Muslim merchants in the rapidly growing new urban centers. In this increasingly international urban environment, Muslims found themselves under pressure to abandon the somewhat particularistic Islamic practices of their communities of origin in favour of more universally integrative forms of Islamic expression. Not surprisingly, these were provided by contemporary Middle Eastern ideas and practices which West African students and pilgrims had discovered in Egypt and Saudi Arabia: culturally and institutionally in the form of médersa education and of new kinds of religious associations such as *Shubban al-muslimin*, and doctrinally in the influences of Salafi interpretations of Islam. These ideas and institutions constituted the raw material with which the young founders of the Bamako médersa and their colleagues began to work in their attempts to refashion Muslim infrastructures in order to integrate them more fully into mid-twentieth-century social, political and economic realities.

To a certain extent, this process was taking place under the impetus of the fundamental changes that accompanied the colonial experience. Many communal aspects of Islamic practice simply did not survive in the new colonial situation because they became redundant. One such example, discussed in Chapter One, was the distinction in northern Ivory Coast between the Jula social categories of *tun tigi* ('warriors') and *mory* ('scholars').[11] The 'warriors', as the term suggests, were concerned with warfare and governance, whereas the 'scholars' were concerned with Qur'anic education, the maintenance and direction of religious institutions, and with providing various other religious services. The 'warriors' were rather lax Muslims, who drank openly and prayed irregularly, and whose initiation rituals were directly modeled on those of the non-Muslim Senufo. The social category of 'warrior' simply lost its *raison d'être* in the colonial context, although it is arguable that it was replaced structurally and functionally by the new class of French-educated civil servants of the colonial and post-colonial regimes. These civil servants (*fonctionnaires*), the overwhelming majority of whom are at least nominally Muslim, were (and are) often criticized by certain Muslims as being religiously lax; they are accused of praying irregularly (if at all) and of drinking alcohol. These alleged failures to conform with Muslim norms are often attributed to the influences of secular, French-language schooling. Arguably, the *poro*-style initiation of the Jula 'warrior' has been replaced for the *fonctionnaire* by the explicitly non-Muslim process of French schooling.

---

[10] See J.-L. Amselle, *Les négociants de la savane*, and his *Logiques métisses. Anthropologie de l'identité en Afrique et ailleurs* (Paris: Payot, 1990).
[11] See Launay, *Traders without Trade*.

The emergence of the Muslim *fonctionnaire* played a significant role in the evolution of Muslim ideologies after the Second World War. Clearly, the phenomenon of the lax Muslim was not new in West Africa, but it provided one focus for Muslim thinking about the directions 'Islam' must take in order to respond to the new situation. Although Muslim *fonctionnaires* were not representatives of Islam as such, they were Muslims in positions of public responsibility and consequently attracted the criticism of persons who wished to resist both French hegemony and the influence of secularism in public affairs. The social tensions created by these circumstances gave vent to political conflicts that were expressed by some Muslims in religious terms. Robert Launay has demonstrated that these conditions led to religious orthodoxy becoming an ideological issue in urban areas with ritual and doctrine becoming the focus of discourse.[12] But the médersa movement was also a feature of the same process: it was a Muslim contribution to a debate about education and socialization in a rapidly changing social milieu.

If the Malinké-Jula network provided one of the first significant footholds for Salafi doctrine in West Africa other networks, and new associations, evolved in somewhat different socio-economic contexts. One of these was centered on the activities of Mahmoud Ba, who not only inspired the founding of a large number of médersas, but who brought together young students trained in these new schools from Senegal, western Mali and Mauritania and encouraged them to continue their studies in the Middle East, where of course he also maintained very important contacts. These initiatives were reinforced and carried forward by the *Union Culturelle Musulmane* (UCM) founded in Dakar in 1953 by Cheikh Touré and others who had studied in North Africa and the Middle East. Mahmoud Ba's formal association with the UCM is unclear, although the organization applied to assume the sponsorship of the Kayes médersa after it had been closed by the French. As was mentioned in the previous chapter, the contemporary Falah movement in Senegal, which receives much of its financial support from elements within the Senegalese commercial community, traces its origins directly to him.

The career of Cheikh Touré is itself illustrative of the process here under discussion. Born in 1925, his early education included training in both French and Arabic languages; he has written extensively in French. In 1949, he attended the *Institut des études islamiques* in Boutilimit, which was part of the French médersa system, and in 1952 he received a scholarship to study in the French médersa in Algiers. Within only a few months, the scholarships for Africans were withdrawn (one wonders if there was any political signficance in this fact) and Touré was meant to return to Dakar. Before his departure, however, he was contacted by certain of the Algerian *'ulama*, who invited him and his fellow-students to the institute directed by Abd al-Hamid Ben Badis in Constantine, '... where we had the opportunity to initiate ourselves into the

---

[12] *Ibid.*, pp. 126-7. See also Launay, *Beyond the Stream*.

activities of the Islamic movement with the *Jama'at al-'ulama* and to read the press.'[13]

These experiences in Algeria were the direct inspiration for the founding of the UCM, whose major aims and activities were educational, although it developed an increasingly political, anti-French stance during the 1950s as the agitation for independence intensified. There was also a doctrinal, anti-*marabout* and anti-Sufi dimension to their program, which was expressed in its most extreme form by Cheikh Touré himself in his short book, *Afin que tu deviennes un croyant*.[14] But the official statutes of the UCM placed most of their emphasis on education:

to unite all the Muslims, male and female alike, in order to allow them to know and help one another better and to perfect their religious formation;
to utilize for this purpose modern education and pedagogy, such as lectures, religious and artistic performances, movies, excursions, camping, etc.;
to create and develop libraries, to set up local headquarters for the members, to found and manage schools;
to struggle against all influences prejudicial to the educaton of the children;
to combat, by all appropriate means, shameful exploitation by charlatans, fanaticism and superstitions – in short, to cleanse Islam by getting rid of all corrupting influences and practices;
to help the students with gifts in kind and in cash and with parcel packages;
to send students wherever they can perfect their education.[15]

This is an exceptionally mild document as compared with the general resolutions passed by the UCM's conference in December 1957. These included demands for the construction of *écoles arabes*, official recognition of their social contribution, and public grants which would enable graduates of these schools to continue their studies abroad and who should then be found administrative positions upon the successful completion of their higher studies. The conference also called for the dissolution of the *Bureau des Affaires musulmanes* to be replaced by an elected body of Muslims to advise the administrative authorities; a cease fire in Algeria was also called for.[16] The increasingly strident tone of the UCM demands was part of the political fervour which built up during the years preceding independence and which led one colonial official to remark that the UCM was using religion to conceal its true objective 'to convert the Muslim masses to Marxism'.[17] By this time the UCM had become perhaps the most important inter-territorial 'modern' Muslim association in French West Africa, with branches in Senegal, Soudan, Guinée, Ivory Coast,

[13] See Gomez-Perez, 'Associations islamiques à Dakar', p. 6, where she quotes an autobiographical article by Cheikh Touré in a Dakar monthly, *Le Musulman*, May 1989. The specific reference to Ben Badis is from Sylla, 1986).
[14] Cheikh Touré, *Afin que tu deviennes un croyant* (Dakar: Imprimerie Diop, 1957).
[15] Quoted in Kaba, *The Wahhabiyya*, p. 236.
[16] CAOM, Affaires Politiques, 2260, dossier 2, Bulletin de Renseignements, 3 Feb. 1958: Notice d'information, Le congrès de l'Union Culturelle Musulmane.
[17] *Ibid.*

Upper Volta and Togo. In Soudan, *Shubban al-muslimin* had dissolved their association in order to become integrated into the UCM.

The situation with Saada Oumar Touré in Segu was again different. Although he called upon the advice and assistance of a small group of friends and advisors as he developed the new curriculum for his médersa, he was not the founder of any new association, nor was he the centre of any semi-formal network of activities, even when his students began to establish their own médersas. No significant functional or ideological relationships seem to exist among the many former students of the Segu médersa, although many of them are full of praise for their teacher and mentor. One major reason for this absence of organizational initiative on Saada's part may well be his continued allegiance to the Umarian branch of the Tijaniyya Sufi order. As a loyal disciple of Madani Tal, one of his own academic teachers as well as his Sufi master, it is not clear how he could have initiated any kind of new organization or association which would not have challenged the authority of the Tijani leadership. Indeed, his educational experiments were opposed at first by many leaders of the Segu community, and it seems likely that his support by the Tijani hierarchy accounts in part for his success in keeping his médersa open.

The question of the relationship between Saada Oumar's status within the Tijaniyya and the nature of his activities as an educational reformer and social activist is worthy of further exploration. By contrast with Saada, Mahmoud Ba and the Azharists had located their médersas in cities where they were strangers and where as outsiders they were relatively independent of family and local social constraints; indeed, it will be recalled that Mahmoud Ba moved his médersa from his home village to Kayes, and that the Azharists settled in Bamako after not being allowed to open a school in Kankan. In addition, neither Ba nor the Azharists were associated with the Sufi brotherhoods whereas Saada Oumar was from a family that was closely associated with the Tal of Segu. Consequently, although Saada Oumar was extremely innovative and even aggressive in the development of his médersa, he was much more constrained by the limited social and political space in which he could manoeuvre.

This situation had less to do with the inherent nature of Sufi organization as such, than with Saada's lack of autonomy and perhaps authority within the Tijani hierarchy. As previously suggested, he could not have taken any organizational or associational initiatives without challenging in some way the local Tijani leadership. But other Tijanis were themselves involved in the many changes that were taking place during this time, notably the Niass branch of the Tijaniyya which was centered in Kaolack, Senegal. From the 1930s under the leadership of Ibrahim Niass, son and successor of the founder of this order, the Niass Tijaniyya began to grow into an international organization which was acquiring adherents right across West Africa to the Republic of Sudan; its most significant membership outside of Senegal is in Nigeria, and today it has branches even in the United States among African-American Muslims. Of relevance to the present discussion is Ibrahim Niass's restructuring of the brotherhood in the late fifties into a modern-style association to which he gave the name *Ansar al-din*. Sections were created, one per village, one or more per city as needed, each of which elected a president, vice-president, secretary-general, treasurer, etc. The sections in turn were meant to elect representatives to a supreme council that would oversee the entire organization through regular meetings in Kaolack. These sections tended to become grouped regionally into sub-associations. One such in Kano State, Nigeria, known as *Fityan al-Islam*, was formed in 1961 and by 1986 claimed no less than 1,200 sections, each with a *zawiya* and a school, providing for the dispensation of religious education to a total of more than 100,000 children.[18] Ibrahim Niass was responsible for many other innovations in Sufi organization, including the popularisation of recruitment and of appointment to responsible office (such as *muqaddam*), the elevation of the status of women in the order, and a somewhat radical political policy which aligned him with leaders of the pan-African unity movement of the 1960s such as Gamal Abdel Nasser and Kwame Nkrumah. In fact, the Niass Tijaniyya was much more popular and influential outside than within Senegal.[19]

But of course, the most influential pole of attraction for many West African Muslims during this period, as has consistently been the case throughout Muslim history, was centered on the Middle East, especially the cities of Cairo, Mecca and Medina, which played a role for Muslim students and intellectuals analogous to that of Paris for young persons educated in the French colonial schools. The intellectual and political stimulation of this international environment has already been noted in the cases of Mahmoud Ba and the Azharists. But the French began fully to appreciate the signficance of these influences only in 1952 when Marcel Cardaire accompanied West African pilgrims to the Middle East as an official representative of the French West African government. His mission was to collect intelligence 'on the origins of Wahhabi propaganda in French West Africa and the contacts which might exist between active movements in the Middle East and the Islamic community in French West Africa'.[20] The information gathered on such missions was deemed invaluable, and agents were assigned to accompany the pilgrims throughout

[18] Ousmane Kane, 'La confrérie Tijaniyya réformée à Kano', mémoire de DEA, University of Paris V, 1987, pp. 42 and 65.

[19] For another example of the early development of such associations, see Stefan Reichmuth, 'Education and the Growth of Religious Associations among Yoruba Muslims – the Ansar-Ud-Deen Society of Nigeria', *Journal of Religion in Africa*, XXVI, 4 (Nov. 1996), pp. 365-405.

[20] This reference to 'Wahhabi propaganda' indicates that by 1952 the French administration had concluded that Wahhabism was a danger to be reckoned with. Quoted from AMI, 'Rapport du Capitaine Cardaire, Commissaire du Gouverncur de l'A.O.F. au Pèlerinage à la Mecke en 1952'. Information from this report is also to be found in Cardaire, *Islam et le terroir africain*. The report is also cited and quoted in Alliman Mahamane, 'Le mouvement wahhabite à Bamako (origine et évolution)', mémoire de fin d'études, l'ENSup, Bamako, 1985, pp. 39ff.

the mid-1950s; Cardaire went again in 1955.[21] In 1952 Cardaire visited Lebanon and Syria as well as Cairo and Jeddah, although the focus of his interest was on West Africans then present in Egypt and Saudi Arabia; his interpretation of what he discovered set the tone for French Islamic policy in Soudan for the 1950s.

Cardaire's report noted that 104 Soudanese were resident in Cairo in 1952, all of them presumably students at al-Azhar. His report does not give the impression that the Soudanese community in Cairo was formally organized within itself in any way, although some sense of shared identity no doubt brought these young men together through the common experience of studying abroad. No particular leaders or prominent individuals were identified, save one Souleymane Camara who acted as spokesmen for the students when Cardaire met with them as a group.[22] Camara is mentioned here because his comments to Cardaire were carefully recorded and are of interest to the present discussion because they illustrate the extent to which events in West Africa were followed and debated in this student milieu. Cardaire noted the deep suspicion with which he was greeted by the students, and Camara had been put forward as a spokesman by the group precisely to pose questions about the motives for Cardaire's mission. The discussion turned to the closure of the Bamako médersa:

'They have closed the school of Kabiné Kaba, which has distressed all of us here. When we return home, we will be learned persons [*savants*], trained by the first university in the world. We will want to enlighten our brothers who have remained uneducated. We want to tell them the truth, but the government will not allow it'.

[Cardaire responded,] ... 'I am not fully informed about this question, but I know that it was the Muslims of Bamako and the Sharif of Kankan who requested the closure of the school about which you are speaking. A government has to listen to the requests of the majority, doesn't it?'

'True, but that majority is a majority of ignorant persons and fetishers. They must be enlightened (and he tightened his arms on his armchair); we have a mission from God, we have something to say and the government must let us speak. Uneducated persons like the Sharif of Kankan and Talibé Kaba [?] deceive the people. We must be allowed to speak.' ...[23]

Cardaire observed that these remarks were delivered in a somewhat 'messianic style' and that it was precisely these kinds of 'fanaticized' people who were causing political problems in West Africa. There was nothing new in French

[21] CAOM, 19 G 15 'Rapport de M. Sankale sur le Pèlerinage à la Mecque en 1953;' AMI, 'Rapport du Chef de Bataillon Amadou Fall, Commissaire du Gouverneur de l'A.O.F. pour le Pèlerinage de 1954;' and AMI, 'Rapport fin de mission, 2 septembre 1955, par Cardaire, Commissaire au pèlerinage aérien pour 1955'.

[22] Cardaire's 1955 pilgrimage report includes a list of Soudanese students then attending al-Azhar which includes a Soulaymane Camara, born in 1922 in Kankan. AMI, 'Rapport fin de mission, 2 septembre 1955, par Cardaire, Commissaire au pèlerinage aérien pour 1955'.

[23] AMI, 'Rapport du Capitaine Cardaire, ... au Pèlerinage à la Mecke en 1952'.

administrators labeling politicized Muslims as 'fanatics'. But this quotation also eloquently documents how this generation of young students would use their educational experience in Cairo to distinguish themselves in the Muslim community at home. They were the new *savants* who must accept their responsibility to enlighten their fellow Muslims at home; they had gained access to the 'truth' which they were determined to convey as soon as they had the opportunity to speak in public. This kind of discourse was not new either; it was part of the continuing contest amongst Muslim intellectuals to gain control over the definition and dissemination of Islamic knowledge. The young students of Cairo were therefore pitted against both the French and their own elders, whom they were prepared to describe as the older generation of 'ignorant' scholars and leaders.

Cardaire's report conveyed a different impression of the West African community in Saudi Arabia, which by contrast seemed to be even more politicised than the community in Cairo. In any case, he identified a number of very influential individuals, including al-Hajj Mahmoud Ba, about whom he wrote detailed accounts. But his attention concentrated primarily on two men from the Niger-bend region of Soudan: Abd al-Rahman al-Ifriqi, a Songhay from Ansongo, and Mohamed Ali Ag Ataher, a chief of the Kel Antassar Tuareg of Goundam.[24] It was these men, especially al-Ifriqi, who provided a source of leadership that was seemingly absent in Cairo. In the first place, both men were somewhat older than the majority of students. Ag Ataher already had two of his own sons in al-Azhar, and al-Ifriqi, about 44 years of age in 1952, was a respected teacher and director of the *madrasah Dar al-Hadith* in Medina. Al-Ifriqi, who had received a French education, allegedly left for the Middle East following an incident in which he was falsely accused of theft by his French employers in the colonial administration.[25] Ag Ataher had been a *conseiller général* in Soudan, as well as chief of the Kel Antassar, but following an 'argument' with the colonial administration, he departed clandestinely for the Middle East.[26] Cardaire observed that he was very interested in the 'African nationalist movements and the problems of decolonization'. According to his own account, Ag Ataher had for years been pursuing an unrelenting campaign to bring educational opportunities to his own people.[27] For both these men, education had become a means to confront what they considered political domination by non-Muslims.

Cardaire saw the two men playing complementary roles, al-Ifriqi as the

---

[24] Information on these two men has been derived from several sources, firstly from Cardaire's 1952 report on the pilgrimage, *op. cit.*, and his *Islam et le terroir africain*. For al-Ifriqi, see Jean-Louis Triaud, ' 'Abd al-Rahman l'Africain'. For Mohamed Ali, see Mohamed Ali Ag Ataher Insar, 'La scolarisation moderne comme stratégie de résistance', *REMMM*, no. 57 (1990), pp. 91-7.

[25] Interview with Mahmoud Zouber, 17 Jan. 1988, Bamako.

[26] *Ibid.*

[27] Ag Ataher Insar, 'La scolarisation', pp. 91ff.

prestigious religious figure and Mohamed Ali as a political organizer and propagandist:

> Mehemet Ali [Ag Ataher] is like the politician who aspires to a certain authority while Abd al-Rahman [al-Ifriqi] is the pious, religious man who is motivated to convince others through his love of God. … It is a matter of the temporal chief and his chaplain; the first employs his strength and prestige to sustain the concepts of the second.[28]

Cardaire was of course preoccupied with this relationship between the religious and the political, because his mission was to assess the impact of such activities upon West African Muslims. Judging from the evidence, however, he might have got it wrong about who enjoyed the real prestige in this team. The reputation of al-Ifriqi had begun to spread among West African pilgrims since at least the mid-1940s; in 1952, of the 330 pilgrims who were in the group which Cardaire accompanied to Jeddah, 84 visited him in Medina, including almost all the pilgrims from Soudan.[29] Cardaire's impression was that the name of al-Ifriqi was as well known among the barely literate Muslims of West Africa as among the most learned scholars.

Al-Ifriqi's reputation, as well as his religious message, had spread through the pilgrim and student network that extended from the Middle East into all of Muslim sub-Saharan Africa. Most of the persons who were closely associated with him in Saudi Arabia were from the Niger-bend region of Soudan,[30] although there were many others as well. The constant flow of visitors and students provided not only a context for the free exchange of ideas but also the means to communicate with like-minded Muslims in Africa. Persons returning to West Africa carried with them correspondence, messages and even publications; some were recruited as preachers and propagandists by Saudi *'ulama*, for whom money was available to finance such activities. In Cardaire's view, al-Ifriqi and Ag Ataher were at the centre of a network which constituted 'what might be called the "Soudanese dimension" of the Islamo-Arab problem in French West Africa'.[31]

The specific nature of this 'problem', as Cardaire perceived it, was a volatile mixture of Salafi religious doctrine with an enhanced political consciousness and activism. We will discuss the content and impact of al-Ifriqi's doctrinal orientations in greater detail below, but here suffice it to say that he taught the works of Ibn Taimiyya and Muhammad 'Abd al-Wahhab in *Dar al-Hadith*, where he himself had formerly studied. This institution was specifically dedicated to the teaching of foreign, especially African, students; it subsequently

---

[28] AMI, 'Rapport du Capitaine Cardaire, … au Pèlerinage à la Mecke en 1952'.
[29] These included 45 Soudanese, 12 Maures, 12 Senegalese, 2 Voltaics, 4 Ivoirians, and 2 Guineans; Cardaire, *Islam et le terroir africain*, pp. 80-1.
[30] Twenty-seven of 33 individuals named in the 1952 report as associates of al-Ifriqi were identified either as members of nomadic groups or as coming from Sahelian towns such as Ansongo, Gao and Goundam.
[31] AMI, 'Rapport du Capitaine Cardaire, … au Pèlerinage à la Mecke en 1952'.

became the Islamic University of Medina under the directorship of al-Ifriqi's own deputy, 'Umar b. Muhammad al-Fallati.[32] Many of the young persons who subsequently have founded médersas in Mali studied at the Islamic University; indeed, *Dar al-Hadith* and the Islamic University have served as models for the development of the médersa system.

Al-Ifriqi was certainly not unaware of the political implications of his religious teachings, although he did not project himself as a political figure. He was described as 'a pious and very cultivated man, … moderate in speech, ingratiating, readily adopting a conciliatory attitude, refusing all agitated discussion'.[33] When asked by one of Cardaire's pilgrim informants whether his 'Wahhabi propaganda' was political, he responded, 'Take it as you wish; we only see it as the application of Qur'anic law'.[34] And he was certainly surrounded by persons who held very explicit political views. One person who made a particular impact on the visiting pilgrims in 1952 was Ibrahim (also known as Amadou) Sylla, a former railway employee from the Ivory Coast. According to Cardaire, Sylla impressed the pilgrims 'by the violence of his language and the bitterness with which he pressed his teacher [al-Ifriqi] to speak in definitive [political] terms;' Sylla himself advocated a 'revolution' to chase the *Nazaréens* [the Christians] from West Africa.[35]

And al-Ifriqi's own comments on matters of religious doctrine and education were filled with political innuendo. He was opposed to the Sufi brotherhoods in West Africa and was also very critical of those 'ignorant' *marabouts* who, 'with their false knowledge, sustained superstitions among the people which are contrary to Qur'anic law'.[36] And he criticized the French administration for obstructing the evolution of the médersas that proposed to teach both the Arabic language and the principles of the Islamic faith in an appropriately orthodox manner, which are 'necessary for every good Muslim'.[37] But al-Ifriqi was also critical of al-Azhar; he is reported to have alleged that 'there is not a single professor in al-Azhar who does not live off usury'.[38] It may be that he convinced Ag Ataher to remove his sons and a nephew from al-Azhar and to enrol them in *Dar al-Hadith*. This hostility toward al-Azhar was not an isolated instance but reflected the beginnings of an active recruiting campaign

---

[32] Al-Fallati was the author of the obituary upon which Triaud based his biographical article about al-Ifriqi; Triaud, ' 'Abd al-Rahman l'Africain'.

[33] AMI, 'Rapport du Capitaine Cardaire, … au Pèlerinage à la Mecke en 1952'.

[34] *Ibid.*

[35] Cardaire, *Islam et le terroir africain*, pp. 81-2; his 1952 report also presents a brief portrait of Sylla.

[36] AMI, Rapport du Chef de Bataillon Amadou Fall, … au Pèlerinage à la Mecque, 1955.

[37] *Ibid.* During his visit with al-Ifriqi in 1955, Amadou Fall attempted to convince him to return to West Africa to take up a position in the Islamic Institute at Boutilimit. Fall proposed that there would always be 'false *marabouts*' in West Africa so long as their best teachers go abroad to teach elsewhere. Al-Ifriqi politely replied that he would consider this offer.

[38] AMI, Rapport du Chef de Bataillon Amadou Fall, … au Pèlerinage à la Mecque, 1954.

financed by the Saudi government to attract an increasing number of African students to study in Saudi Arabia.

Ag Ataher's itinerary had been quite different. He had been politically active in West Africa for several decades before he travelled to the Middle East, where he was recognised as a prominent figure within the Soudanese community, but especially among persons of nomadic background, in whose interests he reportedly was travelling constantly between Cairo, Saudi Arabia and other Middle Eastern capitals. However, there was a sharp political edge to his activities. He spoke definitively to Cardaire's informants about his decision not to return to his home until the political situation took a more favorable turn and until Muslim judges were appointed on the same terms as French magistrates and were empowered to hear cases in accordance with Islamic legal principles. And in his opinion, there was a specific political value in the education which one could obtain in the Middle East ; he was quoted as saying:

Everywhere that I travel in Arabia, in the Anglo-Egyptian Sudan, in Egypt, I find Soudanese who are studying; they are learning things which they cannot learn with the French. When they have acquired this knowledge, they will return home in order to defend the interests of their country.[39]

This statement is more than a simple observation; it is the expression of a profound political commitment. According to his own account, Ag Ataher had become concerned about the political implications for the Tuareg of French educational policy as early as 1920.[40] It will be recalled from Chapter 1, that this was the period, following the recommendations of Paul Marty, that a debate was launched within the colonial administration about the objectives of the Timbuktu médersa. From this time there was a clear tendency to concentrate recruitment for the French médersas among the nomadic populations and to concentrate recruitment for the French schools among the 'black', sedentary populations.

Ag Ataher saw this educational policy as a manoeuvre to marginalize the Tuareg politically, and he became convinced that the political future of his people would be linked to the acquisition of a modern education. He consequently launched a personal campaign to enrol as many Tuareg children as possible in school, but the plan met opposition on all fronts. In this connection, he assisted in the founding of the *école nomade* in Diré.[41] However, the majority of Tuareg parents refused absolutely to countenance the idea that their children should attend a French school; and the French, for their part, clung to their policy that nomadic children should be educated in the French

---

[39] *Ibid.*

[40] The following discussion is based upon a published interview with Ag Ataher on 21 May 1989; see Ag Ataher Insar, 'La scolarisation'.

[41] Interview with Mahmoud Zouber, 17 Jan. 1988, Bamako. The *écoles nomades* were a kind of compromise between the French schools and the French médersas; they taught the basic secular curriculum as well as religious studies and Arabic. After independence, they were incorporated into the system of *écoles franco-arabes*.

médersas, and even then only a select minority of 'notable' children. No doubt some of the resistance to Ag Ataher's proposals resulted from the sheer ambition of what he was proposing. He advocated the systematic enrolment of all children in school and the development of a curriculum that would, in effect, transform their lives. He held the view that a limited or interrupted education could be worse than no education at all. In a perceptive observation, which would become commonplace in later decades, he spoke about how he was unable to communicate effectively with a group of young men who had been sent down from their schools after a few years:

How could they understand? They had left their tents to attend the colonial school when they were about five or seven years old; they had neither acquired a traditional knowledge which would enable them to understand what I was saying, nor reached an adequate academic level so that they might understand in another manner. And so their entire education was lost on both sides, everything was destroyed.[42]

And the French played upon Tuareg suspicions about the impact that French education might have on their children, and their society more generally:

The French administration profited from this and built their propaganda upon the themes of those who refused to enrol their children: 'Beware of Mohamed Ali [Ag Ataher] who wants to destroy your traditions, turn you into Frenchmen, remove you from your present conditions and sedentarize you, modernize you and transform you into town dwellers!' Imagine!, a Tuareg at this time who is prosperous and knows his desert, if you told him to settle in a village of black town dwellers. It would be like living in a chicken coop. It would not be a village of Frenchmen, or northern Berbers, nor of Arabs, which he might accept. What Tuareg would accept such a thing? Disgusting![43]

The racist overtones of these comments are characteristic of much of Ag Ataher's discourse. His political interpretation of the situation was that French educational policy, whether consciously or not, would mean that with independence the Tuareg would become the political subordinates of the sedentary black populations of Soudan. Supposedly he confronted the Governor-General of French West Africa with such a charge during an interview in Dakar. 'You will soon be gone', he claims to have said. 'And the result is that the Blacks of Soudan and Niger have been educated and not us. That means that you are preparing again our colonization by the Blacks and the Arabs.'[44]

Frustrated in his ambitions to bring education to the Tuareg, Ag Ataher focused his energy on seeking to educate his own children. Here, too, the French seem to have put many obstacles in his way. From his own account, one has the impression of an almost frenetic quest to find an adequate education for his children, seeking to enrol them successively in different schools in Mopti, Bamako, Dakar, Algiers and even Paris. His travels to the Middle East appear to have been part of this search to educate his children, enrolling

[42] Ag Ataher Insar, 'La scolarisation', p. 92.
[43] *Ibid.*
[44] *Ibid.*, p. 93.

them successively in al-Azhar and in Medina. These were the issues which led to the 'argument' between Ag Ataher and the administration, and to his eventual resignation as chief of the Kel Antassar in 1947. He resigned in order to have a free hand in pursuing these objectives.[45]

Clearly, Ag Ataher had many influential contacts throughout the Middle East and North Africa, and throughout his extensive travels he continued to seek support for both his educational and political projects.[46] His story illustrates several important themes which are characteristic of the events here under study. It supports one of the contentions made by many policymakers: that the success of the Islamic médersas could be limited by making more places available in the French-language schools. Secondly, Ag Ataher was not seeking an Islamic education for Tuareg children, but one that would enable them to seize their independence. Education for him was a political project. He found resonance of the same desires among Soudanese in the Middle East, but he does not seem to have been convinced by the doctrinal arguments in vogue there; nor does he seem to have found much support for his educational project. That was made available in Libya, where he claims he was able to enrol over sixty students, including two of his own children. But when he returned to Soudan in 1952, officials were very suspicious of possible Wahhabi influences:

Mohamed Ali ag Attaher, who has just returned from the Hedjaz via Cairo, might be Wahhabi although this is denied by his relatives and does not appear in the correspondence which he has exchanged with them. On the other hand, he has always insisted in this correspondence on the necessity of his fellow tribesmen to develop their instruction and this is probably, at least in part to reinforce his exhortations by his example, that he has enrolled two of his sons in the University of al-Azhar. Perhaps it is more convenient for him to speak of modernism and progress rather than Wahhabism despite the relationships he has with Abdoullaye ag Mahmoud on the one hand [see below] and with Ibn Sa'ud and his theologians on the other.[47]

For Ag Ataher himself such doctrinal issues were of little interest; nor was he willing to engage in this kind of religious discourse to support his objectives.

[45] Echoes of Ag Ataher's efforts on behalf of his sons appear in the colonial record. CAOM, 19 G 13, *Revue trimestrielle des questions musulmanes*. Deuxième trimestre, 1952, reports that three of his sons were in schools first in Mecca and then at al-Azhar. Sankale, in his report on the 1953 pilgrimage, *op. cit.*, states that one son, Muftah, pursued his education in Soudan, then at the Lycée Van Vollenhoven in Dakar and then in al-Azhar. He said that another son, Attaher Abdullah, was a student of al-Ifriqi. Sankale described Ag Ataher as the 'most dangerous' of the Soudanese who had been in the Middle East, and charged that he had been involved in the trade in slaves, an allegation denied by Amadou Fall in his report on the pilgrimage in 1954, *op. cit.*

[46] He spent some time in Libya on his return journey to Soudan in 1952. Just before Mali gained its independence, he exiled himself to Morocco, from where he was extradited because of his suspected involvement in the Tuareg rebellion. He was imprisoned in Mali from 1963 to 1977, after which he returned to Morocco.

[47] CAOM, Affaires Politiques, 2158, dossier 3, Rapport de Mission sur la situation de l'Islam en AOF (3 avril-31 juillet 1952), J. Beyries.

He was very perceptive about how the French employed such concepts as Wahhabism and 'tradition' and also how they used their educational policies in order to maintain political control. In his view, because of colonial propaganda and policies, Tuareg society had been denied the educational tools it required to function effectively in the post-independence period. On the one hand the administration discouraged them from enrolling their children in school saying 'they were going to lose their traditions, and on the other hand [the French] offered them a perverted instruction which led to nothing'. They had become like a 'flock of worn-out sheep'.[48]

Cardaire's 1952 report ends on a pessimistic note, which is not surprising considering that it is filled with thumbnail sketches of active and committed individuals, not so prestigious or influential as al-Ifriqi or Ag Ataher, but who were taking full advantage of the freedom of movement and expression that they had found in the Middle East and who fully intended to return to West Africa and to translate their new ideas into action. Cardaire agreed with the contention of al-Ifriqi, that although the French had closed the Bamako médersa, another would open to take its place, and that when the present students of Cairo and Medina return to Soudan, they would find a ready clientele for their new schools. And so, he counseled, let the 'counter-reform' movement go ahead; if it fails, it will not be the fault of the administration. And let the 'traditionalists' resist the Azharists, since there is little the government can do in order to stop the flow of events. The decrees of August 1945 that were being used to contain the médersas were now a 'dead letter' in his view.[49]

It was with these half-hearted recommendations on record that Cardaire would join with Amadou Hampâté Bâ and others to launch the movement of 'counter-reform'.

The politics of counter-reform

Cardaire's recommendations may have been half-hearted, but he nonetheless energetically directed a campaign within Soudan during the 1950s to block the progress of Islamic reform in all its manifestations.[50] French concern was not aroused so much by reform as such, as by the challenges to their own political interests which were emerging in the Arab and Islamic worlds: Algeria, Nasser in Egypt, Suez, Arab nationalism, pan-Islamism, Wahhabi religious propaganda, to name only some of the more salient issues of the period. Counter-reform emerged in this context, as part of a broader policy to counteract the possible influence of such political ideas and to limit the spread of the

---

[48] Ag Ataher Insar, 'La scolarisation', p. 95.

[49] AMI, 'Rapport du Capitaine Cardaire, ... au Pèlerinage à la Mecke en 1952'.

[50] Cardaire may well have been disillusioned with his duties in Soudan throughout the 1950s; see J.-L. Triaud, 'Le Crépuscule'. This article analyses in detail the administrative structures which were put in place to implement the anti-Islamic policies which had been developed during the early 1950s

Arabic language. Significantly, it was an African initiative that was endorsed and supported behind the scenes by the administration.

Such a distinction may seem to be irrelevant, but the French were careful to appear to be acting within the law, regardless of what they might do clandestinely. Thus it was that the Bamako médersa was closed in 1951 on the legal grounds that the number of hours devoted to Arabic exceeded the legal limits, although the real motivations were political. These same regulations governing the operation of private schools would be used both to marginalize the médersas and to support the counter-reform effort. At the same time, the administration never relied solely on the law to achieve their ends, as the following letter from the Governor General clearly indicates:

> In the regions where traditional Islam is solidly rooted, our benevolent neutrality must continue to operate. Where this Islam is confronted by reformist or modernist tendencies which are likely to disturb the public peace or bring unrest, it is in our interest to make it known among the *marabouts* that our discreet support for them is assured. And along the front of Islamic expansion, it is important to promote a firmer policy through the organization of Christian and animist resistance.[51]

In other words, the government was prepared to use every possible means to achieve its objectives, although this same letter explicitly states that no one should have any 'illusions' that the progress of Islam in West Africa could be more than temporarily slowed down.

The preceding quotation also illustrates what Jean-Louis Triaud has called the 'three-zone theory' of Islamization.[52] Triaud demonstrates that from 1950, when the Ministère de la France d'Outre-mer directed authorities in French West and Equatorial Africa to adopt more active policies to resist and contain the 'danger' of Islam, different policies were proposed for different regions depending upon their degree of Islamization, from which considerations emerged the 'three-zone policy'. The precise definitions of these zones varied during the 1950s, depending upon who was describing them and for what purpose. The predominant pattern was to refer to totally Islamized, partially Islamized, and totally 'animist' zones, although there were variations in the scheme. For example, on some occasions Mauritania, along with northeast Chad, was described as belonging to a totally Islamized and Arabophone zone; and Soudan was variously described as falling within the partially Islamized zone or the fully Islamized, non-Arabophone zone.

One proposal for how the 'three-zone theory' might be applied to policies on Islamic education can be summarized as follows. In the fully Islamized and Arabophone regions, such as Mauritania and northeast Chad, the government might support secondary and advanced Islamic studies in Arabic (as they did in Boutilimit; see below), but in such schools the study of French language and the modern sciences should also be obligatory, as well as 'moral

[51] CAOM, Affaires Politiques, 2256, dossier 4, Lettre du Gouverneur-Général au Ministère de la France d'Outre-mer, 7 July 1950.

[52] J.-L. Triaud, 'Le Crépuscule', pp. 498-500.

and civic instruction'. In non-Arabophone, areas, such as parts of Soudan, Guinea, and Senegal, the government might support programs in which only the Qur'an and essential prayers were to be taught in Arabic, while all other subjects, such as *tawhid* and other religious sciences, would be taught 'only in indigenous languages'. No secondary or advanced Islamic instruction would be supported by government in this zone. In areas of limited Islamization, the teaching of only 'the best known verses of the Qur'an and the essential prayers' would be permitted.[53]

The counter-reform program was developed specifically to counteract the impact of the new médersas and to undermine the appeal of Islamic education in the Arabic language in Soudan, that is, in a partially Islamized and non-Arabophone zone. Originally conceived by Amadou Hampâté Bâ, it was set up and directed by his son-in-law, Abd al-Wahhab Doukouré, who had studied in Zaituna University in Tunis and was literate in both French and Arabic. Technically, this was a private initiative, but the colonial government supported it in numerous important ways, short of directly (and publicly) subsidizing it. The program was not unanimously endorsed in official circles; many administrators were skeptical that it would have any significant effect. But it was finally approved on the basis of the argument that if it did work, it would serve French interests, and if it didn't, the administration would not have to assume any blame for the failure.

The origins of the counter-reform program, like the evolution of the médersas, can be traced to the educational experiences of its major proponent, Amadou Hampâté Bâ. His schooling, however, differed significantly from that of the founders of the médersas; he was educated in French schools to a relatively advanced level and was employed in the colonial administration from the 1920s. He did not receive a classical Islamic education, except for a brief period in Qur'anic school as a child and occasional tuition as an adult, and he did not know Arabic. Virtually all of his religious formation, which he received in the Fulfulde language, he attributed to his religious mentor and Sufi master, Cerno Bokar Saalif Tal.[54] It would not be an exaggeration to say that the faithful transmission of Cerno Bokar's teachings, in both form and content, remained one of Hampâté Bâ's most cherished aims throughout his adult life. The form was an abbreviated catechism of basic Islamic knowledge taught orally in Fulfulde, that is, not in Arabic. The content built upon the basic articles of faith and a few Qur'anic *suras* into a Sufi mystical and ecumenical teaching. The counter-reform program presented Hampâté Bâ an opportunity to fulfill his lifelong aim. Its appeal to the French should be

---

[53] CAOM, Affaires Politiques, 2256, dossier 3, Note d'étude sur l'instauration d'un enseignement coranique et arabe en Afrique Noire, no date.

[54] Hampâté Bâ made constant reference to his debt to Cerno Bokar in many of his publications, but perhaps his fullest portayal of their relationship is found in the two published volumes of his mémoirs: *Amkullel, l'enfant peul* (Paris: Actes Sud, 1991); and *Oui mon commandant! Mémoires II* (Paris: Actes Sud, 1994).

obvious: it would provide Islamic religious instruction which would be completely compatible with French-language schooling, which could be taught in either African languages or French, and which would emphasize the unity of religious experience among Muslims and non-Muslims.

By the 1950s Hampâté Bâ was very well placed in French colonial circles to effect his counter-reform program, the seeds of which arguably began to germinate as early as the late 1930s when he entered into correspondence with Théodore Monod, founder and director of the *Institut français d'Afrique noire* (IFAN) in Dakar. On the advice of French colleagues, Hampâté Bâ had sent Monod a French translation of an oral text taken from Cerno Bokar's Sufi teachings for possible publication. Although the piece was never published, this contact was to lead to both a professional collaboration and an intimate friendship.[55] Monod would eventually arrange to bring Hampâté Bâ to IFAN, from where he was able to launch his illustrious career as a researcher and writer, but Monod would also, during the 1940s, constantly encourage Hampâté Bâ to record as much as he could of Cerno Bokar's life and teachings. Monod was the first person to publish an account of Cerno Bokar and his teachings, and it was with his encouragement that Hampâté Bâ would eventually commit to writing two rather separate aspects of Cerno's teachings. The first was the Islamic catechism which Hampâté Bâ had been taught in Fulfulde, later published under the title *Ma 'd-din* ('What is religion?'), and the second was the 'parables' of Cerno Bokar, which included his spiritual reflections, answers to questions and other religious discourses which Hampâté Bâ committed to writing in about 1946-7. Most Europeans, like Monod, seem to have been much more interested in the latter aspect of the teachings than the former.

It seems highly unlikely that the teachings of Cerno Bokar would ever have been known, much less have gained such wide celebrity as they did, had Hampâté Bâ not translated them into French, and had Monod not encouraged him so enthusiastically to develop this material. Equally important was the fact that the friendship between the two men was based on a deeply shared religious and spiritual commitment with the result that Cerno Bokar's teachings from the first were presented to the French-reading public by a Frenchman who respected their content. (The content of the teachings will be discussed further in the next chapter.) But Monod's influence was also significant in other ways. It was through him that Hampâté Bâ was introduced into French intellectual circles. For example, Monod sent Hampâté Bâ's original French text for comment to Louis Massignon, the renowned French scholar of Sufism. He eventually met Massignon in Paris in 1951, where he spent most of the year on a grant from UNESCO, also arranged by Monod. During this visit Hampâté Bâ met many other intellectuals, including Marcel Griaule, the famous ethnologist of the Dogon, who allegedly first

---

[55] For a detailed discussion of the relationship between the two men, see L. Brenner, 'Amadou Hampâté Bâ, Tijani francophone'.

encouraged Marcel Cardaire to make contact with Hampâté Bâ when he was posted to Soudan, . It was with Cardaire that Hampâté Bâ would jointly write the first full account of Cerno Bokar's life and teachings, *Tierno Bokar, le sage de Bandiagara*, published in 1957.

The publication of this book was the realization of a personal project begun twenty years earlier, but its co-authorship with the chief of the *Bureau des Affaires musulmanes* clearly illustrates the intimate manner in which the religious and the political were intertwined in the career of Amadou Hampâté Bâ. In this, Monod and Hampâté Bâ seem to have been somewhat at odds, because for all of their shared interests in scholarship and religion, they disagreed about involvement in politics. And despite Monod's advice to the contrary, Hampâté Bâ could not resist involving himself with the colonial administration when he concluded that counter-reform might be a vehicle for the dissemination of Cerno Bokar's teachings. At that point, in 1951, either directly or through the agency of Abd al-Wahhab Doukouré, Hampâté Bâ began to lobby for the adoption of what would become the counter-reform program. The first official reference to the ideas of counter-reform, and their relationship to the teachings of Cerno Bokar, appeared in that year with the suggestion that the struggle against the 'growing influence of Arab culture' might be aided by introducing religious education into French schools two or three afternoons per week. Such instruction would be offered in the local languages, 'as was done in Bandiagara by the late *marabout* Tierno Bocar [*sic*]'. Traditional chiefs were said to support the idea.[56]

During 1952 these ideas gained increasing currency in official circles, especially after they were endorsed, firstly by Cardaire who arrived in Soudan early in that year, and subsequently by his superior, Mangin, Chief of *Affaires musulmanes* for the entire confederation of French West Africa. The names of Hampâté Bâ and Doukouré, and favorable assessments of their 'loyalty', began to appear regularly in official reports. Former Governor-General Beyries wrote of Hampâté Bâ:

An unusual personality among the Muslims of Bamako is Hamadou Pate Ba [*sic*], who is attached to IFAN. A bit older than fifty years, he is a Peul from Bandiagara, where he studied with Tierno Bokar, and he has also followed correspondence courses of the *Ecole universelle* and acquired a remarkable knowledge of the French language. He has demonstrated his hostility towards the Wahhabism of Kabine Kaba, but would like a transformation of traditional pedagogical methods based upon the use of local languages in the teaching of the Qur'an in order that students can understand what they read, write and recite. In addition, it is rumoured that he has plans for a religious renewal which would seek a conciliation with Christianity.[57]

Later in 1952 Mangin would argue the case for counter-reform before his colleagues in *Affaires politiques* in terms that had been formulated by Cardaire, now the major advocate of the program in the administration. Both the threat

[56] AMI, Soudan, Rapport Politique Annuel, 1951.
[57] Rapport Beyries, 1952.

of Arabization, Mangin contended, and the counter-current opposing it were very real. Counter-reform could count upon the support of many important African personalities, chief among them Muhammad Sharif of Kankan.

Spiritual direction [of the program], which would be the responsibility of Amadou Hampâté Bâ, would be of the highest quality, and would seek its inspiration from a local culture (*terroir*) the richness of which we can only surmise. The execution [of the program] would be confided to Abd al-Wahhab Doukouré, whom readers will know from the last *'Revue trimestrielle des questions musulmanes'* (2ᶜ Trimestre 1952).[58] The prestige which he has gained from his Arabic studies in Zaituna in Tunis and the authority of the good name of his family, well known in Soudan, Senegal and Mauritania, places all the trump cards in the hand of this young man, who has gone beyond both religious conservatism and Muslim nationalism and embraced a Franco-African humanism which consitutes the ultimate objective of our civilizing work.

The precise contours of the project envisaged are: to favor the creation of Muslim schools where a summary teaching of the Qur'an will be combined on the one hand with religious instruction in local languages, inspired to the extent possible by the lessons of Tierno Bokar, this Peul of Bandiagara who was baptized by Th. Monod as 'an African Saint Francis of Assisi', and on the other with elementary instruction in French (language, arithmetic, accounting, rudiments of science).[59]

Late in 1952 the program was officially endorsed by *Affaires politiques* in Paris:

...a memorandum will be circulated in French West Africa with a view to modifying the situation of the Qur'anic schools. Within the context of the decrees in force, a stimulus will be given, in the partially Islamized zones, for the development of Qur'anic instruction in the indigenous language.

The possible creation of private Muslim schooling in indigenous languages will be studied in accordance with the last report prepared by M. Mangin following his mission to Soudan in August 1952.[60]

In 1953 Cardaire and Mangin produced a subsequent report which presented the counter-reform program in both its pedagogical and political aspects. They described counter-reform as a form of Islamic education in 'indigenous languages and in French [given] by teachers who offer full guarantees [i.e., of loyalty to the French cause] to children in certain public schools'.

Briefly, it is a matter of giving Muslim public school pupils a religious instruction modeled on the catechism that their young Christian comrades receive from the missions. From our point of view, the introduction of this form of teaching will have the following advantages:

[58] CAOM, 19 G 13, Revue Trimestrielle des questions musulmanes, Deuxième trimestre, 1952. The report refers to Doukouré as a young Soudanese whom, although he had studied three years in Tunis, 'neither Arab culture nor Oriental puritanism has seduced'. The same report states that Doukouré had proposed opening a school in Bamako where the doctrines of Cerno Bokar would be taught and where Bambara and Fulfulde languages would be employed as languages of instruction.

[59] CAOM, Affaires Politiques, 2256, dossier 4: Extrait du rapport de mission effectuée au Soudan en Haute Volta et au Niger par M. l'Administrateur en Chef MANGIN, Chef du Bureau des Affaires Musulmanes, Aug.-Sept. 1952.

[60] CAOM, Affaires Politiques, 2256, dossier 4, Procès verbal, réunion du 5 décembre 1952.

– to demonstrate that it is possible to study secular subjects and therefore assure the best conditions for one's material life while at the same time be a good Muslim who has an adequate knowledge of the prescriptions of his religion and the rules of living and prayers which it imposes;

– to prove that in using the indigenous language for the youngest children, and French for those who have begun to understand it sufficiently at school, it is possible, employing modern pedagogical methods and books about Islam printed in French, to acquire an adequate knowledge of one's religion during about four hours of class a week;

– to destroy the prestige of the Arabic language which one notes is presently growing in French West Africa, with all the consequences which that brings with it in both the cultural and political domains;

– to rehabilitate in this manner the public school which is considered atheistic by a great number of good Muslims;

– to prevent the creation of private Muslim education for which it will be impossible to refuse subventions.[61]

The final point refers to an issue of some concern within the administration. Hampâté Bâ and Doukouré had proposed the creation of a new kind of Muslim private school in which basic Qur'anic education would be combined with both religious instruction in local languages and basic literacy and numeracy in French.[62] Mangin had recommended the adoption of this program in 1952, and *Affaires politiques* had agreed the matter should be explored for possible implementation. However, it would seem that a decision was taken in Soudan not to endorse the creation of such private schools for fear that this would create a precedent of which other 'less well-intentioned persons might seek to take advantage'.[63] In other words, if private counter-reform schools were approved, it would be difficult to oppose the opening of Islamic médersas in which Arabic would be the language of instruction. The counter-reform program therefore began in Soudan as a supplementary religious studies curriculum made available to public school pupils after school hours in several selected localities. It seems that the Governor General himself directed that the experiment should begin in those areas where the movement toward Arabization was furthest advanced.[64]

The experiment will begin in places chosen from among those which appear to be the most threatened by Arabization:

– in Bamako, in order to fill the vacuum created, one must accept this fact, by the closure of the school of Kabine Kaba in December 1951;

– in Sikasso, where the majority of the Muslim population has rallied to Wahhabism;

– in Diafarabé, in the midst of Peul country in the Macina, where the expansion of Islam has placed French instruction in a difficult position;

[61] CAOM, 19 G 14, Rapport de tournée effectuée au Soudan, en Guinée et en Côte d'Ivoire, par l'administrateur en chef MANGIN, chef du Bureau des Affaires Musulmanes du Gouverneur Général, accompagné du Capitaine Cardaire, 15 Aug.-Sept. 1953.

[62] This plan was outlined in Rapport Mangin, 1952.

[63] Rapport Mangin-Cardaire, 1953.

[64] Rapport Mangin, 1952.

– in Kayes, if possible, where 13 [*sic*] of Mahmoud Ba's students have followed their teacher to al-Azhar, and from where he will presumably soon return;
– and eventually in Segu and Kankan where we know Arabisation has progressed dangerously during recent years.[65]

A closer examination of these cases illustrates that the operation of counter-reform on the ground, although fully consonant with the spirit of policy statements, varied considerably in practice from the stated guidelines. Unfortunately, alomost no information is available about counter-reform activities in either Sikasso or Kankan.[66] Counter-reform schools were opened in Segu in 1954 and in Kayes in 1955; these cases will be examined in detail below, but suffice it to say here that both were private Qur'anic schools and not supplementary courses offered to students attending public schools. The Bamako school seems to have been the successor to *Radiyu 'l 'ilm*, which had been founded in May 1951 in direct competition with the Azharist médersa by *Saut al-din*, of which Hampâté Bâ was Secretary General. This direct link between *Radiyu 'l 'ilm* and its counter-reform successor is nowhere made in the official documentation, but this may be simply because only Cardaire ever referred to it by its Arabic name. In 1952, Beyries spoke of 'the traditionalist school of Mamadou Touré which for the moment includes almost all Qur'anic students' but which intended to offer a complete education in 'Islamic culture'. The staff consisted of five teachers, among whom was Abd al-Wahhab Doukouré.[67] A school with the same staff, less Doukouré, was listed in a 1956 document that named all the schools associated with counter-reform at that time.[68]

The mention of Diafarabé as the site of a counter-reform initiative may seem anomalous since no threat of either Arabization or Wahhabism existed there. However, Hampâté Bâ was working in Diafarabé at the time, attached to a local branch of IFAN where he was collaborating with Jacques Daget in the research which would lead to the publication of *L'Empire peul du Macina*.[69] Clearly, the authorities had decided to allow Hampâté Bâ to experiment with his own program, perhaps as a reward for his contributions to the evolution of anti-reformist policy. He himself saw this as a much-welcomed opportunity to transmit the teachings of Cerno Bokar to Soudanese school children. But when he wrote to his friend and superior, Monod, from whom he had

[65] Rapport Mangin-Cardaire, 1953.

[66] In 1956 Hampâté Bâ and Doukouré claimed that a counter-reform school existed in Sikasso, 'appartenant à la communauté musulmane, mais son directeur Issaka Diallo est obligé de "faire le transporteur" pour vivre', an observation which casts doubt on how effectively it was operating. CAOM, Affaires Politiques, 2260, dossier 2: Situation matérielle de la contre-réforme au Soudan (établi d'après les déclarations des intéressés), Paris 5 Oct. 1956.

[67] CAOM, Affaires Politiques, 2158, dossier 3, Rapport de Mission sur la situation de l'Islam en AOF (3 April-31 July 1952), J. Beyries.

[68] CAOM, Affaires Politiques, 2260, dossier 2: Situation matérielle de la contre-réforme au Soudan, 1956.

[69] A.H. Bâ and J. Daget, *L'empire peul du Macina (1818-1853)* (Abidjan: Nouvelles Editions Africaines, 1984), first published by IFAN in 1955.

to request permission to participate in these activities, he pretended that the proposition unexpectedly had been made to him by Mangin. In September 1953 he wrote:

> They summoned me to Koulouba to meet with M. Mangin of *Affaires musulmanes.* They proposed to me the popularization of the teaching of Tierno Bokar. They would allow me to try it out in Diafarabé. A room in the *campement* will be made available to me for this purpose. I will begin by giving lessons to children in the Diafarabé school (one hour per day).
> This is a strange change of circumstances [*retour des choses*].
> What is God's ultimate purpose?
> We should leave things to providence ... God always works for our well-being [*Dieu fait toujours bien*].

And then, following a lengthy section in the letter where he thanks Monod for all his previous support and for his much-appreciated assistance in making known the life and teachings of Cerno Bokar, Hampâté Bâ asks him for permission to take on these extra responsibilities. There is a change in tone in the letter from that of friend and religious companion to that of supplicant:

> What am I going to ask you who have given so much?

Here is the civil servant, who is not allowed to take certain initiatives, who is addressing his department chief who alone has the right of authorization.

> I would be pleased to be authorized in writing
> (1) to give lessons according to the teaching of Tierno Bokar to the Muslim children of the Diafarabé School (approved by the authorities);
> (2) authorization to absent myself from Diafarabé whenever necessary either to contact a religious chief or to respond to a summons from the administrative authorities.[70]

Is there not more than a touch of irony in these lines, written by a man who had been politicking on behalf of counter-reform for at least two years?

Hampâté Bâ remained an active participant in the counter-reform program, although it was Doukouré who assumed full-time responsibility for its development, made possible by a salaried position in *Affaires musulmanes* arranged for him by Cardaire. Doukouré's employment was first suggested by Mangin in his 1952 report as a way in which the administration could indirectly support the counter-reform program.[71] Indeed, the administration attempted consistently to limit its support to 'indirect' action, often by ensuring the cooperation of various *commandants de cercle* or sympathetic religious leaders and teachers. They certainly left the way open for Hampâté Bâ and Doukouré to campaign for support for their program.

[70] Letter from Hampâté Bâ to Théodore Monod, 26 Sept. 1953; private papers of Prof. Monod. For the full text of the letter, see L. Brenner, 'Amadou Hampâté Bâ. Tijani francophone'.
[71] *Ibid.* Hampâté Bâ had attempted to obtain a position for Doukouré in IFAN, although adequate funds were not available; a 1956 document refers to him as 'rédacteur d'arabe aux *Affaires Politiques* à Koulouba [Soudan]'; CAOM, Affaires Politiques, 2260, dossier 2: Situation matérielle de la contre-réforme au Soudan (établi d'après les déclarations des intéressés), Paris, 5 Oct. 1956.

In a brief document written in the mid-1950s as part of this campaign,[72] Doukouré explained that the School for Islamic Education (a more palatable public name for counter-reform?) offered a new 'method of Muslim religious education' for teaching three student constituencies: pupils in the public schools, future clerics, and adults seeking further religious instruction. Although the first group constituted the primary objective of counter-reform as it evolved in the mid-1950s, the document makes clear that Hampâté Bâ and Doukouré were nursing somewhat grander ambitions for a fundamental reform of Islamic education.

Our method [of religious instruction] synthesizes the method of complete Arabization, which if applied on its own would constitute a considerable and unacceptable setback for public education in a vast sector, with the maraboutic method, [which has become] static and outdated [*désadaptée*]. [Our method] introduces the excellent innovation of being addressed to schoolchildren while at the same time avoiding the educational backwardness that has so hampered the intellectual advancement [*promotion*] of our youth.

Most of the text is devoted to describing the program offered to public schoolchildren, who 'constitute the number one objective of the teachers of the School for Islamic Education':

... A Muslim instructor attached to an official educational establishment will indoctrinate the children during three hours per week, during free time in their schedules, in a room located near their school. At the end of the academic year, the children will simultaneously sit the examinations for *certificat d'études* and a diploma in religious studies.

(a) Aim. Its essential objective is to provide a profound knowledge of religion, in both letter and spirit, without prejudicing the normal education of the young black Muslim.

(b) Method. It consists in teaching texts of the Qur'an in Arabic to young Africans ; but our major innovation is directed at explaining the texts, books, rites and dogma in the indigenous language.

(c) Advantages. In addition to the knowledge of religion in its spirit, our method also includes:

(1) A certain pedagogical interest, illustrated by the results obtained in different examinations in Soudan ...
(2) A rehabilitation of indigenous languages
(3) A setback for excesses of all sorts resulting from a fragmentary or deliberately deformed knowledge of religion
(4) A setback also for these individual or collective crazes for questionable propaganda and rites, and for which, unfortunately, an incorrect understanding of religion so often offers an unexpected screen [to hide behind]!
(5) And finally, the advantage of averting all risks of divisions or misunderstanding among a youth who are so diversely solicited.

[72] CAOM, Affaires Politiques, 2256, dossier 4, Ecole d'éducation islamique du Soudan Français. The document is undated but internal evidence suggests it was probably written in 1955 or 1956 in conjunction with a campaign for financial support, which is discussed below.

(d) Conclusions. In brief, we intend to promote an experiment of synthesis that is unique in the world, between public western culture of Christian inspiration and a major aspect of African culture which is deeply impregnated with Islamism.

This statement by Abd al-Wahhab Doukouré was in fact an appeal for support from sympathizers throughout the French Union; it ends on a chauvinistic note claiming that the counter-reform program is in complete conformity with the Muslim policy of France, 'the only great Islamic power in the West', and with the spirit of synthesis of the Union Française. And he includes a list of African notables who were supporting the program: Muhammad Sharif of Kankan (inevitably!), the Khalifa General of the Mourides in Senegal Falilou M'Backé (who is thanked for financial aid), the Khalifa General of the Tijanis in Senegal Boubakar Sy in Tivaouane, Seydou Nourou Tal, and Abdullahi Ould Cheikh Sidiyya of Boutilimit in Mauritania.

The preceding document can be understood as a public appeal in the form of a statement of policy, and it should undoubtedly be read in conjunction with another, compiled in 1956, when Doukouré and Hampâté Bâ made formal representations to the Governor General for a government subvention in aid of their program. This second document, on the 'material situation of counter-reform',[73] is interesting for several reasons. It reveals the extent to which Doukouré and Hampâté Bâ had mobilized support and interest for their project, and it provides evidence that already they were clear that any sustained success would depend on developing a sound economic base to support such schools. In other words, the promoters of counter-reform would face the same financial problems as the médersa pioneers. Both systems would rely upon salaried teachers, which would move Islamic education into a different sector of the political economy. In fact, the ultimate success of the médersas, and the failure of counter-reform, would be determined by the ability, or inability, to resolve these economic issues.

This second document was prepared in order to request government funds; it contains no policy statements or political rhetoric, but simply lists material assets (in the form of land and buildings), class sizes and amounts of financial support requested. At the same time, the information provided is uneven, often imprecise, and in many cases reflects wishful thinking more than actual accomplishments. Particularly vague is the designation 'school' (*école*). No mention is made here of the School for Islamic Education, nor is it clear when the term 'school' is used whether it refers to supplementary classes for public schoolchildren or to a self-contained school which is employing the 'new methods' of the counter-reform program; 'school' is also used to refer to Qur'anic schools in which teacher-directors have expressed some interest in the counter-reform program.

Table 3.1 summarizes the information supplied in the document for the

---

[73] CAOM, Affaires Politiques, 2260, dossier 2: Situation matérielle de la contre-réforme au Soudan (établie d'après les déclarations des intéressés), Paris, 5 Oct. 1956.

Table 3.1. SUBVENTIONS REQUESTED FOR FIVE
COUNTER-REFORM SCHOOLS

Assets	No. of students	Sum requested (francs CFA)
BAMAKO		
2 plots of land	ca. 500 [divided into three	1,500,000
2 schools	sections; see below]	
1 adult centre		
SEGU		
1 plot of land	170	300,000
1 school		
KAYES		
1 plot of land	200	400,000
1 school		
SIKASSO		
1 plot of land	not provided	1,000,000
SOFARA		
1 plot of land	school proposed	500,000

five localities for which subventions were requested, presumably the only places where the program was presently or potentially active. Other locations mentioned seem to fall into the category of future prospects, included perhaps to impress the prospective donors! For example, individual Qur'anic school teachers and the numbers of their students are listed for Koulikoro and Bandiagara (a total of about 340 students); these persons may have expressed interest in the program, but the names listed were also persons closely allied with Hampâté Bâ in his personal network of influence.[74] Beyond this, hopes were expressed for the setting up of schools in Kati, Mopti, Ouagadougou, Bobo Dioulasso, and the villages around Say in Niger.

Of particular interest in this document is the way in which counter-reform is associated with the ownership of property. As stated above, with the exception of Bamako, no information is given about the precise operation of the various 'schools' mentioned here; however, it would seem that counter-reform was moving toward the establishment of a network of private schools. School directors (in contrast to the instructors who were meant to provide supplementary religious education to children in public schools) are named in three instances: Segu, Kayes, and Sikasso. In Sikasso, the plot of land was specified as being owned by Hampâté Bâ, and the school as 'belonging to the Muslim community', although its director was 'obliged to earn his living as a transporter'; this juggling of business and educational activities would

[74] For example, Baba Thimbely and Bokary Seck in Bandiagara had been close to Cerno Bokar.

become common in the Islamic médersas as they spread after independence. Although not specified, the land and school in Segu were probably properties of the Thiam brothers, Mamadou and Abu Bakr, who were co-directors of the counter-reform school which, after the collapse of counter-reform, was transformed into a médersa (see below).

The Sofara case is of particular interest. Half a million francs was requested to 'develop the land already obtained' for a school which would cater to 'all the Peuls of Soudan and Upper Volta'. Such a 'school', drawing upon a widely distributed population, was not meant to provide a religious supplement to public education. This land actually belonged to Hampâté Bâ, a fact which is not mentioned in the document itself. Coincidentally (?), he had acquired it on precisely the same day in September 1953 that he wrote to Monod reporting on Mangin's 'proposal' that he might 'popularize the teachings of Cerno Bokar' in Diafarabé.[75] In this same letter, Hampâté Bâ indicated to Monod his wish to develop the Sofara site into a *zawiya* for the transmission of Cerno Bokar's teachings. Perhaps the proposed Sofara school was intended to replace the Diafarabé experiment, which may have been no longer operative in 1956; no mention was made of it in the subvention request.[76]

Slightly more detailed information is provided for Bamako, where three separate courses of study were on offer, those described in Doukouré's earlier description of the School for Islamic Education. Between 150 and 200 public schoolchildren were said to be enrolled in supplementary classes, 50 students were training to be 'clerics', and about 250 persons were taking adult education classes. Six staff were named, although no information was provided about their individual duties;[77] the 1.5 million franc subvention was to be used to build three new classrooms and to purchase 100 new four-seater school desks.

The course of study for the training of future clerics was identified in the 1956 document as preparation for entry to the 'University of Boutilimit'. A detailed discussion of the history of this institution is beyond the scope of the present study, although its aims and origins conform entirely with the counter-reform policy and thinking of the period. Publicly the French presented the 'Muslim University' of Boutilimit as a 'private initiative' by Abdullahi Ould Cheikh Sidiyya, current leader of this influential Sufi family which had

[75] A dated copy of the document of sale was included in the letter to Monod, letter from AHB to TM dated 26 Sept. 1953. See also L. Brenner, 'Amadou Hampâté Bâ: Tijani francophone'.

[76] The following passing mention was made of Macina, the region in which Diafarabé is located: 'Macina – Ousman Doukouré, brother of Abd al-Wahhab Doukouré'. Hampâté Bâ may have terminated his teaching in Diafarabé, and been replaced by Ousman, as early as 1954; a report in that year states the reduction of 'zeal' among his students since his departure for a 'propaganda tour' in Senegal. ANM, I-E-40 (II), Fonds récents, Revue trimestielle, Dec. 1953-Mar. 1954.

[77] Ethnic identifiers were also added in many cases: 'Mamadou Touré (Maure de Touat), Mamadou Konatigui (Bambara), Mamadou Cissé (Marka), Mamadou Soumaré, Alfa Nafogou (son of the imam of Djenné), Aguiyatou Sibi.

cooperated with them for decades. According to French sources, Abdullahi had proposed the idea as a way of reinvigorating both higher Islamic studies and the practice of Islam itself in Mauritania, which he felt were in serious decline. The French were certainly not overly concerned about any decline in Islam as such, and they clearly managed this 'private' venture from behind the scenes and heavily invested in it both politically and economically. Their motives are revealed in a letter written by the Governor General to the Minister of France d'Outre-Mer.

The creation and support for the University of Boutilimit, as you know, responds to a political imperative. It is a matter of satisfying the thirst for Islamic culture manifested by African youth by canalizing their religious and intellectual aspirations toward an establishment which provides us guarantees of loyalty thanks to the choices available to the teachers and to a certain extent [the content of] the curriculum, and by our strategy of moral and material control of the project.

Thus, without pretending to eclipse the universities of the Arab world, of which certain (al-Azhar) are a thousand years old, and without succeeding in totally preventing the exodus of young African elites toward the religious and cultural centres of North Africa and Egypt, we can limit this movement by permitting parents who wish to imbue their children with a more profound Islamic culture to do so within the Federation. At the same time, we can respond to the reproach which is often levelled against us that we oppose the creation of cultural centres based upon teaching the Arabic language and analyzing the Qur'an.[78]

Of major concern to the French was the growing interest among African youth to study in Middle Eastern universities, from which they allegedly risked 'returning impregnated with xenophobic fanaticism and hostility toward the traditional [Sufi] brotherhoods through which African Islam is structured'. And this trend was fuelling a local political problem, 'due to the contrast between the sclerosis of traditional Islam and the dynamism of Wahhabi and modernist tendencies'.[79] The Boutilimit project was supported with these political considerations in mind, and also with a keen eye on public response: 'In order for the project to meet with approval and [gain] moral credence, it must appear to be an enterprise under the authority of Cheikh El Sidy'.[80] And the French supported it with grants totaling 13.1 million francs between 1953 and 1955, by which date the university had an enrolment of 169 students.

Hampâté Bâ and Doukouré never received any of the 3.7 million francs that they had requested, and for which they had no doubt been encouraged

[78] CAOM, Affaires Politiques, 2256, dossier 2, Lettre du Haut-Commissaire de la République, Gouverneur-Général de l'AOF au Ministère de la France d'Outre Mer, 30 Dec. 1955. This file contains extensive documentation on the Muslim University of Boutilimit. See also J.-L. Triaud, 'Le crépuscule', pp. 512-13, n. 62.

[79] CAOM, Affaires Politiques, 2256, dossier 2, Note de présentation sur l'Institut Musulman des Ahel Cheikh Sidia à Boutilimit, no date.

[80] CAOM, Affaires Politiques, 2256, dossier 2, Lettre du Haut-Commissaire de la République, Gouverneur-Général de l'AOF au Ministère de la France d'Outre Mer, 30 Dec. 1955.

to apply by the example of Boutilimit. They had never seriously considered how they were going to finance their educational initiative, and they made the mistake of relying too heavily on government support. Even as early as 1952, when Mangin and Cardaire were actively campaigning for official support for counter-reform, budgetary calculations indicated that available funds would be inadequate to develop such a program to the extent that it could make a significant impact on education in the colony. Only 4 percent of school-age children were enrolled in schools at the time, and estimates suggested that even if all the programs then in progress for the development of both private and public schools were successful, the rate of enrolment would peak at only 8 percent.[81] By 1957 counter-reform was described as 'paralyzed due to lack of resources';[82] the fatal blow came when it lost all official support following the abolition of *Affaires musulmanes* according to the terms of the *Loi cadre* of 1956.[83]

The political aim of counter-reform was of course to provide an alternative to the Islamic médersas and hopefully to erode their appeal. The first counter-reform schools were set up in cities where médersas had been successful: Bamako, Kayes and Segu. Such confrontational policies of course led to an increase in political tensions. In order to develop a broader base of support for counter-reform, Abd al-Wahhab Doukouré set up an association known as *Jam'iyyat al-murshidin* (Association of Spiritual Guides).[84] Founded perhaps as early as 1953, the new association was meant to provide political legitimacy for counter-reform; all the imams of Soudan were said to be electors to its executive committee.[85] The 1956 request for financial support, like most associated activities, was made in the name of the association. According to Doukouré himself,[86] *Jam'iyyat al-murshidin* was seeking to provide an opportunity for Muslim youth to deepen their knowledge of Islam while still attending French school. He claimed, long after the fact of course, that his problem with the médersas was that they taught none of the secular subjects such as mathematics, science and geography, which was why he opposed them. But of course, the French had specifically blocked the teaching of such subjects in the médersas of both Bamako and Segu, while at the same time attempting to limit the number hours devoted to Arabic as well. So it is

[81] Rapport Mangin, 1952.

[82] CAOM, Affaires Politiques, 2261, dossier 3, Affaires Musulmanes, Synthèse de mai 1957.

[83] J. -L. Triaud, 'Le Crépuscule', p. 517, n. 73.. Triaud points out that with the *Loi cadre* of 1956, all the political bureaus were abolished, and their functions devolved to other ministries, often under African direction.

[84] See Kaba, *The Wahhabiyya*, p. 246.

[85] CAOM, Affaires Politiques, 2260, dossier 2, Situation matérielle de la contre réform au Soudan.

[86] The views of Abd al-Wahhab Doukouré contained in this paragraph are taken from an interview with him conducted on behalf of the author by Tierno Oumar Ly, Dakar, 28 Jan. 1988.

perfectly understandable that, as Doukouré explains, the proponents of the new program found it difficult to convince the médersa directors that *Jam'iyyat al-murshidin* was neither against the Arabic language nor against Islam, but concerned to 'create Muslims who would be useful to themselves and to their country'. And suspicions would not have been reduced by the fact that three of the counter-reform initiatives were set up in direct competition with the Islamic médersas in Bamako, Segu and Kayes.

Already in 1953 certain French administrators were convincing themselves of the success of counter-reform. Following the opening of classes in Bamako and Diafarabé, the annual report was sanguine: 'The major result [of the counter-reform initiative] has been to crystallize and to circumscribe the reformist group. In the Soudan, the reformist movement appears thus to have been stalled'.[87] Perhaps in 1953 prospects looked particularly good from the French perspective. The Bamako médersa had been closed for two years, and the Kayes médersa had recently been forced by the administration to close its doors due to the extended absence of al-Hajj Mahmoud Ba. Only Saada Oumar persisted in Segu. However, official optimism was misplaced; the program of the *Jam'iyyat al-murshidin* in Bamako and Diafarabé may have been off to a promising start, but the reformist movement had hardly been stalled.

In the same year, 1953, the *Union Culturelle Musulmane* was founded in Dakar, and in 1955 it formally took up the cause of the Kayes médersa. The episode of the Kayes médersa was one of the first direct confrontations between the forces of reform and counter-reform.[88] Early in 1955, the UCM under the leadership of its local president, al-Hajj Tiémoko Diabaté, requested permission to reopen the Kayes médersa under the directorship of Mahmoud Ba. The administration refused to receive a request in the name of the UCM, and said an application would have to be made in the name of an individual, who in any case could not be Mahmoud Ba. Eventually, in the spring of 1956, authorization was granted for the reopening of the school under the directorship of one Mamadou Salif Diallo.

The administration's formal refusal to recognize any legitimate role for the UCM in this matter was a significant political decision; it was of course yet another ploy to limit the impetus such an association might give to the creation of any new médersas. It was an ineffective policy, of course, because members of the UCM could apply to open schools as individuals, and the UCM could offer all kinds of other support. For example, in Kayes the association was raising money to support the médersa in 1956. But the situation in Kayes also demonstrates the duplicity of French policy. Cardaire had visited

---

[87] AMI, Soudan, Rapport Politique Annuel, 1953.

[88] Information about these events is based primarily on periodic political reports from Kayes region which are contained in ANM, 1-E-21, FR, Rapports politiques et Rapports de tournées, Cercle de Kayes (1914-58). The events were also discussed in interview with Abd al-Wahhab Doukouré, 28 Jan. 1988, Dakar.

Kayes in 1955 to investigate the UCM, whose members he denounced as 'extremists'. Although he could not find a legitimate excuse to keep the médersa closed, he did recommend that a counter-reform school be opened in order to undermine its appeal. Within only a couple of months, such a school was authorised to open under the directorship of al-Hajj Oumar Ly, described as 'a protégé of the administration in Bamako', who had been recommended by Abd al-Wahhab Doukouré. Oumar Ly was also assistant Secretary-General of *Jam'iyyat al-murshidin*.[89] Not only was Ly authorized to open his school, but the administration provided the land and financial resources necessary to launch the project; as Doukouré said, with some exaggeration, 'Whatever we asked from the administration, they gave us'. The fact that a 'protégé of the administration' should be favored in this way, when the supporters of the Kayes médersa had been struggling without success to reopen their school for almost two years, resulted in a 'campaign of denigration' against the counter-reform school which seriously limited its intake of students. Indeed, the discontent and resentment generated by this affair was dissipated only by the authorization, reluctantly granted in the spring of 1956, to re-open the Kayes médersa.

Events in Segu were similarly confrontational. Alarm was expressed about Saada Oumar's activities as early as 1951, as noted in the previous chapter:

> In spite of regulations limiting the number of hours of Arabic teaching in the Qur'anic schools, this instruction is developing every day. So it is that in a school in Segu, a *marabout* recommended to his students to speak only Arabic among themselves.[90]

Saada Oumar was seen as a particular danger, a 'traditional' Sufi Muslim who had adopted modernised teaching methods and become committed to teaching the Arabic language. The counter-reform school set up in 1954 in Segu was specifically designed to attract prospective students away from Saada Oumar's médersa.[91] In fact, the *Jam'iyyat al-murshidin* plan in Segu was rather insidious, since it played upon a lingering dispute between Saada Oumar and the Thiam family which had developed during the late 1940s when they had founded Segu's first médersa together. Government documents only state that Mamadou Thiam had been 'won over by the counter-reform movement' when he filed a request to open a 'Qur'anic school' in which instruction would be dispensed in the Bamana language. Apparently, Mamadou and Abu Bakr Thiam[92] were given all the resources necessary to build and open their school and, at least at first, to run it on a non-fee-paying basis.

[89] In 1981 al-Hajj Oumar Ly would become the president of Mali's first national Muslim organisation, the *Association malienne pour l'unité et le progrès de l'Islam* (AMUPI).

[90] AMI, Soudan, Rapport Politique Annuel, 1951.

[91] Information about the activities of the counter-reform movement in Segu is to be found in ANM, 1-E-40(I) et 1-E-40(II) FR, Rapports politiques et rapports de tournées, Cercle de Ségou (1923-1939) et (1940-1959), and AMI, Ségou, Rapports politiques annuels, 1957, 1958, 1959, 1960, 1961.

[92] Hashimi Thiam, who had been involved in the 1940s with the original Segu médersa had since gone to Cairo to continue his studies. Cardaire noted his presence there in 1955.

Already in 1953, when the counter-reform movement had formally begun, Saada Oumar, or 'the Tal clan' as the political report put it, had expressed its opposition to the teaching of Islamic subjects in Bamana. Before they approached the Thiam family, the counter-reformists had also apparently attempted to 'win over' Saada to the program, and having met with a refusal, they tried to close down his médersa. Saada's recollections of these events are characteristically vivid:

'They created in Bamako a Muslim association which they called *Jam 'iyyat al-murshidin*, the Association of Guides. A Muslim association presided over by a Christian, Captain Cardaire! With Abd al-Wahhab Doukouré as secretary and Amadou Hampâté Bâ as adviser. Against me, a nobody (*un petit*), a good-for nothing who had absolutely nothing! They voted 80 millions to close my médersa and all the médersas that might appear in the country.

Captain Cardaire came to me and said: "I have been to Cairo in my capacity as chief of *Affaires musulmanes* in Soudan. There were 125 African students there who abused me, saying: 'Kafir! When we finish our studies and we return to Africa, we are going to vilify you French and all the false *marabouts* who are there!' These are the people who are going to come and declare war against us and against you, the *marabouts*. We have our aeroplanes and our canons, but you are poor. Join with us to bar the way against these people."

I asked by what means we might do this, and he said: 'By abandoning the Arabic language in Islamic education. God understands Bamana, understands French, understands Sarakollé, understands all the languages.'

I said: "*Mon Capitaine*, I am the first pupil, not the first teacher. Give me the teaching manual in Bamana." Amadou Hampâté Bâ called on me and said: 'I can invent the characters [for transcription]', and I replied: "Invent the characters for another generation, but not for Saada Touré. Here is my authorization; they authorized me to teach Islam in the Arabic language. *Mon Capitaine*, withdraw your authorization. I will return to the vestibule and continue to teach in the fashion of my father and all the other *marabouts*."

They saw that this approach was not going to work. *Les petits* don't want money; *les petits* do not retreat in the face of intimidations. What were they going to do? So they set up their association in our town with a *sharif* as president [Ibrahim Abdoulaye Haidara]. This *sharif* came to see me: "You are hard; you are a scoundrel. You must join our association". I said: "If you are really a sharif, I want to remind you of one of the statements [*hadith*] of your grandfather, the Prophet, who said, 'Love the Arabs for three things: because I, the Prophet, am an Arab, because the [language of the] Qur'an is Arabic, and because the language of the inhabitants of paradise is Arabic.' Therefore, those who want to fight against Arabic, including you as a *sharif*, have abandoned the Arabs, you have abandoned the Qur'an and you have abandoned the Prophet. ... If you are an enemy of the Prophet, of the Qur'an, and of paradise, then I cannot be with you."

So they held a big meeting and decided to create a médersa where the pupils would pay absolutely nothing whereas here, I would be taking money [in fees]. My school would be deserted and abandoned. That is the school they gave to Bokar Thiam and the others; they decided to create this médersa, but it failed lamentably.'[93]

[93] Interview with Saada Oumar Touré, 13 Oct. 1977, Segu.

It is not true that the Thiam médersa failed, unless by failure Saada meant that his own médersa continued to thrive. The French kept score of the comparative enrolments each year:

	Saada Oumar	Thiam
1954	200	60
1955	200	80
1956	300	100
1957	300	100
1958	330	160

In 1959 the statistics for the two schools were combined to a total of 600 pupils, accompanied by a brief comment to the effect that the médersas were continuing to develop. In 1960 the total figure for the two schools was given as 500, and the accompanying comment was very much in keeping with the spirit of a newly independent, secularist Mali:

> The number of students seems to be declining in comparison with their reputation of several years before when religious fashion passed them off within fanatical milieux as the ideal form of teaching. But present circumstances have turned the masses toward progress, and parents now prefer the public schools which open careers for their children which will enable them to earn a living.

Perhaps, but the 1961 report, which included no statistics, observed that due to parental demand, it had been decided to provide a class in Segu to prepare pupils for the *brevet élémentaire arabe*, the elementary certificate in Arabic. By 1961 the Thiam school had become an Islamic médersa, virtually indistinguishable in official reports from that of Saada Oumar; it was destined to become one of the largest and more prestigious in the country. And Arabic became the language of instruction; indeed Abu Bakr Thiam subsequently wrote an Arabic grammar which became widely used in the médersas of Mali.[94] So the Thiam médersa did not fail, as Saada Oumar implied, but the counter-reform campaign in Segu certainly did.

This reference to the *brevet élémentaire* is related to Saada's ultimate victory over his opponents. About 1959 (the precise date is uncertain), and almost certainly in the context of a request by Saada for authorization to teach French, the administration decided to inspect his médersa. To perform this task, they sent none other than Abd al-Wahhab Doukouré. As Saada Oumar put it, they sent this man 'who with Captain Cardaire had been fighting against me for seven years running. They sent him to examine my children; all this was designed to do away with me.'[95] But, according to Saada Oumar's story, when Doukouré examined the curriculum and the organization, and functioning

[94] *Al-Risāla al-naḥwiyya li 'l-madāris al-ibtidā'iyya*. Tunis: Maison Tijani al-Muhammadi, sans date.
[95] This and other quotations from Saada Oumar in this passage are taken from an interview with him on 13 Oct. 1977, Segu.

of the médersa, he offered his apologies, saying: 'I did not know the médersa was organized in this manner. … The conflicts are over. With what I have seen here, if I love God, I can no longer oppose this school.' Thus encouraged, Saada requested that nine of his students be examined for the *brevet élémentaire*, of whom seven passed.

The French Governor was dismayed, and everyone was surprised. [Doukouré] was the representative of the Ministry [of Education], therefore they were obliged to issue those students who had passed with diplomas signed by the Minister himself.

Interestingly, Abd al-Wahhab Doukouré's version of this episode is rather different. He claims some of the credit for 'preparing' these students for the examination and of convincing Saada that the possession of such diplomas would be of value to the students and ultimately to the country.[96] Even if this is so, it only further demonstrates the fullness of Saada's victory over the forces of counter-reform. The success in these examinations was perhaps the most significant event to occur in the history of the médersa movement since its origins almost fifteen years earlier. In 1961, these same students would receive scholarships to study in Cairo and would return to become Mali's first Arabic-speaking civil servants to have been educated in the country's médersas. This, perhaps more than any other single development in the short history of the médersas, increased both their popularity and their legitimacy amongst a large proportion of the population.

The political agitation that focussed on the médersa issue in Segu during the 1950s took on a form characteristic of French efforts at political intervention and control. The political reports of the period give only a sketchy outline of events, but the repeated references to the 'Tal clan' seem significant when juxtaposed to the rising influence of the Niass Tijaniyya and the completely disinterested comments about the Segu Hamallists planning to build a mosque. Only a few years before, such Sufi initiatives would have set off the alarm bells. Now the Islamic threat was perceived very differently. Of primary concern was the fact that Saada Oumar was not only teaching Arabic in his médersa, but he was a 'listener and propagandist for the Voice of Cairo'. In 1956 many Arabic-speakers were listening to Cairo's reports on the Suez crisis: 'The call to jihad made from Cairo has therefore been heard, although we have been unable to obtain any comments from the clan of Saada Touré.'

Saada Oumar allegedly posed a threat that transcended the influence of his médersa, and the authorities decided to attempt to isolate him by mobilizing local sectarian forces.[97] As early as 1954 one report included the observation that the influence of Ibrahim Niass, whose branch of a 'reformed' Tijaniyya was based in Kaolack, was eclipsing that of the Tal family in Segu (another case

---

[96] Interview of 28 Jan. 1988, Dakar.

[97] Saada was close to Madani Tal, the son of Muntaga who was both reigning elder of the Tal and spiritual leader of the Umarian Tijanis in Segu. The French were concerned to avoid Madani and Saada rising to 'spiritual leadership' after the death of Muntaga. CAOM, Affaires Politiques, 2258, dossier 2, Note sur l'Islam au Soudan, 13 May 1953.

of official wishful thinking). There followed a sustained campaign by the *Jam'iyyat al-murshidin*, under the local leadership of Ibrahim Haidara, to join forces with the Niass Tijanis. It is unclear whether Haidara himself was a Hamallist, although this is implied by the wording of certain reports. For example, Haidara had received explicit orders 'to join battle against Saada Touré, a twelve-bead Tijani'. Such a reference to 'twelve-bead' (Umarian) Tijanism only has meaning in contrast to the 'eleven-bead' Tijanism of the Hamallists.[98] In the same context the *Jam'iyyat al-murshidin* was itself referred to as a 'sect'. Whether Haidara was a Hamallist or not, Hampâté Bâ and Doukouré were; and the *Jam'iyyat al-murshidin* was clearly associated by some with Hamallism. And this campaign against Saada Oumar and the 'Tal clan' also explains why local officials could report with such equanimity the activities of the Segu Hamallists during this period, such as preparations to build their own mosque. From the French perspective, what was good for the Hamallists was necessarily bad for the Umarian Tijanis and the 'Tal clan'.

If the conflicts in Segu were protracted and sometimes bitter, they did not erupt into violence. In Bamako, on the other hand, the gathering religious tensions exploded into rioting in May 1957, resulting in scores of injuries and damage to property worth millions of francs. The incident came to be known in Bamana as *Wahhabiya-kèlè*, the 'Wahhabi war', between what by now had come to be known within the administration as the 'traditionalists' and the 'Wahhabis', (or 'modernists', or 'reformists; all three labels were being used interchangeably). The confrontation was precipitated by applications in January 1957 to open a 'Wahhabi' mosque and a new médersa in Bamako, but it occurred in a broader political context in which the fortunes of the 'traditionalists' were clearly in the descendent on more than one front.

The genesis of the *Wahhabiya-kèlè* has been analyzed by both Lansiné Kaba and Jean-Loup Amselle.[99] Kaba's study concentrates more on the doctrinal and political aspects of the evolution of 'Wahhabism', and Amselle's more on the social and economic aspects. Both authors attempt to disentangle the religious from the political strands of the story in order better to understand their separate evolution as well as their complex interrelationship. And both place the 'Wahhabi' initatives of January 1957 in the context of the rising political fortunes of the US-RDA (*Union Soudanaise-Rassemblement Démocratique Africain*) to the detriment of their more conservative opponents, the PSP (*Parti Soudanais du Progrès*).

In the March 1957 elections for the Territorial Assembly, the US-RDA had won 64 of 70 seats; in the preceding municipal elections in the newly created

---

[98] The distinction between 'twelve-bead' and 'eleven-bead' Tijanism relates to the major doctrinal issue which separated Hamallists from other Tijanis: the number of times a particular prayer (the *jawharat al-kamal*) was recited during the Tijani litany. The Hamallists recited the prayer eleven times, whereas all other Tijanis recited it twelve times. The 'beads' referred to the differing disposition of the beads on the rosaries of the two branches of the order.

[99] Kaba, *The Wahhabiyya*, chs. 7 and 8; and Amselle, *Les négotiants de la savane*, pp. 253-65.

communes of Bamako, Kayes, Mopti and Sikasso, the US-RDA had won all the seats. The applicants for the 'Wahhabi' mosque and the new médersa therefore felt they were submitting their requests to authorities likely to be sympathetic to their interests. This was not because all 'Wahhabis' were members of the US-RDA (Amselle observes that many of the most wealthy 'Wahhabi' merchants were supporters of the PSP), but many of the younger and more radical had been attracted by the radicalism of the US-RDA, which promised to reduce French influence and to undercut the 'traditional' authority of both chiefs and *marabouts*. Amselle's analysis places emphasis on the appeal of the US-RDA program to young merchants who wanted to break into more lucrative markets controlled by French and Syrian-Lebanese companies. Kaba's analysis concentrates more on the notion that many young 'Wahhabis' were drawn to US-RDA ideology because it opposed the power of the 'traditional chiefs' and the 'Qur'anic leaders'. Of course, these two interpretations are complementary, and echo the analyses of Cardaire who had earlier posited the existence of two rather distinct sub-groups among the Muslim 'modernists': the 'reformist clerics' and the 'Wahhabi merchants'.

This alliance did not long survive independence, and definitively collapsed as a result of the militant secularism and socialist economic policies adopted by the Keita régime. But it was very strong in the 1950s; several 'Wahhabis' enjoyed considerable influence in the party, and 'Wahhabi' merchants were a source of significant financial and material support. So the requests to open both a mosque and a médersa in January 1957 became the focus of a complex political confrontation. The political fortunes of the PSP, the pro-French party of 'traditionalism', were plummeting. The forces of 'Wahhabism' (and 'Arabism' and 'Nasserism'[100]) looked set to receive a boost from their US-RDA allies. Neither the French, nor the PSP, nor the 'traditionalists', nor for that matter the proponents of counter-reform, could afford to ignore this situation.

The 'traditionalists' in this instance were the 'chiefs, notables and Imams' of Bamako who in February addressed a petition to the Governor to intervene in order to block the granting of the 'Wahhabi' applications. In March a large delegation of 'traditionalists' presented itself at the Governor's offices with the intention of further supporting this petition, but by April the new médersa was already in operation, and the 'Wahhabis' subsequently announced that they would pray in their new mosque on Friday, 17 May. This announcement resulted in a flurry of activity by the 'traditionalists', and through the offices of the *commandant de cercle*, the 'Wahhabis' agreed to renounce their project to hold prayers in the mosque. However, at midday on the 17th a large crowd of 'traditionalists', as well as a contingent of police, gathered at the mosque. When at about 1:15 (the prayers would have begun

[100] All three terms were used in the report of the May 1957 disturbances. ANM, 1 E 7 (II), Rapports politiques et rapports de tournées. Cercle de Bamako (1945-58), Revue mensuelle, May 1957.

at 1:30) a single 'Wahhabi' attempted to enter the mosque, he was attacked; other scuffles ensued, which were followed by a rampage of attacks and pillage against the person and property of 'Wahhabis' in the city. Calm was not finally restored until the evening, the security forces having been rather slow in responding to the situation.

The official report on these events, of which the previous paragraph is a summary, estimated that about twenty homes had been pillaged; it gave no indication of the number or extent of injuries, and it made no mention of the fact that the newly opened médersa had also been sacked and its library burned. According to information gathered from 'Wahhabi' informants by Amselle, who describes these events as a 'pogrom', 278 homes were pillaged and one person died. He also adds that 254 of these homes belonged to US-RDA members or sympathizers. In Amselle's view this violence was intended as an attack against both the 'Wahhabis', and through them, the US-RDA, and had been coordinated by Marcel Cardaire. Amselle's account is of French collusion with local 'traditional' leaders, 'the notables of Bamako', in order to by-pass the elected (US-RDA) officials and to strike directly against the 'Wahhabis'. Cardaire's alleged plan seems to have been activated in May, following the 'Wahhabi' announcement of their intention to pray in the new mosque. He first counselled the chief Imam of Bamako, Umar Kalé, to forbid anyone to pray in his mosque with crossed arms,[101] which was allegedly intended as a signal to commence an anti-'Wahhabi' repression. Cardaire is also said to have convinced the provincial chief of Bamako, Mamadou Koumba Niaré, to rally the 'traditionalists' to join in open combat against the 'Wahhabis'. Niaré is said to have summoned the 'Wahhabi' clerics one by one and 'threatened them with severe punishments if they did not resign from the reformist movement'.[102] Indeed, Amselle's presentation of these events implies that Cardaire played on the recent political humiliations of the PSP in order to strike a blow at the 'Wahhabis'. He is said to have persuaded Niaré of 'the danger that the reopening of the Wahhabi médersa and the development of a movement supported by the US-RDA would pose for the traditions, that is, for the notables of Bamako.'[103]

Ali Koulogo Diallo, former al-Azhar student and director of the newly opened médersa, has also asserted that the 1957 campaign by the 'traditionalists' was orchestrated by Cardaire, Hampâté Bâ and Doukouré.[104] If such violent direct action was a grotesque departure from the self-righteous and

---

[101] Folding the arms across the chest during prayer was a ritual act which clearly and visibly distinguished 'Wahhabis' from other Muslims, who prayed with arms at their sides. The Niass Tijanis also pray with crossed arms. Such a detail of ritual practice of course can assume powerful symbolic significance, such as the difference between 'twelve-bead' and 'eleven-bead' Tijanis. For a detailed analysis of the relationship between ritual practice and social identity, see R. Launay, *Beyond the Stream*.

[102] Amselle, *Les négociants*, p. 256.

[103] *Ibid.*

[104] Ibrahim Baba Touré, 'L'Islam dans ses manifestations actuelles à Bamako', (Mémoire

elevated cultural ideology of counter-reform which had been expressed by Hampâté Bâ and Doukouré, and endorsed by Cardaire himself, it should be recalled that the political stakes were very high in 1957. But it is also true that the débacle of May 1957 was the last gasp of the counter-reform movement. In October 1958, Soudan would become the République Soudanaise, an autonomous member of the French community. The *Bureau des Affaires musulmanes* would be abolished and with it all official support would be withdrawn from the *Jam'iyyat al-murshidin* and their program of counter-reform, which would disappear virtually without trace. Even 'Abd al-Wahhab Doukouré would conclude that the results of their efforts had been insignificant.[105]

Viewed from this perspective, Cardaire's alleged conspiracies take on the appearance of the desperate acts of a dying administration intent to protect the vestiges of French influence against a rising tide of 'Arabism' and 'pan-Islamism'. The proposed 'Wahhabi' mosque in Bamako was seen as the first tangible step to replace the 'traditionalist' Muslim hierarchy. But Ali Diallo's médersa was very different from that of the Azharists, not so much because of its curriculum, but because of the fact that it was sponsored by the UCM, now a Muslim association which extended throughout the federation of French West Africa, and because Ali Diallo espoused an extremely radical political position. He was described in one police report of the period as a 'crypto-communist',[106] and Cardaire had allegedly chased him from his office exclaiming, 'So long as I am here, Ali Diallo will never teach in Soudan.'[107] It is not clear precisely when this alleged incident took place, but it suggests that Cardaire saw Diallo as a 'communist' agent who was being aided by Nasser to foment conflict between the French and the Arabs.

Diallo himself said that he was among those who felt that it was necessary in the 1950s to engage 'Islam' in the struggle for independence and nationalism.[108] But he was a political maverick whose radicalism went much further than most of his associates in the UCM. He was one of only two active leaders in the UCM who were not members of the US-RDA; he was associated with the *Parti Africain de l'Indépendance* (PAI), which was allied with the French Communist Party, and he supported the Movement for Peace in Algeria. Criticism against him began to grow within the UCM on various counts: that he 'was the Azharist most eloquent in Arabic but least interested in Islam',[109] and that he was motivated primarily by self-interest, his primary concern being to control the UCM médersa. Thus, when the school was allowed to reopen

---

de fin d'études, ENSup, Bamako, 1989), p. 33; and interview with Ali Koulogo Diallo, 24 Mar. 1989, Bamako.
[105] Interview, 28 Jan. 1988, Dakar.
[106] Kaba, *The Wahhabiyya*, p. 243.
[107] Mahamane, 'Le mouvement wahhabite à Bamako', p. 55, citing the UCM periodical, *Reveil Islamique*, Oct. 1957.
[108] Interview of 24 Mar. 1989, Bamako.
[109] Diallo's political itinerary during this period is discussed by Kaba, *The Wahhabiyya*, pp. 247-50.

in 1958, he was barred from teaching in it by the UCM. This led to a complete rupture with the UCM, and eventually he joined a tiny and short-lived dissident association known as the *Organization Culturelle Islamique*, whose aims were virtually indistinguishable from those of the UCM. Diallo then applied to establish his own médersa, and having been refused, he opened one without authorization; eventually he returned to the UCM fold.

The significance of the 'Diallo affair' resides in the fact that already in the late 1950s, there was a small but visible faction of radical Muslims whose politics were much more extreme than those of the mainstream 'Wahhabis' or of the UCM. Perhaps this was why Cardaire was so exercised over Diallo and why he went to such extreme lengths to crush the 1957 initiatives for the médersa and the mosque. But the violence of May 1957 did little to alter the general thrust of developments. The UCM launched a campaign to reopen their médersa in Bamako. In their constituent congress of December 1957 they denounced the administration's complicity in the violence and asserted that the men who had been involved in the sacking of the school should have 'no right to mercy nor any rights of citizenship in an Africa which sought to be strong and unified'.[110] And they expressed resentment for the fact that the médersa remained closed and was still awaiting authorization to reopen.

In the spring of 1958 the US-RDA authorities allowed the UCM médersa to reopen under the administrative responsibility of Kabiné Kaba, Muhammad Fodé Keita, and Muhammad Sanusi, but the curriculum now included both French language and secular subjects. This decision in 1958 was the first formal step to integrate the religious studies and Arabic language training of the Islamic médersas with the curriculum of the secular state schools. To a certain extent, it is fair to say that the basic model for this program was that of the French médersas, although the Bamako médersa remained under private control. It will be recalled that the Azharists had been refused permission to institute such a mixed curriculum a decade earlier. But now, as the US-RDA moved toward political autonomy and eventual independence, the party was evolving radically new educational policies to broaden the educational base, which envisaged médersa-type schools (*écoles franco-arabes*) as part of an expanded state system. The authorization to teach French granted to Saada Oumar Touré in 1959 should be seen as part of the same re-evaluation of educational policy. But the Bamako médersa was to acquire another, although somewhat dubious, distinction. In 1959, the US-RDA authorities gave the médersa some land on which to construct a new school building, although within a few years it was nationalised as part of the program to create the new system of *écoles franco-arabes*.[111]

This nationalization was but a single element in the gradual but definitive ascendancy of secularist forces within the US-RDA leadership. By the mid-

[110] Chailley, 'Aspects de l'Islam au Mali', pp. 49-50.
[111] In 1966, the school had an enrollment of 500 students, according to V. Monteil, *L'Islam noir*, 3rd edn (Paris: Editions du Seuil, 1980), p. 302.

1960s médersa directors were becoming increasingly alienated from the Keita régime, but in 1958 they welcomed the opportunity to institute the new curriculum, which in no way compromised the platform of the UCM. Jean-Loup Amselle has offered a differing interpretation of these events.[112] In his view, fundamental socio-economic differences distinguished the 'Wahhabi' merchants from the leadership of the US-RDA which were powerfully expressed in their differing attitudes toward language. Basically, he argues that the teaching of French was imposed upon the Bamako médersa in 1958, which was the opening shot in the subsequent political battle between the French-educated emergent bureaucracy and the Muslim merchant class who were not literate in French. Indeed, he argues that this imposition was a significant defeat for the 'Wahhabis', which would be followed by the nationalisation of the médersa, the closure of 'Wahhabi' mosques and the interdiction of the UCM. But these latter events were all part of the radicalization and secularisation of policy that followed the collapse of the Mali Federation in 1960 when the Republic of Mali found itself isolated in its newly-acquired independence. In the late 1950s the majority of politically active Muslims were seeking full participation in the new political order as Muslims. This was certainly true of those who were instrumental in founding the médersas, who had no objection to the introduction of French and secular subjects in their curricula so long as the schools retained their basic religious orientation, which included the teaching of Arabic; only French restrictions had prohibited them from introducing such subjects earlier. It will be recalled that the French did not recognize 'Qur'anic schools' as educational establishments, and consequently restricted what could be taught in them.

In 1958 a second new médersa was authorised to open in Bamako, that of Shaikhna Yattabary, who had studied in Cairo and had recently moved to Bamako from Ivory Coast. His school was called the *Institut Islamique*, and by the 1980s was one of the largest and most prestigious in Mali. According to one source, ten médersas were operating in the Republic of Mali when the country became independent in 1960,[113] although my researches have definitely identified only seven: one in Kayes (UCM), one in Sikasso, two in Segu (Touré and Thiam), and three in Bamako (UCM, Yattabary, and Ali Diallo [unauthorized]). During the 1950s quite a few new 'Qur'anic schools' had received authorizations to open which may have been experimenting with the new pedagogical methods of the médersas. However, even if we take into account only these seven schools, it is clear that the tactics of counter-reform had failed utterly to arrest the momentum of the médersa movement. As the *commandant de cercle* of Gao observed, when reporting on the rising numbers of Arabic speakers in his area of jurisdiction:

[112] Amselle, *Les négociants*, p. 259.
[113] Oumar S. Touré, 'Etude', 1985.

If one considers the wave of proselytization that is taking place in the other regions of the west and south of the Soudan Republic, and that has been manifested in the proliferation of the médersas, along with the favour that these schools are finding among the population, one can reasonably predict that the influence of the French language in this country is in danger in the near future of facing serious competition from the Arabic language.[114]

This prediction gained further credence when the US-RDA government of the newly independent Republic of Mali announced its commitment to the teaching of the Arabic language (and of English) in schools as a way to implement its objectives of pan-African unity.

For the time being, the future of the médersas looked assured. The conflict over mosques in Bamako was also temporarily resolved by a compromise that was firmly opposed by the chief Imam, Umar Kalé. It was agreed that additional Friday mosques could be opened in the city, and that Muslims should be allowed to worship where they wished, in the manner in which they wished.[115] The disputed mosque was to be administered by a group that included both 'Wahhabis' and 'traditionalists', but within a brief period at least two additional 'Wahhabi' mosques were opened. A parallel dispute about mosques and the selection of the imam erupted in Sikasso during 1957-58, which was resolved in a similar fashion.[116] During this period, the US-RDA leadership sought to resolve these conflicts through compromise and in a manner that would not alienate the more politically active Muslims, who tended to be US-RDA supporters.

This chapter has documented how, during the colonial period, local Muslim history became inextricably entwined with the changes that accompanied the European presence in the region. The introduction of a European factor into the dynamics of Muslim society was not primarily the result of any heavy-handed authority imposed by the French in Soudan, although this did occur on some occasions; virtually all the evidence thus far presented, from the establishment of the first French médersas to the collapse of the counter-reform movement, has shown that despite their pretensions colonial administrators were unable to control Islam and Muslims to the extent that they desired. Nor was the most important aspect of these events any direct confrontation between French power and Muslim resistance; new modes of power relations were emerging through a subtle, complex and contingent process which included a rich mixture of Middle Eastern, French and local influences. The new Muslim institutions which emerged through this process, such as the Islamic médersas and the new-style Muslim associations, both resulted from and contributed to the social and political environment being created in the new colonial situation.

---

[114] AMI, Rapport Politique Annuel (Gao), 1959.

[115] Kaba, *The Wahhabiyya*, p. 216.

[116] *Ibid.*, pp. 197-202; and Chailley, 'Aspects de l'Islam au Mali', pp. 37-41.

The dynamic contingency of this process with its rich mixture of diverse influences inevitably affected the self-perception and self-presentation of Muslims, both as individuals and collectively. For example, Saada Oumar Touré claimed that the inspiration for his médersa experiment came directly from his personal experience in a French school. Mahmoud Ba, whose early médersas were closely modeled on the schools he attended in Saudi Arabia, very soon found it necessary to find new ways to generate support for his activities and began to set up new-style Muslim associations. The founding of the Bamako médersa and of the *Shubban al-muslimin* youth association may have been initially inspired by the experience of students in Cairo, but the realization of these initiatives in West Africa was also necessarily responsive to conditions to social and political conditions there. Indeed, it has been suggested that the original plan for the Bamako médersa to teach French and certain secular subjects, although rejected by the authorities at the time, was in fact modelled in part on the curriculum of the French médersas. When the médersa was finally allowed to reopen under the auspices of the *Union Culturelle Musulmane* in 1958, it instituted a combined Islamic and secular curriculum reflecting the need felt by many Soudanese Muslims to educate their children both religiously and in a manner which would integrate them into the newly emergent political economy. The ultimate objectives of the counter-reform movement, although politically opposed to the Arabization advocated by the founders of the médersas, were fundamentally very similar: to combine Islamic and secular schooling with the aim of preparing young persons to function effectively and productively in contemporary society as 'good Muslims'. And the same *Union Culturelle Musulmane* that sponsored the Arabized curriculum of the Bamako médersa conducted many of its meetings and published its public communications in French.

These complex and sometimes seemingly contradictory permutations resulted from the fact that the persons experimenting with these new institutions intended them to function effectively both socially and politically within the colonial (and postcolonial) political economy, and not outside or apart from it. Such aims could not be achieved without attracting the attention of the colonial authorities, whose interventions may occasionally have blocked Muslim initiatives but which also necessarily evoked responses from the Muslims which both honed their political skills and called upon them to represent themselves and their aims to government representatives. The appearance of new Muslim institutions, and other Muslim initiatives, therefore created a new field of power relations that profoundly influenced how certain Muslims began to represent themselves in the public arena. Self-representations were many and varied, ranging from an al-Ifriqi who completely removed himself from West Africa and commented on conditions there exclusively (so it would seem) through a rethinking of Islamic doctrine, to a Hampâté Bâ whose Islam seems completely compatible with the colonial order. Many other variations between these two extremes have also been explored which together illustrate the diverse manner in which power relations evolved between Muslims and the colonial authorities during this period.

The contingencies of this process are even more salient when one examines the lives of individuals, as can be seen in a comparison of the life histories of Saada Oumar Touré and Amadou Hampâté Bâ.[117] Both were removed from Qur'anic schools and forcefully placed in French schools, but the impact of this experience on the two boys differed completely. Saada claimed this experience *inspired* him to reform the teaching of Arabic language in order that young Muslims would have more effective access to the sources of Islamic knowledge, whereas Hampâté Bâ, among other things, became a proselytizer of Muslim knowledge through the medium of the French language and an opponent of the Arabization of Muslim schooling.

This reading of events is intended to highlight the social basis for the re-thinking of Islam and of Muslim institutions that was taking place. Of course, these changes were accompanied by reflections on Islamic doctrine, which will be explored in the next chapter. But because the médersas were specifically intended to function in social and political spaces created by the colonial situation (by contrast with the Qur'anic schools), their advocates were at least as much preoccupied with the difficult questions of how to achieve their practical aims as with doctrinal issues. These Muslim initiatives were made possible by the social disjunctures created by the colonial situation, the impact of which resulted in social dislocation for some but also presented new possibilities for others.

[117] See L. Brenner, 'Becoming Muslim in Soudan Français' in Robinson and Triaud (eds), *Le temps des marabouts*, pp. 467-92.

4

DISCOURSES OF KNOWLEDGE, POWER AND IDENTITY

This chapter examines the simultaneous emergence of 'Wahhabism' and 'traditionalism' in the Soudan, concepts that functioned in Soudanese discourse as complementary twins. Before the appearance of 'Wahhabism' there was no 'traditionalism'. 'Wahhabism' was a label somewhat indiscriminately attached to a variety of Islamically inspired activities by members of the French administration and certain established Muslim leaders who perceived them as a political threat to their hegemony. At the core of Soudanese 'Wahhabism' was Salafi doctrine, and one can trace the introduction of various elements of this doctrine into West Africa. But Soudanese 'Wahhabism' was not simply doctrinal; both Cardaire and Amselle described early 'Wahhabism' as a religious ideology adopted by young and/or newly converted merchants. These socio-economic factors are recognized by Kaba who, while highlighting religious and doctrinal motivations in his analysis, also demonstrates the contribution of pre-independence politics to the 'Wahhabi' equation.

By the late 1950s the concept of 'Wahhabism' had been fully integrated into the Soudanese discourse about Islam; significantly, however, the term was used in French political reports synonymously, and completely interchangeably, with 'modernism' and 'reformism'. Whatever the religious, political or social content imputed to 'Wahhabism', or its synonyms, it was consistently contrasted to 'traditionalism'. In other words, as the French and Muslim establishments struggled to define and give substance to the threat they perceived in 'Wahhabism', they simultaneously invented 'traditionalism'.[1] At first 'traditionalism' was little more than a residual category; the 'traditionalists' were the critics and opponents of 'Wahhabism'. Subsequently there were efforts to formalize the religious substance of 'traditionalism', especially through the ideology of counter-reform. Thus we find Cardaire asserting that 'Wahhabi' ideas were 'totally foreign to the mentality of black Islam'.[2] 'Traditionalism' also had its synonyms; in addition to 'black Islam' there was 'orthodoxy' and even 'Malikism', that is adherence to the Maliki legal school or *madhhab*.

[1] For analyses of such discursive 'inventions', see T.O. Ranger, 'The Invention of Tradition in Colonial Africa' in E. Hobsbawm and T. Ranger (eds), *The Invention of Tradition* (Cambridge University Press, 1983); and V.Y. Mudimbe, *The Invention of Africa: Gnosis, Philosophy, and the Order of Knowledge* (Bloomington: Indiana University Press, 1988).

[2] Cardaire, *L'Islam et le terroir africain*, p. 108.

The idea that Soudanese 'Wahhabism' was itself an invented phenomenon is not new; virtually every scholar who has studied the subject has asserted that the Soudanese 'Wahhabis' were not *really* Wahhabis because they did not conform strictly to Wahhabi doctrine. The Azharists insisted to Lansiné Kaba that they had never referred to themselves as 'Wahhabis' before coming to Bamako, although they later accepted the label 'because of their agreement with the precepts of this doctrine'.[3] It would be useful to know precisely when the Azharists began to see themselves as 'Wahhabis', because as late as December 1957 the label was being forcefully denounced in public by Karamoko Kane, a Soudanese delegate to the constituent congress of the UCM. Kane challenged the UCM's enemies in a speech to the assembly, charging that ...

...worried by our success, they have taken advantage of the fallacious pretext that we are Wahhabis – a word that I would not know how to define – in order to combat us and, after the bloody incidents of 17 and 18 May 1957, to close our schools.[4]

Kane went on in his speech to praise Islamic culture and civilization, he described as 'rallying points for all Africans who are struggling for the emancipation of their country'.

Even this brief quotation suggests the complexity of the process one wishes to analyze. Karamoko Kane was well aware that the term 'Wahhabism' was being used in a pejorative and derogatory manner to discredit persons of his own persuasion. But his own interests, judging from his remarks, were not limited to religion alone, which in a way was the nub of the problem, because the French were extremely sensitive to any political initiative that might base its appeal on Islamic principles. They had always feared that Islam could in some way become the basis for united opposition to them, a concern that only became exacerbated after 1945 with the rising specter of pan-Arabism and pan-Islamism. So there was no particular surprise when, in 1955, Cardaire labeled the members of the Kayes branch of the UCM 'extremists', although it is illuminating that he justified this description by explaining that the UCM had already managed to attract several adherents of the pro-French PSP to their cause.[5] In those days, the RDA was considered by many members of the French administration to be 'an extremist political party'. 'Extremism' was certainly one of the attributes ascribed to 'Wahhabism'.

Some French commentators were aware of the distortions being perpetrated. M. Chailley, writing in 1962, observed:

It has become commonplace [in Mali] to call Wahhabis those persons who, after their return from the pilgrimage and therefore only a brief stay in Saudi Arabia, believe themselves capable of reforming the Islam of their Soudanese compatriots, which is in fact somewhat heterogeneous. These people are 'reformists' and nothing more, because generally they know nothing about Wahhabi doctrine and do not profess

[3] Kaba, *The Wahhabiyya*, p. 95.
[4] Chailley, 'Aspects de l'Islam au Mali', p. 48.
[5] ANM, 1-E-21, FR, Rapport politque, Kayes, 2ème trimestre, 1955.

it in any way. Their faith becomes intransigeant and they adopt an attitude of intrigue. They are recruited generally from among the wealthy merchants; they set themselves apart and oppose the traditional authorities at every possible opportunity. Politically, they flirt with the most progressive parties.

In the following account [a description of 'Wahhabi' – 'traditionalist' conflicts in Sikasso] we employ the term Wahhabi in the sense given it by the Administration, while emphasizing the extent to which it is inaccurate.[6]

It will be argued here that whatever else Soudanese 'Wahhabism' might have represented socially, religiously or economically, the term fulfilled a pejorative role in the political discourse precisely equivalent to 'fanaticism' early in the century and 'fundamentalism' at the end of the century. It was a term that simultaneously connoted danger and denoted politically active Muslims, that is, persons who expressed their political goals in Islamic terms. It was yet another permutation of a persistent French (and European/Christian) fear and animosity toward Islam, which was as much a product of the imagination as of considered reflections about political policy. Muslims, and Africans more generally, reciprocated these feelings of animosity, although it is quite clear that those who were denounced for their 'Wahhabism' were often precisely those persons who were the instigators of many new initiatives in Soudanese society that drew almost as much inspiration from French as from Islamic models, for example, in schooling, social organization and commercial activity. But the French did not want to be emulated by those who refused to be assimilated into French culture, and the 'Wahhabis' of course expressed all their aspirations in an Islamic idiom. It was as if moving into greater proximity, on any level, only served to deepen pre-existing mutual animosities; the parallel manifestation of this phenomenon was the French fascination with the Otherness of 'traditionalism' and 'black Islam'. What follows is not a psychological analysis, although there is certainly a profoundly significant psychological dimension to this complex series of interactions.

Muslim doctrinal politics: a discourse about ignorance and truth

Doctrinal politics is an intellectual activity that accompanies the political process in Muslim societies insofar as that political process is interpreted and commented upon from a religious perspective. Any attempt to establish political legitimacy on the basis of Islamic principles required that political institutions and political practice be seen to conform with Islamic doctrinal prescriptions. The demonstration that this was so in any given circumstance, or that it wasn't, was the work of the Muslim scholars, the *'ulama*, who were the intellectual guardians of Islamic dogma and doctrine. It is precisely because of this relationship between dogma and politics that any political dispute among Muslims is inevitably accompanied by a doctrinal dispute, and vice-versa; the two are virtually inextricable from one another.

[6] Chailley, 'Aspects de l'Islam au Mali', p. 37.

Of course, the role of the Muslim scholar is not necessarily limited solely to intellectual activity; some of the most effective Muslim leaders in West Africa have been 'scholar-politicians', persons who wielded both the pen and the sword. Still, the most valuable asset of the scholar, or the scholar-politician, is his knowledge and command of the Islamic religious corpus. One can certainly acquire political power without such knowledge, but one could never be recognized as a scholar without it; and religious knowledge is what matters in doctrinal debate. Historically in West Africa, religious knowledge has also given the scholar access to another kind of power, an esoteric power that has enabled him to intervene in social and political affairs without recourse to force, the ultimate weapon of the political leader. The practice of this power is usually referred to in the twentieth-century discourse as *maraboutage*, and it was a power that both the French and the 'Wahhabis' were intent on disclaiming and undermining.

Doctrinal political discourse in West Africa has, of course, produced many ordered and reasoned arguments in support, or in condemnation, of a wide range of social, political and religious configurations. Because many of these texts have been preserved, one is able to trace the development of much of this doctrinal argumentation, an exercise that reveals a number of salient patterns in the discourse. Our purpose here is not to offer a detailed analysis of the evolution of this discourse, but to place the emergence of the 'Wahhabiyya' into a broader historical context. To this end, we will review the doctrinal politics of several West African Muslim movements:

– the Qadiriyya-Mukthariyya Sufi brotherhood under the leadership of Sidi al-Mukhtar al-Kunti;
– the *jihad* of Shaikh 'Uthman dan Fodio;
– the dissemination of the Tijaniyya brotherhood under the leadership of al-Hajj 'Umar Tal, and his *jihad*;
– the Tijaniyya-Hamawiyya brotherhood under the leadership of Shaikh Hamallah b. Ahmad;
– the Soudanese 'Wahhabiyya'.

This list is of course selective; other movements could be included, but these few will suffice for the present analysis. Even this simple list can serve to illustrate the profound rupture with the past that the 'Wahhabiyya' represents in West Africa; for the preceding two centuries, the most significant Muslim movements had been Sufi-oriented, whereas the doctrinal rejection of Sufism was at the heart of the 'Wahhabi' religious initiative. Another more subtle, but nonetheless significant, observation is that all the Sufi-based movements are identified by both the names and the religious personalities of their founding leaders. Of course, the term 'Wahhabi' is also derived from the name of that movement's founder, Muhammad b. 'Abd al-Wahhab, which may account for the rejection of this denomination by adherents of the movement who do not wish to associate their doctrines with any individual Muslim but with the Qur'an and the religious practice of the pious community of the Prophet and his companions; thus, the designation of Salafi doctrine.

In these ways 'Wahhabism' was an innovative movement that broke with the past, but at the same time, the doctrinal politics that accompanied its spread were structurally very similar to those that were associated with the evolution of earlier movements. This is because doctrinal debates operate within a limited context which ultimately reduces all argumentation to a demonstration that the content of a given doctrinal position constitutes a better reading than its competitors of the fundamental Islamic texts (Qur'an and *hadith*). As already suggested, the defense of any doctrinal position depends ultimately on the intellectual capacity of its proponents to propagate and defend it, that is, upon their knowledge and control of the basic sources. And because Qur'an and (reliable) *hadith* are understood by Muslims to contain all the principles and guidelines which human beings can ever know about Islam, then it follows that the best interpretation of these sources will be a 'true' interpretation, and any contradictory interpretations will necessarily be 'false'. Consequently, doctrinal political debate inevitably includes claims and counter-claims about what is 'true', and about which scholars are truly knowledgeable and possess a full command of Islamic texts, and which are 'ignorant'.

We have already seen evidence of this discourse about truth and ignorance in the preceding analysis of the Islamic médersa movement, for example in the comments of Saada Oumar Touré. When Saada was called before the *commandant de cercle* of Segu, he asserted that the Imam who had brought a complaint against him was either 'ignorant or an egoist' for questioning the Islamic propriety of teaching mathematics in the new médersa. Perhaps this was an example of Saada's conviction that it was sometimes necessary to speak the 'bitter truth'. Indeed, he was of the opinion that Islam was weak in Mali because the *marabouts* had been constrained in their freedom to speak the truth, and one of his aims for his médersa was to provide young Muslims with an education which would prepare them to achieve the economic independence which would in turn enable them to speak the truth. Very similar ideas were expressed by West African students in Cairo. Cardaire had noted their intellectual pretensions as students of al-Azhar, who were keen to return to West Africa in order to enlighten their Muslim brethren, 'to tell them the truth', in spite of government attempts to restrict them. In their view, the majority of Muslims were 'ignorant persons and fetishers'; Muhammdad Sharif of Kankan, they claimed, was 'uneducated'. 'Abd al-Rahman al-Ifriqi spoke in very much the same manner, criticizing those ignorant *marabouts* who, 'with their false knowledge, sustained superstitions among the people which are contrary to Qur'anic law.'

All of these comments were doctrinal in that they related ultimately to disputes about the proper interpretation of Islam. And they were all political insofar as the Islamic médersa movement was a political movement in which a group of Muslim intellectuals was seeking to gain control over the definition and dissemination of Islamic knowledge. The historical roots of this kind of discourse penetrate deeply into the West African past, and our purpose here is to demonstrate its continuity with the discourse which accompanied the emergence of the 'Wahhabi' movement, which will be examined more fully below.

The movements led by Sidi al-Mukhtar, Shaikh 'Uthman, al-Hajj 'Umar, and Shaikh Hamallah were similar to one another in several ways which are relevant to the present discussion.[7] First, each of these men was an intellectual whose public career was marked by efforts to redefine the parameters of Islamic knowledge in his own time. This statement requires elaboration. All of them were Sufis, whose notions of epistemology included knowledge derived not only from exoteric, literary and oral sources, which were in theory accessible to everyone, but also from mystical sources, in the form of dreams and visions for example, which were accessible to only a select few. Their doctrinal politics therefore included not only lengthy debates over interpretations of Islamic law and practice, of which the works of Sidi al-Mukhtar and Shaikh 'Uthman offer many examples, but also competing claims based upon mystical insights which were available only to themselves. Both Shaikh 'Uthman and al-Hajj 'Umar received authorizations to launch their respective *jihads* in visions; and Shaikh Hamallah was recognized as a legitimate *khalifa* in the Tijaniyya because of his knowledge of the secret Great Name of God, which had also been revealed to him in a vision.

All of them, with the possible exception of Shaikh Hamallah, about whose formal educational achievements there is some disagreement, were also extremely learned and productive scholars. Sidi al-Mukhtar wrote over 80 works, some of them massive; Shaikh 'Uthman wrote over 100. Al-Hajj 'Umar wrote many less, but among them was his *Rimah*, perhaps the most widely disseminated work by any nineteenth-century West African author.[8] Shaikh Hamallah produced no such literary oeuvre, although this lack was more than compensated in the view of his followers by his mystical knowledge.

All of these persons, with the exception of al-Hajj 'Umar, were very young when they launched their public careers. At the age of nineteen, Sidi al-Mukhtar

---

[7] The ensuing discussion draws heavily upon my own previous analyses of this theme. See L. Brenner, 'Concepts of Tariqa in West Africa'; 'Constructing Muslim Identities in Mali' in L. Brenner (ed.), *Muslim Identity and Social Change in Sub-Saharan Africa* (London: Hurst; Bloomington: Indiana University Press, 1993), pp. 59-78; 'The Jihad Debate between Sokoto and Borno: an Historical Analysis of Islamic Political Discourse in Nigeria' in J.F. Ade Ajayi and J.D.Y. Peel (eds), *Peoples and Empires in African History* (London: Longman, 1992); 'Muslim Thought in Eighteenth-Century West Africa', *Réflexions sur le savoir islamique en Afrique de l'Ouest* (Centre d'Etude d'Afrique Noire, University of Bordeaux I, 1985); and *West African Sufi*.

[8] 'Umar b. Sa'id al-Futi, *Rimāḥ al-raḥīm 'alā nuḥūr ḥizb al-rajīm*, Published in the margins of 'Alī Ḥarāzim, *Jawāhir al-Ma'āni* (Beirut, no date).

experienced the first vision that presaged his mission as a *mujaddid*, or rejuvenator of Islam. Shaikh 'Uthman was in his twenties when he began his preaching campaign to bring Islamic practice into conformity with his interpretations of the *sunna*. Shaikh Hamallah was also in his twenties when he was recognized as *khalifa* by a Tijani emissary from North Africa. Al-Hajj 'Umar's intellectual abilities were recognized in his youth, although his public career did not really begin until his return from the pilgrimage, and his *jihad* not until much later.[9]

Of course, the movements that these men led were affected by a complex array of social and political factors, which we cannot analyze here. Our focus is on the fact that the expansion of each movement was accompanied by one, or several, doctrinal initiatives which simultaneously challenged a pre-existing doctrinal position and sought to demonstrate the superior Islamic knowledge of the leader in question. These initiatives in turn led to confrontations about which of the competing doctrinal interpretations was 'true'. Leaving aside for a moment the role of Sufism in their movements, both Sidi al-Mukhtar and Shaikh 'Uthman devoted much of their scholarly attention to explications of the *sunna*. Both claimed to be *mujaddid*. Sidi al-Mukhtar asserted that he lived in an age of religious decadence, which his community, under his leadership, was destined to rectify. Shaikh 'Uthman's first major work of scholarship, the *Ihya' al-sunna*[10] was a sweeping survey of the shortcomings of contemporary Islamic practice and of prescriptions for putting it right. Either explicitly or implicitly, the activities of these two men challenged the learning and the integrity of other contemporary scholars, whose responses and reactions are unfortunately not often available to contemporary researchers. Shaikh 'Uthman drew particular attention to those he called the 'venal' scholars, the *'ulama al-su'*, who allegedly offered their services in return for material reward, especially at the courts of the backsliding Muslim rulers of Hausaland. He also expended a great deal of effort in criticizing the doctrinal position of a group of scholars whom he called the *mutakallamun*, whose mystico-philosophical theology seems to have caused Shaikh 'Uthman great concern.

Most of the doctrinal literature composed by West African scholars was written in a somewhat theoretical style and was addressed to a broad and nonspecific audience of scholars. The content of such works is usually relatively mild when compared with the confrontational language of direct debate between contending leaders. One example of the latter kind of exchange is to be found in the correspondence between Shaikh 'Uthman and the leaders of his

[9] On the theme of Islam as 'a religion of the young', see Murray Last, 'The Power of Youth, Youth of Power: notes on the religions of the young in northern Nigeria' in H. d'Almeida-Topor *et al.* (eds), *Les Jeunes en Afrique*, tome II: *La Politique et la ville* (Paris: L'Harmattan, 1992), pp. 375-399.

[10] I.A.B. Balogun, 'A Critical Edition of Ihya' al-sunna wa ikhmad al-bid'a of 'Uthman b. Fudi, popularly known as Usuman dan Fodio' (unpubl. Ph.D. thesis, School of Oriental and African Studies, SOAS, University of London, 1967).

jihad and Muhammad al-Amin al-Kanemi, who opposed it and defended the Mai of Borno against attack . One of the most heated exchanges of this debate, which extended over several years, occurred when al-Kanemi challenged the integrity of Shaikh 'Uthman by citing an aphorism to the effect that 'I love the Shaikh and the truth as long as they agree, but when they differ, the truth must prevail'. An angry response to this comment was written by Shaikh 'Uthman's son, Muhammad Bello, who retorted that al-Kanemi had either to be mad or feeble-minded to have made such a reference to his father.

In fact, most of the debate between al-Kanemi and the leaders of the *jihad* was relatively civil and reflected a mutual respect for the learning of the respective disputants. But the bottom line of Shaikh 'Uthman's doctrinal justification for his *jihad* was that a proper Muslim community must be led by the learned *'ulama*, who in this case were himself and his colleagues. In their view, the Mai of Borno had apostasized from Islam, and the only doctrinally sound option open to al-Kanemi was to abandon the Mai and join Shaikh 'Uthman; in other words, to submit to his interpretation of the situation. Al-Kanemi persisted in his refusal, and the conflict continued for a number of years.

A similarly heated confrontation occurred when the *jihad* of al-Hajj 'Umar came into conflict with the Islamic *Dina* of Macina, under the leadership of Amadu Amadu.[11] The major thrust of 'Umar's *jihad* had been against regions and kingdoms which could make little claim to being Muslim, whereas the *Dina* had itself been established by a *jihad* early in the century led by Amadu Amadu's grandfather.[12] Nonetheless, when the politics of the *Dina* threatened 'Umar's own strategic position, he found it necessary to attack it, and in order to justify such a move, he wrote a doctrinal treatise which attempted to demonstrate the religious decline of its leadership and more specifically the intellectual shortcomings of Amadu Amadu himself. The work was a sustained argument designed to demonstrate Amadu Amadu's doctrinal ignorance in extremely abusive language. According to 'Umar, Amadu was an ignorant man who

… has gathered around himself other ignorant persons and who has chosen as his secretary an ignorant man more ignorant than the rest. He then took as a teacher someone who is still even more ignorant than that! As [the poets] have said, 'Among the most astonishing of things that you don't know, is that you don't know that you don't know'.[13]

---

[11] For the *jihad* of al-Hajj 'Umar see Robinson, *The Holy War of Umar Tal*; and Madina Ly-Tall, *Un Islam militant en Afrique de l'ouest au XIX siècle. La Tijaniyya de Saïku Umar Futiyu contre les Pouvoirs traditionnels et la Puissance coloniale* (Paris: L'Harmattan, 1991).

[12] See William A. Brown, 'The Caliphate of Hamdullahi ca.1818-1864: a Study in African History and Tradition' (unpublished Ph.D. thesis, University of Wisconsin, Madison, 1969); and Bintou Sanankoua, *Un empire peul au xixe siècle. La Diina du Maasina* (Paris: Karthala, 1990).

[13] See S.M.Mahibou and J.L. Triaud, *Voilà ce qui est arrivé. Bayân mâ waqa'a d'al-Hâgg 'Umar al-Fûtî. Plaidoyer pour une guerre sainte en Afrique de l'Ouest* (Paris: CNRS, 1983), p. 92.

This kind of personalized diatribe has been very much a part of doctrinal politics in West Africa, and derives from the fact that the legitimacy of Islamic leadership was dependent upon what I have described elsewhere as an individual's 'religious persona'.[14] Religious persona is based upon perceptions not only of a leader's knowledge and learning, but also his personal and religious integrity. The religious persona of Sufi leaders was crucial to their popular acceptance, because mystical knowledge is acquired only through the grace of God. Consequently, they were particularly vulnerable and sensitive to personal attacks, and indeed, any dissent from the mystically revealed doctrine of a Sufi leader is by implication an attack on that individual's personal integrity. On the other hand, the possession of mystical knowledge can focus the attention of a new religious movement on what might otherwise appear to be a very small innovation, as was the case with the Tijaniyya-Hamawiyya, which differed doctrinally from 'Umarian Tijani practice only in the number of times adherents recited the *jawharat al-kamal*, a prayer in the Tijani litany.[15]

Sufi movements and brotherhoods derived much of their social force from the religious persona of their founding leaders. The basic doctrinal thrust of Salafism, and therefore of 'Wahhabism' was in opposition to Sufism and all its associated manifestations. Of course, the 'Wahhabis' developed their own notions of religious persona, which were devoid of all vestiges of the mystical. The discourse about ignorance and truth persisted however, in that those who advocated the new doctrine sought to do so on the basis of the breadth and depth, as well as the 'truth', of their own knowledge. Salafism became the doctrinal core of Soudanese 'Wahhabism' and provided the focus of numerous doctrinal political confrontations from as early as the 1930s.

Jean-Louis Triaud has summarized Soudanese 'Wahhabism' as possessing the following characteristics:

– the symbolic rupture with the majority of the Muslim community by the adoption of external signs (such as praying with crossed arms and, more recently, wearing a Saudi-style beard and clothing) and by the founding of their own associations and mosques;
– the rejection of all forms of popular piety, considered as blameworthy innovations (*bid'a*) or pagan survivals, whether it be funeral practices, the consultation of *marabouts* or the cult of saints;
– exclusive reliance on the Qur'an and the *Sunna* of the Prophet, coupled with a confirmed disdain for the jurisprudential corpus, the knowledge of which has served

---

[14] See Brenner, 'The Jihad Debate', pp. 30ff. Of relevance to this discussion of the legitimacy of Muslim leaders is David Laitin's, *Hegemony and Culture: Politics and Religious Change among the Yoruba* (University of Chicago Press, 1986), in which he compares Muslim personal legitimacy with Christian institutional legitimacy.

[15] See R. Launay, *Beyond the Stream*, for an analysis of relationships between ritual practice and social identity. Launay would tend to describe these doctrinal disctinctions as ideological in that they 'either confer or deny legitimacy to specific social distinctions'; see p. 31.

as an instrument of power for the Islamic establishment and the mechanical reproduction of which has contributed to the decadence of Islam;
– vehement opposition to the Sufi brotherhoods (most particularly the Tijaniyya),
considered to be innovative and heretical sects.[16]

From the perspective of the present analysis, these features can be understood
as the same kind of doctrinal initiatives which are integral to all social and
political movements which define themselves as Islamic; they mark the religious distinctions between the 'Wahhabis' and their Muslim opponents. But
'Wahhabism' cannot be defined in terms of doctrine alone, because it was
also associated with various social and political initiatives.[17] For example, its
leadership was generally young, and at least some of the conflict that attended
its introduction was generational. Politically, many 'Wahhabis' affiliated themselves with the more radical wing of the independence movement, which
tended to be militantly anti-French and was also opposed to entrenched
local African authority. Many 'Wahhabis' were also economic entrepreneurs,
not only in their commercial enterprises but also in their experiments with
fee-paying médersas. Indeed, one of the most widespread charges against
them in the popular discourse has been that they are greedy for wealth.

Some French observers were well aware of the complexity of the 'Wahhabi'
– 'traditionalist' confrontation. In the course of his reflections on the causes
for the violence in Bamako in May 1957, the local *commandant de cercle* observed:

Of course, one finds religious passion, which is one of the most violent which man
possesses (the scandal of seeing the Prophet reduced to the ranks of an ordinary
man by the Wahhabis). But there is also a racial quarrel (the autochtons of Bamako
versus the strangers: the Malinkés and Guineans); social antagonism (poor versus
rich); a political conflict (tradition versus evolution, customary leaders versus newly
elected ones, and even something which might be surprising but definitely exists for
some, continued association with the western world in the face of the rising threat
of Arabism and 'Nasserism').

A few months later the same official returned to these questions, wondering
in his monthly report how a quarrel, which at first glance appeared so insignificant, could become so embittered. He evoked again what he called 'fundamental
social oppositions between poor and rich, merchants and clients, exploiters
and exploited, and … between strangers and authentic original inhabitants'.[18]

On one level, these observations are demonstrably valid; social and political conflicts were repeatedly projected into the religious arena in the form of

---

[16] Triaud, ' 'Abd al-Rahman l'Africain', p. 166.

[17] It should be noted that Triaud shares the view that the term 'Wahhabism' connotes
more than doctrine. He has argued for a controlled usage of the term, however, in order
to trace its doctrinal history in West Africa. The characteristics that he listed conform
with popular usage and are intended to describe how the 'Wahhabis' distinguished themselves
both symbolically and doctrinally from the rest of the Muslim community.

[18] ANM, 1 E 7 (II), Rapports politiques et rapports de tournées. Cercle de Bamako (1945-
58), Revues mensuelles, May and July 1957.

disputes about the appointment of imams, mosques and, of course, doctrine. M. Chailley analyzed the evolution of four such conflicts in the 1950s in order better to understand what he called their 'physiology'.[19] His examples illustrate the complex and seamless web of factors that contribute to these disputes, which for him have no clear beginning or resolution. The causes he identifies are generally a mixture of religious, historical, social, economic, political and generational differences and interests, although he has selected his examples with the intention of looking specifically at ostensibly religious disputes. He concludes that in Soudan/Mali there are no 'pure' religious conflicts – not an astonishing insight since it is difficult to imagine a 'pure' religious conflict in any context. But he goes on to say that religion is no more than a pretext to carry on these long-term disputes on another level.

Even this contention is defensible to a certain extent, although there is a derogatory tone in the way Chailley argues his position, which is no doubt related to the fact that French analyses of such conflicts usually excluded themselves from the equation of their genesis. The French were deeply ambivalent about African religion and about Islam; on the one hand they would denigrate it, and then use it in order to achieve certain political objectives. They would do this while at the same time seeking to project an image that they were themselves above this kind of manipulation. But the French were very much involved in making the 'Wahhabi' movement what it was, perhaps often unconsciously involved, but nonetheless involved. 'Wahhabism', like the Islamic médersa movement, was a phenomenon born of the change brought about by the colonial period; its adherents were seeking to confront and transcend existing conditions, for which Salafi doctrine provided an attractive source of ideological leverage.

'Wahhabism' was structurally very similar to the Hamallist movement which had immediately preceded it: it split the Muslim community into hostile factions, and it was viewed as a serious political threat by the French, whose opposition further enhanced the appeal of the movement. And like Hamallism, the earliest origins of 'Wahhabism' in Soudan were to be found in a series of doctrinal initiatives which have been traced by Lansiné Kaba; the following summary is based on his research.[20] The two earliest advocates of Salafi doctrine in Soudan whom Kaba discusses are Tiekodo Kamagaté, who performed the pilgrimage in the 1930s and returned to West Africa in about 1944, and Abdullahi Ag Mahmud, a Kel es Souk Tuareg who had lived in the Middle East for about thirty years, having travelled there with his father. He returned to West Africa in about 1938.[21]

[19] Chailley, 'Aspects de l'Islam au Mali', pp. 29-41.
[20] Kaba, *The Wahhabiyya*, ch. 1.
[21] Kaba also mentions two other persons as possible early Wahhabis, both in Timbuktu in the 1930s, although the evidence about them is unconvincing. One of them, Mustafa Baba, was one of the teachers whom Fadiga had dismissed from the Timbuktu médersa, and whose criticism and discontent was certainly related to that incident. See *ibid.*, pp. 27-

Kamagaté, who was himself a merchant, seems to have been one of the first persons to introduce Salafi doctrine to the Muslims of the Jula network. According to Kaba, Kamagaté took advantage of his time in the Middle East to further his studies, through which he not only acquired a new expertise in the Muslim religious sciences but also an introduction to Salafi doctrine. Upon his return to Ivory Coast, he began a program of preaching in which he publicly advocated the anti-Sufi interpretations of the Middle Eastern Salafis. He found an enthusiastic audience, especially among 'dynamic young traders and transporters', in Jula centres such as Bouaké, Sikasso and Bobo-Dioulasso. But he also soon encountered a strong resistance, which eventually reached the highest levels of the Muslim hierarchy causing Muhammad Sharif of Kankan to denounce the new doctrines as *kufr*, unbelief, and to 'excommunicate' its advocates.[22] Subsequently the confrontations and conflicts increased, and in 1947 or 1948 Kamagaté was arrested and confined to the small market town of Moriba-Diassa, near Bouaké.

According to Kaba's information, Kamagaté's criticism of the *marabouts* was extreme and highly personalized, in the manner discussed above. It is useful to quote Kaba at length on this matter:

Al-Hajj Tiekodo denounced marabutism as a product of pre-Islamic doctrine and practices. In his view, members of Sufi orders could not be called orthodox; and Sufi practices are against Sunnism. He reproached the brotherhoods for abusing the system of *zawiya* (mystical schools) and for keeping students (*talibe*) for the 'sole purpose of their labor'. He and his followers labeled this as a malicious and noxious exploitation. Al-Hajj Tiekodo made direct attacks against ordinary clerics and major marabu, such as Shaykh Muhammad Sharif of Kankan, for the discrepancy between their lives and Quranic morals, the laxity of their commitment, and their surrender to colonial authorities. The harshness of his diatribes against ordinary marabu corresponded to the deep indignation he felt against their lucrative practices, namely, charm making, divination based on alleged knowledge of the hidden meanings of words, letters, and numbers, healing, and even sand divination. With the same vigor, he criticized the cult of the saints (*wali*)– visits to their tombs and offerings to their memory. In his view, all this belonged to the *jahiliyya*, that is, the pre-Islamic beliefs and practices, and hence should be rejected unequivocally from Islam. In doing so, he ultimately implied that the majority of the local lettered people were half-hearted in their allegiance to the Quranic traditions and hypocritical in their behavior. Therefore al-Hajj Tiekodo proposed an interpretation of the prophecy which took into consideration the nobility of Muhammad's role as a holy messenger and

---

8, and Chapter 2, above. Mahamane, 'Le mouvement wahhabite a Bamako', found an archival reference to an alleged Wahhabi in Mopti in a 1941 colonial report (p. 24), and an informant claimed that the word 'Wahhabi' was first heard in Bamako in 1948 by a Tijani from the Anglo-Egyptian Sudan who had been recruited by the colonial administration (p. 34).

[22] Kaba, *The Wahhabiyya*, p. 44, uses the word 'excommunication' to describe Muhammad Sharif's formal condemnation of Kamagaté. He also places the word in quotation marks, suggesting the uncertainty of precisely what action Muhammad Sharif might have taken.

a statesman, although he urged his followers not to direct any prayers to the Prophet himself for fear of associationism [*shirk*].[23]

This passage provides an excellent example of doctrinal politics. Of course, since Kamagaté did not write anything, and Kaba's information was gathered some twenty-five years after the event, it is difficult to know the precise content of what he preached, but it seems evident that he did not limit himself strictly to argumentation about doctrine. If we add other information provided by Kaba to the preceding description, we can analyze Kamagaté's 'Wahhabism' in relationship to the characteristics outlined by Triaud.

Rupture with the Muslim community. Kamagaté prayed with his arms across his chest, although no information is available about his manner of dress. He does not seem formally to have founded any new associations, and his active preaching preceded the campaign to establish 'Wahhabi' mosques by about a decade. On the other hand, his preaching offerred doctrinal justification for persons to refuse to participate in such elaborate and expensive communal rituals as marriages and baptisms, which was a highly visible and public way in which to separate oneself from the broader community and which led to many serious intra-family conflicts. Indeed, although the crossing of arms during prayer became the most widely recognized symbol of 'Wahhabism', the movement was in general most severely criticized because of the refusal of its members to participate in the public ceremonies and celebrations of their families and communities. Finally, Muhammad Sharif's 'excommunication' of Kamagaté must have had considerable impact: there could be no more profound break with the community than being labeled an apostate by the object of one's criticism.

Rejection of popular piety. The main target of Kamagaté's preaching seems to have been *maraboutisme* and all of its associated practices. Indeed, judging from Kaba's account, Kamagaté seems to have been much less directly critical of devotional Sufism than of *maraboutisme*, especially of the way in which the *marabouts* sought to derive financial gain from their allegedly 'magical practices' which were associated with healing and divination. Certainly, it was in his personal criticism of the *marabouts* that Kamagaté's attacks became most virulent, and which led in turn to the extreme reactions against him. But the significance of Kamagaté's general condemnation of the Muslim 'esoteric sciences' was much deeper than the immediate conflicts that it engendered. His preaching marked the beginning of a new Muslim discourse in Soudan which in many ways was congruent with that of the French and the emergent secular African leadership. Kamagaté's allegations of hypocrisy and magical practices against the *marabouts* were very little different from French attitudes about their general ignorance and superstitious inclination. We can perceive here

[23] *Ibid.*, pp. 37-8.

the very beginnings of a process in which the doctrinal rejection of the 'esoteric sciences' complemented the introduction of formal secular schooling and simultaneously provided a doctrinal opening for Muslims to accept alternate forms of technical and scientific knowledge.

Reliance on Qur'an and Sunna and rejection of the jurisprudential corpus. Kaba's account says nothing about jurisprudence as such, but describes Kamagaté's doctrine as a 'return to the roots of Islam' and a call for 'the revival of the "true Islam"'. This, of course, is precisely what Sidi al-Mukhtar al-Kunti and Shaikh 'Uthman had claimed that they were doing over one hundred years before, although the Sufism which these men had embraced was now itself under attack. But again, we should look at the broader implications of a call for a return to Qur'an and *sunna*, and the rejection of received jurisprudential precedent. The general effect is to create a doctrinal *tabula rasa* that allows for a complete legal reinterpretation of Islam. This break with the past in turn allows for the 'modernization' of Islam, in the sense of refashioning its legal constraints to conform with contemporary social, political and economic conditions. In fact, the process involves a reinterpretation of the past in order better to confront the present.[24] The jurisprudential aspect of this change has not developed very far in Mali, primarily because Muslim legal institutions hardly exist there, but given the space in which to evolve, such a debate could certainly be anticipated.[25]

Kamagaté also emphasized the sovereignty and uniqueness of Allah and the obligation for Muslims to serve Him both individually and collectively. It is not clear whether Kamagaté himself became engaged in any close theological arguments about the nature of God, but he did launch into a criticism of Sufi devotional practices with respect to the Prophet, which were rejected by Wahhabis as leading to *shirk*, the association of created beings with God. Wahhabis viewed the Prophet as an exemplary Muslim, but a human being like all others, and they were particularly critical of Sufi perceptions of the Prophet as intercessor. This point struck closer to the heart of Sufism than any other, both because intercession was central to Sufi doctrine and because many Muslims felt Wahhabi attitudes were disrespectful to the Prophet.

Opposition to the Sufi brotherhoods. Opposition to Sufism has of course been a central element of Salafi doctrine everywhere, and Kamagaté was no exception in this regard. But in Kaba's account, criticism of Sufism was focused more on the social hierarchy of the brotherhoods than on their devotional or mystical

---

[24] On this process, see Amselle, *Logiques métisses*, pp. 62-3, where he argues that 'fundamentalism represents the quintessence of culturalism because it is a phenomenon that uses writing [literacy] to inject the present into the past'.
[25] Of course, there is an extensive oral discourse on these matters, in sermons and public lectures, but compared with countries like Sudan, Nigeria and even Senegal, Malian Muslims have not yet developed modern Islamic jurisprudence very far.

practices. To repeat Kaba's words, Kamagaté 'reproached the brotherhoods for abusing the system of *zawiya*' by profiting from the labour of their disciples, which he condemned as 'malicious and noxious exploitation'. This passage implies that Kamagaté was not against the mystical *zawiyas* as such, but against the alleged abuses that they had come to perpetrate. Interestingly, Kaba records an initiative by a few of Kamagaté's opponents to discuss some of these issues with him, to 'discover the truth',[26] as they put it. It does not appear that these efforts toward compromise progressed very far, but it is certainly of interest to note that they took place.

This brief summary of Kamagaté's doctrinal politics demonstrates how he mixed doctrinal argumentation with social and political commentary; implied in his religious discourse were the elements of profound social and political reform. This kind of social and political criticism would become a key element in the Wahhabi movement, as Muslims began to search for ways to reorganize social production and reproduction in the twentieth century. The Islamic médersa movement played a major role in this process, although we have already seen that the innovations that it brought in education were not limited to persons of Salafi persuasion. And Kamagaté himself was not involved in the educational movement.

Given the nature and content of his campaign, however, it is not surprising that Kamagaté should have been the target of condemnations by Muhammad Sharif and of violent attacks by others. And it certainly seems likely, as proposed in Chapter Two, that Muhammad Sharif's oppostion to the educational projects of the Azharists was engendered in part by his antipathy toward the activities of Tiekodo Kamagaté and his associates. More remarkable, perhaps, was the speed with which these events reached such a high level of confrontational intensity, especially when compared with the very different impact of similar preachings by Abdullahi Ag Mahmud.

Abdullahi Ag Mahmud probably began preaching Salafi doctrine in the Niger bend region shortly after his return from the Middle East in 1938, some five or six years earlier than Kamagaté. Although the doctrinal content of his message was very similar to that of Kamagaté, there are no contemporary reports of serious conflict and confrontation arising from his activities, and Kaba's description of him depicts a rather mild and patient man. He opposed Sufism and condemned the shaikhs of the orders, while insisting that the *marabouts* should earn their living by 'honest work' and not through the manufacture of amulets; he maintained that only God, and not the saints or the Prophet, should be invoked in prayers; and argued in favour of the reform of jurisprudential practice, in that properly trained persons were qualified to practice *ijtihad*, or independent legal reasoning.[27] According to Kaba, Abdullahi's 'method of initiation to the new doctrine was to read and explain

[26] These words were placed in quotation marks in Kaba's text, *The Wahhabiyya*, p. 43.
[27] Governor Beyries, 'L'Islam au Soudan Français', CHEAM 2940, 1956, quoted in Kaba, *The Wahhabiyya*, p. 30.

the Quran (*tafsir*) and to lead his audience to discover the truth and perceive what was intrinsically wrong with the brotherhoods and the religious leaders'.[28]

A 1954 political report, written two years after Abdullahi's death, described him simply as having attempted 'to rethink the religious problem', which led to his being considered heterodox by other Muslims, and 'Wahhabi' by the French.[29] According to one French observer, he had exercised some influence in the Gabéro district near Gao, where the youth had become disinclined to affiliate themselves with the Sufi brotherhoods following his visit there in 1942.[30] The report explicitly deferred from describing this situation as a 'massive adherence to Wahhabism', which may have been the official inclination in 1956 when it was written, a point which takes on particular significance when compared with a 1949 report which refers to Abdullahi as a '*Saoudiste*' who was trying to convince people to emigrate permanently to the Middle East under the pretext of performing the pilgrimage.[31]

Indeed, the major thrust of Abdullahi's message may have been to encourage persons to perform a *hijra*, to emigrate from the Soudan in order to make a new life in the Muslim Middle East. This interpretation is supported by reports about his influence on another Kel es Souk Tuareg chief, Effanfan Ag Oguenett, who, having himself made the pilgrimage in 1938, became preoccupied in the 1950s with sending his children to Arabia for their studies.[32] Effanfan's experience recalls that of Mohamed Ali Ag Ataher, discussed in the previous chapter; both men felt impelled by the combination of local conditions and their own personal inclinations to seek an education for their children abroad. Abdullahi Ag Mahmud may have played a key role in encouraging this situation, and one wonders whether he might not have been influential in convincing 'Abd ar-Rahman al-Ifriqi to leave Soudan for the Middle East.

In any event, by the 1950s a small but active community of persons from the Niger bend region had settled in Saudi Arabia, many of whom had no intention of returning home so long as the political conditions which prevailed there persisted. One of the great attractions to Saudi Arabia at that time was the person and teaching of al-Ifriqi, who had become a major proselytizer of Salafi doctrine. We have already noted his opposition to Sufism and his criticism of 'ignorant' *marabouts*. Jean-Louis Triaud has written an analysis of al-Ifriqi's career based upon an obituary that appeared following his death in 1957, and which provides considerable information about the evolution of his doctrinal position.[33] When al-Ifriqi arrived in Saudi Arabia, at an undetermined date, he

[28] Kaba, *The Wahhabiyya*, p. 31.

[29] ANM, 1-E-17 II FR, Gao, Rapport politique, 1954; also quoted in Kaba, *The Wahhabiyya*, p. 30, note 20.

[30] ANM, 1-E-17 II FR, Gao, Rapport mensuel, septembre 1956.

[31] ANM, 1-E-17 I FR, Gao, Rapport de tournée, 1er trimestre, 1949.

[32] MI, Carnets de Personnalité religieuse-musulmane, Cercle de Gao.

first pursued his studies among Maliki teachers resident in Medina. Four years later, when he might have returned to Soudan, he met an African scholar by the name of Shaikh Sa'id b. Sadiq, with whom he decided to continue his studies. Shaikh Sa'id was a teacher of Salafi doctrine in the Mosque of the Prophet, and al-Ifriqi's association with him marked the latter's 'conversion' to this doctrinal interpretation. According to Triaud, al-Ifriqi now became an official charge of the Saudi (and local Wahhabi) establishment.

He subsequently studied in the *Dar al-Hadith*, where he also acted as interpreter for other Africans studying there and where he himself would one day teach. During one period, in 1944-5, he was sent on a preaching mission to the Hijaz, where his aims were strikingly similar to those of similar persuasion who were preaching in West Africa: to discourage the making of amulets and the performance of votive offerings and of animal sacrifices. His methods were not confrontational and he did not condemn such practices outright; rather he concentrated on instructing the children of the community in Qur'an and *tawhid* with the idea that they might in turn lead their parents to a new understanding of Islam. Al-Ifriqi also wrote several brief works, one in criticism of the Tijaniyya, another as a guide to the pilgrimage, and a third in response to a series of questions posed to him and which includes a defense of the legal practice of *ijtihad*.[34]

As Triaud has remarked, during his active life al-Ifriqi was an extremely influential proselytizer of Salafi doctrine among West Africans. The obituary consistently employs the phrase '*al-'aqidat al-salafiyya*', or Salafi doctrine, to describe the object of al-Ifriqi's studies and teaching, which is why the term has been adopted in the present analysis to designate the doctrinal elements of Soudanese Wahhabism. This usage in the obituary illustrates yet again that the origins of the denomination 'Wahhabi' have been external to the movement that it is meant to designate. If the doctrinal origins of this movement in Soudan can be traced to the various individuals being discussed here, all the available evidence demonstrates that they were only ever called 'Wahhabis' by their enemies and detractors. We have already noted a number of explicit and implicit rejections of this label; and even if some persons did come eventually to accept it, as Kaba has been told, such acceptance remains purely on an informal level.[35] Formally they refer to themselves as Sunnis, or the *Ahl al-sunna*,[36]

---

[33] Triaud, "Abd al-Rahman l'Africain'.

[34] Triaud, *ibid.*, p. 176, gives the three titles as: *Kitāb al-anwār al-raḥmāniyya li-hidāyati al-firqa al-tijāniyya* (Les Lumières miséricordieuses pour montrer la bonne voie en ce qui concerne la fraction tijaniyya); Tawdīh al-ḥājj wa 'l-'umra (Explication du Ḥajj et de la 'Umra), and *Jawābān li-Ifrīqiyyīn* (Réponses à des Africains). The present author has been unable to locate any of these books in Mali, either in public or private libraries or in bookshops.

[35] The name 'Wahhabi' has never, to my knowledge, appeared in the official name of any Muslim organization in Mali. One of their newest 'Wahhabi' associations, formed in August 1991, is called '*L'union des musulmans sunnites pour le progrès islamique*'.

[36] Mahamane, 'Le mouvement wahhabite à Bamako', p. 14, notes other forms of this denomination in local languages: *Sounnatié* and *Sounna Mogho*.

a designation which conforms to the principle that their religious doctrines do not derive from any single interpreter of Islam but from the basic precepts to be found in the Qur'an and the *sunna* of the Prophet.

If Salafi doctrine represents the religious core of the movement which came to be known as Wahhabism in Soudan, this movement was also something more (and perhaps less?) than that. In the first place, Wahhabism was not equally successful everywhere in Soudan. It found its first and most receptive audience among the Malinké-Jula groups to the south, and in the major centres of their trading network: Bamako, Bouaké, and Sikasso, where its adherents very quickly identified and entered into conflict with those opposed to their interpretations and activities. The movement made little impact in the older centres of established Islam, such as Jenne, Timbuktu, Segu and Nioro, where persons attracted to Salafi doctrine tended to avoid direct confrontations with established authority. We noted a similar pattern of behaviour in the case of Saada Oumar Touré in Segu, whose médersa project was opposed by certain religious dignitaries in the city, but who himself was careful never to break with the local Tijani hierarchy to which he was connected both by family and spiritual ties.

It is not that Salafi doctrine was unknown in the Niger bend. The doctrine was widely known, and its introduction often resulted in conflict, which seems however to have taken the form of written debate, primarily in order to defend or to attack the Tijaniyya; no doubt, al-Ifriqi's *Kitab al-Anwar* was a contribution to this debate. Unfortunately, virtually no research has been conducted to date into these texts, many of which have been conserved in Timbuktu.[37] However, even without knowing the detailed content of these debates, it is clear that the Wahhabism of the Niger bend was much less socially and politically confrontational than that of the Malinké-Jula region.

With the exception, that is, of Gao and environs where 'Wahhabism' seems to have been able to establish itself because of the city's significance as a trading centre, and because the region is located on the frontiers of the area of Kunta-Qadiri influence. In fact, one of the most radical expressions of Wahhabism to be found in Mali is located in the Gao region, in the form of exclusivist, isolated communities.[38]

However, during the 1950s confrontational Wahhabism was much more characteristic of the Malinké-Jula region, where in popular perception it had less to do with doctrine than with social dissent, politics, and the quest for wealth. According to Kaba, Wahhabism was the Islam of an upwardly mobile class of (mostly) young men whose newly acquired values and ambi-

---

[37] In the Centre de Documentation et de Recherche Historique Ahmed Baba; for recent research on the doctrinal controversies surrounding the Tijaniyya elsewhere in West Africa, see J-L Triaud and D. Robinson (eds), *L'ascension d'une confrérie musulmane La Tijaniyya en Afrique de l'Ouest et du Nord (XIXe-XXe siècles)*, forthcoming.

[38] See Niezen, 'Diverse Styles of Islamic Reform' and 'The "Community of Helpers of the Sunna" '.

tions severely challenged those of their parents' generation. Adherence to the Wahhabi movement was to a certain extent determined by age and social rank and was clearly a manifestation of existing social tensions and power relations.[39] Because their ideology and behavior struck directly at some of the most sensitive areas of social relationships, the Wahhabis very quickly came to be portrayed as 'anarchist, ambitious, niggardly, and selfish'.[40] For their own part, they put themselves forward as hard-working men who earned their living through their own efforts:

The success of a man is not a miracle; it comes from his courage (that is, his perseverence and endurance) and his intelligence.[41]

The good Muslim must have energy and initiative. It is true that we need God's help, but we must act.[42]

If these bourgeois values might have been welcomed in some quarters, they were much criticized by other Africans because they were accompanied by various manifestations of extreme individualism. For example, some Wahhabis began to refuse to participate in communal and family rituals, such as weddings and naming ceremonies, which in their accepted form required enormous expenditures of money. Like Kamagaté before them, they advocated more simple and less expensive ceremonies, which they defended by reference to Qur'an and *sunna*; but regardless of all the doctrinal justifications which they could bring to bear to support their views, they were never able to avoid the attacks of their critics who charged that they were unwilling to share their wealth with their less fortunate kin and associates. Wahhabis therefore came to be stereotyped as persons who were interested, above all else, in acquiring personal wealth, and Wahhabism became equated in the minds of many with the acquisition of wealth. It became common to hear people claim: 'In order to become rich, one must be a Wahhabi.'[43] Some even went so far as to say that, 'If you don't pray, you cannot earn any money'.[44]

This particular discourse about money and wealth had emerged independently of religious contestation, in the context of French efforts to monetize the economy through various forms of taxation and efforts to encourage commercial production. Of course, it came to focus on the Wahhabis because of their own conspicuous involvement in economic affairs and their contestation of dominant social values, particularly concerning the redistribution of wealth. It was not that Wahhabis refused to share their wealth with others, but they began to do so in different ways, in the form of public endowments in

[39] Kaba, *The Wahhabiyya, passim*, but especially pp. 37 and 70-1.
[40] *Ibid.*, p. 44.
[41] Mahamane, 'Le mouvement wahhabite à Bamako', p. 74, citing al-Hajj Ibrahima Touré, proprietor of a general store in Bamako known as *Mille et Une Merveilles*.
[42] Aly Konta, 'Une approche géographique des pratiques islamiques au Mali. Une étude de cas' (mémoire de fin d'études, l'ENSup, Bamako, 1984), p. 24.
[43] Mahamane, 'Le mouvement wahhabite à Bamako', p. 4.
[44] Amselle, *Négotiants*, p. 243.

financing the construction of mosques and schools, for example. These practices, too, have not occurred without evoking severe criticism and therefore
have often demanded justification, as the following passage demonstrates:

Everything has a beginning and an end. And so it is with every created being: for
every life, there is death. It is the same for the human being, whose beginning is life
and whose end is death, although there are things which distinguish one individual
from another.

For example, if a man is learned and fears God, and he teaches the people, works
with them and spreads his knowledge, then when he dies ... there will always be
those who mention his name and remember his work. His name will be recorded in
history, which is why it is said that the death of a learned man is superior to the life
of an ignorant one.

And so it is with a man who has been blessed with great wealth, who fears God,
prays, fasts, performs the pilgrimage and pays the *zakat* as God has commanded him.
If he does not oppress people with his wealth, but dispenses it in the path of God,
and he gives to the poor and dispossessed, and he builds schools and mosques, then
he deserves to be remembered because he has accomplished important and valuable
works for Islam. Seku Oumar Bathily did all this and more.[45]

This excerpt from a pamphlet eulogizing a deceased benefactor illustrates
how an Islamic gloss comes to be placed on a life of economic success. The
document from which this extract is taken was not written from a specifically
Wahhabi perspective, but it is relevant to the present discussion because the
author in effect argues that in Islamic terms, economic production is equal
to scholarly production so long as one's wealth or knowledge are put to use
in the service of Islam.

It was precisely on these two points that the Wahhabis attacked the *marabouts*.
The *marabouts* were charged with misusing their knowledge, by mixing it with
non-Islamic practices and by perpetuating belief in superstitions, which they
then manipulated in order to play on the credulity of the mass of Muslims
in order to extract money and gifts from them. They were also charged with
taking advantage of their students by exploiting their labour. In other words,
the *marabouts* were alleged to be the exact opposite of the Wahhabis, who
claimed to be pious, hard-working, self-supporting Muslims whose quest
for knowledge was undertaken solely for the intention of better fulfilling the
precise obligations of God's revealed law.

The subject of *maraboutisme* is vast and complex, and deserves a special study
in its own right.[46] The word *marabout* is a French usage (derived from the Arabic *murabit*) which was introduced into West Africa at an early date to describe

[45] Dauda Muhammad al-Amin Jah, *Hayāt al-Hājj Saiku ʿUmar Bachīlī 1928-1981* (Bamako,
issued privately, no date).
[46] Lamin Sanneh's *The Jakhanke Muslim Clerics*, and his more recently published *The Crown
and the Turban*, explore various aspects of what the French called *maraboutisme*. See also
Patrick Ryan, *Imale: Yoruba Participation in the Muslim Tradition: a Study of Clerical Piety* (Missoula,
Mont: Scholars Press, 1978); Benjamin F. Soares, 'The Spiritual Economy of Nioro du
Sahel'; and L. Brenner, *Réflexions sur le savoir islamique en Afrique de l'Ouest*, and 'The Esoteric
Sciences in West African Islam'.

Muslim clerics of all sorts. Because of this etymological history, the word has always carried ambivalent, and often pejorative, connotations. Local usages, such as *alufa* or *karamoko* denote more the function of teacher, and are generally less pejorative. But the Muslim cleric, whatever he might be called, was (and often still is) an ambivalent figure in West African society, because the knowledge he acquired could give him access to a wide range of esoteric powers with which he was able to do either good or ill, to heal or to harm. Even such a highly reputed scholar as Sidi al-Mukhtar al-Kunti, widely respected for his exemplary spiritual achievements, was feared for the power of his curse. In effect, the *marabout*, or the popular perception of *maraboutage*, plays a similar role in Muslim society to that of the witch (sorceror or magician) and witchcraft in non-Muslim African society. *Maraboutage* is blamed for all kinds of problems, from marital difficulties to the rise of social deviance, such as prostitution and juvenile delinquency.[47] On the other hand, it can be attributed all kinds of successes as well, from winning over the coveted object of one's affections to the successful execution of a *coup d'état*.

The Wahhabi campaign against the *marabouts* played upon this ambivalence, and placed great emphasis on the less palatable and more dubious aspects of *maraboutage*. The *marabouts* were accused of being 'parasites' who 'shamelessly exploited' those who put their faith in them. They lived 'off the sweat of others',[48] and 'sucked the blood of their brothers'.[49] As we have seen, these kinds of harsh criticisms dovetailed with a deep current of French disdain for Islam and for the *marabouts*, and the efforts of Cardaire and his allies of the counter-reform movement to soften the image of 'traditionalism' remained marginal and unsuccessful, except perhaps among Europeans. Amadou Hampaté Bâ, for example, attempted to emphasize the openness and flexibility of Islam by observing that, like water, Islam takes on the color of the earth across which it flows. This is one of his most frequently quoted aphorisms, which was intended to illustrate that the particular qualities of 'black Islam' were compatible with the universality of Islamic principles. But to this assertion, the 'Wahhabis' responded that their function with respect to 'black Islam' was 'the same as that of a filter for polluted water'.[50] Saada Oumar Touré, a committed Tijani Sufi, for his part berated the 'Wahhabis' as a 'loud-mouthed clique' in a little book which defended local devotional practices.[51] We have already seen that this kind of embittered exchange was not unusual

[47] See Laurence Couchoud, 'La migration sur place. Etude de la marginalité à Bamako (Mali)' (mémoire de fin d'études de DEA, EHESS, Paris, 1987), pp. 94-5. See also Christine Bastien, *Folies, mythes et magies d'Afrique Noire. Propos de guérisseurs du Mali* (Paris: L'Harmattan, 1988).

[48] Amselle, *Les négotiants*, p. 250.

[49] Mahamane, 'Le mouvement wahhabite à Bamako', p. 28.

[50] *Ibid.*, p. 5.

[51] Saada Oumar Touré, *Al-Tuḥfa bi-mā yajūzu wa-yaḥrumu min at-tadāwī wa'l—'uwadh wa'l-ruqya* (The gift about what is lawful and unlawful as regards medication, talismans and charms) (Tunis, 1987).

in doctrinal political debate, and the 'Wahhabi-traditionalist' confrontation has
been no exception to this pattern.

The French, the Africans and the Muslims: a discourse about the Other

The French colonial and administrative discourse complemented many of
the disparaging views of the Wahhabis about local Islamic practice. This discourse was not only a manifestation of colonial power, but also an instrument
of domination in the way that it conceptualized the social and political landscape. The argument put forward here is that this discourse was structured
primarily by the political imperative to dominate and control the colonial
situation, and was also informed by nineteenth-century notions of social
evolution and French convictions about the superiority of their own culture,
attendant racialist attitudes, and deep-seated, centuries-old animosities
towards Islam. The conceptual framework or ideology that resulted from the
admixture of these ingredients, although fairly simplistic and sometimes
contradictory, served on the one hand to reassure the dominating power of its
own legitimacy, and on the other to implement what V.Y. Mudimbe has referred to as the colonial 'plan of domestication' for the African.[52] As we have
seen in Chapter 2 above, French administrators explicitly stated that 'domestication' (apprivoisement) of young Africans was one of the principal aims of the
French médersas. Their usage of the term may not have differed very much
from that of Mudimbe: a combination of political domination and the recon-
struction of local 'memory' through French-language schooling. The French
wanted to disseminate their own understanding of Islam among African
Muslims.

Differences of opinion and attitude existed among the French, of course,
but three prevailing themes emerge from their discourse: their continuing
preoccupation with maintaining control of the political situation, their
reliance upon notions of black African Otherness to justify their political
domination, and their deep ambivalence towards Islam.[53] We can also perceive
changes in prevailing terminology and perhaps attitude during the colonial
period, although French colonial administrators never lost sight of the fact
that they were in Africa precisely in order to dominate and control the
Africans (and their economic resources). From their point of view, the Africans were meant to submit to the new political order, either willingly or by
force.

[52] See V.Y. Mudimbe, The Idea of Africa (Bloomington: Indiana University Press, 1994),
especially Ch. 2: 'Domestication and the Conflict of Memories'. Mudimbe claims that in
Africa this 'plan of domestication' involved 'a necessary and absolute conversion of
individualities and their psychology', p. 122.
[53] For additional discussions of this discourse see Harrison, France and Islam in West Africa;
Amselle, Logiques Métisses; and Jean Bazin, 'A chacun son Bambara' in J.-L. Amselle and E.
M'Bokolo, Au coeur de l'ethnie. Ethnies, tribalisme et Etat en Afrique (Paris: La Découverte,
1985).

In the immediate aftermath of conquest, the control of blacks seemed to many to pose no problem whatsoever:

> The black is a passive and impressionable being who, with only two of our *tirailleurs* in a single village, will obey, will not even dream of the slightest rebellion, and will scrupulously pay his taxes.[54]

For some this passivity could be attributed to the position of the blacks on the evolutionary scale:

> There exists an abyss of fifty, perhaps one hundred centuries, between that which is suitable and assimilable for the black soul and that which responds to the aspirations of the European soul.[55]

There were some who felt that Islam provided the most promising evolutionary way forward for black Africa:

> The black, in our experience, feels the need to raise himself up, to develop his capacities, but he cannot imitate us, because our mentality and our intellectualism are presently incomprehensible to him. But at his side he has the Muslim whose example is easy to follow and whose religion can easily and comfortably be adapted to his own mode of existence.[56]

> The laziness and indolence of the Negro with respect to the forces of nature are well known; that is why a religion which etymologically signifies submission and complete abandon to the wishes of a Supreme Being will necessarily have an attraction for him, all the more irresistable because it demands only a minimum of effort. ... Islam has the double advantage of giving the blacks a higher degree of civilization as well as a certain inner discipline.[57]

But in the highest echelons of authority, there were those who had their doubts about Islam, and who saw dangers in allowing Muslims an unfettered freedom to fulfill their alleged role in the process of social evolution. The policy of appointing Muslims as local administrative authorities was therefore challenged, in part because, due to their evolutionary proximity to Europeans, they often tended to act too independently.

> More supple, more familiar with how we conceptualize the principle of authority and, it must be said, more disciplined, the Muslims quickly acquire political hegemony in countries where fetishists are often in the majority. It therefore comes about that, without ourselves deriving any benefit for the extension of our own influence, and without being aware of it, [our policy of using Muslim administrators] favors the spread of Muslim clericalism, whereas Islam, if it is led by ambitious or fanatical chiefs, can quickly take on the character, more or less dissimulated, of a movement of protest against all European innovations.[58]

[54] Lt. Governor of Soudan, de Trentinian, *L'Afrique Francaise. Bulletin du Comité de l'Afrique française et du Comité du Maroc*, 1897, p. 213.

[55] A. Le Chatelier, *L'Islam dans l'Afrique occidentale* (Paris: G. Steinheil, 1899), p. 351.

[56] A. Quellien, 'La politique musulmane dans l'Afrique Occidentale Française' (thèse de doctorat, Paris, 1910), p. v.

[57] *Ibid.*, pp. 66 and 90.

[58] William Ponty, Circular of 22 September 1909, *L'Afrique Française. Bulletin du Comité de l'Afrique française et du Comité du Maroc*, 1909, pp. 348-9.

These were the words of William Ponty, the Governor General who formulated the *politique des races*, a policy of divide and rule based on the idea that non-Muslim Africans were less likely than Muslims to launch embarrassing political initiatives. Ponty's incumbency marked the end of French reliance upon local Muslim administrators literate in Arabic and the development of a French-language school system designed to train lower-level administrative employees.

The French médersas were created in this atmosphere, and we have already seen how the administrators responsible for these schools saw their major objective as containing the alleged 'fanaticism' of Islam, of 'pacifying' and 'domesticating' it and 'dissipating it's pretensions'. This kind of language is seldom absent from commentary about the aims and objectives of the médersas. Consider the following quotations concerning the médersas of Jenne and St Louis, taken from a 1910 doctoral thesis written by a man who was of the opinion that Islam represented a step forward in the civilization of West Africa. 'It is universally recognised', he asserted, 'that the Muslims of these regions are superior to those peoples who have remained fetishists in their social organization, their intellectual culture, commerce, industry, well-being, *savoir-vivre*, and education'.

> The médersas [of Jenne and St Louis] are destined to furnish Muslim studies with the methodology which they lack and to guide in the direction of modern ideas the evolution of instruction in the Qur'anic schools, which has heretofore been fanatical and sterile. ... This will give us the opportunity and the means to undertake the interpretation of certain texts which are favorable to our civilizing activities, which might enable us gradually to bring our subjects to a better understanding of us and perhaps to like us. ...

> [The objective of those who teach Islam in these schools will be], to utilize Qur'anic texts in order to combat both the prejudices, which over the generations have taken root among the Muslims, as well as their religious fanaticism, which is a consequence of their ignorance.[59]

Although French policy remained consistent in its objectives of containing and controlling Islam through educational intervention, by the 1920s the idea that Islam might be a 'progressive' force in black Africa was profoundly challenged. The first signs of this challenge were brought to the médersas in 1917, when Paul Marty argued that it was a mistake to educate black Muslims in them; in his opinion, Islam was in fact a 'white' and 'nomadic' religion. Here we find the origins of the colonial notion of a 'black Islam', a particular local form of Islam which was not *really* Islamic at all. This idea was very popular for several decades, right through the 1950s when Cardaire redefined 'black Islam' to conform with the interests of the counter-reform movement. By the 1920s, Islam was being dismissed by some as inimical to French interests, and 'fetishism' was being rehabilitated and renamed, first 'animism' and then 'naturism'. The major formulators of this anti-Islamic, 'pro-animist'

[59] Quellien, *La politique musulmane*, pp. 100, 255-6, and 260.

school of thought were Maurice Delafosse and J. Brevié, both colonial officials who promulgated their ideas in a series of publications.[60]

Delafosse deplored the use of the pejorative term 'fethishism' and in its stead proposed the word 'animism', of which he advocated a more careful study. The favorable role of Islam in West Africa had been exaggerated, he argued, and it was necessary 'to give animism, until now very much misunderstood, the attention and consideration which it deserved given its preponderant situation and its strength'.[61] Islam was not compatible with black African society because the blacks had not yet reached 'the appropriate stage of social evolution. And in any case, the argument continued, Islam was basically a religion of nomads that could only spread amongst blacks if their societies disintegrated.

The anti-Islamic stance of Brevié was even more explicit and extreme. In his view, West Africa was a battlefield on which Arabs and French were fighting for 'the moral conquest of millions of naturists', the term he preferred to Delafosse's 'animist'. Islam was incompatible with black African society, and it had been sustained among blacks only by force; indeed, the Islamization of black Africa would be a 'regression'.

To convert a black to Islam is to plunge him into a moral impasse from which he will be incapable of evolving. The fetishist is perfectible, and very much inclined to accept our direction after he has overcome his initial, instinctive timidity, whereas the Muslim distances himself from us and becomes immobilized by the narrow ideals which his orthodoxy imposes on him, ideals which are anything but favorable to innovation and progress.[62]

Brevié's response to the alleged Muslim threat was to assist the 'naturists' to resist Islam and to enable them to set out along the path of French civilization. It was, he said, 'a question of education, and in that we are past masters, because to colonize, in the French meaning of the word, is to educate.'[63] Consequently, he had little use for the French médersas; he would have been happy to see them disappear, and he was completely opposed to the introduction of modern pedagogical methods in them, as advocated by some officials, for fear of future political ramifications should teaching in Muslim schools actually become 'effective'.

The ideas of Delafosse, Brevié and others were reflected in the long-running debates of the 1920s and 1930s about who and what the French médersas should be teaching; as we have seen, various steps were taken to exclude sedentary (black) children from the Timbuktu médersa and to attract the children

[60] See especially M. Delafosse, 'L'animisme nègre et sa résistance à l'islamisation en Afrique occidentale', *Revue du Monde Musulman*, XLIX (March 1922), pp. 121-63; 'L'Islam et les sociétés noires de l'Afrique', *L'Afrique Française. Bulletin du Comité de l'Afrique française et du Comité du Maroc*, pp. 321-33. Delafosse also wrote a preface to J. Brevié, *Islamisme contre 'Naturisme' au Soudan Français* (Paris: Leroux, 1923).
[61] Delafosse, 'L'animisme nègre', p. 162.
[62] Brevié, *Islamisme contre 'Naturisme'*, pp. 293 and 297.
[63] *Ibid.*, p. 299.

of nomads, in particular nomad 'notables'. The reader will recall that the Governor of Soudan had justified the exclusion of blacks from the médersa by arguing that they only aspired to French schooling anyway. But in reading Brevié, it becomes clear that these were the aspirations which the administration wanted to make available to them, which would set them on the desired course of 'evolution' and at the same time block any nefarious Islamic influences.

Other French voices, more sympathetic to Islam, were also heard. As early as 1906, L.-G. Binger in his book, *Le Péril de l'Islam*,[64] clearly identified some of the fundamental contradictions that informed French attitudes and policies. Binger was an advocate of the dominant social evolutionary theories of his day, but, contrary to what might be expected by the title of his book, he criticized those who continually condemned Islam:

If the Muslim defends his country, his home, his independence, his freedom, he is neither considered a patriot nor a man who sacrifices himself for a generous and elevated sentiment; he is a fanatic.

He regularly says his prayers and merely pursues his religion? He is a fanatic.

One finds him reading his Qur'an, the only book which he possesses? He is a fanatic.

He refuses to serve your interests? It is because of fanaticism.

He meets with his fellow-Muslims in order to discuss the Pentateuch or the Gospels, or perhaps to learn to read his prayers more fluently? That is only with the purpose of exercising, at some later date, his fanaticism.

He allies himself in a war with other Muslims? That is always due to fanaticism and his hatred of the Christian.

In a word, every act by a Muslim, especially those that are contrary to our policies or our interests, can be imputed to fanaticism. But what is most peculiar is that most of the hostile acts that are inspired by this so-called fanaticism would be considered by us at home as the most praiseworthy of qualities, as acts of the highest patriotism, or even of great political consequence.

Binger's observations vividly reveal the contradictions and ambiguities that informed the attitudes of many French toward Islam. By the 1950s, the terms of the discourse had changed: words like 'fanaticism' and 'domestication' were being replaced by the terminology of post-war social science, such as 'modernization' and eventually 'development'. In the context of counter-reform, the French could even discover a model Muslim, in the form of Cerno Bokar, whose teachings as interpreted by Amadou Hampâté Bâ they helped to disseminate. But whether these tactical manoeuvres reflected any fundamental modification of attitude is doubtful.

We have seen that by 1950, the colonial administration, alarmed by the increasing rate of Islamization in Africa and the perceived political threat from the Muslim Middle East, was gearing itself up to confront these renewed 'dangers' to French interests in West Africa.[65] Counter-reform was the back-

---

[64] L.-G. Binger, *Le péril de l'Islam* (Paris, 1906), pp. 31-2.
[65] See Triaud, 'Le crépuscule'.

bone of policies developed in Soudan to counter this threat. The key French player in the development of these policies was Marcel Cardaire, and his writings constitute the fullest exposition, from the French perspective, of what might be called the ideology of counter-reform. In his *L'Islam et le terroir africain*, published in 1954, Cardaire analyzed with considerable insight the socio-political dynamics which were giving rise to the new Muslim movements in Soudan, which in his view could be countered by reliance on the strengths of local 'black Islam'. Cardaire shared an opinion that was wide-spread within the administration that the rapid pace of Islamization in rural areas, as well as the increasing success of reformist activities, were due to the disintegration of indigenous society. As local religious practices fell into disuse in the villages of Soudan, a 'spiritual void' was allegedly opened which was being filled by an Islam that integrated these villages into a wider socio-economic network. Such changes occurred most often, according to Cardaire, in areas where Muslim merchants were opening new markets and where local chiefs saw adherence to Islam as a means for extending their own political authority.[66]

Cardaire's analysis was built around a series of metaphors about the relationship between religions and the earth that nourishes them, thus his reference to *le terroir africain* in the title. Indigenous African religions are nourished by the African soil (a metaphor for local culture) into which their roots have deeply penetrated; Cardaire refers to them consistently as 'social religions of the soil' (*religions sociales du terroir*). Islam, by contrast, is a foreign religion of conquerors and rulers whose conversions have always been superficial; during periods of Islamic supremacy, indigenous religions have retreated to the bush, only to reassert themselves with the decline of state or imperial Muslim power. In recent decades, with the impact of social and economic change, indigenous society and its religion have been breaking down: 'The socio-religious unit [*cellule*] ... is losing first its ethnic purity, and then in turn, its faith and its social coherence.'[67] It is precisely this kind of situation in which Islam finds its appeal: 'The success of Islam is due to the isolation of the "pagan" who sees his social and religious system collapsing.'[68]

In the face of this social disintegration, Africans tend to reorganize themselves into new kinds of associations, which have a 'curious' tendency 'to take on a peculiar religious form on African soil [*sur la terre d'Afrique*]'.[69] Such is the formative influence of the 'African soil', that it has also given birth to a local form of 'black Islam', which for Cardaire was represented broadly by Muslim 'traditionalism' and more specifically by the example of Cerno Bokar and his teachings, as transmitted by Amadou Hampâté Bâ. The 'black Islam' of counter-reform, based as it was on these teachings, 'emanated from the depths

---

[66] Cardaire, *L'Islam et le terroir africain*, pp. 49ff.

[67] *Ibid.*, p. 52.

[68] *Ibid.*, p. 49.

[69] *Ibid.*, p. 27.

of local culture and refused to renounce ancient African society.'[70] There are echoes of the ideas of Delafosse and Brevié in this juxtaposition of paganism with Islam, and most particularly in the construction of a 'black Islam' which is characterized both by its 'African-ness' and, as we will see below, its malleability and receptiveness to French cultural influence. Like the 'naturism' of Brevié, 'black Islam' was 'perfectible'.

Cardaire considered the Islam of the new Islamic movements to be of the 'foreign' variety. He posited the existence of two complementary trends within these movements, 'the Wahhabism of the merchants' and 'the reformism of the clerics'. He was rather contemptuous of what he called 'merchant Wahhabism', whose adherents he referred to as 'religious snobs' who set off on pilgrimage with virtually no knowledge of Islam and adopted whatever doctrine and practice they found in Mecca. (What they found, of course, was a combination of Salafi doctrine and anti-French propaganda which was being preached by fellow West African Muslims such as al-Ifriqi, Mohamed Ali Ag Ataher, and others.) In conformity with his 'disintegration theory', Cardaire described these people as 'uprooted … detribalized … pilgrim-merchants'.[71] Neither the theory nor the descriptions were completely without foundation; Jean-Loup Amselle has analyzed the process of how, during the colonial period, many non-Muslim former aristocrats and farmers took to commerce in order to benefit from the new economic opportunities offered by the colonial situation.[72] In this region, where the Muslim Jula dominated commerce, becoming a merchant meant becoming a Muslim; during the 1950s most upwardly mobile Muslim merchants were identified by their French and 'traditionalist' opponents as 'Wahhabis'.

But if Cardaire was somewhat contemptuous of the religious pretensions of these merchants, he was also well aware of their social and political significance and of the potential power of their newly acquired 'combative Islam,' as he called it. And even if their Islam was not very profound, that of the reformist clerics was. These Cardaire referred to as '*savants*', young men who had studied in Middle Eastern institutions and had returned to West Africa not only as competently trained scholars, but as impassioned proselytizers of new Muslim and anti-French ideas and ideologies. Cardaire described them as follows:

These young people have lived for years in the politically electrified atmosphere of contemporary Egypt. Put in contact with the proponents of an unbridled modernism, mixed also with the partisans of a pure and simple return to the Salaf, they have indiscriminately drawn upon these two contrary sources. They are familiar with the politico-religious arguments that the eastern press tirelessly distills. They have acquired the conviction that God has confided upon them the mission to instruct their

[70] *Ibid.*, p. 160.
[71] *Ibid.*, pp. 127ff.
[72] See J.-L. Amselle, *Les négociants de la savane* and *Logiques métisses*.

compatriots and they are proud of the role that they see themselves playing on the religious scene in their countries.[73]

And Cardaire clearly perceived that the complementary activities of both scholars and merchants would effectively spread the influence of the reformist movement throughout West Africa: a contemporary example of the classic historical alliance between commerce and the proselytization of Islam, in this instance of reformist Islam. The scholars would teach their new doctrines in functional Arabic, using modern methods in modernized schools. The merchants would provide the material base necessary to finance these new schools as well as an extended network of long distance liaison, along the trade routes, among the various nascent centers of reformist activity. For Cardaire, the potential of the reformists lay in this powerful combination of focussed commitment and effective communications:

Clerics from the Soudanese zone and clerics from the southern territories, very often former fellow students, exchange correspondence, books and pamphlets; they consult one another on the programs in their schools and frequently visit one another. In travelling around this immense area one begins to have the impression of a vague unity, an impression that comes from the real unity which exists in the minds of these young *'ulama* who, from Kayes to Ouagadougou and from Mopti to Abidjan, think, reason and act as propagandists formed in the same mold.[74]

But despite the extent of this nascent network, Cardaire noted that the centre of reformist and 'Wahhabi' activity coincided with the centre of the Malinké-Jula network in the region bounded by Bamako, Bouaké, Sikasso and Kankan, which also acted as a refuge for activist reformers chased from the religious cities of the north. Areas dominated by the social and religious hierarchies of the Peul and Tuareg, for example, were more successful in resisting the dissemination of reformist ideas.

All this evidence pointed to the conclusion that the best way to limit these new and politicized forms of Islamic expression was to maintain a strong, integrated, and therefore conservative 'traditional' society. Cardaire did not explicitly formulate his conclusions in this manner, but they can be read very clearly in the sub-text of his book, which might be described as an exercize in contradictory wishful thinking. Contradictory because he was unable, or unwilling, to asess in depth the French colonial input into the process he was analyzing; wishful thinking because he was not convinced that the tide of Islamic change could be stopped.

In the prevailing conditions of the mid-twentieth century, the prospects for Islam in Africa were seen to be better than ever before. What had changed was that now the elements were present which might fully integrate African Muslims into the international Muslim community; these were the possibility of mass literacy in the Arabic language and a growing 'consciousness of

[73] Cardaire, *L'Islam et le terroir africain*, p. 138.
[74] *Ibid.*, p. 144.

belonging to a theocratically orientated politico-religious unit'.[75] In Cardaire's terms, this was an intrusive and alien form of religious expression that must be opposed.

As we have seen, the responses proposed to meet these alleged threats were centered on schooling, and particularly on blocking the spread of Arabic literacy. Cardaire was quite clear about this; even if the desire to learn Arabic was basically religious, knowledge of this language would inevitably lead, in his opinion, to an interest in reading books and newspapers in Arabic and would ultimately 'pose political problems'.[76] He argued that much of the success of the médersas was due to an inadequacy of places in French schools.[77] This was not a new idea; it had its origins in the earliest policy decisions about the French médersas, and it was shared by many French administrators in the 1950s (indeed it would survive right into the 1990s). The Fort Lamy conference of 1956 on 'Muslim problems' concluded that the insufficiency of places in French schools 'favored the expansion of Islam and the diffusion of the Arabic language'.[78] Language policy was therefore a central element in French Islamic policy. The Fort Lamy conference recommended that the teaching of French be improved and intensified in both the secular public schools and the Christian mission schools in order to combat the spread of Arabic.[79]

In Soudan the authorities complemented this course of action with the program of counter-reform, which employed indigenous languages for teaching Islamic sciences in an effort to demonstrate to Africans that they could be good Muslims without knowing Arabic. Cardaire was the official primarily responsible for obtaining French endorsement for this program, and his collaboration with Hampâté Bâ and Doukouré may have been motivated by both his personal interest in their ideas and the fact that counter-reform conformed well with current French thinking about Islam. According to Hampâté Bâ, it was Cardaire who first suggested they co-author *Tierno Bokar, le sage de Bandiagara*.[80] This book, published in 1957, provided an intellectual justification for the counter-reform program. In it was a description of the catechism which Cerno Bokar had devised in order to teach the basics of Islamic knowledge to illiterate Muslims in their own language, as well as numerous examples of his own profound and provocative reflections.

Here was a model of African Muslim educational practice and religious insight which was deserving of attention and respect in its own right, but, like the program which it inspired, it became immediately tarnished in the

---

[75] *Ibid.*, p. 155.

[76] *Ibid.*, p. 121.

[77] *Ibid.*, p. 120.

[78] AMI, Procès-verbal de la Conférence interterritoriale sur les problèmes musulmans, Fort Lamy, 1956.

[79] Mudimbe, with reference to Zaire, wrote: 'French was the domain wherein African traditions were actively eroded in order to permit the growth of a new memory.' *The Idea of Africa*, p. 132. The same was true for the 'plan of domestication' in Soudan.

[80] Bâ, *Vie et enseignement*, p. 9.

eyes of many Muslims because it was made public in the context of the administration's efforts to contain the nascent reformist movement.[81] On the other hand, the appearance of *Le Sage de Bandiagara* seems symptomatic of the times; at the very moment when Europe was emerging from the horrors of a long and costly internecine war and beginning to loosen its imperial grip on Africa, Europeans were awakening to the intellectual richness of African culture. The 1940s had seen the publication of two, now controversial, classics in the field of African thought, Marcel Griaule's *Conversations with Ogotemmêli*, and Placide Tempels' *Bantu Philosophy*.[82] Bâ and Cardaire's *Tierno Bokar* is of the same genre, but has thus far escaped the critical attention attracted by the other two books.

Cardaire's affinity with Hampaté Bâ and Doukouré may also have been motivated by the fact that both were precisely the kinds of products the French had hoped their educational policies would have produced; as Cardaire put it, they were 'considered "sound" by the Administration'.[83] In other words, they were advocates of a kind of 'black Islam' which was 'tolerant, ... favorable to the well-being of the population, and reassuring for the progress of the country'.[84] In the final pages of *L'Islam et le terroir africain*, Cardaire resumes his eloquent metaphorical style in order to present the 'black Islam' of counter-reform as being nourished by the African soil. Hampâté Bâ and Doukouré were 'plunging the roots of their faith into the very depths (*dans le fond*) of their black homeland, ... in order to fertilize the revealed dogma of Orthodoxy by irrigating it with local mystical concepts ... transmitted by black [Sufi] masters who were free from any external influences.'[85]

No matter what its political appeal, counter-reform would associate the teaching of Islam more closely with the state schools than had ever before been the case, and would also be conducted in the indigenous languages, another significant innovation in official French thinking. But Cardaire defended these innovations in his book:

---

[81] See Kaba, *The Wahhabiyya*.

[82] Marcel Griaule, *Conversations with Ogotemmêli: An Introduction to Dogon Religious Ideas* (Oxford University Press, 1965) was first published in 1946 under the title, *Dieu d'eau: entretiens avec Ogotemmêli*. Placide Tempels, *Bantu Philosophy* (Paris: Présence Africaine, 1969) was first published in Flemish in 1946. Although it is arguable that *Tierno Bokar, le sage de Bandiagara*, like Tempels' *Bantu Philosophy*, was written to a European audience and in the service of European interests, it is not really open to the charge of being an ethnophilosophical work since it is the exposition of the thoughts of a single individual that are not generalized to represent the thinking of an entire community. According to P.J. Hountondji, in *African Philosophy, Myth and Reality* (London: Hutchinson, 1983), ethnophilosophy is a style of exposition in which (1) Africans themselves remain mute, that is, an external author 'writes about' their thought on their behalf, and (2) it is assumed that all members of the social or ethnic group in question share a 'unanimity' of thoughts and ideas which are never debated among them.

[83] AMI, Procès-verbal ... Fort Lamy.

[84] Cardaire, *L'Islam et le terroir africain*, p. 108.

[85] *Ibid.*, p. 155.

The utilization of local dialects has the double advantage, according to MM. Bâ and Doukouré, of improving the comprehension of the children and of revitalizing the languages themselves, 'the richness and poetry of which no longer require demonstration'. For these children, religious instruction is more an education than mere instruction. The knowledge of the principles of dogma, theology and law which is included within this teaching will be assimilated more quickly if it is transmitted in the mother tongue.

In the same paragraph, Cardaire presented an argument that may well have clinched his campaign in favor of the counter-reform movement:

[In following this program] the child will therefore be able to devote the majority of its time to 'the amelioration of its life style' and to 'the acquisition of modern knowledge,' [to quote Abd al-Wahhab Doukouré]. Having broken with an Arab culture from which they can expect nothing, the clerics of the counter-reform movement are looking toward a Franco-Soudanese culture which will be French in the practical aspects of general instruction and Soudanese in the exposition of basic religious themes.[86]

A winning combination if ever there was one! An African population educated in all practical matters through the medium of the French language who were at the same time 'tolerant' and cooperative Muslims. Put in these terms, the counter-reform movement was a continuation of the same French Islamic policy that had been in force for decades.

On the other hand, there is also a profoundly ironic element in the collaboration between Cardaire and Hampâté Bâ. The teachings of Cerno Bokar, a once-dreaded Hamallist, were now brought into the service of the French to protect their interests against a new and different threat. Had Hampâté Bâ slyly outwitted the French and used the counter-reform movement in order to achieve a symbolic rehabilitation of Hamallism? This effect may have been more evident among the African population than to the administration, but in any case, Hampâté Bâ never attempted to organize any group of Hamallists around him as such.[87] There was a Hamallist dimension to counter-reform, however, not only because it was based on the teachings of Cerno Bokar and led by Hampaté Bâ and Abd al-Wahhab Doukouré, who also came from a Hamallist background in Mourdiah, but the counter-reformists also used the Hamallist network to mobilize support for their program, especially in Segu. On the other hand, there was nothing whatsoever of specifically Hamallist content in the teachings which Hampaté Bâ had received from Cerno Bokar in 1933, which was before he had converted to Hamallism, as indeed there was nothing of Hamallism in the intellectual underpinnings of the counter-

---

[86] Cardaire, *L'Islam et le terroir africain*, p. 161.

[87] There have been claims that such politicians as Modibo Keita, Diori Hamani, and Boubou Hama had been 'disciples' of Cerno Bokar. There is no evidence that any of these persons ever met Cerno Bokar, and they could only have known of his teachings, like so many others did, through Hampâté Bâ. See Pierre Alexandre, 'A West African Islamic Movement: Hamallism in French West Africa' in R. Rotberg and Ali Mazrui (eds), *Protest and Power in Black Africa* (New York: Oxford University Press, 1970), p. 508.

reform movement, which looked toward the creation of what Cardaire called a Franco-Soudanese culture.

Abd al-Wahhab Doukouré eloquently embraced the idea of such a hybrid culture in the article he published in the official newspaper *Soudan français*, which was quoted at length in *L'Islam et le terroir africain*. The article is a clever comparison of the values of African, Arab and French cultures, in which Cerno Bokar, who is praised as a pious Muslim as well as a progressive humanist, is held up as an ideal representative of black Islamic culture. Not surprisingly, the Arabs do not fare very well in this comparison, written by a man who had himself studied in an Arab university in Tunisia. In his own experience, Doukouré claimed, he had seen many blacks who returned from their studies in Arab countries, well-versed in Arabic literature, but 'totally robbed of their natural simplicity, of their ardent faith, and of the charity which they had seen their elders practice without limit'. Given this reality, why should Africans go to study in Arab countries, especially since the Arabs 'were far from being compassionate toward black Africans'. If it is Islamic values which they seek, these will be found more readily at home, and if it is the knowledge of modern science which they seek, then better to go to France, where the Arabs themselves study these subjects. The article closed with the following recommendations:

To close these few lines, I wish with all my heart, on the one hand, that the Administration of the French Union might understand the desires of its Muslim·subjects and offer to young Muslim students who have been imbued with a solid religious culture the means to go to France where they can take advantage of the progress which has been attained by French learning, and that with the objective of remaining French Muslims.

And I wish, on the other hand, that all Muslims of good will, *who wish to conserve for their country its originality and its local flavor* [*saveur*], might form a group to continue the work of Cerno Bokar Salif. *This group would demonstrate that the black African can find within his own substance* [*fond*] *what is necessary in order to assimilate and transform any assistance coming from outside in a manner which conforms to his own spiritual and material needs.* It would prove that the Black Man, as an element within the Universe, possesses his own capabilities and is able to make his own intellectual and moral contribution to Humanity.[88]

The preceding analysis provides only a tiny selected sampling of the French colonial discourse, but it is representative and it demonstrates that although over the decades there was an evolution toward a less disparaging use of language, for example from 'fetishist' to 'animist', there was a persistence of underlying attitudes. The concepts of 'animism' and 'naturism' were religious and cultural glosses on Ponty's *politique des races*, which itself rested on notions about the inherent political passivity of non-Muslim, black Africans. There is very little substantive difference between Brevié's description of 'naturists'

---

[88] Doukouré, 'Sources', as quoted by Cardaire, *L'Islam et le terroir africain*, pp. 155-7. Cardaire's own emphasis.

as timid but perfectible and de Trentinian's characterisation of blacks twenty-five years earlier as passive and impressionable. Nor indeed between either of these descriptions and Marcel Cardaire's portraits of African *religions sociales du terroir* and of a 'black Islam' which was 'plunging the roots of its faith into the very heart of its black homeland'. Cardaire employed words like 'tolerant and reassuring' to describe 'black Islam', arguably only another permutation of 'timid but perfectible' or of 'passive and impressionable'.

Table 4.1 is an attempt to illustrate the complexities of this discourse in the form of a diagram. The three primary terms of the diagram, African

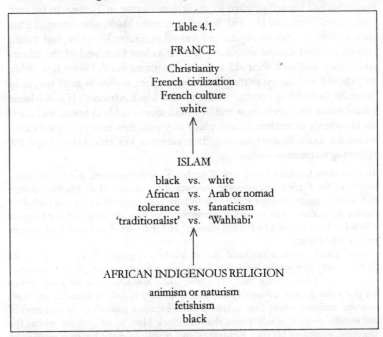

Table 4.1.

FRANCE

Christianity
French civilization
French culture
white

ISLAM

black	vs.	white
African	vs.	Arab or nomad
tolerance	vs.	fanaticism
'traditionalist'	vs.	'Wahhabi'

AFRICAN INDIGENOUS RELIGION

animism or naturism
fetishism
black

indigenous religion, Islam, and secularist France (or European Christianity), linked by arrows pointing upward, suggest the cultural hierarchy proposed by the social evolutionary thought which informed much of the French discourse. The racialist content of the discourse is illustrated by the fact that this social evolution is also posited as a movement from blackness to whiteness. The pairing of opposing terms under the rubric of Islam is another indication of this pervading racialism. The disparaging and pejorative epithets about Islam which litter the French discourse are all semantic equivalents of the 'white' Islam which is alien to black Africa: fanatical, Arab, nomad, 'Wahhabi'. The semantic equivalents of 'black', by contrast, connote comfort and security: tolerant, African, 'traditionalist'. French ambivalence about Islam arose from their perception that, to put it rather crudely, the 'whiter' Islam became, the more it was seen as posing a danger. By contrast, few, if any, fears were ever expressed about possible political threats emanating from indigenous religions.

This analysis provides some insight into how concepts of African Otherness informed the policy needs of the colonial administration and reinforced the psychological needs of the colonial agent. The major need for both administration and administrator was to keep the African at a distance and in a state of passivity. It is in this context that one must understand the simultaneous appearance of 'traditionalism' and 'Wahhabism' in the Soudan. 'Wahhabism', which Cardaire called an *Islam de combat*, was the 1950s version of fanatical 'white' Islam and, according to him, 'totally foreign to the mentality of black Islam'. The best strategy to meet this threat was to keep Islam 'black', in other words, to keep it passive.

Identity as a transformative system

I have elsewhere analyzed identity as a process of naming (naming of self, naming of others, naming *by* others) which is itself located within and determined by the dynamics of a specific socio-political context.[89] Identities are therefore the product of a discursive process operating within a political process; they are constantly being constructed and reconstructed, by self and/or others, through continuing actions and discourse. They are formulated through the appropriation and reassortment of various elements or 'building blocks' which, as in the present case, may be religiously significant, but are also socially, politically and economically motivated. As complex clusters of attributes, they are subject to continuous reordering by self and others depending upon perceived aims, needs and constraints. They reflect political conflict and are representations of alleged social realities rather than essences in themselves.

The emergence of the 'Wahhabi' versus 'traditionalist' conflict in Soudan is an excellent example of how this complex transformative system functions. The conflict was generated, of course, by the forces of social change which began to make themselves felt by the middle of the twentieth century. Certain young men sought to take advantage of these changes, rather than to resist them, in the fields of both education and commerce. Significantly, they chose to do so specifically as Muslims, for example, in their first experiments with médersa education and in the founding of the *Shubban al-muslimin*, the Muslim youth organization that was intended in the first instance to promote a renaissance of Muslim consciousness, especially within the Malinké-Jula commercial network. These initiatives were enough to raise an alarm within certain circles of the colonial administration, where any efforts by Muslims to

[89] L. Brenner, 'Constructing Muslim Identities in Mali'. This approach to the analysis of identity is based largely upon the arguments of J.-L. Amselle in *Logiques métisses, op. cit.*

organize themselves on the basis of Islamic principles was considered a political threat. And when some of these young Muslims, although certainly not all of them, embraced the tenets of Salafi doctrine, there was also a strong reaction from the African Muslim establishment.

It was from these combined reactions that the concept of a 'Wahhabi' movement emerged, although it was an attribution that differed in many ways from how the young Muslim activists saw themselves. The connotations of 'Wahhabism' as the term evolved in Soudanese discourse were pejorative in the extreme: it connoted fanaticism for the French and apostasy for Muslim notables like Muhammad Sharif of Kankan. But the fact that the French had decided that such a movement existed, and that they began to look for evidence of it everywhere in order to contest it, in fact served to elevate the programs of the Muslim activists to another level of political reality. This transformation seems particularly evident when one recalls that many of the conflicts that became identified with 'Wahhabism' were based on generational, family and other local political differences. The creation of a 'Wahhabi' movement in the official mind, and the determination to oppose it, resulted in pulling many people together into a single movement. Similarly, official opposition tended to radicalize persons whose original aims were relatively mild; this seems to have been the case with the Azharists.

What is being argued here is that the 'Wahhabi' movement was formulated through the process of colonial power relations, through the interaction between those first Muslim initiatives and the various reactions to them. Of course, the French did not invent the term 'Wahhabi', which was associated with specific doctrines which had gained prominence in Saudi Arabia, but they did contribute significantly to the 'invention' of the Wahhabi movement in Soudan. The process of invention is much more clear with respect to 'traditionalism', a term seems to have originated within the French colonial discourse and which in one sense is nothing more than a residual conceptual category comprising all those aspects of local Islamic practice which were rejected by the proponents of Salafi doctrine and by those who came to be known as 'Wahhabis'. With the appearance of 'Wahhabism', the French suddenly found a new interest in something they called 'traditional' Islam, which they previously rejected and disparaged but now embraced with enthusiasm. As we have seen, Marcel Cardaire, with the aid of Amadou Hampaté Bâ, formulated a version of 'traditionalism' which conformed with French interests and which he called 'black Islam'.

These religious identities were also reflections of the political patterns which emerged in the 1950s and which opposed the more conservative, and 'traditional' PSP with the more radical (and 'extremist', to use the French term) US-RDA. Certain 'Wahhabis' exercised considerable influence in the US-RDA, which had been one encouragement for the 'Wahhabi' campaign to open their own mosques in Bamako and Sikasso in 1957. The pro-French stance of the PSP therefore contributed to the French inclination to support Islamic 'traditionalism'.

This entire concatenation of naming and counter-naming is full of irony and contradiction. The 'Wahhabis' often refer to themselves as 'Sunnis', whereas many 'traditionalists' prefer to be called 'orthodox'. But, of course, the Arabic word *sunni* is usually translated into European languages as 'orthodox'; the *sunna* of the Prophet Muhammad derives from his words and deeds which are recorded in collected *hadith*, a term which is usually translated as 'traditions'. In one sense, then, all Muslims are 'traditionalists' in that the dynamics of Islamic doctrinal politics requires that any Muslim group assert and demonstrate its capacity to defend and enforce the *sunna*.

But this complex system of transforming identities, which operates largely in the field of discourse, was both the reflection and the product of a deeper set of transformations in the field of power relations where the process of schooling, perhaps more than any other single factor, was beginning to produce new subjectivities. French-language secular education was at the core of French colonial policy, central to their 'plan of domestication', as evidenced in the following statements by Governors General Brevié and Roume:

Colonial responsibility and political and economic necessities impose a double task on our educational undertakings: on the one hand to train indigenous cadres who are destined to become our auxiliaries in all areas and to assure the rise of a carefully selected elite; on the other hand to educate the masses in order to bring them closer to us and to transform their manner of living. ... The content of our teaching programs is not a simple matter of pedagogy; the student is an instrument of our native policy. (Brevié)

We consider instruction to be something precious that one distributes with discrimination and we limit its benefits only to those qualified to receive it. We choose our students firstly from among the sons of chiefs and nobles; it is with these families especially that we have a constant relationship of [administrative] service. The prestige that derives from birth must be reinforced by the respect conferred by knowledge. (Roume)[90]

In the view of these men, the benefits of French schooling were to be carefully controlled and meted out to serve colonial needs and interests. But in fact, the French were unable to control the effects that schooling would have on those gaining access to it. If many Muslims rejected French schooling because they feared it was designed to turn their children into unbelievers, we have seen that its impact could also contribute to the new Muslim initiatives that were appearing. The fact that Saada Oumar Touré learned to read and write French during his four years in French school inspired him to develop a new pedagogy for teaching Arabic. 'Abd al-Rahman al-Ifriqi, according to the author of his obituary, had been liberated from the constraints of *taqlid* by the analytic spirit which had been imparted to him in the French schools.[91] And some of the most influential early 'Wahhabi' publications appeared in French, such as

[90] Quoted in 'L'Enseignement en République du Mali (Dix ans après la réforme de 1962)', Contact Spécial, *Bulletin Pédagogique*, no. 4 (1973), p. 39.
[91] Triaud, "Abd al-Rahman l'Africain', p. 175.

Afin que tu deviennes un croyant, by Cheikh Touré, founder of the *Union Culturelle Musulmane.*[92]

The French language, hailed in 1910 as an 'effective cure ... against [religious] fanaticism', was less than fifty years later apparently contributing to the dissemination of 'fanaticism' in the form of 'Wahhabism'. In the same year, 1910, A. Quellien had remarked that the French médersas were 'destined to furnish Muslim studies with the methodology which they lack'; well, now they had it! On the one hand, the French believed that education was a 'good thing'; but they also believed that there could be too much of a good thing! Witness their treatment of Mohamed Ali Ag Ataher, whose private educational campaign had highlighted the contradictions of official policy.

New forms of Muslim schooling, as developed in the Islamic médersas, would contribute significantly to the production of new understandings of Islam and therefore of new Muslim subjectivities. The médersas would provide a religious education based on a modernized pedagogy of the Arabic language, which in turn would lead to a more rapid and firmer grasp of the essential Muslim texts. The médersas would also demonstrate their capacity to provide a mass education that included secular subjects in addition to religious ones. And schooling would necessarily be at the heart of these changes because only persons who could demonstrate complete and confident control of the basic religious texts could effectively defend the new forms of Islamic expression that were beginning to appear.

In the 1950s few could have suspected just how profound these changes would be, but social and political conditions in postcolonial Mali would dramatically advance the transformation of power relations, and of Muslim subjectivities, which began during the colonial period.

---

[92] Other works include two by al-Hajj Kabiné Diané, *Recueil des cinq piliers de l'Islam,* 2 vols (Algiers: Imprimerie P. Guiauchain, 1956), and *Le Coran: Lumière du Créateur,* 2 vols, 8th edn (Algiers: Imprimerie P. Guiauchain, 1956). Diané was described by Kaba, in *The Wahhabiyya,* p. 10, as 'a prominent Wahhabi educator' and imam in Bouaké.

5

POWER RELATIONS IN THE POSTCOLONY

The focus of analysis now moves to the first three decades of independence, from the achievement of full independence of the Republic of Mali under the leadership of the democratically-elected Modibo Keita (and the US-RDA) in September 1960, to the removal from power of Moussa Traoré by a *coup d'état* in March 1991. The sources available for the study of postcolonial Mali differ considerably from those used for the colonial period and necessitate the adoption of methodologies that tend to be more sociological than historical. Documentation of the kind that allowed us to trace the itineraries of various individuals in the preceding chapters simply does not exist, and evidence for the expansion of the network of médersas can often be derived only from ephemeral sources and survey research methods. Much of the documentation is statistical rather than substantive. Despite these methodological difficulties, our aim remains unchanged: to locate the history of postcolonial Mali in the broader context of the *longue durée* of the history of Muslim societies in West Africa. Our analysis begins with an examination of the social and political features of the postcolony itself.

Although independence was greeted in Mali with expressions of euphoric optimism by much of the population, the subsequent thirty years proved to be a period of profound social, economic and political conflict which sporadically erupted into open violence; the various *coups d'état* , both failed and successful, which peppered these years might be considered symptomatic of the turbulent nature of the political struggle which was in progress. Moussa Traoré came to power in a *coup* against the Keita government in November 1968; he and his comrades imposed a military government until June 1979, when the Malian Second Republic was declared immediately following the establishment of the single party which would govern it, the *Union Démocratique du Peuple Malien* (UDPM). After the fall of Moussa Traoré in 1991 as the result of another *coup*, Mali entered a new phase of political experimentation with democratic institutions. The Third Republic was declared in 1992 following a period of transition; a new constitution was adopted by referendum, and municipal, legislative, and presidential elections were held. One of the first principles adopted by the transitional authorities was freedom of association, which had been systematically suppressed for the preceding thirty years.

Islam, and the Islamic médersas, were not central to the evolution of political events during this period. Both nonetheless played a significant, if

169

somewhat obscured and largely misunderstood, role in the internal social dynamics of the country. In 1960, the seven or so existing Islamic médersas may have accounted for as many as 3,000 pupils, perhaps six percent of the total primary school enrolment. The French primary schools had an enrolment of about 50,000 pupils, accounting for slightly less than ten percent of the school-age population.[1] It was a small beginning for the founders of the médersas, but they had achieved it in little more than a decade against sustained opposition from both the colonial authorities and certain elements in the Muslim establishment. Indeed, compared to what the French had achieved in over half a century, it was a very impressive beginning, and with the arrival of independence under the leadership of the US-RDA, the Muslims had reason to be sanguine about the future of their schools.

Many adherents to Wahhabism had expressed strong anti-French and pro-independence sentiment, and some had been active in the independence struggle and in the US-RDA, which had in turn supported their campaigns for the médersas. Lansiné Kaba has demonstrated how Wahhabi members of the US-RDA influenced the party's political programs and informed their meetings with an Islamic content which often made their radical proposals more acceptable to many Muslims.[2] More skeptical analyses suggest that perhaps the US-RDA had found the Wahhabis useful for opposing the forces of 'traditional Islam' (allies of the more conservative PSP) as well as to help cement alliances with Arab North Africa in their pan-African, anti-imperialist campaigns, but that in reality this was an unholy alliance which could never have withstood the test of time.[3] In fact, any hopes that the Wahhabis, or indeed Muslims in general, might have nursed about the public role which Islam would be allowed to play in the newly independent Republic of Mali were firmly dashed as events unfolded during the 1960s, and the hard-line left-wing Marxists of the US-RDA managed to assert their control over the party and the government.

This was not simply an ideological shift in emphasis; it had real effect in terms of policy. The Bamako médersa was nationalized into the state school system to become the first of a newly established system of *écoles franco-arabes*, which was envisioned eventually to include all the Islamic médersas. The plan was for these schools to teach, in both the French and Arabic languages, a curriculum which would be completely secular. The French médersa in Timbuktu was incorporated into this system, and became a *lycée franco-arabe*. The médersa of Saada Oumar Touré was similarly designated for 'secularization', and was

---

[1] Joseph-Roger de Benoist, *Le Mali* (Paris: L'Harmattan, 1989), p. 154; and 'Vers un plan d'action pour les systèmes éducatifs des pays du Sahel'. working document prepared for the meeting of Ministers of Education of the Sahelian countries. Bamako, 15-18 Jan. 1990. Prepared by P. Jarousse and A. Mingat of l'IREDU-CNRS (Université de Bourgogne), p. 6.

[2] Kaba, *The Wahhabiyya, passim*, but especially pp. 127 and 230ff.

[3] Froelich, *Les musulmans*, p. 315.

[4] Interview with Saada Oumar Touré, 13 Oct. 1977, Segu.

only saved from this eventuality by the military *coup d'état* of 1968 which removed Modibo Keita and his government from power.[4]

The impact of government policy on the economy, and particularly on the merchants (and thus on many Wahhabis) was if anything even more drastic. With the collapse of the Malian Federation in 1960,[5] which had united Senegal and Mali in a federal state, the Malian government unilaterally cut off all trade with Senegal. This decision was a disastrous blow to Malian commercial interests, whose major trading partner was Senegal. It was to be followed, in 1962, with an even more serious economic decision, the adoption of a nonconvertible Malian currency. The commercial community and others opposed to the government, including many leaders of the now banned PSP, publicly demonstrated against this decision. The reaction was brutal and repressive; some individuals, including several leaders of the opposition PSP, were condemned to death for their opposition to the government, and no less than 22 merchants were sent to the notorious prison of Kidal in the northern desert.[6]

These economic decisions emanated from a 'revolutionary' Marxist ideology in which there was no room for 'reactionary bourgeois' merchants, much less for religious principles, as preached by either the 'Wahhabis' or the 'traditionalists'.[7] These years saw the entrenchment of an official and militant secularism in Mali that served to a certain extent to redefine the public religious landscape in the country. The confrontation between 'Wahhabis' and 'traditionalists' was now made more complex by new tensions that placed Muslim 'secularists' in conflict with other Muslims. Official secularism proclaimed religion to be a personal affair, which should be no concern of government unless public security was put at risk by religious conflict. Organizations such as the *Union Culturelle Musulmane* were banned, and as we have seen, the private Islamic médersas were scheduled for secularization.

Official Marxism would disappear with the *coup d'état* of 1968, but secularism would persist, both in official government documentation, and more importantly in the attitudes of a vast majority of public civil servants and government officials, most of whom had been educated in the French secular schools. It was this class of bureaucrats who came to dominate independent Mali; they were the true inheritors of the French mantle of authority, acquiring along with it positions of relative wealth and privilege. Islam consequently became officially invisible during the 1960s, and remained so throughout the 1970s, precisely when the network of private médersas was experiencing a period of rapid expansion. It was not until 1980 that the government of Moussa

---

[5] See William, J. Foltz, *From French West Africa to the Mali Federation* (New Haven, CT: Yale University Press, 1965), and Cheick Oumar Diarrah, *Le Mali de Modibo Keita* (Paris: L'Harmattan, 1986), pp. 19ff.

[6] Amselle, *Les négociants*, p. 264, and Diarrah, *ibid.*, pp. 68-71, 161-2.

[7] Boubacar Daba Traoré, 'Le Panislamisme en Afrique noire (cas du Mali)' (Mémoire de fin d'études, ENSup, Bamako, 1987), pp. 59-60. This *mémoire* is full of the 'revolutionary' rhetoric of the First Republic, which portrayed religion as 'anti-revolutionary' by its very nature, an illustrative example of the 'secularist' discourse in postcolonial Mali.

Traoré took note that the médersas now accounted for a significant proportion of primary school education (between 20 and 25 per cent) and decided
it must intervene in the situation. The decision was taken formally to recognize as educational establishments those médersas that met certain
requirements of curriculum content and standards in the provision of
school facilities. The response among médersa directors was mixed; some
welcomed this change of policy as a long-awaited official recognition of the
value of médersa education, while others rejected it as a politically motivated
initiative to undermine and compromise what they claimed were the basic religious objectives of the médersas. The most contentious issue was how to
develop a balanced curriculum for the médersas that would allow for
teaching both the secular subjects of the public *école fondamentale* and the religious subjects of the médersa without compromising either.

This shift in policy was development-led, precipitated by a major
intervention by the World Bank and other international aid agencies designed
to resuscitate what was by now deemed to be Mali's dramatically inadequate
and rapidly decaying system of public education. Of particular relevance to the
present analysis is the fact that, in constructing this multi-million-dollar,
multi-national aid program, the international aid community paid virtually
no attention to the underlying social dynamics which had produced a rapidly
expanding network of Muslim private schools in the country not only without
government support, but in the face of almost total official indifference.
Ironically, a major aim of this vast educational intervention was to encourage
the spread of private schooling in Mali in order to increase the percentage of
children attending school at minimal government expense; the médersas,
of course, were privately financed in their entirety and had never cost the
government a penny! Furthermore, between 1960 and 1991, médersa enrolments expanded at more than double the rate of the state schools.[8] The possible
reasons why a patently successful, self-motivated, non-government
experiment in private education over a period of more than twenty years was
virtually ignored by the international aid community will be explored below
in Chapter 7.

Nor is this the only irony which emerges in Malian policies (or non-poli-
cies) relating to Islam. The growing attraction of médersa education was due
in part to the decision of the Marxist regime of the First Republic officially

---

[8] Educational statistics in Mali have been extremely unreliable in the past, but even allowing for inaccuracies, the basic differential patterns of growth are clear. Official figures
calim that just below 30 per cent of primary school-age children were enrolled in schools
in 1991. Of these 59,117 were in médersas and 327,452 in state schools. A comparison
with enrolment estimates for 1960 of 3,000 and 50,000 pupils respectively illustrates that
the médersas expanded at more than double the rate of the state schools in the post-
independence period. Statistics are taken from the *Annuaire des statistiques scolaires, 1990-1991*,
Ministry of National Education, Republic of Mali. For a broadly similar assessment of
the statistics, see 'Rapport final. Table Ronde Nationale sur l'éducation de Base pour
Tous d'ici à l'an 2000', Bamako, 3-7 Sept. 1991.

to recognize the teaching of Arabic in the state schools, and its assistance in obtaining grants for some of Saada Oumar Touré's students to continue their studies in Egypt, who upon their return to Mali received positions in the civil service. It was thus demonstrated that a médersa education could also lead to a position in the public sector, independent Mali's most coveted source of wealth and status. Malian secularist policies did not hinder Muslims from organizing the resources necessary to meet their social and economic needs in a manner that they felt compatible with their understanding of their religion. Nevertheless, the impact of the official invisibility of Islam in a predominantly Muslim country remains an anomaly that calls for further exploration.

Knowledge and power in the Republic of Mali

The few médersas which existed at the time of independence were early manifestations of a current of socio-political thought and action which would seek to reformulate Islamic cultural resources in order to survive and perhaps thrive in a self-proclaimed secular polity. For purposes of convenience, we will refer to this phenomenon as the médersa movement, although it never took the shape of a unified self-conscious association with clearly defined and shared objectives. Indeed, the movement grew in a somewhat inchoate fashion and only began to cohere to any degree at all when the médersas became the object of government attention and médersa directors were compelled to respond to official interventions in their affairs, through a process which was comparable to the evolution of 'Wahhabism'.

The growth of the médersa movement must therefore be analysed in the context of its socio-political environment. Whereas it is true that much of the inspiration for these new kinds of schools came from elsewhere in the Muslim world, especially Egypt and Saudi Arabia, and that similar forms of educational reform were taking place throughout the Muslim world, the precise nature of médersa schooling and its impact in Mali were most deeply affected by local social, economic, and political conditions in post-independence Mali.

The history of Mali's first three decades of independence can justifiably be described as one of social differentiation, political disenchantment, and economic decline. The euphoria and hope that were so evident in 1960 had given way to widespread despair by the late 1980s, when research for this book began. By that date, Mali was in a state of extreme economic destitution and ranked as one of the poorest countries in the world, and the incumbent government, which gave every impression of being politically as well as economically bankrupt, was presiding over what many Malians perceived to be the progressive disintegration of the institutional infrastructure and social fabric of the country.

The socio-political structure of postcolonial Mali can best be described as a hierarchical clientelist system with a 'state bourgeoisie' perched at its summit.

The state bourgeoisie was comprised of those employed in the government and the civil service, the *fonctionnaires* or bureaucrats, as well as influential members of the Party, either US-RDA or UDPM, or the military contingent which governed in the years immediately following the 1968 *coup d'état*. Such persons were in positions of considerable authority and influence depending on the positions they held, and they also enjoyed more or less direct control over, and therefore access to, various state resources.

Clientelism ordered social relations throughout the country on all levels of society, and clientelist networks provided the most effective means available for amassing and redistributing social and material resources. Indeed, the colonial and postcolonial state in Mali, as the primary distributor of the country's most valuable resources (in the form of education, jobs and wealth), was the focus of the most prosperous and powerful of these clientelist networks, which were plugged into the state through the state bourgeoisie. These networks permeated official administrative institutions, although they were quite separate from them; at times the networks operated through administrative institutions and at times they competed with them. Jean-Loup Amselle has demonstrated how, especially since 1968, well-placed members of the state bourgeoisie, in alliance with various merchants, managed to accumulate large personal fortunes by, in effect, pillaging the state.[9]

The social roots of clientelism are no doubt to be found in lineage forms of social organization, and 'family' or lineage connections continued to provide the most fundamental framework of social and political relationships in post-independence Mali. But new frameworks of clientelist relationships also emerged which could cut across lineage associations, such as political or religious affiliations, or classmate friendships (Malians often refer to belonging to the same school class: *la même promotion*; according to some observers, this kind of social affinity may be a contemporary manifestation of age-grade associations).

Clientelist networks had also been important during the colonial period, as has been illustrated in the preceding chapters. Saada Oumar Touré could never have maintained his médersa experiment in Segu without the support of Muntaga Tal, his local patron. And Amadou Hampâté Bâ's counter-reform program was made possible because he had a patron in the administration in the person of Cardaire; whatever the political objectives of counter reform, it will be recalled that money and jobs flowed through the counter-reform network as a way to reward those who participated in the project. Indeed, the development of Hampâté Bâ's career from the 1930s to the 1950s depended largely on his ability to gain the support of well-placed patrons in the colonial

[9] J.-L. Amselle, 'Fonctionnaires et hommes d'affaires au Mali', *Politique Africaine*, 26 (1987), pp. 63-72; 'Socialisme, capitalisme et précapitalisme au Mali (1960-1982)' in H. Bernstein and B. Campbell (eds), *Contradictions of Accumulation in Africa* (Beverly Hills: Sage, 1985), pp. 249-66; and 'La corruption et le clientélisme au Mali et en Europe de l'Est. Quelques points de comparaison', *Cahiers d'Etudes Africaines*, 32 (4), 128, 1992, pp. 629-42.

service. However, this pattern of relationships between patrons in government and their clients would expand in the postcolony, with the sole difference that now it was Malians who were the new patrons, the members of the new 'state bourgeoisie'. This resurgence of clientelism may be in part due to the fact that lineage social organization is inherent to the local cultural heritage, which the colonial and postcolonial political environment tended to reinforce.

In times of relative prosperity, and especially in conditions of an expanding ecnomic base, a clientelist system can operate effectively enough as a means both for redistributing resources and for mediating power relations among its various levels and segments. By the 1980s, however, the Malian system was in crisis as a result of a drastically reduced resource base. Not only were the national coffers empty, but the country had still not fully recovered from the impact of two extended bouts of serious drought which had severely damaged agricultural production and also decimated herds. In addition, the effects of structural adjustment were also beginning to be felt; entry to the civil service had been severely restricted, and persons were being removed from jobs in the civil service or from rapidly contracting public sector enterprises. And even those who managed to hold on to their jobs found themselves in increasingly perilous economic straits; the less well-placed members of the state bourgeoisie found their positions of relative privilege being rapidly eroded.

One symptom of the economic pinch was the decision in 1983, to reintegrate the Malian currency with that of other French-speaking West African countries by adopting the franc CFA.[10] At the time of this reform, one French franc was equivalent to 50 francs CFA and to 100 Malian francs. It was therefore anticipated that with the reform, the numeric value of prices and salaries would be halved in Mali; in other words, 100 Malian francs would become 50 francs CFA. The salaries were duly halved in numeric terms, but the prices retained their numeric values. What had formerly cost 100 Malian francs now cost 100 francs CFA (popularly referred to during this period as *Comment Faire Avec?*). In other words, prices doubled overnight.[11]

Furthermore, the government treasury had been virtually empty for some time, and government employees were receiving their monthly pay-cheques every three months or so, thus effectively cutting the income of all civil servants by a further one-third. In these conditions, the clientelist networks began to come under increasing pressure, as those in favored positions were less and less able to satisfy their many supplicants who, as they were turned away, abandoned their loyalty to their patrons. For persons outside or less well placed in the networks (such as lower-level civil servants) the basic issue became sheer survival and finding enough food to feed themselves and their

[10] It will be recalled that twenty years earlier, Mali had withdrawn from the franc zone, a decision that resulted in serious public violence and repressive reactions from the Keita government.

[11] See Amselle, 'Socialisme, capitalisme et précapitalisme', p. 263.

families. By contrast, anyone who was fortunate enough to occupy a position of influence was using it, if possible, to further his/her own economic interests. The *fonctionnaire* who was never to be found on seat was a kind of standing joke, but a joke that reflected economic realities. He or she was out hustling, not only for their own personal interests, but because they in their turn were going to be hustled, by family, friends and clients who were looking for jobs, favours, money or just food. By the late 1980s the government barely seemed to be functioning; but insofar as the society and the economy held together, it was precisely this kind of 'free enterprise' which kept them ticking over.

Such 'enterprise' ranged from the legal to the criminal and fraudulent. But the lines of distinction between what was considered acceptable or unacceptable behavior were often difficult to discern. Few were the individuals in positions of responsibility who escaped accusations of corruption; but at the same time, fewer still were those who would refuse to use the influence of their family or friends to meet their own needs or pursue their own interests. As economic and social conditions deteriorated, the discourse of derision increased among the disaffected. Trust in the government or the administration evaporated, and charges of corruption were rife. But the entire situation was also riddled with a profound ambiguity; charges of corruption and proclamations of generosity are often simply opposite sides of the same coin in the currency of clientelism. The general impression was that if one received favors and support from a patron, then he/she was praised for being generous; if one was refused, the same patron might well be denounced as corrupt.

By the late 1980s this same ambiguity and ambivalence were evident in popular attitudes toward the state and the government of Moussa Traoré, who himself, his family and his closest allies were widely perceived as having been the chief beneficiaries of the plundering of the state coffers. In many contexts, both governance and administration had ceased to function effectively (schooling was one such area), and it was often difficult to distinguish between the formal structures of the state and the clientelist networks through which much of the real economic and political power of the state was exercised. The exercise of power, like access to wealth, was dispersed throughout both bureaucratic and clientelist hierarchies and tended to collect in nodes at certain points; at the same time, the power exercised at the apex of this system, often referred to locally as *le Pouvoir*, was formidable and could be wielded with devastating ferocity, as occurred on several occasions during these first decades of independence. Indeed, violence, or the threat of violence, both real and symbolic, pervaded the socio-political system. Thus the popular perception of *le Pouvoir* in Mali was of an ambiguous and vaguely defined collectivity of persons who on the one hand could deliver social and economic benefits to clients who were well-placed in the networks, or on the other hand, could be exploitative and oppressive.

Postcolonial Mali therefore fits well into Jean-François Bayart's analysis of postcolonial politics in Africa, which he describes as a struggle to determine who would dominate and who would be subjugated in the emergent new political order. The postcolonial state was transformed into a vast, virtually private, resource which dominant groups plundered in order to construct and maintain their dominance, through a hybrid structure of bureaucracy, 'free enterprise' and clientelism.[12] Bayart seems to suggest that this production of social inequality was a conscious political act; dominant groups sought to identify and 'domesticate' those that they would dominate and exploit. This idea of political 'domestication' recalls French colonial rhetoric, and although Bayart does not use the same French word as the colonial officials (*apprivoisement*), the connotations of his language are strikingly similar:

> The central problem of the dominators south of the Sahara is, if one can put it this way, to discover their dominated, to compel them to settle down in a domestic social space where their domination and exploitation will become more evident.[13]

This literal, and perhaps clumsy, translation has the virtue of effectively illustrating Bayart's view that social inequality has been (and is) actively produced and reproduced through an inherently violent political process.

Some of the harshest and least compromising descriptions of *le Pouvoir* in postcolonial Africa that appear in the academic corpus have been written by Achille Mbembe.[14] At his most severe, Mbembe equates political power with the management of violence in the context of an intensifying struggle for access to limited and diminishing economic resources. The most vivid and horrifying extremes of this scenario have occurred, according to Mbembe, in the political manipulation of famine, such as those that devastated much of the Sahel, including Mali, in the 1970s and 1980s. Food aid was diverted to the benefit of commercial and bureaucratic profiteering, which resulted in the obscene juxtaposition of ostentatious investment in Bamako with the effective condemnation to death of thousands of nomads in the Sahel, for whom the aid was originally destined.[15] In such conditions, a literal struggle for survival took place about who would eat and who would go hungry, a confrontation, as Mbembe puts it, between the power to kill and the refusal to die.[16]

---

[12] J.-F. Bayart, *L'État en Afrique. La politique du ventre* (Paris: Fayard, 1989), published in English as *The State in Africa : The Politics of the Belly*, tr. by Mary Harper, Christopher and Elizabeth Harrison (London and New York: Longman, 1993). Unless otherwise indicated, all quotations are taken from the French edition. The points being made here are discussed on pp. 146-7.

[13] *Ibid.*, p. 309.

[14] See, for example, J.A. Mbembe, *Les jeunes et l'ordre politique en Afrique noire* (Paris: L'Harmattan, 1985); Achille Mbembe, *Afriques indociles. Christianisme, pouvoir et Etat en société postcoloniale* (Paris: Karthala, 1988).

[15] See Amselle, 'Socialisme, capitalisme et précapitalisme', pp. 258-9, and Comité Sahel, *Qui se nourrit de la famine en Afrique?* (Paris: Maspéro, 1975).

[16] Mbembe, *Afriques indociles*, pp. 62 and 156ff; and *Les jeunes*, pp. 234-5. The political ramifications of these events were to erupt in the form of the 'Tuareg rebellion' in the

In a later article, entitled 'Provisional Notes on the Postcolony', Mbembe further pursued the permutations of this theme of violence. The notion of 'postcolony', he explained,

… identifies specifically a given historical trajectory – that of societies recently emerging from the experience of colonization and the violence which the colonial relationship, par excellence, involves. To be sure, the postcolony is chaotically pluralistic, yet it has nonetheless an internal coherence. … The postcolony is characterised by a distinctive style of political improvisation, by a tendency to excess and a lack of proportion as well as by distinctive ways in which identities are multiplied, transformed and put into circulation. But the postcolony is also made up of a series of corporate institutions and a political machinery which, once they are in place, constitute a distinctive regime of violence. In this sense, the postcolony is a particularly revealing (and rather dramatic) stage on which are played out the wider problems of subjection and its corollary, discipline.[17]

In this article, Mbembe refers to the authoritarian exercise of power in the postcolony as the *commandement*:

I use the term *commandement* in the way it was used to denote colonial authority, that is, in so far as it embraces the images and structures of power and coercion, the instruments and agents of their enactment, and a degree of rapport between those who give orders and those who are supposed to obey them, without, of course, discussing them. Hence the notion of *commandement* is used here as the authoritarian modality *par excellence*.[18]

The preceding chapters have provided some insight into the ideology and practice of the authoritarian institution of *commandement* during the colonial period,[19] which was established and sustained by the ultimate sanction of force of arms. The reader will recall that students of the French médersas were being trained to serve in the *commandement indigène*. But neither the concepts nor the practices of power in the postcolony were beholden solely to the colonial experience.

If the term postcolony, as glossed by Mbembe, suggests a specific interest in tracing the evolution of the colonial heritage of violence and domination in its postcolonial forms, their precolonial antecedents can by no means be ignored. The analyses of Mbembe, Bayart and others depart from a focus on European-based policies of 'neo-colonialism' as such, and place primary emphasis on the internal dynamics of African societies as a profoundly determining factor in their postcolonial social and political evolution. This shift

---

early 1990s; see Hawad, 'La *teshumara* antidote de l'Etat', pp. 123-38, and Elleli Ag Ahar, 'L'Initiation d'un *ashamur*, pp. 141-52, *REMMM*, no. 57 (1990) *Touaregs, exil et résistance*.

[17] Achille Mbembe, 'Provisional Notes on the Postcolony', *Africa*, 62 (1), 1992, p. 3.

[18] *Ibid.*, p. 30, note 7.

[19] The title of Amadou Hampâté Bâ's second volume of mémoirs, *Oui mon Commandant!* is specifically intended to reflect the fact that one never said 'No' to one's administrative superior, although episodes in the book illustrate very well how in practice what one said and what one did might be quite different!

in emphasis is perhaps the direct result of adopting an analytical problematic which views contemporary African societies in their historical perspective.[20]

For example, modes of state power, as well as the resources available for a fuller exercise of this power, were certainly transformed during the colonial period. However, local concepts and perceptions of power and power relationships tended to persist among the vast majority of the population, as evidenced in the clientelist networks themselves. For example, local concepts of power, such as the Mande *fanga* or the Peul *laamu*, connote both the power seized by superior force of arms and also the inherent or inherited right to such power. According to Shaka Bagayogo, it is popularly accepted that the possession of *fanga* requires no justification; to possess it proves that one deserves it. As one of his informants told him, 'Power is unlike anything else. Power is power. A sovereign is not like any other man; he knows neither friend nor enemy.' According to this view, the sovereign holds right of ownership over all he controls: 'In the past, the country and everything in it belonged to the sovereign, just like the toad and everything in its stomach belongs to the hornbill.'[21]

To employ a metaphor of 'eating' to describe the exercise of power is by no means unusual in Africa. The concept is inherent to Bayart's analysis of postcolonial politics, as reflected in the title of his book, *L'État en Afrique. La politique du ventre*, translated into English as *The State in Africa : The Politics of the Belly*. On one level this title recalls the omnipresent African metaphorical association between power and 'eating', or the accumulation of wealth. But it is also meant to evoke the other side of the equation of what is perceived as the effective exercise of power: reciprocity. Ideally 'power eats and causes others to eat.' This phrase neatly encapsulates the ideology of clientelism which informs the structure of power relations in Mali, and a central problematic in Bayart's book is an analysis of how the exercise of state power is deeply enmeshed in the complex web of personalized clientelist networks through which circulate both social and material resources.

If precolonial concepts of power have persisted into the postcolonial period, the precolonial 'aristocratic' classes no longer necessarily hold power in Mali. The colonial interlude eroded the position of those 'born to power' and also instituted new forms of delegated administrative authority and power. Claude Fay[22] has described the way in which rural Peul perceive those

---

[20] For a similar perspective, see for example, J.-P. Olivier de Sardan, *Les sociétés songhay-zarma (Niger-Mali). Chefs, guerriers, esclaves, paysans...* (Paris: Karthala, 1984), and J.-L. Amselle, *Logiques métisses*.

[21] These observations are quoted in Shaka Bagayogo, 'L'Etat au Mali: représentation, autonomie et mode de fonctionnement' in E. Terray (ed.), *L'Etat contemporain en Afrique* (Paris: L'Harmattan, 1987), pp. 93 and 102. Bagayogo explains that toads constitute the principle element in the diet of the hornbill! See also J.-L. Amselle, 'La corruption', pp. 637-8, where he traces the historical antecedents of the predatory state in Mali.

[22] Claude Fay, 'La démocratie au Mali, ou le pouvoir en pâture', *Cahiers d'Études africaines*, 137, XXXV-1, (1995), pp. 40-1.

contemporary *commandants*, who on the one hand may hold only delegated authority, but may nonetheless behave as if they were the warrior princes of old. Peul distinguish three categories of local *commandants* according, so to speak, to their 'eating habits'! First are the 'sucklings of power', those who were nursed at the breast of power, who are 'proud of their origin and show it and know how to cope with the peasants'. According to a Peul proverb, 'One must have suckled power to be able to exercise power'. These persons 'eat' of course, but within reason and also avoid 'eating' their age-mates. The second category are the 'hunters' or 'seekers of power', sons of the poor or the *laamaabe*, subjects or persons whom one commands. 'The white man taught them to read, they seek power but they don't forget the hardship (*fatigue*) of their own elders.' Some of them therefore 'eat' with restraint, but others are abusive and 'eat' to excess. Finally, there are the 'things of power' (*choses du pouvoir*, Fulfulde, *kulleji laamu*) 'who "are here because of a piece of paper and leave by a piece of paper", who know French but do not know how to command, who are afraid of everything, who "take nothing and bring nothing", which is the exact opposite of the habitual task of power, which is "to eat and to cause to eat".'

These comments and insights evoke the clientelist ideology of hierarchical reciprocity and illustrate the rich field of referents associated with the notion of 'eating'. We see here an acceptance of the legitimacy of the state, even one based on clientelist hierarchies and personalized in the form of a *Pouvoir* whose members have a right 'to eat', that is, to collect taxes and tributes, so long as they provide for the welfare of their clients and also maintain security and order.[23] By contrast, there is simultaneously a profound suspicion that this same *Pouvoir* might 'eat to excess', that is, abuse its position through acts of predation and repression. These observations reveal yet again the ambiguity and ambivalence that pervades power relations in Mali.

Fay's analysis also reveals an explicit disdain for those who gain access to power through 'reading and writing'. The relationship between power and knowledge in this context is patently clear. All Malians are fully aware that those who retain posts in the state bourgeoisie are the products of French-language schooling who belong to a privileged social class which was invented during the colonial period through the process of schooling, even if they don't conceptualize their observations in these terms. Acquisition of a western education has therefore become an indispensable and unavoidable requirement for access to the institutions of governance. Persons without such training might still exercise forms of social authority and influence, but they cannot accede to positions in government or administration. Schooling

---

[23] Welfare should here be understood in a very broad sense; for example, according to Fay, the qualities of Moussa Traoré as a leader were questioned in part because he ruled during years of severe drought in the 1970s and 1980s, whereas the man who removed him from power, Amadou Toumani Touré, was interim president of Mali when the country enjoyed some of the most abundant rains in years.

therefore created a profound gap between those who manage the institutions of the state and its unschooled subjects, especially in the rural areas. The 'unschooled' could be integrated into the clientelist networks that were dominated by the state bourgeoisie, for example, through marriage, family ties, and commercial relationships, but for those outside these networks, French-language schooling, as well as the knowledge of writing and of French language which it transmits, became symbols of profound difference and were perceived by many as the weapons of an intrusive and often oppressive state.

French-language schooling in Mali has been and remains a very scarce resource; by 1991, less than 30 per cent of children of primary school age were enrolled in schools (including médersas) and only 25 per cent of these had the likelihood of successfully completing primary school. One of the most tangible impacts of this uneven distribution of French-language schooling in Mali has been the production of social inequality, rather than the 'development' which much public rhetoric promises. In fact, state schools are seen by many of those who are furthest distanced from the apparatus of the state, especially in the rural areas, as dangerous and invidious institutions. Any analysis of schooling in the postcolony must therefore highlight this ambiguity.

In his recent study of schooling in a rural area south of Bamako, Etienne Gérard argues that schooling has played a central role in the evolution of forms of political domination in the twentieth century:

In societies like those of Mali, the cultural arbitrariness represented by the school was imposed primarily through the vehicles of writing and the French language. Employing these two fundamental tools, the school transmitted new knowledges and formulated new procedures for their transmission. Concurrently, the State appropriated writing and the French language as instruments of social control, domination and the monopolization of power: the law came to be enforced through the writing down of [legal] codes, the establishment of specialized [legal] organizations, and through the medium of the Courts of Justice and the police.

Attitudes to education and schooling must be understood in the context of these relationships and orientations. In an oral society, the imposition of writing constitutes in itself a kind of 'symbolic violence'; the legalization of practices or the monopoly of power authorized by the mastery of writing and the French language also directly affects power relations between the State and communities.[24]

According to this argument, state power in the twentieth century, in the form of colony and postcolony, came to be expressed through written, as opposed to oral, codes. Acquisition of literacy in the French language became associated with higher social status which (until the 1980s) virtually guaranteed access to a position in the state governing apparatus. The foundations for this transfor-

---

[24] Etienne Gérard, 'L'Ecole déclassé. Une étude anthropo-sociologique de la scolarisation au Mali. Cas des sociétés malinkés', thèse de doctorat (nouveau régime), Université Paul Valéry, 1992, p. 8. A revised version of this work was published as *La tentation du savoir en Afrique. Politiques, mythes et stratégies d'éducation au Mali* (Paris: Karthala/ORSTOM, 1997).

mation were laid down during the colonial period, when schooling was aimed at training the sons of chiefs and notables and at forming lower-level employees for the colonial administrative services. French-language schooling therefore originated as an arm of colonial policy designed to prepare Africans to serve the needs of *commandement*, to use Mbembe's term.

With independence, the stated aims of the educational system would change dramatically. With its Educational Reform of 1962 the Keita government set about to broaden the base of education and to 'de-colonize' it. The oft-cited five objectives of the Reform were to create (1) quality education for the masses; (2) an education which would produce, with the maximum economy of time and money, all the leaders required by the country; (3) an education which would guarantee a cultural level such that its diplomas would be equivalent to those of other modern states; (4) an education based not only on specifically African values but also on universal values; (5) an education which would decolonize the mind.[25] In reality, the objectives of the reformed educational system were no less designed to serve postcolonial political objectives than had been colonial policies. A ministerial document on the reform stated that: 'A true decolonization is at one and the same time political, economic, and cultural. It is much easier to change the political and administrative structures of a country than to change the way its people think and act. It belongs to the education system to accomplish that difficult and painful process of transforming people's minds.'[26] Education would therefore play a central role in the 'socialist revolution' that the US-RDA wished to bring about in Mali, and students would constitute its vanguard. 'To form citizens for the new socialist society, we need an education system that trusts students. School must prepare students fully to play their role as citizens, treat them as human beings and moreover, consider them as equal to teachers.'[27]

However, one might reasonably ask what 'decolonization of the mind' actually meant? Whose minds had been colonized, and in what ways? Raising these kinds of questions reveals some of the profound contradictions which lurked at the core of the rhetoric about (and the real impact of) national education. Modibo Keita's nationalist campaigns for independence made much of the fact that colonial education (along with other political and administrative structures) had existed for the sole benefit of the colonists and had turned many Africans into irresponsible and passive persons who were no longer capable of taking initiatives. Furthermore, he contended, 'intellectual colonization has inexorably accomplished its task of destroying our national heritage and

---

[25] Pierre Guedj, 'Le système éducatif malien: sa structure et ses principes de base à travers l'analyse de la réforme de l'éducation et de ses prolongements', *Etudes et Documents* (Ecole Nationale d'Administration, Bamako), no. 4, April 1986, pp. 3-4.

[26] 'La réforme de l'enseignement au Mali', Ministère de l'Education Nationale, 1965, quoted in Soumaila Diakité, 'Education, the State and Class Conflict: a Study of Three Education Policies in Mali' (unpubl. Ph.D. thesis, Stanford University, 1985), p. 160.

[27] 'Premier séminaire de l'Education Nationale', 1964, quoted in *ibid.*, p. 167.

corrupting our élites'.[28] One of his major aims was the reassertion of both the 'African personality' and Mali's 'national culture'. But precisely who had lost their 'African personality', and how could a system of French-language education restore 'national culture', if indeed either of these had ever existed in reality? And was a Marxist inspired socialism compatible with either of them? These kinds of questions do not seem to have been posed by postcolonial leaders, or if they were, no one paused very long to reflect upon them.

The expansion of school provision was a widely popular policy, and school enrolments expanded rapidly in the first flushes of enthusiasm following independence.[29] More important, perhaps, was the transformation of the public discourse on education. French language education, which in the colonial period was allegedly 'aimed at nothing less than the depersonalization of our people',[30] now became central to the program of national salvation. Schooling would now be available equally to all children, at least in principle; indeed, sending one's children to school was now formulated as a kind of national duty, and families were made to feel ashamed if they did not have at least one child in school.[31] The socialist rhetoric of the US-RDA, which portrayed education as serving the cause of national liberation, would eventually give way to a more liberal rhetoric under Moussa Traoré in which the value of education was praised in terms of individual liberation. By the mid-1980s, a Ministry of Education publication would speak of schooling in the postcolony as 'an inalienable and free right for everyone to emerge from the fog of illiteracy and to receive general and technical training'.[32] And of course, education was at the very center of the developmentalist thinking which has so profoundly affected postcolonial policy-making in Mali, as elsewhere in Africa.

But despite the rhetoric and the ambitious policies, the actual impact of French language schooling on the ground was always ambiguous. Schooling under the US-RDA was rapidly subsumed to the quest to secure the 'revolution'. The 'decolonization of minds' was in fact implemented in the form of an ideological indoctrination designed to serve the policy objectives of the Keita government, and students were called upon to execute some of the most extreme forms of political action advocated by the radical wing of the US-RDA. Because of this politicization of students, they and youth more generally became the focus of much of the popular disillusionment that

---

[28] Quoted in Cheick Oumar Diarrah, *Le Mali de Modibo Keita*, p. 89.

[29] According to Diarrah, *ibid.*, p. 88, primary school enrolments more than doubled between 1960 and 1964, from 54,540 to 113,448. This expansion is discussed more fully in Chapter 7.

[30] 'L'Enseignement en République du Mali. Administration. Organisation. Missions', Ministère de l'Education Nationale, 1985, p. 20.

[31] Gérard, 'L'école déclassée', p. 30.

[32] L'Enseignement en République du Mali. Administration. Organisation. Missions', Ministère de l'Education Nationale, 1985, p. 39.

eroded support for the Keita régime.[33] More prosaically, but nonetheless significantly, civil servants, who constituted little more than one per cent of the total population, made up 99 per cent of the government.[34] The roots of the state bourgeoisie were already deeply implanted.

As the schooled appropriated more and more power and wealth in ensuing years, the idea became generalized, at least among much of the literate population, that literacy was a positive and unambiguous 'good' and that illiteracy was equivalent to ignorance and powerlessness. Gérard calls this process the 'mythification' of literacy.[35] But it was not all a myth, of course, since schooling had become a key factor in power relations. And for many Malians, especially those who had not received it, schooling retained its colonial connotations, despite the postcolonial rhetoric: 'If you have been to school', one informant told Gérard, 'you will be the *tubab* [white man] of another.' 'People who don't know how to read think they are going to be eaten. And it is us (the educated) who are going to eat them. They are the meat that we eat.'[36] Quite contrary to its intentions, developmentalist rhetoric reinforced these perceptions of social and political difference by seeking actively to eliminate them: the extension of schooling to all children would allegedly bridge the educational gap and lead to a wider and more equitable distribution of social and economic benefits. But in fact the Malian state was unable to deliver schooling to all, and what it did manage to deliver became progressively less effective.

Such facts did not, however, inhibit the Ministry of National Education from disseminating fantasies in the guise of policy statements. In 1985 an official publication stated that, 'The state guarantees, in principle, for all its citizens from the age of six or eight years, a primary education which is free, secular and obligatory.'[37] This statement was no more than a hollow mantra intoned by official spokespersons. The words 'in principle' do impart some sense of reality to this declaration, but in fact primary education was neither free, obligatory, nor since 1985, secular, this being the year that administrative responsibility for the Islamic médersas was assumed by the Ministry of National Education. Schooling had never been obligatory; the percentage of primary school enrolments peaked in 1980 at about 30 per cent, and fell consistently for the remainder of the decade.[38] And schooling was certainly

---

[33] See Shaka Bagayogo, 'Les jeunes et l'état au Mali ou les revers d'une désarticulation', *Jamana* (Bamako), no. 35 (Mar. 1994), pp. 16-25, and Oumar T. Ly, 'La structuration du concept de "jeunesse" dans le discours de l'Union Soudanaise du RDA (1947-1962)' in H. d'Almeida-Topor *et al.* (eds), *Les Jeunes en Afrique*, II, pp. 85-99.

[34] Diakité, 'Education, the State and Class Conflict', p. 169.

[35] Gérard, 'L'école déclassée', pp. 80 and 105.

[36] *Ibid.*, pp. 204-5.

[37] 'L'Enseignement en République du Mali. Administration. Organisation. Missions', p. 1.

[38] Ministère de l'Éducation Nationale. Institut Pédagogique National. 'Etude sur la demande sociale d'éducation en milieu rural au Mali. Réalisée par IPN en collaboration avec l'Institut

not free, but required many of those who wanted it for their children to make enormous sacrifices, as illustrated by this report of an interview with a father of four:

He [the father] had just paid the 'registration fee' of 1,750 francs CFA for his fourth child, Toumani. It was urgent because the announcement from the Parents Association [*Association des parents d'élèves*, APE] was unequivocal: 'Given the limited number of places available, the parents of pupils are encouraged to hurry …' On your mark! Get set! Go!

[Toumani's father] was still waiting for his July salary. He would also have to pay the APE 1,750 francs for each of his other three children, in installments at least, but without which they would be expelled from class precisely at the time of their examinations.

Toumani will need to be equipped with a desk (2,000 francs)[39], a book satchel (1,000 francs), a spelling book (960 francs), a slate (230 francs), a pencil box for his chalk (260 francs), an eraser (160 francs) and a ruler (100 francs). All in all, leaving aside the things that will have to be replaced during the year (like books), the total bill comes to 48,980 francs CFA.

In addition, he will have to provide four completely new uniforms, not *yuguyugu* (used clothes), at least of equal value to those of the neighbouring children. When will all our schoolchildern, rich and poor, wear the same uniform?

[Toumani's father] spoke continually, more to unburden himself than to inform me. He is a nurse, first cycle, second class, eleventh echelon, married, four children, living in rented accommodation, sixteen years of service. Monthly net salary: 34,435 francs [approximately 70 pounds sterling at the time].

He will buy what he can. Sali, who is repeating his seventh year, will save him about 12,000 in book purchases. No one can dare to pretend that all children have an equal chance in school.

'Who would dare to claim that education is free nowadays?' he sighed.[40]

Toumani and his family lived in Bamako, where the percentage of school enrolments was the highest in Mali, although even here, access for all children was by no means guaranteed. Personal economic circumstances determined which children would or would not attend primary school; clearly children from poor families had much less opportunity for schooling than did those from more well-to-do families. Nor could schooling be accurately described as an 'opportunity' in the mid-1980s. Deciding to send one's child to school, especially in a city like Bamako, was more like making a tactical move in a complex strategic game which one had very little chance of 'winning' but

---

Malien de Recherches Appliquées au Développement (IMRAD). Avril 1989. This decline in percentages may well be due, in part, to demographic factors, since the population was growing while the public schools were unable to absorb more children. But it is also true that médersa enrolments were increasing during this period, although these were not included in official statistics because médersas were not considered 'schools' before 1985.

[39] Primary schoolchildren were expected to furnish their own desks (*table-banc*) at this time.

[40] A. Barry, *Jamana*, no. 5 (1985), p. 49.

from which one could not comfortably withdraw. Only schooling could lead to regular salaried employment, but the job market had shrunk to such an extent that the majority of young persons leaving school were unemployed. As Mbembe claimed, schooling was training people for unemployment.[41] Participation in the commercial sector did not necessarily require schooling, and the collapse of recruitment into the civil service had eliminated the major window of opportunity to which most school leavers aspired. Even if urban populations were becoming suspicious about the official line on schooling, in planning for their children's future, they had few alternatives to investing in their education.

By contrast, the alleged benefits of schooling had never been very widely accepted among Mali's rural populations. Of course, all peasants did not reject schooling; for one thing, many recognized the practical values of literacy in managing their own affairs as well as in dealing with a state infrastructure which was based upon written codes and documentation. Many were also prepared to invest in the schooling of at least one child in the hope that he (almost always a male child) would successfully complete his education and later be in a position to assist the family financially, or at least to be able to protect the interests of family or village in their dealings with the agents of the state bureaucracy. But there was also always profound suspicion and resistance to schooling in rural areas, even in the enthusiasm of the early 1960s when the Keita government introduced its ambitious educational reforms. French-language school was a colonial, white man's institution that from its inception had been designed to train persons to work in the administrative apparatus. The idea that such a school could serve the interests of the rural community was therefore at best considered novel, and at worst incomprehensible.

In the event the 1962 educational reforms never delivered what they promised in the rural areas; as elsewhere in the country, school places and enrolments increased until 1980, when they began to decline; the quality of schooling, never very high in the rural areas, also declined. Parents discovered that most children who had attended school even for only a few years but who did not succeed in their studies (the overwhelming majority) often wanted to abandon the village (and the family) for town or city. Such parents thus lost both their children and their investment, since, as we have seen, sending a child to school was costly. Rural resistance to schooling therefore increased, and some local administrators, like their French colonial predecessors, resorted to coercive measures to ensure that school places were filled. School therefore became for many parents a symbol of repression rather than a path for 'development'.

These observations are illustrated by a study commissioned by the Ministry of National Education in 1989 to evaluate the reasons for the low demand

[41] He referred to students as *'chômeurs en formation'*; see Mbembe, *Les jeunes*, p. 64.

for primary schooling in rural areas.[42] The findings of this study were based on interviews with 440 parents in four different rural communities (in the regions of Kayes, Koulikoro, Mopti and Tombouctou). Although 80 per cent of the respondents agreed that 'schooling' was important, only 45.5 per cent said they would willingly send their children to a state primary school. The study concluded that this apparent paradox was due to the fact that school could no longer provide a guaranteed economic payoff in the form of salaried employment. The content of the study does not unequivocally support this conclusion, in that only six per cent of respondents saw training for a job as an important consideration for sending children to school. Nonetheless, it was argued that rural parents would be willing to sacrifice to send their children to school if the real benefits derived from it were adequate. In fact, the study fails to address the cultural and political issues which pervaded perceptions of schooling in rural Mali at the time.

There seems little doubt that the low opinion of state schools held by many rural parents resulted in part from the sheer failure of the educational system to provide successful school careers for their children. However, the study did not pursue in depth the question of what the parents would consider to be 'success'. The report was written from an urban perspective and placed primary emphasis on schooling for jobs, whereas many rural parents were overwhelmingly concerned with the ways in which primary school experience undermined the maintenance and reproduction of a rural labor force and the coherence of rural society. Similarly, stock explanations for failure were put forward by the authors of the report, such as the lack of adequate economic and pedagogical resources, without addressing basic questions about the kind of schooling which would be appropriate to the needs of a rural population. The structure of the study itself reflects the nature of the gulf which separated the urban educated classes from the rural masses; the report was formulated around the implicit assumption that schooling is schooling and should everywhere be the same.

However, the image of the state primary school that was painted by these rural respondents was of an institution which, far from serving the interests of the community and providing opportunities for their children, drained it of both human and economic resources. Like in Bamako, rural schools also required a significant investment from parents, who had to construct and maintain them, as well as to purchase the furnishings and supplies for them. Because of poor and irregular payment of salaries, rural parents were often expected to supplement the income of local teachers with grain and other foodstuffs. Schooling also interfered with the provision of domestic labor that was normally provided by children of the household. And finally, the economic sacrifice required to keep a child in primary school was increased

[42] Ministère de l'Éducation Nationale. Institut Pédagogique National. 'Etude sur la demande sociale d'éducation en milieu rural au Mali. Réalisée par IPN en collaboration avec l'Institut Malien de Recherches Appliquées au Développement (IMRAD). April 1989.

many fold if he or she passed primary school examinations and won the opportunity to continue studies in a regional capital or in Bamako, where expenses could be expected to be even greater. For the tiny percentage of individuals who successfully completed school and found paid employment, the rewards could often be considerable, but for most rural parents schooling, especially when it was imposed on them, came to be seen as a handicap in the struggle for survival.

Comments in the report document the depth of discontent that these conditions produced, especially when schools failed so utterly in their mission. The extremes of failure were illustrated in a case study of a village school in the Mopti region where, during the preceding twenty-four years, only one child had succeeded in continuing studies beyond primary school. According to the report, this school had had no positive educational impact whatsoever, and parents remonstrated that the local teachers were less interested in teaching than in employing their pupils to till their fields.[43] The authors of the report observed that the peasants in this village were no longer prepared to give even a single *sou* for the support of this school, and would never have done so 'if the threat of the administration had not been hanging over the heads of the parents'. Similar conclusions were reached in the Kayes region, where it was said that parents had 'no intention of sacrificing their children to please a government that had done nothing to ameliorate their fate.' A completely separate study, undertaken in the community of Touba, northeast of Bamako, cited very similar views from a local dignitary about the operation of the state schools: 'Registrations in the French school are drawn from the administrative census list and are not based upon the wishes of the parents; otherwise, there would not be a single child enrolled in Touba.'[44]

For many parents, the promise of schooling for their children was transformed into a vector of state intrusion, and even exploitation, in their lives. For example, in the late 1980s, a local development tax was introduced in Mali, of which 30 per cent was designated for the support of local schools. In 1991, an international aid worker had occasion to visit some sixty rural schools in Ségou and Sikasso regions. Not a single one of these schools had received even a single franc of their share of the local taxes that had been collected in their communities.

But neither economic hardship nor alleged exploitation were the features of school which were most vehemently condemned by respondents to the 1989 study; most resentment was aroused by the social impact of schooling. As one person observed, schooling brings about 'a total break with customary social life' in the village.[45] Acculturation into the school environment results in

---

[43] Of course, this is a time honored practice in West Africa, where Qur'anic school pupils were normally expected to work in the fields of their teachers.

[44] Yoro Diakité, 'L'impact de la religion sur la politique socio-économique du Mali: étude comparée des cas du Touba et Kiban à travers l'islam' (mémoire, fin d'études, ENA, Bamako, 1987), p. 58.

[45] *Ibid.*

de-culturation from the village environment. Some parents alleged that the school leaver was 'marred for life, not knowing at eighteen years of age how to do the kinds of jobs that children of eight can easily carry out.' 'Those who have been to school don't do anything; ... they are neither white nor black, and are generally lost.' Furthermore, school was also blamed for producing behavior which was considered undesirable by parents; children who had been to school were said no longer to respect their parents, nor the community values of the village, nor social conventions and mores, such as the rules of marriage. Particular concern was expressed about the impact of schooling on girls and the (allegedly) associated increased incidence of premarital pregnancy among schoolgirls. According to some parents, schools produced 'social misfits ... who incline towards delinquency: vagabonds, bandits, thieves and cheats'. Equally reprehensibly, schools were also responsible for producing those 'vile government agents ... [such as] the police, the officials from the Ministry of Water and Forests, and the *chefs d'arrondissement* who oppress [the peasantry] with exorbitant taxes.'

The disillusionment about state schools in rural Mali which followed the first flushes of enthusiasm in the 1960s may well have been due in part to the factors mentioned in the 1989 study: the radical reduction of recruitment into the civil service and the increasing difficulty of school-leavers to find paid employment, the rising costs of schooling which the government expected parents to assume, and the sheer inefficacy and perceived inappropriateness of the schooling offered. But, as already suggested, the authors of this study began from the assumption that schooling as they understood and had experienced it was of unquestioned universal value, and they therefore failed to confront and assess the fact that schooling policies and practices in the rural areas had also produced a deep current of political dissatisfaction and tension.

Etienne Gérard's study effectively evokes the contradictions and nuanced ambiguities which have been associated with schooling in rural Mali, where the possible advantages of schooling are constantly weighed against immediate needs and interests. State schools, like other state institutions, are treated with suspicion when they threaten local institutions. Schooling in the rural areas is strongly associated with governance and administration and with a state that functions through the medium of written documentation. The agents of the state, like civil servants and school teachers, arrive in rural areas 'by a piece of paper' and leave 'by a piece of paper'. Rural communities welcome schooled allies who can assist them in dealing with such agents, but the schooling which the state offers does little, in their view, to support the local social and political order.[46] Combined with these factors is the lure of the city; the extensive rural exodus of primarily young people who are swelling the cities is also reinforced by the ideology of schooling, since the economic prospects opened by schooling are still primarily associated with work in urban areas.

---

[46] Gérard, 'L'école déclassée', p. 474.

Thus far our analysis of the ambiguities associated with French-language schooling in Mali has focused on the unevenness of its availability and the suspicions and hostility it has aroused among those who have felt marginalized from it. But the political implications of schooling become much more salient when we examine the group that has benefited most from schooling, those who have reached secondary and higher levels of education. Not only has access to power and wealth been limited for the most part to this educated minority, but, as argued by Gérard, the literacy and knowledge of French language acquired in school have provided them with the tools through which they can exercise social control and impose their political domination.

The students have wielded their political muscle repeatedly during the postcolonial years. We have already alluded to the key role assigned to students, and youth more generally, in the programs of radical political and social change envisaged by the US-RDA. Most students were therefore opposed to the *coup d'état* led by Moussa Traoré in 1968, and students became an active focus of political dissent from 1968 until the removal from power of Moussa Traoré in 1991. They organized a strike as early as April 1969 and another in 1971, both of which were severely repressed. And between 1977 and 1980 they precipitated the most severe political crisis which the military government had experienced since it had seized power. These upheavals began in 1977 with protests against a new policy of restricting entry to higher education on the basis of examinations. They intensified in 1978 when the government was unable to pay teachers' salaries and student stipends on a regular basis, and they reached their tragic climax in 1979-80 when the student leader, Abdoul Karim Camara, was killed while in police custody and hundreds were arrested in the course of violent repressions.

Government reaction to this challenge was to adopt a policy of divide and rule, reinforced by a series of strict measures designed to constrain student activities. Secondary education was regionalized, requiring all students to attend secondary schools in the region of their residence, thus redistributing the high concentration of students in Bamako throughout the country. The militant student organization, the *Union Nationale des Etudiants et Elèves du Mali* (UNEEM), founded in 1972, was dissolved and the only legal forum for the public expression of student views became the *Union Nationale des Jeunes du Mali* (UNJM), an organization which was in effect the youth arm of the the UDPM. Students were subjected to close surveillance, and those found guilty of creating a disturbance were subject to immediate suspension and possible expulsion from school.[47]

[47] For further discussion of these events see S. Diakité, 'Education, the State and Class Conflict', Ch. VI; Cheick Oumar Diarrah, *Mali. Bilan d'une gestion désastreuse* (Paris: L'Harmattan, 1990), pp. 41-3; Moussa Konaté, *Mali. Ils ont assassiné l'espoir* (Paris: L'Harmattan, 1990), pp. 43-53;. and Pierre François, 'Class Struggles in Mali', *Review of African Political Economy*, no. 24 (1982), pp. 22-38.

A new student organization did not emerge until 1990, when the *Associa-tion des Elèves et Etudiants au Mali* (AEEM) was founded as part of the burgeoning democratic movement which would result the following year in the removal of Moussa Traoré from power, and eventually in the establish-ment of Mali's Third Republic. Although students, and youth more generally, played a central role in the political struggle to oppose Moussa Traoré and to establish a democratic form of government, their militant actions after 1991 posed one of the most profound political challenges that the nascent Third Republic would have to face. Student actions were directly responsible for the resignations of two successive Prime Ministers, Younoussi Touré and Abdoulaye Sow, in 1993 and 1994. Students resorted to violence on a number of occasions, in 1993 setting fire to the National Assembly and the Ministry of Education, and completely destroying the facilities of the Jamana publish-ing house and cultural cooperative;[48] they also sacked the private homes of a number of prominent officials, including that of the President of the Repub-lic. In 1994, when student violence resumed, the government took action reminiscent of 1980: students were arrested and schools were closed until calm could be restored.

Central to these disputes and confrontations were economic issues. In one of its first official acts in April 1991, the transitional government that took power after the fall of Moussa Traoré formally agreed to act on 26 student grievances and demands which the AEEM had placed before the previous government. The *Mémorandum* containing these demands touched on many aspects of education in Mali, but the points that would become the focus of political contestation were related to the level of scholarship aid and the criteria for its distribution. The *Mémorandum* may have been endorsed in good faith by the transitional government in recognition of the essential contribution and profound sacrifice which students had made to the move toward democrati-zation then in prospect, but it soon became clear to responsible officials that the parlous financial state of the national treasury (as well as the constraints of the structural adjustment program) would not permit the full implementa-tion of its terms.

The AEEM contended, with some justification, that in a country as poor as Mali, schooling was dependent upon state subventions and scholarship aid. But they never seemed prepared to explore the economic implications of their demands for the educational system as a whole. Since independence, disproportionate amounts of national resources had been devoted to educat-

[48] The *Coopérative culturelle d'édition et de diffusion Jamana* was created in 1986 under the lead-ership of Alpha Oumar Konaré, the first president of the Malian Third Republic. In 1993 the cooperative consisted of 100 members. Jamana was involved in numerous pub-lishing activities, including *Les Echos*, which in 1989 was the first independent newspaper to appear during the regime of Moussa Traoré. It was a target of violence because of its association with President Konaré, and probably because of the critical editorial policy of *Les Echos* toward the radicalization of the student movement. See *Les Echos*, 9 April 1993.

ing the tiny percentage of youth who successfully reached secondary and advanced levels of education. Table 5.1 illustrates the fact that in the late 1980s, almost 60 per cent of the Ministry of National Education (MEN) budget was allocated to secondary and higher education students (there was no university in Mali at this time), although they represented only 19 per cent of the total school population.[49]

Table 5.1. PERCENTAGES OF ENROLMENTS
VERSUS BUDGET ALLOCATIONS

	% of total enrolments	% of MEN budget allocation
Primary School (years 1 – 6)	81	35
Secondary School (years 7-12)	17	38
Higher Education	2	19

The bulk of secondary and higher education expenditure was allocated to scholarship aid. For example, in 1992-3, 70 per cent of the higher education budget was devoted to scholarship aid and other student support, and only 30 per cent to personnel and maintenance.[50] One calculation attempted to demonstrate that if the amounts dispensed for scholarships were halved over five years, the savings could provide the financial means to more than double primary school enrolments.[51] The reader will recall that total school enrolments averaged less than 25 per cent of children of school age in the late 1980s.

One conclusion to be drawn from these statistics is that, taken as a group, secondary and higher education students in Mali represented a highly privileged, yet tiny, minority of the population. They were the fortunate few who had succeeded in a highly inefficient school system, and they were relatively well-off economically. Being a student was often more remunerative than having a job, the highest level of scholarship being more than double the minimum wage,[52] a situation that suggests that remaining a student as long as possible could become an attractive economic strategy, especially when there were so few jobs available for qualified graduates. And in fact, a sustained line of criticism against the radical student leadership had been that the longer they could disrupt the schools, the longer they could enjoy the benefits of their scholarships. A contrary argument advanced in support of the students was that they constituted a disadvantaged class for whom

[49] The statistics in the paragraph are taken from 'Projet de Consolidation', IDA-USAID, 19 Nov.-1 Dec. 1989. The remaining 8·per cent of expenditure went to administrative expenses and to state support for private schools, primarily subventions to Catholic schools.
[50] See *Le Républicain*, 9 Feb. 1994, p. 7.
[51] Nagognimé Urbain Dembelé in *Les Echos*, 13 Oct. 1993, p. 3.
[52] *Les Echos*, 18 June 1993, letter from Abdoul Traoré dit Diop, p. 5.

scholarships were a matter of survival. This may well have been true for students who came from very poor families, but both arguments lead to a similar conclusion: that high on the political agenda of the AEEM was the retention of privileged access to a shrinking national resource in the form of state scholarships.

The preceding discussion illustrates that the impact of French-language schooling in Mali has been both vastly uneven and deeply ambiguous. For the most part, schooling had not been seen by rural populations to serve their interests, whereas urban populations, despite the despairing prospects of unemployment faced by most school graduates, often seemed to see no alternative to sending their children to school; schooling was an investment they could ill afford not to make. By the late 1980s, the curious situation arose that one of the most tangible benefits of schooling was simply to be a student and to receive scholarship aid! The private employment sector was not expanding; in 1987 it was estimated that as many as 94 per cent of salaried employees in the country were still working in the civil service. In effect, the budget of the Ministry of National Education was being expended in order to reproduce the state bureaucracy. It is for these kinds of reasons that schooling in Mali became such a highly politicized domain; access to it was severely limited while the rewards it offered, while shrinking in availability, could nonetheless be great. Consequently, students have proven to be one of the most astutely politically conscious groups in Mali, very ready to protect their interests at any sign of erosion in their favored position.

Of course, students as a group cannot justifiably be described as simply self-interested. But a clear understanding of where their interests lay in this political context further illustrates the ambiguities which pervaded their situation. Cheick Oumar Diarrah's adulation for the students who took action in 1980 was repeated by many others in 1991: he praised them for their 'fearlessness, their inflexible will, their capacity for sacrifice, their love of social justice and freedom, which had given to Africa and to the world a superb example of courage in their struggle against an authoritarian régime.'[53] But even if this evaluation of student action is justified within a specific political context, neither such rhetoric nor such courageous deeds should be allowed to obscure the fact that the interests of students were not necessarily shared by the vast majority of the population, especially the rural population. Such contradictions are at the core of the political reality of schooling and its impact.

Schooling, therefore, is not the apolitical institution which official policy and developmentalist rhetoric often imply that it is. During the colonial period, the French never seriously attempted to hide the political aims of their educational policies; during the postcolonial period, the universalist ideology of education captured the official imagination to such an extent that government officials were unable to assess the real social and political impact that schooling (or its absence) was having on the society.

[53] Cheick Oumar Diarrah, *Mali. Bilan d'une gestion désastreuse*, p. 55.

Nowhere was this blindness to reality more evident than over the Islamic médersas which, as already mentioned, were officially invisible during the first two decades of independence; médersas were not recognized as teaching institutions and were subsumed to the administrative authority of the Section des Affaires Religieuse of the Ministry of the Interior, and official policy was designed to avoid any intervention in 'things Islamic' unless there was a clear threat to public order. Yet, during this period of official 'blindness', médersa enrolments expanded at something like twice the rate of the state schools!

Islamic resurgence and the materialization of Islam

The rapid expansion of the Islamic médersas between 1960 and 1980 poses two central questions for exploration: what were the root causes of this expansion during this period of time, and what was its significance in terms of power relations in the postcolony? The remainder of this book is devoted to exploring these questions and the complex range of issues raised by them. But first, we should explore two significant subsidiary questions. By what process were the médersas brought into public and official view? And why were they greeted with profound official hostility?

That such hostility was widespread is evident in the following statement, contained in one of the first official reports into the Islamic médersas, published in the early 1980s:

The médersa teacher has undergone a pedagogical training given by the Muslim League, of which he is a committed adept and active member. ... If the *marabout* is a good Muslim who undergoes a solitary struggle with the sole aim of disseminating knowledge of the Qur'an, the médersa teacher is affiliated with a highly structured expansionist sect whose activities extend well beyond the borders of our country. The curriculum of the médersa leaves no doubt about the objective of his [political] program.[54]

The views expressed here are representative of a pervasive and influential line of secularist thought in the Ministry of National Education and in the administration more generally. The quotation illustrates several important points. First, it is based on misinformation: in fact, relatively few médersa teachers would have had any formal association with an international Islamic organization, much less have been trained by one. More significantly, it clearly reflects the political contours of much official thinking about schooling, which was based on the unexamined premise that French-language schooling was apolitical, whereas médersa education posed a potential political threat. But perhaps the most intriguing aspect of the quotation is the fact that its content is politically symmetrical with criticisms made by those who felt distanced from, or threatened by, French-language schooling. Change the wording slightly, and one could imagine a similar statement from a Malian

---

[54] Schools inspector quoted in 'Médersa au Mali. Documents d'informations', Direction de l'Enseignement Fondamental, 1983-4., II, p. 25.

peasant or a committed Muslim criticizing western-oriented secular education. What could be a more 'highly structured expansionist sect' than French-language schooling which, according to some, produced those 'vile government agents' who acted as the vectors of oppressive government power in rural areas, and which allegedly transformed Muslim children into amoral unbelievers and delinquents?

There were some government officials who thought the médersas could serve the cause of 'national development', but only if the dangers they posed were strictly limited by government controls.

What must concern us above everything else is the future of the hundreds of thousands of young Malians who are likely to attend the médersas and Qur'anic schools in the near future, given the rapid expansion of Islamization. These children expect us to offer them the opportunity to become enlightened Muslims, effective citizens [*des citoyens à part entière*], effective producers and agents of national development, not blind and dangerously fanaticized masses who will be even more susceptible to exploitation.

And so, just as it is appropriate to assist and encourage those teachers and founders of schools who present the required guarantees for [providing] a valid education, so it is necessary legally to prohibit the incompetents and swindlers from cheating the people.[55]

Both these quotations recall French colonial perceptions about Islam. The fears expressed about 'fanaticism' and the possible threat of international Islamic political influence could have been lifted from the colonial discourse. Other terms have changed, even if their political import remained consistent; 'contributing to national development' has been substituted for 'loyalty to the French colonial project' as the all-encompassing normative referent for formulating official policy. But some new terms have been introduced into the discourse which reflect the political dynamics of the postcolony; reference to swindlers and cheats is characteristic of discourse generated in a clientelist political environment which thrives on special favors, breeds corruption, and nurtures contempt for those with whom one is not allied politically.

More fundamentally, these critical statements seem to reveal the suspicion among some that the success of the médersas might represent a form of popular dissent from the projects of the state. They reflect a fear that the médersas might produce schooled adults who might not easily be subjected to government authority, or perhaps more specifically, to the constraints imposed by those who controlled the state bureaucracy. And indeed, the problem was real, not because the médersa constituencies were likely to make a direct claim for political power in the form of an Islamic state, something virtually never proposed in the Malian context,[56] but because the médersas

[55] 'Rapport du Comité Restreint au Conseil Supérieure de l'Education Nationale sur les médersas et les écoles coraniques en République du Mali' in *ibid.*, III, 54.
[56] Never proposed but often suspected as a hidden agenda. See S. Bagayogo, 'L'état au Mali', p. 117, where he refers to the 'wind of fundamentalism [*intégrisme*]' blowing across

appealed predominantly to those populations who were largely marginalized from or opted out of the state system of French-language schooling, either due to social condition (such as the peasantry) or by conscious choice (such as those committed Muslims who viewed French-language education as anathema).

This occupation of marginal space, or dissent from the national educational project, is an example of what Jean-François Bayart has described as 'popular modes of political action', or a 'politics from below', which can take diverse forms but does not aim at directly challenging state power:

> ... revolts, refusal to grow certain crops or underproductivity, strikes, abstention from elections, migrations, recourse to the sacred, contraband, the blossoming of what is often called the informal economic sector, so-called spontaneous habitations, individual or collective escapisms, the wide circulation of news which is not controlled by official media, delinquency, undermining the authorities [*le pouvoir*] with biting humor or by alluding to transcendent [powers] of a religious or messianic nature, contentious participation in the structures of political control ...[57]

As will become evident in the chapters that follow, the médersa directors at no time sought political power as such, but they did attempt to maintain their autonomy, and they did so in the name of Islam. Criticisms about educational standards in the médersas, or moves by government to control them, were often condemned as attacks on Islam, as if whatever was done in the name of Islam should automatically be exempt from critical scrutiny, from the government or anyone else. This tactic, of course, was the reverse side of the coin of secularism; the médersa directors had long enjoyed the benefits of official neglect, and they did not intend to surrender them without a struggle. Many did indeed see themselves as fulfilling a religious duty by educating young Muslims, and they did not understand why government should suddenly take an interest in their activities, which also constituted their means of livelihood. And so from the 1980s the médersas became a focus of political tension.

These events unfolded in a broader context of increasing public and official interest in (and growing concern about) Islam and Islamic affairs resulting from various local and international developments. During the 1970s the Malian religious landscape was radically transformed; public space, especially urban space, was increasingly 'Islamized' as a result of an explosive growth in the Islamic institutional infrastructure. The number of médersas was increasing rapidly, and some of them were impressive, purpose-built, modern structures. But the most visible sign of these changes was in the construction,

the country. See also an analysis of a debate about the relationship of Islam to the state which appeared in the mid-1980s in several issues of *Jamana. Revue culturelle malienne* in L. Brenner, 'La culture arabo-islamique au Mali' in René Otayek (ed.), *Le Radicalisme islamique en Afrique subsaharienne. Da'wa, arabisation et critique de l'Occident* (Paris: Karthala, 1993), pp. 182ff.

[57] Bayart, *L'état en Afrique*, pp. 258-9.

not of médersas (many of which are quite non-descript) but of new and often opulent mosques. Between 1968 and 1983 the number of mosques in Bamako increased from 77 to 203.[58] The rate of construction was dramatically higher in the rapidly growing outskirts of the capital. In Commune I, on the eastern side of the city, 34 new mosques were built (or work on them was begun) between 1974 and 1987; during the same period the population of the commune more than doubled, while the population of the entire city of Bamako increased by one third.[59] The creation of Friday mosques experienced a similar rapid proliferation. In 1968 there was only one, the *Grande Mosquée*, located in the center of Bamako; in 1986 there were 41.[60]

The pattern of urban Islamization, and of the Islamization of urban space, was in part a continuation of the process of Islamization that had been underway since the colonial period. As we have already seen, due primarily to the activities of the largely Muslim commercial networks, West African towns and cities became the foci of both Islamic expansion and innovative ('reformist') Islamic thought during the colonial period. As the urban population burgeoned in the postcolonial period, Muslim infrastructures became one of the most effective conduits of social integration for the rural populations moving to the cities. Several of the mosques built in Commune I during the 1970s and 80s were established to meet the needs of formerly non-Muslim communities. According to one observer, not to be seen to practice Islam in Bamako became 'a sign of dishonour'.[61] Etienne Gérard has remarked on the rural impact of this urban Islamization; he found that the rapid Islamization which accompanied the social dislocation resulting from the construction of the Sélingué dam, south of Bamako, was reinforced by the local image of Bamako as a centre of progress and civilization, 'the seat of money, political power and of Islam'.[62] To become Muslim was, in a sense, to become urbane and 'modern'.

The progress of Islamization had been slowed neither by French colonial policy, nor the secularist ideology of the Keita régime. Following the *coup d'état* of 1968 the new military government adopted what has been described as a

---

[58] Fodé Doumbia, 'Les mosquées à Bamako', *Jamana*, no. 13 (May-June 1987), p. 36.
[59] The population of Commune I increased from 51,588 in 1976 to 122,513 in 1987; during the same period, the population of Bamako increased from 419,239 to 646,163. See Recensement Général de la Population et de l'Habitat (du 1er au 14 avril 1987). Population Urbaine (Résultats Provisoires), July 1987. The data on mosque construction is derived from a survey conducted by the author in 1991 on the history of mosques, Qur'anic schools and médersas in Commune I, which is discussed in the next chapter.
[60] Fodé Doumbia, 'Les mosquées à Bamako', p. 34.
[61] Fodé Doumbia, 'La répartition géographique des établissements du culte musulman dans le district de Bamako', (Mémoire de fin d'études, l'ENSup, Bamako, 1984), p. 24. For a detailed resumé of this mémoire, see Jean-Louis Triaud (after Fodé Doumbia). 'Bamako, la ville aux deux cents mosquées,' ou la victoire du 'secteur informel' islamique', *ISASS*, no. 2 (1988), pp. 166-77.
[62] Gérard, 'L'école déclassée', p. 529.

'laisser faire, laisser passer'[63] attitude to Islamic affairs. This new policy (or non-policy?) coincided with the 1973 Arab oil boom. Petro-dollars began to flow into Mali, as into other parts of the world, in order to finance both private projects, such as the construction of médersas and mosques, and public ones, such as development projects. By the end of the decade, mosques were said to be 'sprouting like mushrooms' in Bamako, as confirmed by the figures cited above.

It has been calculated that during the decade 1973-83, well over $600 million was lent or given to the Malian government by several Arab countries[64] and by the Islamic Development Bank, the Arab Bank for Economic Development in Africa, and the Organisation of the Islamic Conference.[65] Although relatively few of the projects financed in this manner could be interpreted as having a specifically Islamic objective,[66] such official aid was looked upon by some with suspicion as a possible conduit for increasing external Islamic influence on the country. Such concerns were only reinforced by the success of the Islamic Revolution in Iran in 1979.

Of perhaps widespread concern was the money which changed hands privately between Arab or Muslim donors and local recipients, and which went to build many of the new mosques and médersas. Most persons responsible for the construction of such establishments, many of which were quite ostentatious in style, were very careful not to disclose their financial affairs in public, thus fueling speculation about precisely how much money was received, where it came from, and how it was expended. The following, mildly candid, disclosure was quite unusual:

> We receive assistance from certain wealthy merchants in the city; we also organize collections within our *quartier*, although clearly this is insufficient. All the mosques that are built in a style similar to our own are financed by Arab funds. We do not obtain this aid through the Government, because it is not an Arab government that gives it to us. These are private donations that are the fruit of personal relationships.[67]

---

[63] *Ibid.*, pp. 116-17. See also Alliman Mahamane, 'Le mouvement wahhabite', which claims that the military government ignored the rapid increase in mosque construction so long as public order was not disturbed.

[64] Qatar, Kuwait, Algeria, Iraq, Libya, Saudi Arabia, and United Arab Emirates.

[65] Ousmane Oula, 'Pouvoir et religion (cas de l'Islam au Mali)', (Mémoire de fin d'études, l'ENSup, Bamako, 1984).

[66] Among these was a grant to transform the *Centre de Documentation et de Recherche Historique Ahmed Baba* (Tombouctou) into an *Institut régional d'études islamiques*. This center was originally established by a grant from UNESCO for the collection and preservation of Arabic manuscripts in West Africa. In fact, the center never did become a religious studies institute. The Central Mosque in Bamako was built with funds donated by Saudi Arabia, and what was perhaps the most imposing new Islamic structure in Bamako when it opened in 1987, the *Centre Culturel Islamique* was built with donations from Libya and the United Arab Emirates. The center complex includes a médersa, a medical centre, a sports centre, and a mosque.

[67] Fodé Doumbia, 'La répartition géographique', p. 50.

This person went on to explain that the bulk of donations for the mosque had come from the relative of a Saudi diplomat and 'a Kuwaiti friend'. Building costs had now reached something like 70,000 French francs, he continued, exceeding the original estimates, although this did not seem to pose a problem for the mosque committee since gifts received already exceeded 74,000 French francs, not counting the 'substantial' Kuwaiti contribution. Judging from other available information, however, it would seem that this mosque was being built at a bargain price! Fodé Doumbia has estimated the total cost of 75 mosques constructed in Bamako during this period to have been 3,445,688 French francs, or about 460,000 French francs per mosque.[68]

Donations from Muslim benefactors, both public and private, thus began to play a significant role in the Malian political economy that ultimately contributed to shifts in policy. Muslim (especially Arab Muslim) oil producing states were apparently willing to share their new found wealth with other Muslim states through grants and loans. At the same time, private funds began to flow through clientelist networks that extended beyond the national borders and, perhaps more significantly, which often operated outside the direct control of the higher echelons of the state bureaucracy and *le Pouvoir*. Whereas some Muslim merchants and religious figures used their connections with international Muslim benefactors to initiate or enhance their relationships with representatives of the state, it is also true that a concern to control the flow of these new sources of money was a major factor which influenced the government to modify its Islamic policies.

Reorientation of policy was also encouraged by internal causes. The postcolonial situation had not only quickened the pace of Islamization generally, it had also served to heighten existing political conflicts among Muslims. Tensions between Wahhabis and 'traditionalists' had by no means disappeared. The reader will recall the severe violence which had erupted in 1957 when the Wahhabis had attempted to open their first mosque in Bamako. Similar though less severe incidents were repeated in many towns in subsequent years as the Wahhabis sought to give material expression to their doctrinal identity in the form of mosques; by 1984 there were 28 Wahhabi mosques in Bamako.[69] In the *quartier* of Badalabougou, just south of the Niger River in Bamako, Wahhabi and 'traditionalist' congregations built opulent new mosques literally within yards of each other; this pattern of symbolic confrontation was repeated across the city, even if in a less extravagant and less costly manner.[70]

The discourse that surrounded this 'battle of the mosques' reflected not only internal doctrinal conflict between Wahhabi and 'traditionalist' tendencies, but also the deep social fissures which were emerging at the time. No aspect

[68] Fodé Doumbia, 'Les mosquées à Bamako', p. 35.

[69] *Ibid.*, p. 33.

[70] At least four of the new mosques in Bamako's Commune I were built as the direct result of conflicts.

of these developments escaped comment and criticism. Some Muslim scholars condemned the multiplication of Friday mosques as contravening the precepts of Islamic law. Others claimed that the proliferation of mosques divided the Muslim community, although those who built them often defended their actions in the name of Muslim unity. One Muslim scholar was quoted as saying that there were too many mosques in Bamako, and that their proliferation, far from denoting religious fervor, was 'a sign of misunderstanding and selfishness'.[71] This harsh judgment seems to have been borne out by many of the justifications offered for building mosques so closely to one another in Bamako:

> 'The imam over there is not suitable.'
> 'We are not the same, because they are Wahhabis'.
> 'The man who built this mosque wants to become the chief of the quartier'.
> 'These people built their mosque because they are rich.'[72]

Critics of this wave of mosque-building raised questions about why the economic windfall provided by the oil boom was not being directed toward assuaging the fundamental social and economic needs of the society. One such critic wrote:

The spiritual formation of the Malian population is dependent first and foremost on its survival. As the adage says, 'A hungry stomach has no ears'. Malians are more in need of employment, regular salaries, housing and food than mosques, médersas and an Islamic Cultural Center.[73]

Another critic asked whether it was not possible

... to make our Muslim leaders more sensitive to their responsibilities so that they slow down the multiplication of mosques in favor of health centers. The *jama* (people) are ill, and they are not unaware that, while praying is a good thing, so is sound health.[74]

As if in response to this question, someone who was asked directly why the Muslim community did not collect the *zakat* for purposes of social welfare, replied:

... right now any attempt to sensitize Malian public opinion [to the need for social welfare] would be futile because we are living through a period when people trust one another less and less.[75]

As a result of this intensification of Islamic activity, and in an effort to both control and redirect the political energy generated by it, the government decided to intervene directly in Islamic affairs with the creation, in 1980, of the *Association Malienne pour l'Unité et le Progrès de l'Islam* (AMUPI). The creation of

[71] Fodé Doumbia, 'La répartition géographique', p. 79.

[72] *Ibid.*, p. 85.

[73] Adama Traoré, *Jamana*, no. 7 (1986), p. 3.

[74] Sory Ibrahim Touré, *Jamana*, no. 5 (1985) p. 3.

[75] Fodé Doumbia, 'La répartition géographique', p. 83. The *zakat* is an alms payment prescribed by Muslim law that is collected for the benefit of the Muslim poor.

AMUPI was an intergral part of the corporatist state now being constructed by the recently established single party, the UDPM. The UNJM, created during this period with the intention of controlling youth and especially student activities, was discussed above. The *Union Nationale des Femmes Maliennes* (UNFM) and the *Union Nationale des Travailleurs du Mali* (UNTM) were also set up with similar aims of containing political activity and controlling the formation of public opinion among these social groups.

Such corporatist arrangements were an effective way to maintain control and extend influence in a clientelist political structure. The organizational structure of AMUPI reflected precisely that of the UDPM, and all office holders, from the National Executive down to regional and often local levels, were hand-picked, presumably by government or Party leaders, in a manner designed to balance what had come to be known as the '*deux tendances*', the Wahhabi and 'traditionalist' factions. The National Executive of AMUPI consequently included some rather extraordinary combinations of Muslim personalities. For example, al-Hajj Oumar Ly, a man of strong 'traditionalist' credentials, was appointed National President; he had been associated with Hampâté Bâ in the counter-reform movement as assistant Secretary-General of *Jam'iyyat al-murshidin* and as the director of the counter-reform school opened in Kayes in the 1950s (see Chapter 3). The Secretary General was none other than Muhammad Fodé Keita, a man of equally strong 'Wahhabi' credentials and one of the founders of the first Islamic médersa in Bamako.

The political trade-off which was negotiated in these circumstances was eminently clientelist: the leaders of AMUPI would hopefully be seen to occupy positions of considerable prestige within the Malian Muslim community and would be expected to find a way to subdue the continuing conflict among Muslims, as well as to regulate the proliferation of mosques and médersas. The existence of a national Muslim organization was also deemed very important for attracting Muslim financial contributions and aid, which the AMUPI leadership would help to facilitate; this role could, of course, give them access to such funds. Predictably, accusations of diversion of AMUPI funds to personal ends were made against officials at all levels of the organizational structure;[76] even if these allegations were difficult to confirm, there was much cause for suspicion. Between May 1980 and August 1987, AMUPI officially declared a total income of 65,213,597 francs CFA. Of this, 11,551,865 francs CFA was collected within Mali from donations and the sale of membership cards, and 53,661,532 francs CFA was received from external donors, including the World Islamic League of Mecca, the Islamic *Da'wa* of Libya, and the government of Egypt, as well as a number of private donations from Kuwait (over 14,000,000 francs CFA), which were designated for building an AMUPI headquarters. Total expenditure for the same period was 34,618,982 francs CFA, over half of which was expended on salaries and travel costs both

---

[76] A number of alleged incidents of misappropriation of funds were recorded during field research, none of which could be independently confirmed, of course.

within and outside Mali.[77] No record exists, of course, of any private financial arrangements that may have been facilitated through AMUPI connections.

The clientelist foundations upon which AMUPI was established were therefore clear: taking up an official position in AMUPI (which also implied at least tacit endorsement of the UDPM) could generate both personal prestige and real income for those who were willing to take on the task of acting as intermediaries between agents of the state and the Muslim community (or Muslim communities). The official aims of AMUPI, as stated in Article 4 of their *Statuts*, were quite different, of course:

(*a*) to develop and reinforce Unity, and relationships of Islamic brotherhood and solidarity, among all Muslims of both sexes in conformity with the prescriptions of the Holy Qur'an, in order to permit them to support one another in perfecting their religious education.

(*b*) to employ modern methods of information, education and pedagogy to achieve this aim.

(*c*) to create and develop libraries, and to provide localities for the use of the Association, and to found and manage schools.

(*d*) to rid Islam of all noxious influences and corrupt practices and to return it to its original purity.

(*e*) to assist students in obtaining scholarships to further their studies or for training courses and to send them wherever they will be able to complete their education.

Other language in the *Statuts* sought to highlight the 'religious' as opposed to the 'political' aims of the organization. Article 5 states: 'The Association, which is strictly religious, rejects any political preoccupation foreign to Islam.' And Article 7: 'The activities of the Association are essentially religious and educational; AMUPI will labor for the consolidation of Islamic Unity and work for the awakening of Islamic culture and consciousness among all Muslims.'

From the moment of its creation, AMUPI was plagued by the political tensions generated by the contradictions between its announced public aims and its internal clientelist structure, by the profound factionalism which divided Muslims, and by the parlous social conditions then prevailing in Malian society. In addition, AMUPI was given, and accepted, a remit which it could not possibly fulfill because it was not given the means to do so. To be fair, it was no small accomplishment that the organization actually survived at all, so profound were the divisions that pervaded the National Executive. Oumar Ly was quite candid about these problems in his *Rapport d'activités* during AMUPI's constitutive congress in 1987, and about his own personal doubts that the association would hold together given its 'stormy and disappointing' early meetings resulting from the 'spirit of factionalism' (*esprit de*

---

[77] 'Rapport financier' in 'Programme et textes de base', Congrès Constitutif, AMUPI, Nov. 1987, Bamako.

tendance) which prevailed in them. He had much to say about Muslim unity, knowing full well that, to the extent that it existed, it was very tenuous indeed. Most observers were also fully aware that the achievement of such unity, even if it might bring a degree of much-desired social harmony, was very much in the interests of the UDPM and *le Pouvoir*, for whose political purposes AMUPI had been created. Therefore, the claim that AMUPI renounced political activities was accepted by virtually no one, and the organization was consistently viewed and often disparaged as an arm of government.

In his *Rapport d'activités* Oumar Ly was at pains to deny any intervention in AMUPI affairs by government. He did admit that Moussa Traoré had supported the formation of the organization; what Ly did not say, but which everyone knew, was that under the prevailing political conditions such an organization could not exist wihout the express approval of Traoré. Still, according to Oumar Ly, the role of the government in the formation of AMUPI had been limited to acting as a catalyst. 'Not only did [the government] not intervene at any level in the selection of AMUPI leaders, nothing subsequently had been done which could be interpreted as the kind of dependent relationship which exists between a department and its subordinate offices or between the Central Executive Office [of the UDPM] and the democratic organizations'.[78]

This statement was both true and not true. At the time of its creation, AMUPI had been given a kind of administrative remit to regulate mosques and the médersas but without any authority to act, except presumably through negotiation. A few years later, the government shifted the administration of the médersas from the Ministry of the Interior to the Ministry of National Education and began to intervene directly in their affairs, in effect by-passing AMUPI administratively, but effectively placing them in the middle of the resulting political imbroglio. (These developments will be analysed in Chapter 7.) Consequently, few persons viewed AMUPI as anything other than a political entity, either as an arm of government policy, or as a focus for advancing the interests of certain Muslim factions.

Furthermore, the Congress expressed its explicit gratitude to Moussa Traoré in the form of a special motion, which is an excellent example of the kind of public rhetoric produced in a clientelist single-party state:

– Considering: the determining role played by the Chief of State, General Moussa Traoré for the Unity and the Progress of Islam in Mali;
– Considering: the special attention he has never ceased to accord to the religious communities of Mali;
– Considering: the mandate that he gave to the Minister of Territorial Administration and of Basic Development [the Ministry of the Interior] which led the Muslim community to a consensus which permitted the birth of AMUPI.

---

[78] Discours au Congrès constitutif de l'AMUPI par El Hadj Oumar Ly, Bamako, Nov. 1987. 'Democratic organizations' was the current euphemism employed to refer to the Party and the various associations, like AMUPI, which it had created.

– The Congress addresses to General Moussa Traoré, President of the Republic, Malian Chief of State, the expression of its deepest gratitude.[79]

This resolution, and the discourse surrounding the entire AMUPI episode, reminds one of Achille Mbembe's comments on public discourse in the postcolony:

What one says is neither what one thinks or does. What one does is neither what one thinks or says. One talks about what one would never do, and one does what one would never talk about. In other words, there is no public discourse about what is actually done, and public discourse describes things that have never taken place. The one camouflages the other and expresses itself in terms of its own opposite.[80]

The pertinence of this observation is confirmed by the fact that AMUPI's Constitutive Congress occurred in November 1987, at the height of the confrontation between médersa directors and the government over the decision to absorb the médersas administratively into the Ministry of National Education and to impose a new curriculum on them (see Chapter 7). This issue was not on the formal agenda of the Congress despite the fact that AMUPI was officially recognized as 'respresentative' for the médersas in all their dealings with the Ministry! This fact illustrates the many contradictions which pervaded AMUPI's creation and subsequent functioning, which in turn provide a good example of the complex ways in which 'Islamic issues' interpenetrated and interacted with broader social and political issues in the postcolony, and of how they were expressed or suppressed in the prevailing political environment.

Whatever the objectives intended with the creation of AMUPI, and regardless of the political role its leaders did or did not play, the fact is that through this officially sanctioned Muslim organization, Muslims were formally accepted into the clientelist structures of Party and state where they were expected to speak and act *as Muslims*. In reality, however, they were rarely permitted to do so, and when they were, they were expected to limit their remarks to certain authorized themes. For example, 'unity' was a perfectly acceptable topic of discourse, the achievement of which was completely compatible with the UDPM project. AMUPI's contribution to unity was to be in the resolution of disputes, and especially in diminishing conflictual relations between Wahhabis and traditionalists, although these in reality were only symptoms of much deeper social divisions within the society which· derived from differences in wealth, schooling and social status. One political function of AMUPI was arguably to divert attention from these more profound problems by highlighting Wahhabi – traditionalist conflict. Similarly, AMUPI spokesmen could speak about 'progress', which fully conformed with the many developmentalist programs in which the government was engaged. They could not talk about 'politics', however, as their *Statuts* clearly stated.

[79] AMUPI. Programme et textes de base, Congrès Constitutif, Nov. 1987, Bamako.
[80] J.A. Mbembe, *Les jeunes*, p. 233.

The rules of this game were nowhere written down, nor could these 'guidelines' be found articulated in any government policy, but they were nonetheless effectively, if tacitly, enforced. Even when the government absorbed the médersas into the Ministry of Education, the médersa directors found it almost impossible to discuss Islamic education with ministry officials, a refusal that became the focus of their grievances and protests. It was almost as if Islam had been brought officially into the public arena in order better to marginalize it; so long as Muslims, and their institutions, remained semi-autonomous they were less subject to control. Integrated into the networks of power relations that were articulated through state and Party, Muslim institutions and Muslims themselves could be more effectively controlled.

It was extremely difficult to avoid being drawn into this game, even if one clearly understood the ultimate effects of playing it. Of course, the only players were those of already relatively privileged status who were fully versed in clientelist politics, even if they were neophytes in the game of the 'politics of the politicians'. And one might join the game for different reasons: in the expectation of personal gain, to enhance one's social status, or even for perfectly selfless reasons in the hope that one might actually 'do some good'. But in the 1980s, regardless of the omnipresent rhetoric to the contrary, the game was not about unity, progress, or even development, but about gaining access to power and wealth, and for many it was a very rough game.

Bayart has defined politics as a pluralistic contest to accumulate wealth, to manipulate hegemonic shared meanings, and to seek autonomous power.[81] This definition can be helpful in providing a framework for further analysis of the preceding discussion.

Let us begin by examining the pluralism of postcolonial Malian politics, which is perhaps the most complex factor to describe and to analyze because political contestation (as defined here) ranges over so many different categories of social difference. Much emphasis has been placed on the determining role of clientelism in the socio-political order in postcolonial Mali as an effective means for amassing and redistributing social and economic resources. Political competition and contestation among (and within) separate clientelist networks is common, since groups and individuals often compete to control the same resources, but a more salient theme in the present study is the contradiction between the ethos of personal reciprocity which is inherent to clientelism, and the ethos of interest group politics and institutional governance which is associated (at least ideologically) with the modern nation state. Here, the struggle to amass wealth coalesces with the politics of meanings.

[81] Jean-François Bayart, 'Le politique par le bas en Afrique noire. Questions de méthode' in J.-F. Bayart, A. Mbembe, C. Toulabor, *Le politique par le bas en Afrique noire* (Paris: Karthala, 1992), p. 47.

Although no one in Mali ever publicly advocates clientelism as a form of governance, neither does anyone doubt its fundamental political significance; and although governance is only ever represented publicly in terms of rule-governed national institutions, everyone knows that it has been pervaded almost completely by the ethos and practice of clientelism during the first 30 years of independence. Both the extreme radicalism of the US-RDA in the 1960s and the democratic movement of the early 1990s might arguably be interpreted in part as ideologically generated efforts to replace clientelist structures and with institutional forms of governance.

The overwhelming majority of those who participated actively in these movements received some form of contemporary schooling, most of them of course in French-language schools. We have also seen that success in schooling, especially French-language schooling, provided almost sole access to positions in the state bureaucracy as well as to the highest level of government and administration. These facts alone demonstrate the profound political implications of schooling as an institution which has created social difference in Mali and, especially during the first decades of independence, has provided a small minority of the population with access to a new means of gaining wealth (government jobs) and a new means to establish a dominant role in power relations through the exercise of bureaucratic authority. In other words, schooling was essential to the creation of new forms of power relations which depended primarily on literacy and other skills which could be obtained almost exclusively only in modernized schools.

However, if schooling contributed (at least theoretically) to the possibility of rule-based institutional forms of governance, clientelism continued to flourish and to define the contours of the real political economy. The 'schooled' incumbents in the state bureaucracy were absorbed into the clientelist networks and used their positions as conduits for amassing and redistributing wealth and influence. On all levels of government and administration, official business was often conducted 'unofficially' in transactions that ranged from small bribes for the completion of minor administrative matters to the granting of major contracts to wealthy businessmen. The boundaries between public and private interests were completely blurred, creating profound ambiguities and uncertainties about the nature of governance in postcolonial Mali, as reflected in the vagaries that characterized public perceptions of *le Pouvoir*. One could never be completely certain who was participating in *le Pouvoir* at any given time since it could include the (often anonymous) patrons and clients of those in government or the higher ranks of the state bureaucracy. The most notorious 'unofficial' participant in *le Pouvoir* after 1968 was the wife of Moussa Traoré, Mariam, who attained enormous wealth and influence and who by turns was widely respected, feared and hated.[82]

---

[82] For an excellent description of the complexities of this system, as well as a penetrating analysis of its social and cultural context, see Amselle, 'La corruption'.

Given the fact that the postcolonial socio-political order was fundamentally about amassing and redistributing wealth and influence, it is not surprising that matters of policy were not high on the political agenda during most of the thirty years of independence under consideration. The radicalism of the US-RDA had ended in dramatic failure, although aspects of this socialist ideology persisted in some quarters. The military regime of Moussa Traoré was concerned primarily to retain its grip on state power, and the creation of the single-party corporatist state of the UDPM was little more than a restructured expression of clientelism.

This absence of policy-making is relevant to understanding official attitudes to Islam. It does not seem that Moussa Traoré and his various governments ever purposefully abandoned secularism, as was charged especially following the creation of AMUPI and the formal recognition of the médersas. The available evidence suggests that no one in government ever seriously reflected on the matter from this perspective! The introduction of Muslim affairs into the public arena was a more gradual and natural process. In the first place, the overwhelming majority of persons in government and administration in postcolonial Mali were themselves Muslims, even if most of them were also French-language schooled. Furthermore, the Muslim presence by now was pervasive in Mali, especially in Bamako, and even the most ideologically fervent secularists rarely condemned Islam as such, a significant change from the attitudes of many French who combined their secularist politics with a deep animosity toward Islam. Islam was now more readily and openly accepted as integral to Malian culture.

On the other hand, the emergence of militant international Islamist movements in the 1970s and 1980s gave rise to considerable concern in secularist quarters, recalling French preoccupations about the political implications of Wahhabism in the 1950s. Critics also claimed that Muslims were gaining increasing political influence through their clientelist associations with *le Pouvoir*; most of the wealthiest merchants and businessmen in Mali were Muslim. These fears were deepened by the flow of money into the country as a result of the oil boom which helped to finance the rapid expansion of Muslim institutions, and which certainly contributed to the decision to establish AMUPI as a national Muslim organization.

These developments had profoundly political implications. Local Muslim constituencies were being reinvigorated with injections of new wealth and (as was evident from the 1980s) a rapidly expanding network of modernized Muslim schools, many of whose graduates would also aspire to enter the state bureaucracy. Through AMUPI, Muslims had also been given a legitimate political voice in the public arena.

Whereas debates about these developments in Mali centered on perceived threats to secularism versus the rights of Muslims to pursue their religion, in fact the underlying political issues were related to those signaled in Bayart's definition of politics which opened this discussion. Local Muslims now had access to new 'Muslim' wealth, which they were using to enhance Mali's Muslim institutional infrastructure, including the médersas, whose successful products might be expected to compete for social and political recognition with their French-language schooled compatriots. The more alarmist critics of these developments expressed fears of 'fundamentalism' and of the danger of a possible demand for the establishment of a Muslim state. In fact, the materialization of Islam and the expansion of the médersas was rooted much more in grass roots social change than in national politics, which was largely irrelevant to the interests of most of the médersa constituencies, as will be demonstrated in the next chapter.

The oil boom had enabled certain Muslims to extend their clientelist relationships beyond Mali's borders to tap a new resource of wealth that not only benefitted them personally, but also flowed through them into the broader Muslim community. This new source of wealth shifted the political balance in Mali, not only because it was Muslim money for ostensibly Muslim projects, but simply because it was new money! This development was a classic case of what Bayart calls extraversion, the mobilization of external resources to reinforce internal positions of power.[83] According to Bayart, schooling has been a major resource of extraversion in twentieth-century Africa, an assertion that is fully supported by the situation in Mali where French-language schooling has been the single most powerful force for creating social and economic difference. However, in the 1970s and 1980s the near monopoly of modernized schooling enjoyed by French-language schools was threatened by the rapid expansion of the médersas. The influx of new money created the promise of new opportunities and attracted new 'human resources' in the form of students, teachers and aspiring directors to the médersa enterprise, changes which contributed to the new political tensions which were beginning to emerge around 'Islam'.

---

[83] See *L'Etat en Afrique*, pp. 41ff, 104ff and *passim*.

6

THE DYNAMICS OF MEDERSA SCHOOLING

The expansion of the médersa network

The médersa network of schools expanded at about twice the rate of the state schools in postcolonial Mali.[1] No records, either official or unofficial, exist which document this rapid expansion, and even after the first official statistics began to appear in the early 1980s, they have been incomplete and inaccurate for several reasons. Firstly, the nature of the phenomenon itself, as something of a grass-roots movement, has meant that médersas have appeared and disappeared with great frequency as young (and sometimes, not so young) educational entrepreneurs have attempted to establish their own educational enterprises. Secondly, from the mid-1980s, when official policy toward the médersas became more firmly formulated, the Ministry of National Education began to list only formally 'recognized' médersas, that is, those which fulfilled newly promulgated standards of operation, including such matters as the physical facilities offered, number and training of teachers, and most importantly, an agreement to adopt the new government-approved curriculum. In fact, 'recognition' depended almost exclusively on the adoption of the ministry's newly distributed curriculum, which was strongly resisted by some directors, especially by Saada Oumar Touré in Segu. The political confrontation that surrounded this issue meant that some médersas were eliminated from the census for political reasons, which was certainly the case for the 1987 statistics. However, médersas which did not achieve official 'recognition', for whatever reasons, are nowhere listed, with the result that there is no official record of the full range of médersa activity, including those aspiring to be 'recognized', and indeed, those who positively did not wish to be 'recognized'. Finally, the sheer inefficiency of the educational inspectorate meant that many médersas simply escaped detection; the wide variations in numbers of schools listed from year to year suggests uneven census coverage.

These variations in census coverage can be illustrated by a survey of médersas in Bamako's Commune I, carried out in 1991.[2] The base line of the survey was taken from a list of médersas compiled by the local section of

[1] See above, Chapter 5, note 8.
[2] This survey was carried out with the assistance of Malik Almamy Yattara under the auspices of the Islam in Modern Africa Project, SOAS; the aim of the survey was to explore the origins and current operation of mosques, médersas and Qur'anic schools in the administrative district of Commune I in Bamako.

AMUPI, which named 36 médersas in 1988. The 1991 survey confirmed the existence of 27 médersas by actually visiting them and interviewing their directors or other teachers. In the same year, the Ministry of National Education's *Rapport de rentrée des médersas* (enrolment reports submitted at the beginning of the school year) named only 17 médersas in Commune I, of which only six appeared on the same ministry's *Liste de médersas reconnues* (i.e. 'officially recognized' médersas).[3]

Table 6.1 provides published census figures for the médersas through 1992. The annual fluctuations in these figures further illustrate their questionable reliability. The wide disparity between the 1991 figures provided respectively by CPLA (*Centre pour la Promotion de la Langue Arabe*), and the ministry is of particular interest in this regard. CPLA·is a department within the ministry; their offices and those of the statistics department are only a few yards apart across a courtyard. And yet, the two offices neither cooperated nor communicated about their respective activities; this semi-autonomous attitude among departments within the same ministry, combined on occasion with a definitive refusal to share information, was characteristic of the bureaucratic culture of Mali in the 1980s.

Table 6.1. MÉDERSA ENROLMENTS

	Total médersas	Total enrolments	Source
1981	170	41,957	MEN[1]
1983	288	62,203	MEN[2]
1987	273	58,260	CPLA[3]
1989	318	67,449	CPLA[4]
1990	354	62,317	CPLA[5]
1991	277	60,210	CPLA[6]
	379	64,957	MEN[7]
1992	358	66,348	UNICEF[8]

[1]Ministère de l'Education Nationale, 'Médersa au Mali. Documents d'informations', 3 vols (Direction de l'Enseignement Fondamental, 1983-4), I, p. 2. These statistics, gathered by the Ministry of the Interior, represent the findings of the first official enquiry into médersas in postcolonial Mali.
[2]*Ibid.*, II, p. 101.
[3]'Situation des médersas au Mali, 1986-7'.
[4]'Renseignements statistiques sur les médersas (1988-89)'.
[5]'Renseignements statistiques sur les médersas (1989-90)'.
[6]'L'enseignement arabo-islamique dans le système éducatif du Mali', 1991.
[7]Ministère le l'Education Nationale, *Annuaire des statistiques scolaires, 1990-1991*.
[8]UNICEF, 'Projet: Promotion de l'enseignement dans les médersas', 1992. The source for these figures is not given, however, other statistics cited in this document are taken from the 1991 CIPLA document and it is possible these figures were also provided by CPLA.

---

[3] The 'Liste de médersas reconnues' was drawn up by the Bureau des Projets in the Ministry of National Education to indicate which médersas could apply for aid under the *4ème Projet Education*, a major international aid intervention in primary education in Mali, which is discussed in Chapter 7.

UNICEF estimated that during the 1990-1 school year, médersa students represented a total of 19.1 per cent of the total number of children in school in Mali; during the same year, only 30 per cent of school-age children were enrolled in schools.[4] Of course, if the basic statistics are unreliable, then such percentages cannot be reliable either; estimates of the proportion of médersa enrolments ranged from about 15 to 25 per cent during the 1980s. However, whatever the precise percentage, enrolments were not insignificant, and one motivation for officially recognizing the médersas as educational institutions in 1985 was the indisputable evidence of their contribution to the schooling of Malian children. Indeed, the first official study of the Malian médersas in 1983 argued that when one grouped enrolments in the primary schools, the médersas, and the Qur'anic schools together, the percentage of children receiving schooling in Mali rose from 22 to 30 per cent.[5] If reliable statistics about médersa enrolments were difficult to establish, one can only wonder at how the Qur'anic school figures were acquired! In any case, subsequent published statistics have never included Qur'anic schools as educational institutions.

The causes for the expansion of the médersa network were many and complex. Of course, the original impetus of the first pioneers of the médersas, which we have traced in earlier chapters, remained. Their commitment to developing a modernized form of Islamic education that could respond to the changing conditions of the twentieth century was shared by many of those founders of médersas who have followed in their footsteps. And, indeed, the strong religious commitment expressed by the early médersa pioneers has also persisted, and is usually stated by most persons associated with the médersas as the primary cause for both setting them up and sending one's children to them.

However the postcolonial social and political environment also profoundly affected the evolution of the médersa network in that the founders of new médersas had to respond to the conditions that were created by each successive political regime. The first fillips to expansion came from the socialist government of the US-RDA, under the leadership of Modibo Keita. It will be recalled from the discussion in Chapter 3, that between October 1958 and September 1960, when the future Mali existed as the République Soudanaise, the US-RDA had made a number of concessions to its Wahhabi political allies. The Bamako médersa had been allowed to reopen under the direction of the *Union Culturelle Musulmane* and to incorporate secular subjects into its curriculum; a number of other médersas had also been allowed to open. During the 1960s, after the creation of the République du Mali and after the US-RDA had taken a more radical turn, the alliance with the Wahhabis dissolved, and the forces of secularism came to the fore in the party. However, the situation remained somewhat ambiguous with regard to the médersas because, in spite of the pressures towards secularism, there was also support for the teaching of Arabic language,

---

[4] UNICEF, 'Projet: Promotion de l'enseignement dans les médersas', 1992
[5] 'Médersa au Mali', III, p. 2.

which was considered by many in the US-RDA to be a language both of African nationalism and of pan-African unity. Consequently, the teaching of Arabic (as well as English) was encouraged in Mali's schools, and the Educational Reform of 1962 made specific reference to médersas, which were defined in Article 10 as 'primary schools [*écoles fondamentales*] in which the study of Arabic begins from the first year.'[6]

This definition perhaps reflected the ambiguities and tensions present within the US-RDA and in fact was full of foreboding for the Islamic médersas. The definition made no mention of Islam or of religious studies, and implied that the médersas would function as state primary schools in which Arabic would be the language of instruction, although this last point was not made explicit.[7] In fact, the intention of the government was not to suppress the médersas, as the French had attempted to do, but to secularize them, and most of them were saved from this fate only by the *coup d'état* of 1968 which removed Modibo Keita and the US-RDA from power. According to Abdullahi Sangaré, Minister of Education during the early years of the US-RDA régime, this policy was aimed at 'demystifying' Islam by spreading the knowledge of a 'secularized' modern Arabic language.[8] The naiveté of such a policy might be arguable, but there is no doubt that it received both political and financial support from the Arab countries of North Africa, and especially from Gamal Abdel Nasser in Egypt, who at the time was pursuing a similar policy of secularization.

This Arabic language policy was effected through the creation, not of médersas, but of a number of *écoles franco-arabes* in Bamako, Sikasso, Djenné, Mopti, Sévaré and Timbuktu. The French médersa in Timbuktu became the Lycée Franco-Arabe, in which it was intended that graduates of the Franco-Arab primary schools would continue their studies. The Bamako médersa was nationalized and transformed into an *école franco-arabe* and religious studies subjects were completely eliminated from the curriculum; as mentioned above, other médersas seem to have escaped similar treatment only through the timely intervention of the 1968 *coup*.

A major legacy which the US-RDA left to the médersas, in addition to the support they offered them during the party's earlier, less radical, phase, was their legitimation of Arabic in the state schools, something the French had resisted for decades. They had also endorsed the teaching of French language and secular subjects in the médersas; in effect, they recognized the médersas as educational institutions, something else the French had avoided. After the

[6] Décret no. 235/PG-RM, 4 Oct. 1962.

[7] The Reform of 1962 also envisaged the eventual use of African languages as the language of instruction in primary schools.

[8] Interview, 29 Dec. 1987, Bamako. Sangare also claimed that this policy was promoted by certain Wahhabi members of the US-RDA, which illustrates that internal Islamic politics were also at issue. Sangare further stated that due to his support for Arabic language teaching, he was later pushed out of office by the Marxist wing of the party who argued that such a policy would contribute to the spread of Islam.

1968 *coup*, the existing médersas, largely ignored by the new military government, continued to develop in this direction, and new ones opened. But perhaps the most important legacy of Mali's first independent government to the médersas was the financial aid it obtained from the Egyptian government in 1961 to send twelve graduates of Saada Oumar Touré's médersa in Segu to pursue further studies in al-Azhar in Cairo. When these persons returned to Mali in 1968 with their diplomas, they were integrated into the civil service in the same manner as their colleagues who had studied in French-language schools, thus demonstrating that an Arabic-language education could also lead to integration into the state bureaucracy. In fact, such opportunities would prove to be severely limited, but this did not prevent seeds of hope being sown.[9] This episode established a pattern which would prevail for many years: primary school study in the médersas of Mali, followed by a quest for scholarship aid for a minority of successful students to continue further studies abroad in either North Africa or the Middle East. The translation into lucrative employment of diplomas and degrees obtained in such institutions, however, would prove to be difficult, except in the religious vocations or in teaching. These developments also introduced an element of ambiguity into the médersa system which has characterized it ever since. Were the médersas to become an alternative route to upward mobility and integration into the emerging middle (and politically dominant) class of bureaucrats, or were they to be schools devoted primarily to religious education. This issue was to become increasingly significant as the movement entered its expansionist phase, which was produced by the petrol boom.

During the 1960s, a number of new médersas were opened, some of which would grow into quite large institutions, such as *al-Hilal al-Islamiyya* and *Nahar Djoliba* in Bamako; founded respectively by Sufiyana Dramé and Amadou Kansai, by the late 1980s these schools consisted of a large central school facility and a number of smaller affiliated satellite schools. However, available evidence suggests that the appearance of new médersas during the first decade of independence was slow and tentative, perhaps as a result of the growing uncertainty surrounding government policies and intentions. What is very clear, however, is that rapid expansion of the médersa network began from 1973, coinciding with the Middle East oil boom. The impact of the 1970s oil boom on Islamization in Mali was discussed in the previous chapter. During the 1970s and 1980s, money flowed into Mali from both individual donors and Islamic governments to finance both improvements in existing médersas and the construction of new ones. Assistance was also given for operating expenses and books, and some Arab governments sent teachers. It is probable that every major médersa in Mali received some sort of financial aid from abroad during this period, and its impact was profound and often highly visible: the facilities in some of the new médersas were sometimes superior to those in the state schools.

[9] See L. Brenner, 'La culture arabo-islamique au Mali', esp. pp. 176-80.

This flow of money also increased the public visibility and prestige of the directors (and/or) founders of these médersas, illustrating their ability to attract finance through international Muslim clientelist networks, and of course also enabled them to attract clients within Mali. One of the most important measures of a director's success was his ability to obtain scholarship aid for his students to continue their studies abroad.[10] Success in these activities also attracted much criticism from those who opposed the process of Islamization and Arabization that the médersas represented for them. However, the private acquisition of foreign financial assistance was completely compatible with the political and economic structures that prevailed in Mali during this period. As we saw in the previous chapter, among the range of government motivations in setting up AMUPI was to control, encourage, and perhaps even to tap into this flow of funds; all the participants, as well as the critics, of these developments were fully aware of this fact, no matter what their ideological inclinations. The indisputable fact was that the founders and directors of the larger médersas were playing the clientelist game very well indeed.

The influx of Arab and Muslim money also seems to have encouraged the growth of the grass-roots médersa movement, not simply because of the hope that any founder or director of a médersa might gain access to some of the financial aid which was currently available, but because the idea became widely accepted that creating a médersa could be a lucrative economic endeavor. One of the most significant defining characteristics of the médersa, as compared with the Qur'anic school, is that it requires some degree of capital investment to set up; it is a business enterprise and it is approached as such. All médersa directors/founders may place religious motivations at the top of their list of reasons of why they have chosen their vocation, but any lengthy discussion about the operation of their médersa will very soon turn to the financial question. Most médersa directors have not become wealthy, nor can they expect to do so, but they manage to generate an income which distinguishes them from the vast majority of persons who are economically less well off.

In fact, the médersa network became a kind of self-contained economic sub-system in Mali; the only work most médersa graduates could find in the 1980s was either to teach in another médersa or to set up one themselves. Interestingly, the médersas have been criticized for this, the usual charge being that médersa training does not prepare one for a productive job. For example, one critic has argued that the médersas are:

... maladapted to Malian socio-economic realities. For the most part, these schools do not manage to train the kind of productive personnel which the country needs. Rather, they simply insure their own reproduction by continually producing médersa teachers.[11]

---

[10] For an overview of the general pattern of scholarship distribution as recorded in government sources, see *ibid.*, pp. 192-5.

[11] Seydou Cissé, *L'enseignement islamique en Afrique noire* (Paris: L'Harmattan, 1992), p. 157.

Not to put too fine a point on it, few contemporary institutions in Mali were better adapted to the socio-economic realities of the country in the 1980s. True, the médersas were not producing the kind of graduate required in many areas of the economy, but neither were the state schools, which had much less excuse for their failure; the médersas had not been set up with such a goal in mind. In any case, the productive jobs alluded to in the preceding quotation were simply not available. But the médersas were responding to a profound need in the country by providing primary educational skills to a significant portion of its children, and they were doing so at no cost to the state. The entire network of médersas had been developed by independent educational entrepreneurs, who were not only providing themselves with an income but also employing many others as teachers in their institutions. What precisely was the nature of the 'problem' if the médersas continued to recreate themselves, since even by 1991, the Malian schools were still only able to enrol 30 per cent of its children? The real question was whether the Malian economy could support the continued expansion of the médersas as profitable and sustainable business enterprises. In the late 1980s, there were strong doubts within the international aid community that this would be possible,[12] although this assessment did not halt the implementation of the *4ème Projet Education*, one of the major objectives of which was to encourage the development of a system of private French-language primary schools in the country.

In fact, much of the criticism that was leveled against the médersas was equally applicable to the state school system, and much of it was politically motivated in that the major underlying concern about the médersas in the minds of most critics was that they were Islamic. But of course, for those parents who sent their children to the médersas, their Islamic orientation was their primary attraction. This observation brings us to another major cause contributing to the expansion of the médersas: their positive appeal to a large segment of the population. Most assessments of why parents increasingly chose to send their children to médersas have been made in negative terms, and usually with reference to their rejection of the state schools. Here is a representative example:

– the attitude of certain Muslims who are deeply opposed to the French-language school which they consider to be a place that produces non-believers. These Muslims prefer to send their children to the médersa, where they will learn Islamic moral conduct that will at the same time guard against their adopting western models of behavior or, in any case, values that are contrary to those of the Muslim religion. [...]
– the present crisis in the French-language school that is providing less and less opportunity for a graduate to find paid employment. As a result, some people prefer to move toward the médersas, where, so they say, one at least has the chance to know one's religion, and to achieve 'the Other world'. [...]

[12] See Jonathan Haughton, 'Financement et réforme de l'éducation au Mali' (World Bank, 1986), p. 73.

– the rapid growth of population has made it impossible for the state schools to absorb all the children of school age. The médersa therefore constitutes the last chance.[13]

These assessments are not incorrect; indeed, there is ample evidence to demonstrate that many parents chose a médersa for their children in precisely these terms. And the last reason cited, that the popularity of the médersas was simply due to an inadequate number of places in the state schools, had been circulating since the colonial period. Marcel Cardaire made precisely the same argument in the 1950s when no more than ten médersas existed:

It is certain that these Arabic language schools, whether reformist or traditionalist, owe a great part of their success to the restricted number of places available in the European schools. The custom of 'going to school' has become well established among the populations of African cities. A good number of children frequent the modern Qur'anic schools because access to both official and private [French] establishments is forbidden to them. If the 'French school', of all sorts, could open new classes, these would be filled with these children, provided that they could find elsewhere a sufficient religious education.[14]

Whereas this argument may be valid in certain specific contexts, it has been employed mostly by persons opposed to the médersas seeking to explain away their positive appeal.

Perhaps the most important positive reason for sending one's child to a médersa has been related to the role which Islam, and the médersas as an Islamic institution, have played as mediators of social change in twentieth-century Mali, primarily for those who were marginalized socially and politically during the colonial and postcolonial periods. One clear indication of this process is the comparison of social backgrounds between children in the médersas and in the state schools. Studies carried out during 1990 and 1991 in four of Bamako's largest médersas and in two state schools revealed that 49 per cent of the fathers of children in the state schools, but only 18 per cent of the fathers in the médersas, were classified as *fonctionnaires* (civil servants).[15] Two

---

[13] Cissé, *L'enseignement islamique*, pp. 128-9.

[14] M. Cardaire, *L'Islam et le terroir africain*, pp. 120-1.

[15] These studies focused on the *second cycle* of primary education (years 7, 8, and 9); the total number of respondents was 296 in the state schools and 588 in the médersas. The studies were undertaken under the auspices of the Islam in Modern Africa Project, School of Oriental and African Studies, University of London, and constituted final year *mémoires* for students at the Ecole Normale Supérieure, Bamako: Tacko, dite Oumo, Maiga, 'Les jeunes et l'école: cas des adolescents scolarisés de Sogoniko (District de Bamako)', mémoire de fin d'études, ENSup, Bamako, 1990; Soumaïla Coulibaly, 'Les jeunes et l'école (étude de cas [Ecole Mamadou Konaté])', mémoire de fin d'études, ENSup, Bamako, 1990; Talfi Ag Hamma, 'Les jeunes et les médersas. Etude d'un cas: Institut Islamique Yattabary', mémoire de fin d'études, ENSup, Bamako, 1990; Hamadoun Tolo, 'Les jeunes et la médersa. Cas de l'Institut Islamique Naharu Djoliba de Bamako', mémoire de fin d'études, ENSup, Bamako, 1991; Boukary Traoré, 'Les jeunes et les médersas: cas de la Médersa Sabil al-Hidaya de Niarela, Bamako', mémoire de fin d'études, ENSup, Bamako, 1991; Cheick Amadou Tidiane, 'Les jeunes et les médersas: Etude de cas: Institut Islamique Khaled Ben Abdul Azız (District de Bamako)', mémoire de fin d'études, ENSup, Bamako, 1991.

additional studies were completed in 1992 which involved intensive inter views with the parents of 32 families who had enrolled at least some of their children in médersas.[16] Among this group of respondents, six had been to French-language school, seventeen had atttended only Qur'anic school, and eight had not attended any kind of school; only one person, a mother, had attended a médersa for three years, and she had also attended a state school for four years.

Although the sample represented in these studies is relatively small, the overall pattern which emerges is clear and would hold for médersas in other social contexts: the overwhelming proportion of children attending médersas in the early 1990s came from families in which the parents had not attended French school, were very often illiterate and did not speak French. These findings should not lead one to the conclusion, however, that such families necessarily systematically rejected French-language schooling; the predominant pattern in Bamako for large families of this social background was to send some children to the médersas and others to the state schools. At the same time, a strong current of resistance to French-language schooling did exist, as illustrated in the preceding chapter. Some of this resistance had its roots in a specifically Islamic ideology, as suggested in the quotation above, and as clearly illustrated in the earlier chapters of this book. But by the late twentieth century, much of this resistance was also deeply rooted in the very structure of power relations, especially in the rural areas, where deep suspicions about the state schools persisted. Such schools were seen by many as another intrusive and oppressive arm of the state; perceptions of their alien nature were reflected in depictions of them as *tubab* (white man's) institutions which taught, largely useless and socially disruptive, *tubab* knowledge to their children.

During the 1970s and 1980s the médersas developed into an institution that could help to bridge the social gap between the (French-language) schooled and the unschooled segments of Malian society. Even the most rudimentary médersas provided basic literacy and numeracy skills to children; the larger and better equipped médersas also provided a curriculum in secular subjects which, while not as extensive or as sophisticated as that offered in some state schools, nonetheless exposed children to these areas of learning. Many médersas also taught French as a subject, as well as the Arabic which they employed as the language of instruction. Absolutely critical to the success of the médersas was that they taught these subjects in an institutional and cultural environment that was comfortable and acceptable to parents of the social categories described above.

Which brings us back to the mediating role of Islam in the postcolony. Etienne Gérard, in his study of schooling in the canton of Baya south of

---

[16] These two unpublished studies were also sponsored by the Islam in Modern Africa Project: Hamadoun Tolo, 'Les Filles et la médersa (Cas des Instituts Naharu Djoliba et Sabil al-Hidaya de Bamako)', 1992, and Boukary Traoré, 'Le déferlement massif des jeunes vers les institutions islamiques (médersas)', 1992.

Bamako, has demonstrated how conversion to Islam in this area was a response to the social disruption caused by the construction of the Sélingué dam; Islam provided a new focus for social unity which replaced that destroyed by the dam project which had resulted in the destruction of many villages. The ambiguities of the situation that he describes are very revealing. On the one hand, the state intervened locally to build a dam in the name of 'development'. The social dislocation that resulted from this project led to widespread conversion to Islam as a means to compensate, both socially and ideologically, for the social damage to local communities wrought by the project. At the same time, at least part of the appeal of Islam derived from its association with progress and 'civilization', as represented in the local image of Bamako as a center of Islam and of modernity. In other words, on the one hand people condemned and opposed the disruptive 'modernization and progress' which was imposed upon them by the state, while on the other they were attracted to the imagined opportunities offered by the Islamized urban center of Bamako.

Gérard claims that similar attitudinal patterns apply to schooling. French-language schooling was perceived in this region as creating social divisions; the sacrifices of parents who sent their children to school resulted in the creation of a social elite, and for many, the loss of their children as productive members of the family and of the village. The médersas, according to Gérard, were not perceived as creating these social differences, although they did transmit the basic literacy and numeracy skills expected of schooling. In effect the médersas were seen to provide a form of schooling that contributed to social transformation without the kind of social fragmentation and political differentiation associated in the minds of many with the state schools.[17] As we will see below, a very similar attitude prevailed among Bamako parents who sent children to médersas.

The central focus of Gérard's study is an analysis of the failure of the Malian state school system to translate its educational ideology into practice. As we have seen, the promise of quality education for all became in reality a form of schooling which created social inequality; according to Gérard, the very skills the schools were to transmit, such as literacy and knowledge of the French language, became symbols of political and social difference. Prevailing postcolonial rhetoric equated schooling with human progress and illiteracy with backwardness; the US-RDA policy of guaranteeing employment to successful graduates encouraged the general belief that this was the only value to be associated with schooling, and when this guarantee disappeared in the 1980s, so did the *raison d'être* of French-language schooling in the minds of many parents.[18]

In addition, by the 1980s the state school system was in an advanced state of decline. Enrolments were dropping, the failure of the system to educate

---

[17] Gérard, 'L'école déclassé', pp. 556-7.
[18] Etienne Gérard, 'Entre Etat et populations. L'école et l'éducation en devenir', *Politique Africaine*, no. 47 (Oct. 1992), p. 62.

young children was becoming increasingly evident, and morale among both teachers and students was low and falling lower. The student upheavals that occurred in 1979-80, and the associated teacher strikes, had further undermined public confidence in the schools. By comparison, the médersa network was still expanding, although more slowly by the mid-1980s. The médersas were not plagued by the disruptions afflicting the state schools, and many parents began to feel that their children, especially young children, would be more safely and securely placed in the médersas..

The robustness of the médersa network, and its evident educational significance in Mali, led to formal recognition of the médersas as teaching institutions and the transfer of their administration from the Ministry of the Interior to the Ministry of National Education. The decision to make this change was taken in 1982, and the regulating order in council was promulgated in 1985. The order in council formulated a new definition of the médersas: 'The private médersas are primary schools (*écoles fondamentales*); religious instruction is authorized in them'. The order also stated that 'Arabic is the language of instruction in the private médersas', and that they would be 'represented by AMUPI'. These stipulations would arouse considerable controversy and confusion among both the supporters and the critics of the médersas, but we will leave the analysis of this situation to the next chapter. The major point to be made here is that the médersas were now formally recognized as teaching institutions by the state – for all the good or ill that this change in status would bring about for those associated with the médersas.

The socio-economic roots of médersa schooling: changing religious subjectivities

The preceding analysis has focused primarily on selected comparisons between the médersas and the state schools. However, the innovative nature of médersa schooling can best be appreciated when it is compared with the training offered in the Qur'anic schools; after all, the original aims of the pioneers of the médersa movement had been to reform and improve the teaching of the classical religious studies curriculum, not to compete with or replace French-language schooling. Furthermore, the médersas have emerged out of the Qur'anic school system; the vast majority of the directors of the médersas which were founded in the 1970s and 1980s received their basic religious education in Qur'anic schools.

Chapter One presented an analysis of Qur'anic schooling in its historical context; the present discussion will explore how contemporary social and economic conditions have affected the transmission of Islamic religious knowledge in the médersas.[19] The major rôle of the Qur'anic school in Mali, as elsewhere in the Muslim world, is and has been to provide basic religious training for Muslim children: recitation of the Qur'an and the fundamentals

[19] The following discussion is based in part on L. Brenner, 'Two Paradigms of Islamic Schooling in West Africa' in H. Elboudrari (ed.), *Modes de transmission de la culture religieuse en Islam* (Cairo: Institut Français d'Archéologie Orientale, 1993), pp. 159-80.

of Islamic ritual obligation. Before the choice of attending a médersa presented itself, virtually all Muslim children seem to have attended such schools at least for a few years, although only very few continued for further and advanced studies. Parents confided their children to Qur'anic teachers to fulfill their religious obligations, but also in the expectation that their children would be 'educated' in the broadest sense of the term. In most cases this seems to have meant to train them to be submissive, respectful and obedient. The infamous reputation of the Qur'anic teacher for the physical punishment meted out to his charges is only one aspect of this process of socialization. The children were completely under the teacher's direction; they worked around his house and labored in his fields. Parents were expected to give gifts to the teacher at certain stages of their children's educational progress, but the image which Qur'anic teachers projected of themselves was that teaching was a religious obligation. Malian Qur'anic teachers interviewed by this writer in the 1970s and 1980s insisted firmly that they were never *paid* for providing this educational service, which they claimed was as a religious obligation; other studies, however, have demonstrated that many Qur'anic school teachers receive regular payments which range between 10 and 100 francs CFA weekly per student.[20] Payment in money seems to be a relatively recent phenomenon, certainly induced by the evolution of the money economy, and perhaps by the example of the médersas. In any case, the Qur'anic school was always structured in a manner which provided income for the teacher and his family.[21]

The tiny minority of students who continued their education beyond the Qur'an to the *majlis* proceeded to the study of 'books', usually beginning with small works of *tawhid* and *fiqh*, and later moving on to the study of more scholarly books of *fiqh*, *hadith* and *tafsir*. The students of 'books' were usually adolescents, and they might leave home to study with teachers in other villages and towns. Considerable value was placed upon leaving home to study, although many students studied with their own relatives, especially if they were members of learned families. The study of 'books' and the religious sciences could last for years; there was no structured or standard course of study, and the student followed his own needs, possibilities and interests.

By the late twentieth century the Qur'anic system had become a mere shadow of its former self. Even those who would defend it as an effective institution for transmitting Islamic culture to the young and for memorizing the Qur'an do not expect it to produce the intellectual leaders of contemporary Muslim society, a function that has been co-opted in Mali during this century first by French schools and European universities, and more recently by the Arabic-language médersas and universities. Nor is this situation merely the

---

[20] See S. Cissé, *L'enseignement islamique*, pp. 96-7; and Oumar Diallo, 'Etude sur les écoles coraniques à Sikasso', mémoire de fin d'études, ENSup, Bamako, 1987, p. 27.

[21] For the relationship between slave production and Muslim education, see L. Sanneh, *The Crown and the Turban: Muslims and West African Pluralism* (Boulder, CO: Westview Press, 1997), Ch. 3 'Slavery, Clerics and Muslim Society'.

passive result of the rapid evolution and elevated status acquired by French-language and médersa schooling. As we have seen, there had been an active campaign by the French to disparage (as well as to undermine) Qur'anic schooling during the colonial period, thus creating a current of criticism in official circles which was reinforced by the attitudes and actions of Muslim educational and religious reformers. Not surprisingly, the pressures towards marginalization and the voices of disparagement continued to prevail during the postcolonial period.

One reason why this was so, especially among those who worked in the Ministry of National Education, was because Qur'anic schooling did not conform to their own image of *proper* schooling. It is worth quoting at length a lively and evocative description by Seydou Cissé, which succeeds in imparting much of the atmospheric 'flavor' of daily life in the Qur'anic school.

... Classes take place amost anywhere, in the entrance room [of the teacher's compound], inside or alongside a mosque, in the open air, on the sidewalk, in the market place, in the shade of a tree in full foliage, in front of the shop of a teacher-merchant [*marabout-commerçant*], etc. If this situation facilitates the teaching of children, one must also recognize that almost no Qur'anic school possesses sufficiently functional and viable infrastructures.

During class hours, one can see the children sitting side by side, very close to one another reciting Qur'anic verses. All ages and levels mixed up, they sit on mats, on sheep skins, even on the earth, holding in their hand a book or a [wooden] slate on which are written several Qur'anic texts. Seated in a semi-circle, facing the teacher, the boys are generally in front, the girls behind them. This image recalls the arrangements for prayer in the mosque, where the women locate themselves behind the men. Alongside, ordinary life carries on, an incessant coming and going around the children who are trying to learn. Women on the way to market stop for several minutes to greet the teacher, without noticing that they are interrupting the concentration of the children. A donkey in the neighborhood begins to bray loudly. The pounding of pestles, the cries of babies, the idle chatter of passersby only serve to disturb the atmosphere of work in the Qur'anic schools.

Undoubtedly, in order to compete with these external stimuli, the pupils try to see who can recite their texts in the loudest voice. This general atmosphere continues until the end of the class. When the teacher announces: 'It's time; you can return home', there is a veritable brouhaha as the pupils rush to place their tablets in the teacher's entry room before departing in all directions, shouting. Often, unknown to the teacher, the shouts end with arguments.

The older students, those who are pursuing advanced instruction, come to consult the teacher individually. At the door of the entry room, they take off their shoes. When they see the teacher, they doff their caps, bow, and shake the hand of the teacher [enclosing it] between their two hands, gestures which are signs of reverence. 'Sitting with folded legs on a mat or a prayer skin, the student reads his text, and the teacher comments on it. The teacher assumes different postures during the lesson. He might sit or lie on a mat or rug, or stand up when he wishes. When the presentation of the text is finished, the student retires in a reverential fashion, bowing again. He will sit in a corner of the entry room in order to listen to the commentaries on the text of one of his colleagues, or he might occupy himself with his own studies. The students will approach the teacher one by one in this orderly fashion.

The Qur'anic school is practically never empty. It is always lively. All day long, pupils and students are present. The Qur'anic school teacher has a very full schedule, although he may employ certain students to assist him in his teaching.[22]

The contrasts between this description of a Qur'anic school and the conditions which prevail in the médersas are considerable, starting with the physical environment. Médersa students are grouped into graded classes, which normally each meet in self-contained and purpose-built classrooms. The class and the classroom are the basic building blocks of the médersa and one of the most marked features which distinguishes it from the Qur'anic school. Many médersas began with only one or several classrooms, and then expanded by adding a new classroom each year as the most advanced class progressed. Depending upon the financial means of the founder, médersas vary considerably in their construction, ranging from a few classrooms made from straw mats with a simple roof covering, to large, purpose-built school buildings containing quite sophisticated facilities.

But regardless of the simplicity or the extravagance of the médersa itself, the classroom everywhere constitutes the basic teaching unit, in which the students sit at desks in rows, facing a teacher who presents lessons, often written on a blackboard, that the students copy into their notebooks with ballpoint pens rather than on wooden slates with reed pens. The pedagogy often lacks sophistication, consisting for the most part of students, individually or as a group, reading aloud the lesson that the teacher has written on the board. Even if questions are asked of the students, allowance is rarely made for discussion or elaboration; emphasis is placed on memorizing the contents of the lessons, rather than on analysis or synthesis, leading to the criticism that the médersas are perpetuating the pedagogy of the Qur'anic schools.[23] To a certain extent these claims are true, both in terms of pedagogical method and in terms of curriculum content; for example, like the Qur'anic schools, most médersas place considerable emphasis on the memorization of the Qur'an, without comprehension, during the first years of médersa schooling.[24]

However, the ethos of the médersa is profoundly different from that of the Qur'anic school, and this difference is reflected in virtually every aspect of the structure and functioning of the médersa, including how the Qur'an itself is learned. No matter how much emphasis is placed on memorizing the

---

[22] S. Cissé, *L'enseignement islamique*, pp. 120-2.

[23] Criticisms of médersa pedagogy can be found in *ibid.*, pp. 151-3; Alfousseyne Diakité and Mori M. Konaté, 'L'enseignement arabo-islamique dans le district de Bamako (place, fonction, incidences scolaires et sociales), mémoire de fin d'études, l'ENSup, Bamako, 1985), pp. 43ff; and Oumar Kane, 'L'enseignement islamique dans les médersas du Mali' in B. Sanankoua and L. Brenner, *L'enseignement islamique au Mali* (Bamako: Editions Jamana, 1991), pp. 87-104.

[24] See O. Kane, 'L'enseignement islamique'. It should be noted that similar criticisms were made about pedagogical practice in the state schools at the time.

Qur'an in the médersa, it is inevitably taught as only one among a wide range of other subjects. According to some critics, this structure of the academic program has resulted both in an inadequately profound teaching of the Qur'an, and in its displacement from the central role which it should play in all Muslim academic studies, both religious and secular.[25] Perhaps this criticism is being endorsed implicitly by the number of parents who send their children to Qur'anic schools during school holidays so that they can supplement their médersa instruction in Qur'an; some have even criticized the médersas for 'not teaching religion'!

A major difference between Qur'anic and médersa schooling is the complete absence, in the latter, of the esoteric dimensions of Qur'anic instruction. Geert Mommersteeg[26] has described how, both explicitly and implicitly, the student in the Qur'anic school is imbued with a sense of sacred respect for the Qur'anic text, and for the power of its very words and letters. These words are recited not only in prayer, but are written into the amulets which the *marabouts*, who are often themselves Qur'anic school teachers, produce for protection and healing. Even the ink used to write these words is believed to contain this sacred power and is carefully preserved in the water used to wash the wooden slates of the students. Qur'anic school students must learn to recite and to write these sacred words absolutely correctly; error is almost equivalent to blasphemy. The severe discipline was therefore intended to train the child to be appropriately respectful both to the sacred text and to the teacher, through whom the student can receive the special blessings (*baraka*) accorded to those who complete their Qur'anic studies successfully. The behaviour of the advanced students described above by Seydou Cissé illustrates how such training of young children is translated into a pattern of reverential behavior in the presence of the teacher, who in this context is treated as a holy personage.

These features are almost completely absent from the médersa. The Qur'an is still treated as a sacred text, of course, but its teaching is not associated in any way with esoteric powers. Quite the contrary, since this 'subject' is learned in virtually the same manner as every other subject in the curriculum (whether effectively or not), be it religious or secular. Médersa discipline is still strict, but it is a discipline designed to maintain order in classes that can exceed 80 children and in schools with sometimes more than a thousand children. It is not a discipline which is intended to associate behavioral deference with religiosity (although these behavioral forms have by no means disappeared), and whereas médersa teachers may be obeyed, perhaps even respected, they are not in any sense revered as holy personages. They are 'professional' teachers, or at least they aspire to be recognized as professionals, with all the implications that that status implies in the late twentieth century.

[25] *Ibid.*, pp. 101-2.
[26] G. Mommersteeg, 'L'éducation coranique au Mali: le pouvoir des mots sacrés', in B. Sanankoua and L. Brenner, *L'enseignement islamique au Mali* (Bamako: Editions Jamana, 1991), pp. 45-61.

Of course, many of those who have moved into médersa education, especially those of Wahhabi persuasion, have been seeking precisely to bring about these kinds of changes. Such persons have opposed on doctrinal grounds the idea that the words of the Qur'an contain esoteric powers, along with all the practices associated with this idea, such as the confection of amulets and the special respect accorded to the *marabouts* because of their alleged intercessionary powers. Their curricula and teaching practices would therefore eliminate all such features from their schools as a matter of doctrinal principle. But the majority of médersa founders and directors have not been Wahhabis,[27] even though the features of an 'esoteric Islam' of the sort characteristic of the Qur'anic schools are absent from all médersas. This fact suggests that the disappearance of these features has at least as much to do with the nature of médersa education itself as with doctrine.

Oumar Kane, himself schooled in the médersas, has published an almost unique criticism of médersa curriculum and pedagogy 'from the inside', as it were.[28] What is most interesting about his article is the tensions it reveals, both within the structure of the curriculum and in Kane himself, between schooling as a process of intellectual training and as religious formation. On the one hand, Kane is critical of inept or poor pedagogy which does not provide proper (or sometimes any) training in intellectual skills, either in the teaching of secular 'scientific' subjects, or in the techniques for determining sound or unsound *hadith*. On the other hand, he criticizes the teaching of theology for being little more than an intellectual process 'with no relation to the heart, failing to touch the feelings or to develop the religious spirit',[29] thus echoing a concern expressed by others that the médersas 'do not teach religion'. These contradictions clearly illustrate how the médersas are functioning as institutional mediators of social, intellectual and religious change in Mali through the medium of religious schooling. And this process of mediation is much more significant socially and politically than the doctrinal differences between Wahhabis and 'traditionalists' that are also articulated through the religious studies curricula of the médersas, because every day médersa directors and teachers, whether consciously or unconsciously, and regardless of doctrinal orientation, experience the tensions evoked by Kane's article in their teaching and administration.

But perhaps the most powerfully determining factor in generating differences between the Qur'anic schools and the médersas is that each is embedded in different socio-economic sectors of the Malian political economy. The most prestigious of the médersas are fully integrated into the cash economy. They

---

[27] Seydou Cissé studied 20 médersas in his thesis; the directors of 8 claimed to be Wahhabi, 6 Tijani, 5 Qadiri, and 1 *'tarbiyya'* (Tijaniyya Ibrahimiyya); see S. Cissé, 'L'Islam et l'éducation musulmane au Mali', thèse de doctorat d'État, Strasbourg, 1989. p. 355. This pattern seems to be borne out more generally, although no systematic study has been made of the doctrinal affiliation of médersa directors.

[28] O. Kane, 'L'enseignement islamique'. The publication of this article was fiercely criticised by some médersa directors as being 'against Islam'.

[29] *Ibid.*, p. 97.

are large (1000+ students), private, fee-paying institutions, with modern facilities; their administrations are necessarily highly bureaucratized. Their survival depends on the successful sale of the product they offer and the careful management of the income they generate from fees. Most directors 'market' their product by emphasizing the religious content of their curricula, and the popular appeal of the médersas derives largely from the fact that they provide an 'Islamic' form of schooling which differs from, and in some ways complements, that offered by the state system. As will be seen below, many factors are taken into consideration by parents when deciding where (or if) to enrol their children in school, and the directors of médersas compete in this 'market'.

By contrast, the Qur'anic school operates within a communal socio-economic environment. Most are single-teacher operations, organized around the personal needs and inclinations of the teacher; there is no bureaucratic structure and none is required. The economic benefits which the Qur'anic teacher derives from his vocation do not come from fees, but from the employment of his students as farm labor (at least this was the predominant pattern in the past, and remains so in most rural areas). Simply put, the médersas are integrated into the cash economy whereas the Qur'anic schools are not.

Similar economic factors are at play even in the operation of the more modest médersas that do not have large staffs and do not require elaborated bureaucratic administrations. The 27 médersas visited in the 1991 survey of Islamic institutions in Bamako's Commune I[30] had an average enrolment of 236 students in six classes, or an average of 40 children per class. The average size of the 24 Qur'anic schools visited was 44, slightly larger than the size of a single class in the médersas.[31] The directors of the larger Qur'anic schools have assistants to help with the younger students, but as one Qur'anic school director said, 'there are no classes in the Qur'anic school'. However, there seems to be a notionally operative number of children which one person can effectively teach, which operates in both the Qur'anic school and médersa contexts, even if the actual number of students one might be required to teach at a given time can be quite high. This is revealed not only by the averages given above, but also by the expansion pattern of the médersas; many médersa directors first opened their schools with one or two classes of about 40 children each (although the precise number varies), and then expanded the school each year by building a new classroom for the newly entering class. Most of Mali's médersas have evolved in this manner, and have not been constructed as purpose-built school buildings.

This notion of expansion is itself significant; persons who intend to found a médersa set out with a plan to invest in their project over a number of years in order to establish an economically viable school. When asked about future

[30] See note 2, above.
[31] Many Qur'anic school directors also noted that their enrolments fluctuate seasonally, rising especially during médersa holidays, and falling during the rainy season when their students (and often themselves) are busy with farming activities.

projects they had in mind, 15 of the 27 médersa directors interviewed in the Commune I survey described specific plans for the further expansion of their schools. Of the 24 Qur'anic school directors asked the same question, only three spoke of specific plans for expansion, although four others expressed the wish to turn their Qur'anic schools into médersas. Perhaps more revealingly, when asked how they had financed their schools, 12 Qur'anic school directors stated explicitly that no financial arrangements had been required for them to open their schools, which were located for the most part in their own homes, whereas every médersa director spoke about how he had raised the money to build the first classrooms. Sometimes these initial investments were modest, but they were nonetheless recognized as investments. At the very least, to set up a médersa one needs to arrange for a properly furnished and arranged classroom; a Qur'anic school can be opened virtually anywhere, and most are usually situated in the director's home.

The economic constraints of managing a médersa profoundly affect relationships between directors and parents, who enter into a contract to pay the fees charged by the médersa for their children's schooling. The regular payment of fees constitutes the economic life-blood of the médersa: on it depends the regular payment (as well as the level) of the salaries of teachers and staff, the maintenance of the school facility, and the possibility of further expansion. A study completed for the World Bank in 1986 concluded that the future economic success of the médersas would depend on the ability of directors to collect a high percentage of the fees owed them, some rates of payment being as low as 30 to 40 per cent of total fees due.[32] By the early 1990s the financial situation was reaching crisis proportions for some médersas; an administrator in one large Bamako médersa complained that their establishment was owed two million francs CFA in back fees.[33]

It would not be an exaggeration to claim that the tensions surrounding the fulfillment of this contractual arrangement, which requires the exchange of cash for teaching Islamic knowledge, have led to some of the most persistent and serious problems faced by médersa directors. On one level, of course, parents knowingly enter into this contract; they are fully aware that 'modern' schooling costs money. But on another level, they have not surrendered the

---

[32] See J. Haughton, 'Financement et réforme de l'éducation au Mali'. Haughton's calculations were based on an average of 50 children per teacher (an average calculated on the basis of 1983 statistics, which as we have seen, were not very reliable); he also based his assessments on the assumption of a teacher being paid an average of 18,000 francs CFA per month, which seems rather high based on other figures available. Although such calculations are useful for assessing the overall economic viability of the médersa network, they do not reflect the actual conditions in which specific médersas operate; these vary considerably based on such factors as location (rural or urban) or nature of financial base (dependent solely on fees, or supported by signficant contributions from either the local community or wealthy donors; a few médersas charge no, or very low, fees). Still, the basic conclusion of the report remains valid; the médersas can function as viable economic enterprises only if directors can regularly collect the fees owed them.
[33] Boukary Traoré, 'Les jeunes et les médersas', p. 17.

idea that the transmission of religious knowledge to their children is a religious duty, and that the teachers who perform this function assume an important religious responsibility. The director of a small médersa complained that many parents who find it difficult to pay their fees plead in the name of Islam to accept their children into the school. Such a request, of course, refers to the concept of the Qur'anic school teacher as a servant of God, a *marabout*. 'But', this director explained with some despair in his voice, 'I'm a teacher, I'm *not* a *marabout.*'

The director is also a businessman, and the children of parents who do not pay their fees are liable to be expelled from the school. Many parents understand this business relationship and enter into the médersa contract with a consumer's attitude that they should be getting the service for which they have paid. Directors then complain that they and their teachers are liable to be treated as servants! As one teacher complained, 'If a médersa teacher hits a child, the parents might possibly come to complain; they might even insult the teacher in front of the children, and the teacher loses all respect.' The fact is that parents do not confide their children to the médersa teacher in the same manner as they did to the Qur'anic school teacher, who was (and for many still is) expected to 'educate' a child morally and socially as well as to instill in him or her basic religious knowledge. Physical punishment, as well as many other hardships, were an accepted and integral part of this process. But, as stated above, teachers are not *marabouts*, and they cannot expect to be treated as such; nor, for the most part, do they really wish to be treated as such.[34]

The institutional structure of the médersas therefore evolved in consonance with the constraints of the cash economy, as was evident at every level of their operation: the charging of fees, the employment of salaried teachers, and the investments required for capital and operating expenses. This fact is also reflected in the orientation of the graduates of these schools. Médersa schooling has never gained, nor sought, a reputation as a guaranteed path to paid employment like the French-language schools, nor have parents sent their children to médersas primarily for this reason, although those who have been schooled in the médersas, and especially those who have obtained higher diplomas and degrees, certainly seek paid employment on the basis of their schooling. The two most saleable skills which the majority of médersa graduates have to offer is their knowledge of Arabic language and their Islamic knowledge, both of which are essential for the most popular form of post-médersa employment, as médersa teachers. Both can also be useful for integration into the civil service, for example in the Department of Religious Affairs of the Ministry of the Interior, and in CPLA, which exercises administrative

---

[34] Etienne Gérard, 'L'école déclassée', p. 549, found in the area where he conducted his research that parents were expected to give over complete control of their children to the médersa teachers and also to undertake to reinforce the Islamic teachings transmitted to them in school. Whereas such expectations may obtain in some médersas, they do not represent the general pattern.

responsibility over the médersas, but such posts also require knowledge of the French language, that many médersa students have not studied to an advanced level. Knowledge of Arabic has won some médersa graduates jobs in North Africa and the Middle East;[35] it is also an advantage for those who place more emphasis on their religious qualifications and seek positions as imams or as preachers, for example, on radio and television. The expansion of the médersas has arguably created a new kind of 'Islamic jobs market'.

Of course, Islamic knowledge had always been an economic (and political) asset; Muslim clerics had been applying their Islamic knowledge to purposes of economic gain for centuries, as teachers, as providers of religious services, and as practitioners of the Muslim healing and divining sciences. But the absorption of the médersas so definitively into the cash economy meant that the evolution of Islamic schooling was integral to the materialization of Islam discussed in the preceding chapter. Both the search for financial support to build or expand the médersas, as well as the distribution of much-coveted scholarships for further study abroad, operated through the clientelist networks which structured socio-economic and power relations, with the consequence that médersa schooling, and 'Islam' itself, were deeply implicated in the minds of many in the 'politics of the belly'. Such attitudes were evidenced in repeated references to the relationship between money and religion which peppered public and private discourse.

The social constituencies of the médersas

Founders, directors and teachers. The founders of médersas in Mali were educational entrepreneurs, both in their experimentation with new forms of pedagogy and in the financial engagements that they undertook in order to bring their ambitions to fruition. With time, the venture of opening a médersa may have become less risky politically and socially, but not economically, especially as the promise of Arab aid faded during the late 1980s. But whatever the prevailing conditions, opening a médersa was not a decision which could be lightly taken; perhaps Qur'anic teachers would express similar views about the decision to start a Qur'anic school, although a Qur'anic school could open with very few students and could operate in a manner which impinged very little on a teacher's normal social and economic activities.

Certainly the first pioneers of the médersa movement, Mahmoud Ba, the Azharists, and Saada Oumar Touré, were prepared to take risks; they had to struggle against numerous opponents to their project, not least the French colonial administration. In addition to their entrepreneurial spirit, and perhaps their courage and ambition, these persons also shared experiences which had dislodged them from the dominant mores of the social and cultural milieu into which they had been born and had opened them to new ways of

---

[35] Saada Oumar Touré's son, Oumar, was the first director of CPLA, and then obtained a position at ISESCO in Rabat.

thinking about and engaging with their social and political environment. For Mahmoud Ba and the Azharists, this break came in the form of their educational experience in the Middle East, and for Saada Oumar, his brief encounter with French schooling.

A similar pattern is evident in the biographies of those who opened médersas in the 1950s and 60s. Shaikhna Hamallah Yattabare, founder in 1958 of what would become the *Institut Islamique* in Missira, Bamako, studied in Egypt and other Middle Eastern countries in the 1940s, and then traveled extensively in Africa teaching and preaching (and presumably trading). In the early 1950s he opened a médersa in Abidjan, from where he was able to send a number of students to al-Azhar; in 1958 he moved to Bamako and opened a médersa in Niaréla quartier, which moved to its present site in 1976, consisting of the médersa itself (which includes a *lycée*), a mosque, and living quarters for teachers, all built with Arab aid.[36] Sufiyana Dramé, who first opened his médersa, *al-Hilal al-Islamiyya*, in Bamako in the 1960s with two classes and about 60 students, had previously studied for a number of years in Egypt; by 1988 he directed a network of satellite schools, as well as the main school in Bamako, comprising more than 50 classes.[37]

Sabil al-Hidaya, in Niaréla quartier, Bamako, was originally founded as a Qur'anic school and was transformed into a médersa in 1973 by Bakoroba Dramé, who had himself pursued only a Qur'anic and *majlis* education. However, he was aided in this transformation by his older brother who had received a university degree in Islamic law in Saudi Arabia and had lived in Egypt for a number of years before returning to Mali to assist with the directorship of the médersa. The administrative staff also includes one person who was educated solely in the state schools and does not speak Arabic. By 1985 the médersa offered instruction through the level of *lycée*, having grown at the steady rate of one class per year since it opened; in 1991 it enrolled 1600 students.[38]

The significance of one's educational experience in the founding of a médersa is even more clear when one compares the educational background of Qur'anic school teachers with that of médersa directors. None of the 24 Qur'anic school directors interviewed in Bamako's Commune I had been exposed to any other

[36] Interview with Abd al-Aziz Yattabare, 7 Jan. 1988, Bamako. Abd al-Aziz took over the directorship of the médersa after the death of his father in 1985. His own itinerary is illustrative of the careers of second-generation directors: he received a scholarship for *lycée* in Lybia (1976-9) and then continued for his *licence en droit* at the University of Benghazi; he had hoped to continue studies in international law in France when he was called back to Mali following the death of his father. Interview, 26 Mar. 1987, Bamako; see also S. Cissé, 'L'Islam et l'éducation musulmane au Mali', p. 592. See also Alfousseyne Diakité et Mori M. Konaté, 'L'enseignement arabo-islamique dans le district de Bamako (place, fonction, incidences scolaires et sociales)', mémoire de fin d'études, l'ENSup, Bamako, 1985, pp, 49ff; and Talfi Ag Hamma, 'Les jeunes et les médersas. Etude d'un cas: Institut Islamique Yattabary', mémoire de fin d'études, ENSup, Bamako, 1990, pp. 5-6.

[37] Interview with Sufiyana Dramé, 5 Jan. 1988, Bamako.

[38] Boukary Traoré, 'Les jeunes et les médersas: cas de la Médersa Sabil al-Hidaya de Niarela, Bamako', mémoire de fin d'études, ENSup, Bamako, 1991, pp. 10-20.

educational experience than that offered in Qur'anic and *majlis* schools; only five of the 27 médersa directors interviewed fell into this category. All the others had experienced a variety of schooling, most predominantly in a médersa, but also including French and Franco-Arabic schools. A similar pattern is apparent when one compares previous or concurrent areas of economic activity of those interviewed in the Commune I study. All but two of the Qur'anic school teachers had been or were involved in work which has historically been associated with Qur'anic teaching: farming, trading, and tailoring (four persons also claimed to have been *marabouts*); the other two had been a dock worker and a bicycle repairman. Among the médersa directors, twelve had been previously employed in other médersas, and two others had been teachers in the state system. Only three described themselves as farmers, as opposed to nine of the Qur'anic school teachers. Travel experience is another indicator of difference. Travel in the search for knowledge as well as to seek one's fortune (*partir à l'aventure*) is common in West Africa. Only five respondents in the survey claimed not to have traveled at all, one médersa and four Qur'anic school directors. Only one Qur'anic school director had traveled outside West Africa, to North Africa, whereas eight médersa directors had done so, mostly to the Middle East (seven), but also one to Europe.

The following account by a young man of his own academic itinerary, while certainly not typical, does illustrate what is meant by the phrase, *partir à l'aventure*. Yusuf was born in Bamako in 1953 and began his Qur'anic studies with an uncle. When, at about the age of nine or ten years, his family moved to Segu he was enrolled in the médersa of Saada Oumar Touré, where he successfully completed the full primary cycle and received his *diplôme d'études fondamental*. He then taught for a year in the médersa before returning to Bamako and teaching in the médersa of Sufiyana Dramé. However, Yusuf felt stifled in this atmosphere, and he left for Ivory Coast where, after unsuccessfully attempting to open his own médersa, he taught in a médersa in Abidjan for a couple of years. He then moved on to Lomé for a couple of years and somehow managed to obtain the funds necessary to travel to Saudi Arabia. It was now 1978; Yusuf had no specific plans for what he might do in Saudi Arabia, but he visited Mecca, Medina and finally Riyadh where he was able to enrol in an institute to improve his Arabic language and then qualify for entry to King Saud University in Riyadh, from where in 1986 he obtained a bachelor's degree in education with a specialization in Arabic language. On his return to Mali, he first taught in two different médersas in Bamako, and then in the *lycée* at Markala, before receiving an appointment in the Ministry of National Education as a schools' inspector for Arabic language.[39]

Of course, not all médersa students manage to develop their careers in the same manner as Yusuf, and although he did not succeed with his médersa in Ivory Coast, he did eventually obtain a post in the Malian civil service. Most

---

[39] Interview, 22 Mar. 1987, Bamako.

successful students end up finding employment as médersa teachers. Seydou Cissé's profile of 100 médersa teachers is very revealing. Of this sample, 77 were under 30 years of age, and 51 were unmarried, a factor of considerable significance in a gerontocratic society in which adulthood is defined, not in terms of age, but in terms of marital status and economic independence. The youth of these teachers no doubt explains their complaint that many parents do not show them adequate 'respect'. And it may be that many médersa teachers cannot afford to marry because of their meager incomes. Also of interest is the fact that Cissé's sample revealed that 61 teachers had received no formal training in French language (which does not necessarily mean they do not speak French), but more significantly, because of its pedagogical import, only 18 teachers had received secondary or higher qualifications in Arabic language; 82 had only completed their studies to the level of the DEF (nine years of schooling). More than half the sample had less than five years' teaching experience.[40]

Cissé's study also revealed considerable discontent among the teachers, primarily because of the very low salaries that they were paid. However, even if these salaries were in fact exploitative, those who managed to gain employment in a médersa were in fact fortunate in comparison with the vast majority of their contemporaries who were out of work. This comment is not intended as a justification for low salaries, but as a counterpoint to Cissé's conclusion that most médersa teachers take such jobs as a last resort. No doubt, they would take something else if it offered a better income or opportunity; but given the nature of Mali's economy in the 1980s, they were doing relatively well. Furthermore, the more ambitious among the teachers did not seem to have been quite so despondent: 'This job is just a pastime for me, I want to continue my studies. I am teaching to earn my living, have a bit of money and leave to study in an Arab country.'[41] Another Yusuf in the making?

There is no doubt that in the 1980s, when Cissé conducted his research, the future economic prospects of most of these young teachers were grim. However, not so grim as the prospects of the Qur'anic teachers, most of whom, according to Cissé, saw the future of their vocation as 'gloomy':

... With the competition from the French schools and now the médersas, the Qur'anic teachers seem helpless before the future. In addition, the growth of materialism in the society undermines the influence of their establishments. People are only interested in what will bring them money, whereas the Qur'anic schools are centers of material poverty. The quest for material well-being which prevails in the contemporary world opposes the principle of austerity which pervades the Qur'anic schools. Those few Qur'anic school teachers who are optimistic think that the future belongs to those who work for the truth. According to this principle, the Qur'anic schools

[40] S. Cissé, 'L'Islam et l'éducation musulmane au Mali', pp. 370ff; unfortunately most of this detail was omitted from the published version of this thesis.

[41] S. Cissé, *L'enseignement islamique*, p. 135.

can·only·know a radiant future. This view is based on the idea according to which the truth is always victorious, even if it is overtaken for a time by lying.[42]

This reference to 'truth' as part of the Islamic discourse will already be familiar to the reader; the discourse about money and religion seems to have blossomed in the postcolonial period in the context of the expanding cash economy.

Parents. In the absence of parents deciding in large numbers to enrol their children in them, the médersas would not exist. Parents might therefore be considered the social constituency most essential to the success of the médersas, even though they are least involved in, or affected by, their actual operations. We have already explored parental attitudes to the médersas in several contexts, but it is necessary to revisit this theme in order to assess more specifically their explanations for why they have sent their children to the médersas.

As noted above, available evidence suggests that the overwhelming majority of parents who send their children to médersas are illiterate, perhaps as many as 80 per cent.[43] This observation might not at first glance appear significant, since this is approximately the rate of illiteracy in the country as a whole. However, the rate drops to less than 50 per cent, and often much lower, in the French-language schools, which reveals a difference in social background between those who have decided to send their children (or some of their children) to médersas and those who have opted for the state schools. Indeed, available evidence suggests that parents who have received French-language schooling are much less likely than other parents to send their children to a médersa.

In interviews with 32 parents of families with children in médersas in Bamako,[44] only eight were literate, six in French as a result of their studies in the state schools, and two in Arabic, an *imam* and a *marabout*, as a result of many years of *majlis* studies. However, within this same sample, only eight heads of family had decided not to send any of their children to state schools, usually because of a very strong religious hostility toward them. The general pattern of enrolments represented by this study was therefore not at all unfavorable to the state schools. The 32 families accounted for a total of 338 children among them! Of this total, 252 had been sent to school (the majority of the others were not yet of school age), of which 31 had gone to Qur'anic school, 124 to médersas and 97 to French-language schools. These figures suggest that illiterate parents do not systematically reject French-language schooling for their children; in fact, the majority of parents who send some of their children to médersas also send some to the state schools. Etienne Gérard came to similar conclusions in his rural study,[45] where schooling strategies are based on different considerations from those in urban areas.

[42] *Ibid.*, p. 97.
[43] See note 16, above.
[44] These interviews were carried out by H. Tolo and B. Traoré; see note 17 above.
[45] Gérard, 'L'école déclassée', pp. 413-5.

However, the willingness of illiterate parents to send their children to the state schools should not obscure the fact that at the same time they hold profoundly different opinions about these two kinds of schools. The most commonly cited reason for sending a child to a médersa was religious, because in the médersa one is taught about Islam and how to fulfill one's religious obligations. The second most often cited reason was that the médersa teaches both French and Arabic, which was clearly seen to be an advantage; in fact, some parents explicitly made the point that the médersa was in this regard preferable to the state school, in which one could only learn French. Some parents associate knowledge of Arabic with religious piety: 'In the médersa one learns Arabic and French. And when one learns Arabic one fears God, which is not the case with other languages.'[46] Beyond such general comments, nothing specific was said about the content of either the médersa or state school curriculum. The assessment generally shared by all the parents was effectively summed up by one mother who explained that the médersa teaches religion, while the state school 'offers work'.

However, the parental views expressed in interview suggest that the 'religion' which they want for their children is equivalent to a kind of socialization which will endorse and reinforce their own social status as elders in the gerontocratic social structure of which they are a part. Similarly 'work' is a symbol of the expansion of the cash economy, which for them is associated with values and social behavior that they find threatening and of which they often disapprove. This is clear evidence of generational tensions, to which schooling is one of the major contributing factors.

According to the many parents who hold these views, the French language schools 'pervert' children; children who attend them become lazy, lose all shame, and 'spend their time drinking tea, listening to music, and dancing'.[47]

Children who go to the state school think their parents know nothing, that they are not civilized. They think this civilization will gain them access to Paradise. But they don't pray, they take drugs, and they drink alcohol. All this is forbidden by religion, but most of these young people do them.

As deplorable as the drugs and alcohol may be, it is the alienation and rejection which they feel from their children which affects parents most deeply and engenders in them a sense of resentment and loss. 'We lose our children to the French school; they no longer listen to us, they trample on our customs, and even worse, they pray rarely if at all.'[48] One widow clearly expressed such feelings in describing the behavior of three of the children of her deceased husband (perhaps the children of one of her co-wives; this was not made clear in the

---

[46] Parent quoted in Gérard, 'L'école déclassée', p. 534. This parent's views about the power of language are comparable to those of William Ponty about the qualities of French, quoted in Chapter Two, n. 4.

[47] Unless otherwise indicated, the quotations cited here are from interviews conducted by Tolo and Traoré in Bamako during their research in 1991-2.

[48] Diakité et Konaté, 'L'enseignement arabo-islamique', p. 35.

interview). They had received diplomas from the state schools and were now employed:

They succeeded [only] for themselves, because they do very little for the family. My co-wife and I are forced to manage as best we can [*se débrouiller*] in order to feed the family. We decided [after the death of our husband] to enrol [our three younger children] in the médersa because of the attitude of their older siblings, who did everything they could to dissuade us. But that's not what we wanted. We enrolled them in the médersa because the older children who went to school and now have work have no consideration for us, although their father, when he was alive, did all he could to ensure their success, but now that they have succeeded they have forgotten us.

In stark contrast, so it is alleged by certain parents, children who go to the médersas 'never forget their parents'; they are taught to be more disciplined, polite and respectful of their elders and consequently are themselves respected by others because of their knowledge of Islam. As the widow just quoted said of her children in the médersa, 'they are different from their older siblings [who went to the state schools]; at least for now they feel compassion for us and help us with our work, and they don't do the kinds of things which we deplore.'

Nowhere are these attitudes about social roles and socialization more clearly expressed than in parental discussions about schooling for their daughters. As Hamadoun Tolo found in his study, most parents who enrol their children in médersas consider that 'the "salvation" of the woman is located in the home and not with academic studies, which appear to be the prerogative of men.'[49] Most girls are sent to the médersa in order to learn the basic requirements of their religion so that they will be good wives. As one father explained, he sent his daughter to the médersa so that 'she might become a good religious woman, one who respects her husband.' The equation of religious education for girls with the production of submissive and respectful wives was clearly expressed by the only *marabout* interviewed in the Tolo-Traoré study:

I have never attended the state school, and I never liked the state school because it does not cultivate in the child love of God and of His Prophet, much less love for religion. In fact, I have in my household a concrete example of this: my third wife. She went to the state school, and when I married her she neither prayed nor respected me; she considered me to be an ignoramus. A lot of time was necessary to bring her to reason. Now she is beginning to understand because she is a bit older; she is 32 years old. She is the only one to cause me problems; I am fully satisfied with the behavior of the other wives. They never contradict my decisions; they have never been to the state school. ...
I did not send my daughters to the médersa because they have no need to learn all that the pupils are taught there. They only need to learn to read the Qur'an, to practice their religion and to respect a husband. Because whatever her religious faith, a

[49] H. Tolo, 'Les Filles et la médersa', p. 22.

woman who does not listen to and do what her husband asks her to do will find it difficult to gain access to Paradise. And even her father will have to answer to God if he has not sent her to Qur'anic school or the médersa.

This is certainly an extreme view; in this man's opinion, even the médersa teaches more than a 'good Muslim wife' needs to know! However, the basic content of this commentary is not uncharacteristic of the attitudes of most parents who send their children to the médersas, and perhaps of many who send their daughters to the state schools. One father, a mason by trade, sent thirteen of his eighteen children to the state schools, not one of whom succeeded in receiving even a primary school diploma. Nonetheless, he claimed, 'One cannot say they have failed in life, even if they are not civil servants. All the girls are with their husbands, and only one son does not have work.' After this record of academic disappointment, however, this father decided to send his remaining five children (four boys and one girl) to the médersa.

Predictably, given the prevailing attitude that the appropriate 'career' for a woman is as wife and mother, the overall percentage of female enrolments in school is generally lower than for males, and this is true in both the state schools and the médersas. The proportion of female to male pupils in the two systems is virtually the same in the first cycle of studies (years 1-6) at about one-third girls to two-thirds boys in 1990-1. However, in the second cycle (years 7-9), the percentage of girls in the médersas drops to about 20 per cent, although it remains at about 35 per cent in the state schools.[50]

These declines in female enrolments in the middle and latter years of schooling seem to be related to the desire of parents to control their daughters' behavior as they reach adolescence and also to ensure for them what the parents consider to be 'appropriate' marriages. The differing rates of withdrawal of older girls from school in the state schools and the médersas may also be related to the differing social backgrounds of the parents; the evidence suggests that parents who have themselves been schooled are more prepared to see their own children, including their daughters, pursue their studies for more extended periods of time. It is therefore significant that larger numbers of girls are being sent to médersas even for a period of six years, during which time they will learn at least some rudiments of literacy and numeracy; the evidence suggests they will then be more likely to want to see their own children in school.[51]

However, virtually none of the parents interviewed in the Tolo-Traoré study spoke in such 'developmentalist' terms. They were much more concer-

[50] MEN, 'Annuaire des statistiques scolaires, 1990-1991', 1992, pp. 22 and 270.
[51] This point was made in a report commissioned by USAID, D.M. Miller, 'Literature Review: Girls' Primary School Education in Mali: Benefits, Determinants and Pilot Projects' November 1990. Miller also pointed out that the literature he reviewed on Muslim societies did not suggest that Islamic belief itself inhibited girls' schooling, but that 'social practice found in Muslim cultures often necessitates institutional adaptation of the Western mode of education to enable girls' participation'.

ned about the immediate needs of their own and their children's lives, and schooling for almost all of them was perceived as either a preparation for paid employment (French-language schooling) or as a training for properly conforming to Islamic principles as a responsible adult (the médersas). And as we have seen, most parents interviewed felt there was a profound contradiction between these two options, since the first undermined the social values allegedly supported and reinforced by the second. Although most allusions made by parents to the teaching of religion in the médersas were little more than formulaic references to learning one's obligations as a Muslim or to preparing for one's eternal life in Paradise, we have seen that such statements reflect a concern to maintain and reproduce one's own social and cultural condition.

The overall impression arising from their comments is that the médersa was seen by many parents as a contemporary substitute for the Qur'anic school. This attitude was explicitly stated in the comments of one mother:

It is not only because of my husband that I send the children to the médersa, but also because of God. We are in this world for only a brief period of time whereas life in the hereafter is eternal. We have all come to earth to obey God; how can one obey Him if one doesn't know what He requires us to do? That's what the médersas teach our children. Also, a parent who neither puts his child in the Qur'anic school nor the médersa in order that it learns about Islam will have to answer to God for his or her actions on the Day of the Last Judgment. ... I want my children to become *grands marabouts* and to teach other children the Qur'an and to pray correctly. The money [they earn] in this fashion will suffice to feed them. And even if it doesn't suffice, they will find something to eat; God will never abandon them.

Once again, we see the juxtaposition of money with religion appearing in a discussion about schooling choices. A similar association appears in a response by the *marabout* cited above when he was asked his opinion of other *marabouts* who were now sending their children to the state schools:

In life each of us has his own manner of thinking and acting. They are free to do with their children as they wish, but what is certain is that this is not what they have been taught. They prefer money to religion because they think that their children who have attended the state school will find work and be able to feed them one day. However, we are all fed by God. Of course, as you say, God has commanded us to work honestly to earn our daily bread. I work [as a *marabout*] and I tell you that we eat 300 kilos of rice a month, without counting the cost of *condiments* [i.e. the contents of the sauce]; who is the civil servant who can come by that honestly each month? However, there are nights when I go to bed without even the cost of *condiments* for the next day. And the next morning, before 10 o'clock, a servant of God will pass by to give me some money. Do you think that is just luck? No! God never abandons His faithful servants.

This, and indeed many of the preceding comments, illustrate how social tensions are reflected in the discourse about both religion and schooling. The issues at stake refer not only to 'work' or 'money' versus 'religion', but also to the larger social order and whether one's children will be fully and properly 'educated' so they become the kind of responsible and productive adults their parents wish them to be. These questions are shared in both rural and urban areas, although the social and economic constraints, as well as the expectations of what schooling can offer, vary in these two contexts. Furthermore, the entire schooling scenario is filled with contradictions. For example, the *marabout* here quoted sent his four sons to the médersa and his three daughters to Qur'anic school; the reader will recall that in this man's opinion, girls do not need to learn all the things that are taught in the médersas. But what he did not explain is why he decided to send his sons to the médersa and not to the Qur'anic school. Perhaps he shared the hopes expressed by several other parents, that their sons (*never* their daughters) who attended the médersa would become great 'Arab intellectuals'. But even if this decision was taken solely in the hope that his sons would learn Arabic more quickly and efficiently while completing their religious studies, the fact is that their economic futures, if successful in the médersa, would very likely be based in the cash economy. Could the *marabout* have been unaware of this likelihood, and could the same have been true of all the other parents who seemed to look upon the médersa as little different from the Qur'anic school?

We are unable to answer these questions, since none of the parents assessed the situation from this perspective. However such questions do point to a profound contradiction at the very core of the médersa phenomenon. Whereas parents send their children to the médersa in the expectation that these schools will transmit and reinforce social values more akin to those associated with Qur'anic schooling, the médersas themselves represent an innovative system combining religious with secular schooling which is managed by a socially and economically entrepreneurial class of (predominantly) young men. These parents may well be enrolling their children in the médersas, but most of them are highly unlikely ever to have founded one themselves!

Still, it seems unlikely that parents are unaware of the implications of their schooling choices, even if they choose to discuss their decisions in a selective manner. For example, they all knew that contemporary education costs money, and all the parents interviewed in the Tolo-Traoré study were prepared to pay for it. As one parent said, 'Before, no one paid to study, but nowadays one has to pay to study; the essential thing is that the child studies.' Such a commitment to schooling is more an urban than a rural attitude. However, sending a child to either a state school or a médersa necessarily involves parents in a cash exchange relationship, and some parents clearly make their choices based on the estimated costs of each option as well as an assessment of where their child is most likely to succeed. There is no clear consensus among parents on which option is less expensive, and costs seem to vary considerably based on where families live and which schools are available for their children. However, there does seem to be a general view that children are less likely to fail in the médersa than in the state school, and that even if children can be expelled from the médersas for inability of parents to pay the fees, it is often possible to 'make arrangements' with médersa directors to keep the child in class.

One of the most striking patterns to emerge from the Tolo-Traoré study was the number of families in which the parents seemingly began to send children to the médersas only after they, or other of their children, had failed in the state schools. Of course, the médersa network only began to expand significantly in the 1970s, and médersa schooling may not have been available to the older children in many of these families. But there is absolutely no doubt that the state school system was failing utterly to fulfill the objectives stated by the reform of 1962, as well as to meet the expectations of its public. This fact is documented by the accounts of many individual families, as well as by various government and international aid agency statistics.

To give just one example of the extreme inefficiency of the system, it was calculated in the mid-1980s that for every 100 children who entered the first cycle of primary education, only 25 would continue to year seven; for every 100 children who entered the second cycle, only 29 would receive the *diplôme d'études fondamentales*; and only one-third of those entering the *lycée* for secondary education would succeed in the *baccalauréat*. The inefficiency of the system can be illustrated in another way: for every child who successfully completed the first cycle of his/her elementary schooling (the first six years), an investment of 22.9 student-years was required.[52] This situation had a devastating impact on public confidence in the school system, and was translated into disaster in many families; in one recorded case, only one child out of 23 sent to school actually received a diploma!

Of course, in addition to the sheer inefficacy of the schools themselves, the high failure rate may also have been due to the fact that those parents who had not themselves been to school were unable to assist their children with their schoolwork. 'I can't read, how can I help them?' The general attitude seems to have been that the children should simply get on with their schoolwork as best they could; as more than one parent said, 'What is essential is that they go to school.' The fact that the médersas rarely either failed students or required them to repeat a year made them appear more successful; in any case, this was the impression among most parents. Table 6.2 is based on figures taken from studies conducted among second cycle students in four médersas and two state schools;[53] it indicates a significantly higher rate of repetition in the state schools. Unfortunately, however, these studies did not ask students to specify in which schools they had repeated years, although it was clear that many médersa students had been transferred into them after a history of failure in the state schools.

52 J. Haughton, 'Financement et réforme de l'éducation au Mali', p. 37.
53 See note 15, above.

Table 6.2. PERCENTAGE OF PUPILS HAVING REPEATED
AT LEAST ONE YEAR OF SCHOOL[1]

MÉDERSAS	7th year	8th year	9th year
Institut Islamique, Yattabary	66.6	53.4	50.0
Médersa Sabil al-Hidaya	47.4	6.3	35.4
Institut Islamique Khaled ben Abdul Aziz	36.7	13.9	43.8
Institut Islamique Nahr Djoliba	60.5	68.4	45.5
STATE SCHOOLS			
Ecole Mamadou Konaté	69.4	82.4	84.6
Ecole Sogoniko	64.4	72.7	75.0

[1]These figures are taken from a limited sample based on a single class from the 7th, 8th and 9th years in each institution.

In the end, of course, students in the médersas must sit examinations to obtain their diplomas, just like their colleagues in the state schools, which is the final test of success or failure. The rates of success and failure in the examinations themselves is surprisingly similar in the two different institutions, as indicated in Table 6.3, although these statistics do not indicate that the real number of médersa students who actually sit these examinations is very small.

Table 6.3. COMPARATIVE SUCCESS RATES IN PRIMARY
SCHOOL EXAMINATIONS, 1991[1]

	Médersas	State schools
CFEPCEF *(Certificat fin d'études premier cycle, enseignement fondamental)*	57.17	59.98
DEF *(Diplôme d'études fondamental)*	36.76	37.38

[1]MEN, 'Annuaire des statistiques scolaires, 1990-1991', 1992, pp. 238 and 276

As mentioned above, the attitude that all children should go to school, and the economic constraints to send children to school, are greater in the cities than in the rural areas. No matter how much parents might disparage the money economy and insist that God will provide for the person who is properly religious, very few of their children seem prepared to endorse this fatalistic opinion, as we will see in the next section of this chapter. And one suspects that very few urban parents select a school for their children without considering the long-term economic implications of their decision. However, the situation in the rural areas seems to be different. Etienne Gérard concluded in his study of rural education that schooling constituted only one part of a broader social and economic strategy. The choice of whether one placed a child in school, and which kind of school, depended on a number of factors such as: labor needs in the fields or in the home, proximity to the administrative center and the perceived value of having a French-speaking member of the family who can deal with the administration, and also communal pressures 'to be Muslim' in a community which is in the process of recent and rapid Islamization.[54] In Gérard's view the predominant strategy was to 'acquire the mix of elements necessary for social mobility on the one hand and on the other, integration with one's peers'.[55] Enrolment strategies also depended on family size, and larger families could afford to diversify and send some of their children to each kind of school. At the same time, however, parents tended not to send all their children to school, as was often the case in the cities. In the view of these parents, although schooling could have some useful results, one also had to remember that a child who failed in school was rarely successfully reintegrated into the village.[56] Although Gérard concluded that most parents in his study did not adopt a conscious strategy of enrolment for their children, and tended to respond to circumstances as they developed, it is true that some parents did purposely enrol their children in the different kinds of schools so that the family as a whole could benefit from each experience. He quoted one father of seven children who sent two to state school, one to the médersa and one to the Qur'anic school: 'I put these children in each type of school because there are two roads [public and Muslim]. If you put them on one only, they don't see the other. If you put them on both, they will walk along the two.'[57]

Students and youth. When we turn to the views of young people, not surprisingly we find that their attitudes about schooling, and more importantly about life in general, often differ profoundly from those of their parents. However, many of their attitudes do not differ very significantly among themselves, at least, not based on the kinds of schools they attended. It is true that those who attended the médersas or the Qur'anic schools tended to express greater interest in their religion, and to claim to 'pray regularly' more often than those who attended the state schools, thus seemingly justifying their parents' hopes that they would receive an effective religious education. This conclusion is based on interviews conducted during 1990-1 with approximately 200 young persons between the ages of 18 and 25 in two *quartiers* of Bamako, Banconi and Magnambougou.[58] This was a period of considerable political upheaval

---

[54] Gérard, 'L'école déclassée', pp. 426, 449, 457 and 532.

[55] *Ibid.*, p. 402.

[56] *Ibid.*, pp. 402ff. Also see the discussion about rural schooling in Chapter 5.

[57] *Ibid.*, p. 415. Some parents adopt similar strategies in the urban areas.

[58] The findings from these interviews were written up in the following unpublished reports: Soumaila Coulibaly, 'L'incidence du travail sur les rapports entre les jeunes et

in Mali, and the primary focus of the interviews was to encourage respondents to discuss their own social and economic situation at this time of political uncertainty. Religion was touched on in the interviews but was not emphasized more than other topics. It therefore seems appropriate to begin this discussion with an analysis of the issues which evoked the greatest concern among all the young persons interviewed in Bamako, no matter where they had been schooled, or even if they had received very little or no schooling at all: concerns about their immediate and future social and economic welfare. Their primary preoccupation was how to acquire material income, which in their view profoundly affected every other aspect of their lives, including their relationships with both their parents and with members of the opposite sex, their prospects for marriage, and most importantly, their social status as responsible adults.

Adulthood in Mali is defined, not by biological age, but by the productive capacity of a man economically to sustain a legal marriage and of a woman to have children; in other words, full adulthood is intimately tied up with being married. This normative expectation persists in urban areas today where 'productive capacity' has become materialized in the form of a cash income, even though the vast majority of young men are unemployed, or seriously underemployed, which in turn means that they risk remaining dependent upon their families at an age when they would expect to be economically independent. This situation in turn poses obstacles to possible marriage, because the costs associated with marriage are beyond the reach of so many young men (although the studies on which the present discussion is based provide evidence to suggest that an increasing number of young urban women were prepared to contribute economically to sustaining a marriage by taking paid employment).

The target population in the 1990-1 studies was young persons between the ages of 18 and 25, precisely that group who would be anticipating their transition to 'adulthood' in the near future. Perhaps not surprisingly, their concerns were clearly informed by normative expectations formulated along gender lines: the young men were primarily preoccupied with finding lucrative work, and the young women, if they were not already married, with finding a husband. And both described what they considered their grim prospects in similarly poignant terms. According to one unemployed young man: 'Unemployment is the worst enemy of man; one who doesn't work is reduced to nothing.' A young single woman observed: 'Marriage is an obligation for a woman who wants to be respected; without marriage, a woman is nothing.'

---

leur environnement social: points de vue des jeunes', 1992; Kader Maiga, 'Jeunes, grins et mouvements sociaux (Le cas de Magnambougou, District de Bamako)', 1992; Tacko dite Oumou Maiga, 'Les Jeunes face au mariage et au chômage. Cas des jeunes de Magnambougou (District de Bamako)', 1992. See also L. Brenner, 'Youth as Political Actors in Mali' in Pearl T. Robinson *et al.* (eds), *Transitions in Africa: Expanding Political Space* forthcoming, upon which some of the following analysis has been based.

The study focused on a local Malian social institution known as the *grin*, which has emerged in recent decades and may be unique to that country. A *grin* consists of a small group of people, usually but not necessarily young, who meet together every day literally to pass the time. Total membership in a *grin* is small, usually no more than six or eight. There is nothing formal about a *grin*; membership can vary, although there seems to be an observable consistency of attendance. People come together for many reasons, because they live near to one another, or because of various shared interests. Some *grins* are mixed by sex, although in the sample under discussion here membership was primarily single-sex and male. Most meet in the proximity of the home of the central member of the *grin*, although some gather at this person's work place, if it is conducive to such a gathering, for example, at a motorbike repair hut. The central member, sometimes referred to as the '*chef*' of the *grin*, is often someone who can afford to provide tea and sugar on a regular basis, although in many *grins*, the members chip in to buy the requisites for tea-making.

The preparaton and drinking of tea is the focal activity of every *grin*; it would be rare indeed to see a *grin*, which are visible everywhere in Bamako, without a charcoal brazier placed at the centre of the gathering. In addition to drinking tea, the major activities of the *grin* are talking about anything and everything and listening to music, the cassette player or less frequently the radio being almost as essential as the charcoal brazier. The members may play cards or engage in similar amusements, but for the most part, the *grin* is a place to relax; it is an informal space where people come together to seek companionship, drawn by one or another affinity, and therefore provides an excellent forum in which the prevailing and persisting concerns of youth can be freely expressed in all their confusion and complexity. It is extremely rare to find a *grin* organized around any kind of productive or goal-oriented activity.[59]

Significantly, the *grin* has attracted the disapproval and criticism of parents, teachers and other authority figures who have alleged that young people simply are wasting their time in such groups and should be more productively occupied elsewhere. It will be recalled that one of the reasons given by parents for sending their children to the médersa was to ensure that they did not spend

---

[59] An important exception to this pattern was a *grin* composed of young unemployed college graduates which was responsible, on 15 October 1990, for initiating the first public march to demonstrate against Mali's single party government. About fifteen young men marched through the center of Bamako carrying banners on which were written such slogans as 'Down with the UDPM'. They were arrested and beaten, but their initiative immediately preceded, and may well have helped to precipitate, the emergence into public of the clandestine opposition movement which had been actively organizing and plotting for some years against the régime of Moussa Traoré. This *grin*, under Keita's leadership, eventually became the nucleus of a new youth association which subsequently joined with other organizations in a 'democratic alliance' whose aim was to introduce multi-party politics into Mali. This *grin* was selected for study specifically because of these political activities, but such goal-orientated activity is in fact uncharacteristic of this social institution. See Brenner, 'Youth as Political Actors'.

their time drinking tea and listening to music, an apparent reference to the *grin*; their view seemed to be that these activities were generated somehow by the experience of state schooling, or by the values transmitted by state schooling. However, research findings on this subject are equivocal. A survey of second cycle students (years 7, 8 and 9) in four médersas and two state schools revealed that a much larger percentage of médersa than state school students claimed to be members of a *grin*.[60] By contrast, the membership of the *grins* actually studied in 1990-1 included only slightly more than ten per cent of persons with a médersa background, perhaps because of the locations in which the study was carried out.

Many adults perceive the *grin* as the gathering place for lazy, irresponsible and even delinquent youth. For the youth, however, the *grin* is a privileged space that they have created for themselves and to which they can retreat from the many pressures which they feel, including those which originate in the context of family. The adult discourse about the *grins*, as well as the youth discourse within them, therefore reflect the tensions of power relations between the generations.

Perhaps the most pervasive impression given by the comments of young people in these interviews was the sense that they felt themselves caught in a kind of double bind. The overwhelming majority of them were out of work and unmarried (both male and female). They were seeking to become self-sufficient adults while at the same time many of them were completely dependent on their families for food, lodging and even spending money, a situation which tended to arouse all sorts of conflicting emotions (apparently among both parents and youth). As one young man of 18 years said, 'Without my family I would die of hunger.'

The emotional weight of this double bind was clearly articulated by a number of respondents, all of whom were unemployed and living with their parents:

'I make do, but I am not happy living with my family, because I am no longer a child. Children are meant to be taken care of, but now I have grown up and I am supposed to be able to ensure my own independence. Unfortunately, I am unable to do so.' (Male, 25 years, attended state school to year 4)

'I am not working; I busy myself with a small orchard which the family owns, but I earn virtually nothing from it. All the income goes to my father and many times he gives me nothing. And even those few times when he does give me something, it's too little. ... If I had the means I would never live with my parents, because I have never gained anything from doing so; I am always being abused and scorned.' (Male, 25 years, brief attendance at Qur'anic school)

'I am not working, and this situation is very upsetting, because I can do nothing for myself. ... I live at the expense of my parents, whereas at my age I should be capable

---

[60] Over 60 per cent of boys and 38 per cent of girls in the médersas, as compared to 30 per cent of boys and 15 per cent of girls in the state schools surveyed claimed membership in a *grin*. These figures are taken from the mémoires cited in note 15 above.

of facing up to my own responsibilities instead of being a burden for my parents.' (Male, 20 years, attended médersa for an unspecified length of time)

'I see myself as completely useless in this situation; it is as if I exist for nothing. I live at the expense of my parents, and I am here only to eat because I make no contribution to the family. [...] When one lives as a parasite, one is completely unimportant, one is marginalized.' (Male, 25 years, no schooling)

'I must be able to face up to my responsibilities. I do not wish to live like this, but because of lack of income I have no choice. ... If there are many children in a family with little means, the children tend to become disobedient. If a father is unable to provide health care, feed and clothe his children, there will be a loss of authority. ... Can one demand something from someone if you haven't done anything for him? Beyond that, one must recognize that the society is in crisis; there is no longer a clear line of behavior to follow. Everything is topsy-turvy and no one knows who is supposed to do what. For the youth, anything that does not advance them should be abandoned, such as traditional obligations and blind obedience [to one's elders].' (Male, 24 years, higher school diploma)

'There are many parents who do not try to understand why their children are not working. They believe it is their fault that they don't have work, and all day long there are insults and humiliations that finally drive their children away from home or push them to getting involved in all kinds of vices. There are a lot of delinquents here [in the *quartier* of Banconi]. ... We, the youth of today, are no longer prepared blindly to respect this social order because times have changed. Our elders must understand that; what was acceptable before is no longer the case today, especially with the hard times we are suffering.' (Male, 25 years, higher school diploma)

This selection of quotations clearly illustrates how unemployment among Mali's urban youth increases tensions within families, regardless of schooling experience or the lack of it. There is also a hint in the last two quotations of a pattern which was very evident in this study: that those with more extensive schooling are prone to take a more political stance about the relevant issues, and indeed, to organize politically.[61]

At the same time, one encounters a fascinating contradiction in the attitudes of young persons of the same age group who are still in school; many were not only quite content to be living with their families, some actually felt it was their parents' responsibility to take care of them so long as they were in school.

'Given the fact that a student is not capable of anything, I think that living with the family provides one with an inestimable support. What can a student do, what can he become outside the family or without his parents? In any case, for me, living with the family and with my parents has many advantages, the only drawback being the petty quarrels that take place.' (Male, 19 years, in 9th year of state school)

'I live with my parents because of my inability to confront my own problems. A student is obliged to live like this, even if this represents an extra burden [for the family]. After all, it is our parents who put us in school, so they are obliged to support us until the end of our studies.' (Male, 18 years, in 8th year of state school)

[61] Of course, these interviews took place at a time of intense political agitation, especially among the youth; see Brenner, 'Youth as Political Actors'.

The expectation, almost insistence in some cases, that one's parents are obliged to support one during school seems to conform with more general attitudes among older and more advanced students in the state schools about their own status. Not only should their parents support them, but students have a right to state scholarships to finance their studies. As we saw in the preceding chapter, the issue of scholarship support has consistently been a major rallying point for political activism among students.

This almost willing dependency is then combined with elevated expectations about one's own social status and the kind of employment one should have. The 1990-1 studies indicated that young persons without formal school qualifications were more likely to have some kind of work, no matter how occasional, than those with qualifications. A considerable proportion of unemployed persons with diplomas, although they tended to be quite ambitious about the kinds of projects they would like to launch (for which funding or financing was almost impossible to obtain), had in fact become imbued with a self-image which deterred them from seeking work which they considered beneath themselves. After all, not many years before, their diploma would have automatically earned them a job in the civil service, and many still saw such a job as another of the 'rights' of the successful graduate. This situation gave rise to a profound sense of despair in some:

'I very much regret having pursued such lengthy studies. If I had gone to a professional school, I might have been able to get by on my own. Now, however, I am a good-for-nothing living at the expense of others. I feel truly diminished. [...] After so many years of study, everyone's wish is to be autonomous. I really deplore this situation, but what can I do?' (Male, 25 years, unemployed graduate of the *Ecole des Hautes Etudes Pratiques*)

'My life is like a kind of hell in which I have been left to myself and my problems. I feel completely destitute. [...] I would like to be independent and to be able to face up to my problems. Somebody can offer you lots of assistance, but they can never satisfy you completely. Nothing can replace being self-sufficient, being independent.' (Male, 22 years, agricultural diploma)

But what is the source of despair for one may be the source of resentment for another. One must not forget that young persons with diplomas represent only a tiny yet relatively privileged minority of the Malian population, a fact which is not lost on the vast majority of young people who have not been to school, or have not succeeded in their schooling and who possess no formal qualifications. This resentment was expressed in only muted form in the interviews conducted for the 1990-1 studies, perhaps because the researchers themselves were members of the same privileged class, but there were certainly criticisms about apparent government readiness to respond to the demands of unemployed graduates, who in the view of their critics had vastly more promising prospects than themselves. Similarly, there were bitter observations about how privilege (such as schooling) was inherited from father to son; if one's parents were wealthy or well-placed, so would be the children; and about how one's prospects of finding work depended more on family or personal connections (that is, on one's position in the clientelist networks) than on one's own abilities:

'Today when one seeks work, especially under the old régime [of Moussa Traoré], you have to be well connected, otherwise it is very difficult to find anything. For example, you can go to look for work in a factory or somewhere, but they won't take somebody who works well, but someone who has a relative that they know or a long arm. Many people say that there is work but that the young people don't like to work, but that's not true. [...] I have made many applications for work, but even if you are first in line, when someone comes after you who has a well-heeled relative, he is more likely to get the job. There is nothing you can do.' (Male, 23 years, no school, laborer)

'I don't work at all. I play the American game, making do [*Je fais l'américain, la débrouillardise*]. Really this is no place. If your parents aren't powerful, you have no place here. And there is no way out.' (Male, 22 years, unemployed, no information on schooling)

In fact *la débrouillardise*, a life of making do and getting by, had replaced the prospects of sustained productive work and regular income for most urban Malian youth by the late 1980s. And if what most of the respondents to the 1990-1 interviews claimed to be doing to earn money fell into the category of 'respectable' work, there is no doubt that many other illegal options were also being pursued, from petty theft to highly organized banditry.[62] And many dreamed of a way out, of travelling to other parts of Africa, to France, and in one case even to the United States, to seek their fortune, to *partir à l'aventure*.

The pervasive necessity for so many young people to pursue a life of *la débrouillardise* placed increased pressure on the clientelist networks and in turn highlighted their critical role in the dynamics of power relations in Mali. People became increasingly aware of who was forced to ask for (and who was in a position to offer) money, food, jobs, scholarships, etc. The pressures of this situation were considerable for the young graduate who had passed through school with the expectation that once he (or more rarely, she) had acquired a diploma, he would be elevated above the fray, but now found himself facing the danger of both social and economic marginalization. The more one became forced into a life of making do, the more one lived day to day and the more one found it necessary to focus on immediate and short-term economic objectives. This is a major reason why the topic of money dominated the conversations in the *grins*. Money became a pervasive metaphor for discussing the politics of domination. Money was alleged to be at the heart of all social relationships *and* to be the root of all evil. 'Nowadays,' observed one respondent, 'all relationships are based on money; if someone doesn't work, doesn't earn anything, he must keep his head down'. And another said, 'Someone who has no money enjoys no respect. Everything is

[62] For an excellent study of marginal youth in Bamako, see Laurence Couchoud, 'La migration sur place. Etude de la marginalité à Bamako (Mali)', mémoire, fin d'études de DEA, EHESS, Paris, 1987.

for sale, even love; love has become a kind of commodity, and women only hang around those who have money.'

In fact, the discourse on gender relations eloquently illustrates the way in which money became a metaphor for discussing power relations, in this case, between the sexes. Stereotypes abound in this discourse: according to the men, women are only interested in money; according to the women, the men are only interested in sex. And these stereotypes prevailed despite the fact that the fundamental preoccupation of virtually all of the unmarried women was to find a husband! This discourse also provides an excellent example of how a particular social group (in this case men) project the source of their difficulties onto a second group (in this case women) whom they feel they dominate, or have the right to dominate.

In the opinion of certain men,

'Many women behave very badly; they want to have what they need without working.'

'We [the unemployed] are social rejects who do not have the right to a wife. Women don't like us because we don't have any money. [...] Girls are not serious; the only thing that counts in their eyes is money.'

'Nowadays, many girls prostitute themselves in order to get money. They don't do anything and don't try [to find work]. They don't want to tire themselves out and yet they want to have everything.'

'Nowadays girls are ready to do anything for money; they change partners like they change clothes.'

'Girls behave very badly, but I don't think they have any choice. Even the boys behave badly, but the girls have no other means [to earn money] except to sell themselves, but that is better than the theft that the boys take up.'

By contrast certain women say:

'Men are dangerous. They speak all kinds of sweet words in order to have us, and once that is accomplished it is hell.'

'I am wary of most men. You have to avoid them so as not to fall into their trap. I can do all kinds of things with a man, but when he starts to speak about certain things, I tell him exactly what I think.'

The general gist of women's comments was that men are women chasers who, once 'they have satisfied their desires', abandon their women friends, or even their wives, to continue the chase elsewhere.

This discourse of mutual derision must be juxtaposed with the fact that both men and women want to be married and to establish a family in order to integrate themselves into adult society. Given the preceding comments and the social pressures to get married, the conflicting feelings produced by this situation must be considerable. The reader will recall the statement of one young woman quoted above that 'without marriage a woman is nothing'. Finding a husband is a prevailing preoccupation among young unmarried women; indeed, many see marriage as a solution to their own personal problems, both economic ('I want someone to support me so that I can escape from this poverty') and familial ('so that I can be liberated from the overwhelming burden of housekeeping work').

Given the prevailing social and economic conditions in Mali, as well as the nature of gender relations, such hopes seem naive, to say the least. Oumou Maiga's study of the relationship between unemployment and marriage explored varying gender expectations in marriage.[63] According to her findings, whereas most young men in her study felt that marriage was beyond their means, they nonetheless held out hope not only that they would eventually marry, but in many cases that they might actually manage one day to have more than one wife, an ambition which reflects both their dreams of becoming men of status and how such status is dependent in part on a man's relationship to women. By contrast, most of the women in her study were already married and almost unanimously stated their preference for monogamy.

One young unmarried woman described her ideal husband as a 'faithful man, who can meet the needs of the household; that is to say, I don't want a man who is unemployed, lazy, and who doesn't want to do anything.' In the economic conditions which prevailed at the time, this cannot be taken as an offhand comment; nor should the view expressed by another woman, who insisted that a husband should not leave his wives and children at home in order to go wandering about. By contrast, one man described the ideal wife as a woman who will 'respect her husband, his relatives and friends, be very welcoming, be always clean, know how to cook, avoid being too jealous, be faithful to her husband, and give him total freedom as absolute chief of the household.'

Where women and men seemed to differ in their views about marriage was first about monogamy and what they meant by faithfulness between spouses, and secondly, about the economic contribution and independence of a wife. Everyone agreed that a successful marriage must be based on a sound economic foundation, and of course wives had always contributed to the economic productivity of the family through their labor in the rural context, where such activity was defined by the cultural parameters of the household and the village. The situation was different in the urban context, however, and many men did not accept that their wives should find independent work in the job market, despite the fact that many wives wanted to contribute to the economic welfare of the family through their own work. Attitudes about these matters tended to vary with extent of schooling.

Almost all the married women surveyed in Oumou Maiga's study were housewives, although a significant number of them had formed themselves into small collectives (usually with unmarried women, as well) in order to engage in economic activities which could be carried out in the domestic situation.

[63] Tacko dite Oumou Maiga, 'Les jeunes face au mariage et au chômage'.

Four such collectives were studied: hair-dressers, dyers, manufacturers of clay earrings and manufacturers of a kind of bead belt worn by women. None of these enterprises brought in more than a bit of spending money, but they contrasted sharply with the individualized search for employment which predominated among young men in the study, who generally did not seem attracted to collective forms of work. These differences in gender orientation toward work might also be compared with the varying attitudes toward the kinds of work highly schooled young men were prepared to accept, which were discussed above. These young women, whose independence was constrained by their social condition, nonetheless demonstrated a certain degree of initiative not always evident among the men, especially among highly schooled men.

These observations bring us back to the question of how power relations are reflected in gender relations. The preceding comments about sex, sexuality and marriage, and their relationship to money, reveal a sub-text about ambitions to dominate or to escape domination in the context of gender relations; they reflect a struggle about who will possess whom. Achille Mbembe has reflected on power relations from this perspective, where the female body is employed, or represented, as an economic resource or as a means to economic viability.[64] One of the prevailing underlying themes of the Malian verbal 'battle of the sexes' seems to be about whether men or women will control women's bodies, a discourse that is precisely parallel to the discourse about work where the issue of who will possess whom is articulated in terms of one's position in the clientelist networks.

A similar struggle is also evident in the discourse about family. 'Today, our parents place money above their relationship with their own children, to the extent that if you want to remain on good terms with them, you must be seen on a regular basis to be giving them a little something. Otherwise, they will abuse you with all sorts of names'. This situation makes the condition of economic dependency on one's parents all the more painful. I have myself observed a situation in which the head of a household insisted on being given his two sons' unopened pay envelopes each month so he could extract what he thought appropriate from their wages. This form of domination was possible only because the young men still lived and ate in their father's household, although one was married with several children. The fact that the unmarried son always opened his pay envelope before giving it to his father was the source of considerable tension and mutual resentment. This is just one more small example of the struggle to dominate or to escape domination which constitutes power relations on various levels of Malian society. All these discourses arise from the same social context, and therefore each reflects the other. Perhaps it was a personal awareness of this fact that led one Bamako informant to observe that 'one needs to be married to really understand the realities of contemporary Mali.'

[64] Mbembe, *Les Jeunes*, pp. 133-7.

Alongside the kinds of social and economic pressures that we have been discussing, religion took a definite second place among the concerns of the urban youth interviewed in 1990-1.[65] Not surprisingly, their attitudes about religion were often expressed in relationship to their social condition, and many of them clearly felt that religion would begin to play a significant role in their lives only when they were older and (they hoped) better established socially:

'Given present social difficulties I am unable to practice religion as one understands it, because I am unable to apply all the rules at the present time. I am confronted with such problems that I cannot respect religion as I would wish; perhaps in the future I will be able to respect them.' (Male, 22 years, in technical training school)

'I am a Muslim, but not practising. […] Right now I have too many problems, and I prefer to devote my time to reflecting on seeking a solution to them.' (Male, 25 years, diploma from Ecole Normale Supérieure)

'If you see someone practising their religion, it is because their mind is at peace. If you have no income, how can you practise a religion? Where can this belief take you? Nowhere! I don't practise anything.' (Male, 22 years, no school, unemployed)

This last comment represents the most negative view about religion expressed in these interviews and is the closest anyone came to taking a position against religion as such. But even here, the speaker seems to imply that should his prospects improve, he might also begin to practice his religion.

Another attitude was expressed which runs parallel to this first, but is almost its inverse: if for some young persons the prescriptions of Islam are too demanding to be followed when one is burdened by problems, for others they are rejected because they prohibit one from enjoying the freedom of youth!

'I love the Muslim religion, but I don't practise it for the moment. The youth of today, we cannot practise the Muslim religion and at the same time pursue certain forbidden activities.' (Male, 20 years, in school)

'Diverting girls and practising religion don't go together. Once I have filled my stomach, I only think of visiting my girlfriends!' (Male, 18 years, in school)

The idea that the full practice of Islam is reserved for one's more mature years is not new, even if here it is being expressed in relationship to a set of very contemporary preoccupations. Young men (but not usually girls) have always been allowed a certain degree of latitude in their behavior before they marry, especially if this takes place beyond the knowledge and view of their parents;[66] the practice of *partir à l'aventure* seems to conform to this social attitude. When one marries and 'settles down', however, one is expected to conform to normative social values, among which is the proper practice

---

[65] It should be noted that none of the respondents was currently a Qur'anic school or *majlis* student, who might be expected to have different views about the role of religion in their lives.

[66] For an excellent analysis of the relationship between the behavior of youth and social proximity to parents and family, see Laurence Couchoud, 'La migration sur place'.

of Islam. However, there are many other more specific indications of the notion that one's Islam is expected to mature with one's age. For example, Amadou Hampâté Bâ speaks in his memoirs of his own successive conscious 'conversions' to Islam, which began when he was in his early twenties; what he describes is a gradual process through which his religious sensibilities were deepened.[67] Such experiences are not unusual among religiously inclined persons in all cultures; one of our research assistants in Mali recounted that he had 'begun to pray' following a dream in which he had died and his father, a *marabout*, refused to pray for him.[68]

There was also a stream of criticism, tinged with idealism, which informed the comments of these young persons. Many of them endorsed Islam, but with reservations, the 'Islam is a good thing, *but ...*' syndrome!

'Islam is a good thing according to what we are taught, but what is deplorable is that certain Muslims participate in shameful activities; they use Islam to deceive people.' (Male, 18 years, in year 9 of school)

'Islam is good in itself, but some people use it for other purposes that are not good.' (Male, 24 years, left school in year 7, unemployed)

'Islam is a good thing, but its principles are very difficult. If one could keep strictly to them, one could live a faultless life. Islam teaches wisdom, but unfortunately many people pray and still do abominable things.' (Male, 25 years, attended Qur'anic school, working as a butcher)

'Islam is a good thing but many people are Muslim for ulterior motives; in this way Islam becomes a means of deceiving people, to profit from the kindness of others.' (Male, 19 years, attended médersa 5 years, manual labourer)

'I am a Muslim in my heart, but I see how the Muslims behave and I decided not to pray. I cannot go along with hypocrisy. My faith is not so deep that I can pray just for the show of it. I feel myself to be a Muslim deeply within myself, but I don't practise it. I don't know how to describe it. But I know that one day I will end up praying, because it is necessary. One must have faith in God even if He doesn't exist; one must invest oneself and have faith in something.' (Male, 25, working as a freelance journalist)

Almost all these kinds of critical comments come from persons who attended state schools, perhaps justifying the views of those parents who felt that this form of schooling undermines religion. Conversely, most of those who made unequivocally positive statements about Islam had been educated in the médersas or Qur'anic schools. One former médersa student said:

'Islam, through its practices, fashions the conduct of the individual and brings him close to God. Islam signifies happiness, love, solidarity, tolerance and pity. It incarnates the virtue and wisdom without which life is impossible, and it prepares man for a better tomorrow.' (Male, 22 years, studied in a médersa for three years, now working in commerce)

[67] See A.H. Bâ, *Oui mon commandant!*, pp. 63-4; 104-6; see also L. Brenner, 'Becoming Muslim in Soudan Français' in Robinson and Triaud (eds), *Le Temps des marabouts*, pp. 467-92.
[68] Interview with S. Coulibaly, 19 Oct. 1991, Bamako.

But a young man with a diploma from an agricultural institute expressed very similar sentiments:

'Islam in a good thing; it is a special science which is at the service of humanity, for the well-being of humanity. … Islam is of great importance because it brings people together and reinforces love, solidarity and concord among them. Islam consoles mankind.' (Male, 24 years, diploma from agricultural college)

By contrast, one former médersa student, when asked what he thought of Islam, replied, 'I have nothing to say about this because I am not a good Muslim.' Another young man, whose only schooling was a brief stint in a Qur'anic school when he was very young, similarly felt unable to respond to a question about Islam: 'I know nothing about this subject. … People make a lot of noise about Islam, but in the end one doesn't know what is true and what is not.'

The overall impression given by these interviews is that young people generally express less interest in religion than their parents, an attitude which is perhaps not surprising in a gerontocratic society in which high status religious roles were almost always reserved for older males. A more pertinent question, in relationship to the present analysis, is to try to determine the extent to which the type of schooling actually affects religious sensibilities. At first glance, the 1990-1 studies would suggest that it does. Almost 85 per cent of those interviewed who had attended either médersas or Qur'anic schools claimed to 'pray regularly', or at least 'sometimes', whereas only about 60 per cent of those who had attended the state schools made a similar claim. These findings suggest that parents might have been justified in thinking that attendance in the state schools could undermine a child's religious orientation.

However, the reader will recall that our analysis of parental attitudes suggested that many parents sent their children to the médersa in order to reproduce the social order as they understood it, and that the parental discourse on religion was a lightly veiled critique of contemporary social change. Does the médersa act as a barrier to such change? The preceding analysis suggests that the impact of the médersa as an institution is quite the contrary, since it provides an opportunity for young people to challenge the received social pattern; as we have seen, the médersa movement is a dynamic contemporary phenomenon which has been led by young persons from its very beginnings. Not many of the persons involved in developing these schools seem to have approached either their ambitions or their future prospects with the view that if they were good Muslims, 'God would provide' for them.

Nor did one find this attitude being expressed by many urban youth in the early 1990s, even if many of their parents still embraced such forms of religiosity. Only a few young men voiced such a sentiment, and always with reference to the difficulty of finding paid employment; as one of them said, 'Only God has the solution to this problem; me, I have none'.[69] Similarly, a young

---

[69] Male, 19 years, unemployed, Qur'anic school education as a young child.

woman who had been schooled in a médersa for only a few years, faced her preoccupations with marriage with a similar attitude:

'Right now the problem of finding a husband makes me afraid. [...] There is no solution in sight, but whenever we talk about it among ourselves, we console ourselves by referring to the general opinion that says that God has promised a husband for every woman.' (Female, 20 years, schooled in a médersa through year 3)

Whether this attitude was acquired in the médersa or not, it is certainly one which is taught there. Indeed, according to Islamic tenets marriage is a religious obligation for a woman, and the following excerpt from an essay by a female médersa student in Sansanding in her 8th year vividly illustrates how gender values are transmitted in some médersas:

'At the end of my studies I want to become a good housewife, very obedient to my husband, in order to benefit from God's pardon both in this world and the next. The Prophet (Blessings and Peace be upon him) said: "If I had to command one person to bow down before another, I would say it should be the wife for her husband."'[70]

One cannot know the extent to which these sentiments represent this young woman's true feelings; it seems likely that she was simply writing what was expected of her in a school essay. Certainly, none of the women in the Bamako study expressed this kind of opinion; they didn't seem to think there were any men around worthy of this kind of respect! Perhaps it is significant that this médersa was located in Sansanding and not Bamako! But these are certainly the kinds of values which many parents want communicated to their children in the médersas.

Chapter 5 concluded with an exploration of the expansion of the médersa network as a political movement in the terms of Jean-François Bayart's definition of politics as a pluralistic contest to accumulate wealth, to manipulate hegemonic shared meanings, and to seek autonomous power. That chapter explored how certain well-placed educational entrepreneurs in the médersa movement managed to tap into the flow of money from local and international donors and investors to help finance their burgeoning Islamic project. This chapter focused more on an analysis of the broadening social and economic base of the médersas and how they opened up a new domain for the accumulation of wealth in terms of jobs for teachers and viable businesses for directors. Institutionally, the médersas were firmly rooted in the postcolonial cash economy; their founders and directors (at least implicitly) endorsed the 'modernizing' and developmentalist pressures of the postcolonial state, but proposed that there was a specifically 'Muslim' way to achieve such aims. A contestation of meanings emerged precisely from this point. The médersas were 'modernized' Muslim schools which offered an alternative to French-language secular schooling; the médersa project therefore did not pose any

[70] S. Cissé, *L'enseignement islamique*, p. 204.

direct challenge to the state, but it certainly signaled dissent from the educational policies of the state.

The question of autonomy is less clear because the médersa constituencies have never sought autonomous power in the classical sense of the term, although they did enjoy a certain autonomy because of their marginalization. The success of médersa schooling in Mali owed absolutely nothing to government or to the state, and even if a few benefactors or founders of médersas have enjoyed clientelist connections with members of *le Pouvoir*, the broad social base of the movement cannot be explained in terms of such relationships. This distancing from the state, and even from *le Pouvoir*, was not the result of a conscious policy or strategy on the part of the médersa directors; it had been imposed on them from the 1940s when decisions were taken not to recognize the new médersas as educational institutions. By the 1970s and '80s, when the social impact of the médersas became patently clear and the state could no longer ignore them, many directors responded to the prospects of state intervention in their affairs by seeking to transform their marginalization into an explicit form of autonomy in the name of Islam. This political confrontation is analysed in Chapter 7.

This pattern of low-keyed dissent and distancing from the state is an example of what has been described as a 'popular mode of political action', a 'politics from below'.[71] The introduction of médersa affairs into the national political arena was the result of government action, not of any purposeful campaign on the part of the médersa constituencies. Once the issue of the médersas, and more broadly of Islam, had entered the public domain the concern most frequently expressed by critics was that the médersas nurtured *intégriste* or 'fundamentalist' ideas which might later form the basis for a challenge to the secularist constitution of the state. The social dynamics underpinning this critical discourse was a continuation of what had begun in the 1950s when the French and others were so preoccupied with Wahhabism: it was a reaction to shifting political configurations in which Muslims were adapting to the dominant political order through Islamic idioms. The terms of the discourse had been modified: the racialist undertones of French attacks on Wahhabis as 'fanatics' had been replaced in the 1980s by secularist attacks against certain Muslims as *intégristes*. But the articulation of these attacks in terms seeking to distance oneself from an 'Other' seems similar.

These comments are not intended to deny the possible emergence of a 'fundamentalist' movement in Mali, although none had appeared by the 1980s, but to draw attention to the fact that the most profound significance of médersa schooling has thus far been, not in any move toward *intégrisme*, but in its particular manner of mediating social change, which is of course integral to its function as a 'popular mode of political action'. The political implications of médersa schooling are therefore important, even if they are

[71] See Bayart, *L'état en Afrique*, pp. 258-9, and J.-F. Bayart, A. Mbembe, C. Toulabor, *Le politique par le bas en Afrique noire*.

not to be found in any 'fundamentalist' challenge to Malian modes of governance. In fact, the findings in this chapter demonstrate that the impact of médersa schooling has ramified through Malian society in a complex variety of ways, certainly challenging secular institutions and schooling, but posing a much more profound challenge to Muslim institutions like the Qur'anic schools and, through the reform of Muslim schooling, contributing to the reformulation of Muslim self perceptions.

The médersas have acted as mediators of social change by providing (modernized) schooling for large numbers of children who might not otherwise have received it, both by increasing the number of school places available and by appealing to parents who do not wish to send their children to the state schools. The evidence also suggests that many parents who have not themselves attended school are more prepared to send their children to a médersa than to a state school, usually for religious reasons. Many such parents see the médersa as being 'for religion' and the state schools 'for work'. However, our analysis of youth discourse suggests that their children, particularly when they are older, become more concerned about economic than religious matters.

These generational differences between expectations and realities are important. One of the major reasons for the expansion of the médersa network has been the capacity of the médersas to provide income for both teachers and directors. No parent interviewed stated these careers as reasons for sending their children to a médersa, although they account for the overwhelming majority of occupations of former médersa students. Although this tendency for médersas to reproduce themselves has been disparaged by some critics, in fact it has both increased the number of available school places and served to introduce many young people into a 'modernized' sector of the Malian political economy: the médersas are fee-paying institutions which employ salaried teachers, supported in the larger institutions by a bureaucratic staff and administration.

These examples illustrate the extent to which the médersas socialize their students into a world very different from that of their parents, how médersa schooling trains young people for insertion into a 'modernizing' socio-economic environment, and how the médersas differ as socializing institutions from the Qur'anic schools. But even if the médersas serve to enable their students better to respond to the social and economic constraints of contemporary Malian society, they remain religious schools and their primary emphasis is on transmitting Islamic religious knowledge, which is precisely the focus of the attacks of their critics who fear that such schooling can only lead to the rise of *intégrisme*.

But the médersa constituencies seem to have been more concerned with social integration than with political *intégrisme*. Despite the many differences in the schooling they have received, médersa students and their state school counterparts share for the most part the same problems and ambitions: both want to transform their successful schooling into viable employment and an improved social status. The history of French-language schooling in Soudan français and Mali had created expectations among graduates that they were meant to administer and possibly to govern. Similar ambitions and attitudes emerged among médersa students, although not to the extent of students in the state schools,[72] perhaps because the ethos of the médersas was not focussed on this objective.

However, the status expectations of médersa students did increase the longer they managed to remain in school, although the extremely high dropout rate meant that the majority of ambitions were frustrated. For example, in the médersa *Sabil al-Hidaya* almost 90 per cent of the students in the second cycle expressed the desire to continue their studies into the *lycée*, whereas in fact only 24 per cent of them managed to do so.[73] Similarly, whatever one's ambitions as a younger student, the reality was that the public sector was not where médersa graduates were finding work. Among twenty students who passed the *baccalauréat* from the *Institut Islamique de Missira* in 1989 and 1990, three had received scholarships to continue their studies abroad (in religious subjects), three had found employment in commerce, twelve were teaching in médersas, and two women were continuing with typing courses.[74] This example also illustrates a more general pattern: not unexpectedly, the further médersa students pursue their studies, the more they tend to move toward 'religious' specializations, whatever their ambitions might have been as younger students. Their médersa schooling, in effect, places them on a particular path of educational development in Arabic and religious studies from which it is very difficult to deviate as their studies advance.

Which brings the discussion back to the tensions between integration and *intégrisme*. Much of the evidence evoked in this chapter has documented the extent to which the médersas have functioned as institutions mediating social change and social integration in Mali; virtually no evidence exists to support allegations that the médersas have served as training grounds for political *intégrisme*. The next chapter documents the politicization of the médersa constituencies in the name of 'Islam', not for ideological reasons but in reaction to heavy-handed government intervention in their affairs. The issue of contention was the demand that the médersas integrate the programme of secular subjects of the state schools into their curriculum; the crisis arose not so much from the demand itself as from how it was implemented. The evolution of these events illustrates how power relations in postcolonial Mali could very well shift the ambitions of the médersa constituencies from integration to *intégrisme*.

---

[72] Over 80 per cent of second cycle students in one state school aspired to become civil servants, whereas the proportion ranged between 60 and 40 per cent in the médersas studied. See S. Coulibaly, 'Les jeunes et l'école', pp. 175; 185; Talfi Ag Hamma, 'Les jeunes et les médersas', p. 91; B. Traoré, 'Les jeunes et les médersas', p. 73.

[73] B. Traoré, 'Les jeunes et les médersas', p. 73; H. Tolo, 'Les filles et la médersa', p. 9.

[74] Talfi Ag Hamma, 'Les jeunes et les médersas', p. 87.

7

ISLAM, THE STATE AND THE IDEOLOGY OF DEVELOPMENT

THE POLITICS OF MUSLIM SCHOOLING IN THE 1980s

In the 1980s, the government decided to integrate the médersas into the national school system. This decision to recognize the médersas as 'educational establishments' stemmed from two complementary sources: the corporatist political thinking which informed the creation of the single party state in the 1970s, and the developmentalist ideology which the government adopted in the guise of policy-making. Considerable evidence exists to demonstrate that the change in status of the médersas was ultimately precipitated by the adoption of the *4ème Projet Education* which was launched in the late 1980s, led by the World Bank and implemented by a consortium of international aid agencies. The actual implementation of the decision to modify the administrative status of the médersas was a complex and deeply ambivalent process through which party and state sought to capture the energy and initiative of the médersa movement for their own political purposes, while at the same time acting to ensure that any implied formal association with 'Islam', through AMUPI and the médersas, would not provide a political opening for Muslim-based dissent from their national project. This ambivalence was reinforced by the attitudes of many of Mali's aid partners, particularly certain French and Americans, who either officially or personally (or both) were deeply suspicious of anything 'Islamic', despite the fact that they were meant to be assisting in the 'development' of a Muslim society. These attitudes sometimes combined with what might be termed a developmentalist mentality which tacitly seemed to exclude the possibility that 'development' could take place in the absence of the authority and expertise of properly trained 'development experts'.

The logic of corporatism, implicitly embraced by the recently-created single party state, required that all of Mali's social constituencies, as well as all forms of social action, should be 'represented' by officially condoned bodies which were linked, no matter how loosely, to the structures of the UDPM. The construction of the party and its extension throughout the country was accompanied by a democratic rhetoric which presented the UDPM as 'the voice of the people', whereas in reality the primary aim was to ensure that no aspect of national life should escape the surveillance and control of either the party or the state. As already discussed in Chapter 5, the decision to 'appropriate Islam' through the creation of AMUPI in 1980, followed from this logic, and the difficulties which consistently plagued AMUPI's existence derived directly from the contradictory circumstances which had led to its creation. Presented to the public as an organization which would 'represent' Mali's Muslim constituencies, and oversee Muslim affairs, its creation also extended the control of *le Pouvoir* and its clientelist allies over a segment of Malian society which had hitherto been operating in a largely independent manner.

The decision to integrate the médersas into the national educational system followed the same logic, and its implementation was affected by similar contradictions. Government put forward many sound and convincing reasons why the médersas should no longer be allowed to operate as fully independent institutions, free from any regulatory controls: they were schooling a significant proportion of primary school children; the curricula of the médersas, as well as the quality of pedagogy they provided, varied considerably from one institution to another; they did not offer standardized examinations; and it was the responsibility of government to assure the quality and standards of schooling offered to the Malian public. But when the state bureaucracy proceeded to effect this integration, their actions took on the hallmarks of an operation to 'domesticate' the médersas and their associated social constituencies, 'to compel them to settle down in a domestic social space where their domination and exploitation would become more evident', to paraphrase Jean-François Bayart.[1]

Not surprisingly, this initiative on the part of the state was met with resistance from some of the médersa directors, who as a result began to organize themselves around specifically Islamic issues. A politicization of Islam thus ensued; convinced that government intervention in their schools was designed to undermine the religious focus of their curricula, the resisting directors turned to 'Islam' to justify and defend their protests. At the same time of course, there were other directors who accepted the intervention without dissent, often because of the possible perquisites they might obtain from some degree of integration into the clientelist networks of *le Pouvoir*, no matter how fragile or tenuous this might be. To this political mix were added the criticisms of those secularists who opposed any recognition or endorsement of political constituency based on religious affiliation; in their view the médersas should have remained totally independent of direct government intervention and regulation.

As will be demonstrated below, this entire episode demonstrates how 'Islam', although formally banned from public political discourse in Mali, nonetheless affected the dynamics of power relations in this Muslim society. This is certainly not surprising in a political confrontation which involved the

---

[1] J.-F. Bayart, *L'Etat en Afrique*, p. 309; see note 13, Chapter 5.

médersas, but the point is most effectively demonstrated, not by the Islamic response of the médersa directors to the government challenge, but by the manner in which government representatives and administrators dealt with the médersas. Many of them were disparaging and dismissive of the médersas, and it will be argued that their pejorative attitude toward Islam served more to politicize this affair than anything done by the médersa constituencies themselves.

The second factor which motivated the Malian government to intervene in the médersas was the developmentalist ideology that it had embraced as the inspiration for its social policy. By the 1980s, Mali was struggling with the effects of structural adjustment imposed by the International Monetary Fund and the World Bank, a set of programs which were aimed primarily at liberalizing the economy through privatization and at reducing the levels of public expenditure, especially by lowering levels of government employment. We have seen how these policies had caused severe political reactions among students in 1979-80, and we have examined some of the social effects on educationally qualified young people of the extensive unemployment brought about by the reduction of civil service jobs, combined with the failure of the private sector to expand. Such policies had their supporters as well as their critics, but our interest here is not in discussing their efficacy or advisability, no matter how justifiable structural adjustment may or may not have been as a strategy for moving Mali out of its economic crisis. Our interest is in the ideology of development which came to pervade the consciousness of an increasing number of Malians in the postcolonial period, and which substituted a kind of 'developmentalist rhetoric' for any serious debate about social or economic policy.

By the 1980s, there was virtually no issue of public concern which was not discussed and evaluated with reference to 'development': economic productivity, unemployment, urban 'delinquency' and street children, health care, demography and family planning, the status of women, and of course schooling. Every program, every project, which addressed any of these kinds of issues was conceptualized and presented to the public as an aspect of 'development policy', although at the same time, virtually all of these programs had originated with, and were financed by, foreign governments or international aid agencies (non-government organizations – NGOs). In other words, the essential content of social and economic policy was imported from abroad, and often applied by foreign 'experts'. It is perhaps arguable that, given the economic plight of the country, such dependence on foreign 'assistance' was unavoidable, but it is equally arguable that such dependency was completely compatible with the interests of those well placed in the state bureaucracy, the party and associated clientelist networks.[2] Plugging into the international

---

[2] In this sense, development aid can be seen as a resource of extraversion; see Chapter 5, n. 83.

aid network was a natural extension of the structures of clientelism into the international arena, although like so much else, not without contradictory implications. The flow of aid may well have helped to sustain members of *le Pouvoir* in a position of domination within the country, but it also revealed their own ultimate political and economic dependence. This fact may have affected Malians more deeply than one might suspect; as one Malian observed, 'Everyone in this country begs, starting with the State.'[3] It is noteworthy that 'begging' in the streets was a widely discussed social issue in Mali in the 1980s, precisely because it was alleged by many to be a serious barrier to 'development'.

However, the central issue addressed in this chapter is the anomaly that the developmentalist ideology which had come to pervade Malian public discourse systematically eliminated, or ignored, the Malians themselves as the initiators of anything which either the government authorities or the development experts would be prepared to recognize as 'development'. Of course, during the 1980s this developmentalist ideology operated in the context of the single party state, and it seems best to begin our explorations with the political implications of this fact for the médersas.

The domestication of the médersas

Order in Council no. 112/PG-RM of 30 April 1985 decreed that the médersas would henceforth fall under the administrative responsibility of the MEN, although they would be 'represented by AMUPI'.[4] This arrangement was typical of the current political project of the single party state: the médersas would fall under the administrative authority of a ministry ultimately responsible to the government, and they would be 'represented', as decreed by the same legislation, by an organization which was itself a creature of the party. Of course, the government and the party were one and the same, but the fiction was disseminated that AMUPI, as the legally recognized association 'representing' all Muslim interests, could better represent the interests of the médersas than the directors themselves. Although médersa directors did hold responsible positions in AMUPI, we have seen that this association was crippled by internal divisions, and that it enjoyed absolutely no authority among most Muslim constituencies, both because it had been given no powers of sanction and because most people saw it for what it was, an organ of *le Pouvoir*. AMUPI never succeeded in representing the médersas in any matter of significance.

Administrative authority over the médersas resided in the *Centre pour la Promotion de la Langue Arabe* (CPLA), a bureau within the Department of Primary Education in the MEN; it had been created in 1979 with the appointment of

---

[3] Quoted in L. Couchoud, 'La migration sur place' p. 31.
[4] According to S. Cissé, *L'enseignement islamique*, p. 130, the change in administrative responsibility was decided by the Council of Ministers in April 1982, although the formal legislation was not promulgated until 1985.

the first *Inspecteur général d'arabe*, Oumar S. Touré, the son of Saada Oumar Touré, founder of the first Segu médersa.[5] The creation of CPLA presaged government interest in controlling the médersas. In 1981, the first census of the médersas was taken. In 1982, the Council of Ministers decided that the education ministry should assume responsibility for the médersas, and plans were set in motion to revise the relevant legislation in order to bring both the creation and functioning of the médersas into line with the state primary schools, and a special committee was set up to enquire into the matter and make recommendations to the Minister of National Education.

The results of these enquiries and deliberations were published in 1983-4.[6] It was recommended that the médersas should remain private, although they would be required to conform to the new regulations concerning their operation. Arabic would be the language of instruction, although French (and eventually the national languages) should be taught as a subject. The religious orientation of the schools would be respected, although the teaching of secular subjects would have to be included in the curriculum and taught to the standards that applied in the state schools. And finally, it was recommended that AMUPI would have a predominant role in ensuring that the médersas conformed with these new arrangements. Somewhat ominously, however, Djimé Diallo, the retired schools inspector who presented these recommendations, predicted that there would be considerable resistance to this program, to which the Minister of National Education replied that thus far he had been able to calm the many people who had already come to him with their worries and complaints, and that in any case the government would not be concerned with either the organization or the management of the médersas, which in fact would be the responsibility of AMUPI![7] These remarks seem to have been made in an effort to reassert the government's commitment to secularism by distancing the ministry from the internal affairs of the médersas, although the reality would be quite different, and profound ambiguities were destined to plague this new policy.

Another source of ambiguity, more conceptual than operational, and indeed more profoundly significant, was the persistent confusion, often laced with tension, which accompanied almost all discussions about the médersas. Once government decided to regulate the médersas, they would have to be formally defined as institutions, which in turn raised a number of questions. One of the most contentious of these was whether the médersas should be classified primarily as religious schools, as the médersa constituencies viewed them, or as a special category of primary schools (*écoles fondamentales*). The

---

[5] Oumar Touré was among the first generation of médersa graduates; he was also among those to receive a scholarship to study in Cairo in the early 1960s, and was integrated into the civil service upon his return.

[6] 'Médersa au Mali. Documents d'informations', 3 vols (Direction de l'Enseignement Fondamental, 1983-4).

[7] *Ibid.*, III, pp. 3 and 46.

government intention seems to have been the latter, as reflected in the wording of the 1985 Order in Council: 'The private médersas are primary schools; religious instruction is authorized in them. ... Arabic is the language of instruction.'

Whether this choice of words was intended to satisfy all parties, or to signal an official commitment to secularism (by citing the médersas as an exception), it was not successful in assuaging doubts; quite the contrary, since it aroused the suspicions, if not the hostility, of everyone concerned. Certain directors were incensed (this is not too strong a word!) that a government which had done nothing to develop the médersas could now claim to 'authorize' the teaching of religious subjects in them; many also expressed the fear that such 'authorization' could at any time be withdrawn; the secularization policies of the US-RDA had not been forgotten. Those who had drafted the legislation seem to have searched for a wording which on the one hand would include the médersas in the primary school system, while at the same time 'respecting' the existing religious studies curriculum; legislation of this sort had existed for the Catholic schools since the colonial period. Secularists, however, strongly objected to this exception, which they condemned along with the creation of AMUPI as the abdication of the state's commitment to constitutional secularism.

The new decree also gave rise to a debate about the wisdom of formally recognizing Arabic as a language of instruction in the médersas, now classified as *écoles fondamentales*. Of course, Arabic was originally employed in the médersas as the language of instruction because of its fundamental religious importance for Muslims, although the political implications of its use were also clear to the médersa pioneers, as indeed they were to the French. The political weight of the Arabic language was subsequently reinforced during the independence movement, with its associated pan-Africanist ambitions, and further deepened with the explosion of Arab aid in the 1970s. Suddenly, so it would seem, the government realized that it had at its disposal a valuable resource in the médersas which could be used to attract aid, precisely because these schools employed Arabic as their language of instruction. This is evident from the fact that the first department set up to oversee the médersas as teaching institutions was called the *Centre pour la Promotion de la Langue Arabe*, which was directed by the Inspector General of Arabic in the MEN. CPLA was charged with responsibility:

– for the training of all personnel who teach the Arabic language in the Republic of Mali;
– for the production of pedagogical materials for teaching Arabic;
– for the elaboration of Arabic curricula, their continuing adaptation and their proper application;

– for gathering suggestions relating to the improvement of Arabic teaching;
– for coordinating and overseeing the activities of the *écoles franco-arabes*;
– to consider proposals to open new schools;

– to promote Arabic as a language of instruction and of culture.[8]

Significantly, perhaps, the médersas were not mentioned in CPLA's original remit, no doubt because at that time the médersas, as officially-defined religious institutions, were still under the administrative authority of the Ministry of the Interior. However, when the first official studies of the médersas were launched in 1982, they were set in a conceptual framework which emphasized the fact that the 'teaching of Arabic' had reached unprecedented levels in Mali;[9] the major objective of these deliberations was to devise a program which would improve the teaching of Arabic and of secular subjects in Arabic (as well as to develop a curriculum for teaching French as a subject of study).

This emphasis on Arabic language was also reflected in a report completed for UNESCO by Oumar Touré in 1985, entitled 'Study on experiments underway and on the present state of the use of the Arabic alphabet in both formal and informal instruction in Mali.'[10] The report touched on all the institutions in Mali which, both past and present, taught Arabic, including the Qur'anic schools and the *écoles franco-arabes*; there was even a section on the French médersas. But the major focus was on the Islamic médersas, their history and their present needs. Perhaps not surprisingly, Oumar Touré devoted considerable space to recounting how his father had developed the teaching of Arabic language in his médersa through his own initiative, never having studied Arabic abroad; the aim of this exercise was to demonstrate the commitment of Malians to learning this language. Although the Islamic content of the médersa curriculum was not ignored in this report, neither was it given much prominence.

But of course, such a tactic did not really hide, nor was it Oumar Touré's intention to hide, the fact that the primary objective of the médersas, at least for their directors, was to transmit knowledge of Islamic religious studies. However, by defining médersas as 'primary schools in which Arabic is the language of instruction', the government may well have intended, if not to divert public attention away from the fact that the médersas were religious institutions, at least to emphasize the fact that its interest in them was primarily to respond to the educational needs of the country as officially defined. After all, Arabic was an official language of the United Nations; and UNESCO and UNICEF were both agencies which interested themselves in education and were prepared to support schooling in Arabic as well as in French. In the view of these two agencies, basic educational skills and knowledge could be transmitted equally effectively in either language. The government's official endorsement of the Arabic language for schooling seems to have been

---

[8] S. Cissé, *L'enseignement islamique*, p. 130; Diakité et Konaté, 'L'enseignement arabo-islamique', p. 38.
[9] 'Médersa au Mali', I, p. 2.
[10] Oumar S. Touré, 'Etude sur des expériences en cours d'éxecution et sur l'état actuel de l'utilisation de l'alphabet arabe dans l'enseignement formel et non-formel au Mali' Rapport à l'UNESCO, 1985.

informed by similar considerations, plus the fact that Arabic was an African and international language which could serve as a valuable asset in both government and commerce. But this kind of argumentation and justification could not hide the fact that Arabic was also the revered language of Islam and of Islamic knowledge, which the government was much less prepared to acknowledge publicly, and which further deepened the suspicions of many medersa directors about its ultimate intentions.

And, indeed, it was precisely the fact that the médersa was an Islamic institution which aroused the greatest suspicion among many officials, some of whom were not reticent about airing their concerns publicly. For example, the final report of the first government study of the médersas in 1982-3, included the following statement (cited above in Chapter 5):

> What must concern us above everything else is the future of the hundreds of thousands of young Malians who are likely to attend the médersas and Qur'anic schools in the near future, given the rapid expansion of Islamization. These children expect us to offer them the opportunity to become enlightened Muslims, effective citizens [*des citoyens à part entière*], effective producers and agents of national development, not blind and dangerously fanaticized masses who will be even more susceptible to exploitation.
>
> And so, just as it is appropriate to assist and encourage those teachers and founders of schools who present the required guarantees for [providing] a valid education, so it is necessary legally to prohibit the incompetents and swindlers from cheating the people.[11]

Here we have several significant juxtapositions, for example, between 'agents of national development' versus 'fanaticized masses', and between presumably legitimate 'teachers and founders of schools' and 'incompetents and swindlers'. The point is not that there may not have been 'incompetents' and perhaps even 'swindlers' involved in médersa schooling; the point is that such language was never used with reference to the state schools where, as we will try to demonstrate, conditions and practices comparable to those in the least palatable médersas also existed. Similarly, in the early 1980s there was little evidence of the existence of 'fanaticized masses', or even the threat of their emergence in Mali, although political 'terrorism' was of course a major international issue. Nonetheless, this statement, as part of the official report on the médersas, helped to set the public tone for the government intervention that was to follow.

In March 1985 the MEN published an overview of Malian education, in which the médersas were mentioned almost as an afterthought, at the end of a lengthy description of the state primary schools. This document is of particular interest, because it appeared concurrently with the Order in Council that formally extended government control over the médersas:[12]

---

[11] 'Rapport de la Comité Restreinte au Conseil Supérieure de l'Education Nationale sur les médersas et les écoles quraniques en République du Mali', in 'Médersa au Mali', III, p. 54.
[12] 'L'Enseignement en République du Mali. Administration. Organisation. Missions' (Bamako: Ministère de l'Education Nationale, 1985).

The médersas. The médersas are primary schools in which the study of Arabic begins from the first year.

The médersas, the Franco-Arabic schools and the Qur'anic schools all have a common goal, the expansion of Arab culture in our country.

In 1981, a census of these establishments determined that more than 127,252 students receive an education in them.

This figure represents 36.62 percent of the enrolments in primary school and demonstrates the great interest that people have in this form of education for their children.

The level of enrolments in the primary schools, the médersas and the Qur'anic schools [taken together] gives a more accurate idea of the educational efforts made by the Government and the Party in the struggle against illiteracy.

Furthermore, [by including the médersas and Qur'anic schools] the enrolment rate among children of primary school age [years one through six] would be approximately 30 per cent instead of 22 per cent if one takes into account only the state primary school.

Given the large number of children enrolled in the médersas and the Qur'anic schools, their [government] regulation is necessary in order:

– better to regulate the content and level of educational content [of their curricula],
– to harmonize nationally the activities of all our educational institutions.

This document speaks volumes about attitudes then current within the ministry, and presumably in other official circles. It totally misrepresents the objectives of both médersas and Qur'anic schools by ignoring their religious orientation and by alleging that their aim is to spread 'Arab culture'. Nor does the author seem to have discerned a basic contradiction in suggesting that, whereas the educational contribution of these institutions had only recently been 'discovered', credit for this contribution should go to government and party. The main point of the passage seems to lie in a number-crunching exercise, apparently designed to demonstrate that the rate of school enrolments and illiteracy in Mali was not as bad as was generally thought. It would seem that this document was prepared for public consumption, as a kind of overview of ministry activities in the mid-1980s, perhaps as an introduction to the Malian educational system for aid workers arriving to participate in the *4ème Projet*. Whatever its purpose, the views expressed in it reflect attitudes held by persons in responsible positions in the ministry.

These kinds of attitudes, as well as the ambiguities and uncertainties surrounding government intentions, produced considerable anxiety among many within the médersa constituencies, but these concerns were as nothing when compared to the reaction created by the authoritarian and aggressive manner in which the MEN actually intervened following the 1985 Order in Council. Here was an example of the *commandement* in action, of a ministry and its agents expecting that their authority should be accepted without question or discussion. Here also was an example of how the tactics and strategies of power relations in a Muslim society could be articulated around various competing perceptions of Islam.

In 1986, the first official directives based on the new legislation were distributed, along with a new curriculum for the first cycle of the primary school (the first six years).[13] It was also announced that examinations for the primary school certificate[14] and entry into the second cycle, which would be based on this curriculum and administered in Arabic, could be taken on a voluntary basis at the end of the academic year 1985-6, although at the end of the next academic year, in 1987, they would be obligatory for all médersa students. It is not clear precisely when the new curriculum was distributed, but it was certainly well after the 1985-6 school year had begun.

The protests from directors were immediate: they alleged that the new curriculum subverted the central religious objectives of the médersas by not allowing adequate time for proper coverage of religious studies subjects; the médersas could not possibly prepare their pupils for examinations in secular subjects for which the proper teaching manuals and materials were not available in Arabic, nor did they have enough properly trained teachers to cover all these subjects. And their resentment only deepened when they discovered that the proposed examinations included no questions at all on religious studies.

Not surprisingly, the most militant of those who resisted government intervention in the operation of the médersas was Saada Oumar Touré in Segu.[15] He claimed that the new curriculum had been drawn up without any consultation with the médersa directors, and that in effect CPLA was incompetent to take on such a task. He also attacked what he considered the suspicious language of Article 3 of the 1985 Order in Council: 'The private médersas are primary schools; the teaching of religion is authorized in them.' The objective of the médersas was to teach Islam, Saada Oumar asserted, not 'religion'; would this article allow someone to open a school for teaching Bahai'ism, or even communism, and call it a médersa? And he wondered how the government could 'authorize' what for forty years had been a fact!

Saada's reaction might have been predictable except for one intriguing fact: his own son, Oumar Saada Touré, had been responsible for developing this curriculum when he was director of CPLA, a position from which he had now resigned in order to take up a post at ISESCO in Morocco. Oumar Saada flatly refuted the claim that the new médersa curriculum had been drawn up in the absence of consultation with médersa directors. According to him, in its search for a new standardized curriculum for the médersas CPLA had assembled all the directors of the Bamako médersas at a meeting at which they compared the curricula from many of Mali's leading médersas (including

---

[13] *Al-manhaj al-rasmī li 'l-madāris al-ahliyya al-'arabiyya (al-marḥala al-ibtidā'iyya)* [*Programme officiel pour les médersas populaires arabes (Premier Cycle)*]. Centre de Promotion de la Langue Arabe, Ministère de l'Éducation Nationale. 1986.

[14] *Certificat fin d'études du premier cycle, enseignement fondamental.*

[15] The following discussion is based on an interview with Saada Oumar Touré in Segu, 29 March 1987.

that of Saada Oumar) with those from such institutions as al-Azhar, the Islamic Centre of Khartoum, and the University of Madina. These programs were then juxtaposed with the curriculum of the Malian *école fondamentale* with the aim of developing a single curriculum for the médersas which would combine a sound religious education with a level of 'scientific' training equal to that offered in the state schools; of course, Arabic would be the language of instruction in the médersas.[16]

Perhaps it is significant, given the subsequent course of events, that only directors of Bamako médersas were invited to these consultations; and one suspects that Saada Oumar Touré and his son may not have agreed on these matters of reform. In any case, Oumar Saada had left his post at CPLA before the reforms were promulgated and was not responsible for their implementation. And perhaps his absence made it all the easier for his father to react as he did. Saada Oumar allegedly informed the regional inspector of education that the students in his médersa would not be sitting the newly introduced examinations. In addition to the substantive objections already mentioned, he argued that the curriculum had not been distributed in a timely manner which would allow directors to modify their programs to conform to it, even if they were of a mind to do so, and that one could not expect students to sit an examination for which they had not been properly prepared. Furthermore, he added, even when the curriculum was received, well after the start of the school year, much of it was illegible because it had been poorly reproduced.

Saada Oumar also took action in his role as regional president of AMUPI by convincing all the médersa directors in Segu to sign a letter to the national president of AMUPI stating that the new curriculum was unacceptable because it was not in accord with the Islamic objectives for which the médersas had been established, and that it would have to be revised in cooperation with the directors themselves.[17] He further argued that this threat against the médersas was in fact a threat against the basic interests of Islam, and that AMUPI must act now to defend the 'rights' of the médersas and of Muslims in general, and that they must pursue their cause to the end. The only hope for the Muslims was to unify through AMUPI, which after all had been established to promote the *unity* and *progress* [Saada Oumar's emphasis!] of Islam. His own strategy, he explained, was not to say 'no' to the government, but at the same time to defend his 'rights'. He claimed that he had always predicted that Muslims in Mali would not unite until they were under the whip; now

[16] Oumar Saada Touré, personal communication, 6 December 1991. His comments were made in response to my assertion that the Malian government had 'promulgated its reform and published its curriculum without any consultation whatsoever with the médersa directors'. See L. Brenner, 'Médersas au Mali. Ttransformation d'une institution islamique' in Sanankoua and Brenner, *L'enseignement islamique au Mali*, p. 83.

[17] Although I never saw a copy of this letter, this part of its contents were confirmed in interview with Oumar Ly, national president of AMUPI, 19 March 1987, Bamako. Interestingly, Oumar Saada asserted in his comments to me: 'I challenge anyone to tell me that the program that was drawn up was not Islamic.'

they were! And if the government were to try to attack Islam, well, the Muslims knew very well how to defend themselves!

Perhaps the defiant tone of some of these remarks was more extreme because they were expressed in the privacy of his own home, but there is no doubt that Saada Oumar publicly united the Segu directors against the new curriculum. The initial response from CPLA was simply to ignore Segu. CPLA, too, had received a letter from Segu, which according to them had 'mentioned faults' in the curriculum, but without suggesting counter-proposals. 'They refused to participate in the examinations last year, which in any case were voluntary. But if they continue to resist, we will simply close their médersas. Not by sending in the police and locking the doors, but by refusing to recognize their diplomas and refusing to allow their students to participate in competitions for scholarships. And if this happens, the schools will simply disappear.'[18]

Not only did the resistance continue, but it spread to Bamako, although not with the same unified force as in Segu. In the first place, there was no advocate for the médersas in Bamako with the same religious and political stature as Saada Oumar, most of the directors there being much younger. Furthermore, there were many more médersas in Bamako, and their directors represented a broad range of often conflicting views about their role and objectives. Not only were there doctrinal divergences, but some directors felt that cooperation with the government would benefit their schools and were quite prepared to accept the new curriculum. Finally, unified political resistance in Bamako may have been more difficult to organize because of the pervasive presence there of the state bureaucracy, the party, and their agents. In Bamako one was more directly susceptible than in a place like Segu to both the punitive and the seductive attentions of *le Pouvoir*.

Nonetheless, a resistance movement did develop in Bamako, primarily because of the stubborn attitude of the minister of education, who dug in his heels and refused to negotiate; he insisted that the ministry would set policy, not the directors of médersas. This confrontational situation brought together a number of médersa directors who organized themselves into a new association, the Union of Arabo-Islamic Médersas,[19] which followed Segu's lead in writing a letter to AMUPI to protest the new curriculum. The members of this organization also joined with Segu in boycotting the 1987 examinations, which were meant to be obligatory for all médersa students.[20] The boycott further deepened tensions, and CPLA responded just as they had threatened;

[18] This is a paraphrase of comments by M. Dikko, assistant director of CPLA, 23 March 1987, Bamako.

[19] *Ittiḥād al-madāris al-'arabiyya al-islāmiyya.*

[20] These included the médersas directed by Sufiyana Dramé and the *Institut Islamique*, directed by Abdul Aziz Yattabare; among the major Bamako médersas to allow their students to sit the examinations were the *Institut Islamique Khaled Ben Abdul Aziz* and *Institut Islamique Nahar Djoliba*.

students from the boycotting médersas were not allowed to compete for state-controlled scholarships for study abroad. The confrontation grew into a stalemate that extended well into 1988, when the minister of education finally ordered CPLA to sit down with a committee of directors to consider a curriculum drawn up by the Union of Arabo-Islamic Médersas as a possible basis for compromise.[21] By then, however, the ministry had also begun to impose other sanctions on the non-cooperating médersas, such as not allowing their staff to attend re-training programs for médersa teachers, and a campaign to impose strict adherence to regulations concerning class size and hygiene.[22]

The creation of the Union of Arabo-Islamic Médersas illustrates the political dynamic which had been created by this confrontation. The médersa directors had never previously felt the need to organize among themselves, but now their interests were being directly threatened, and they were being politicized around a specifically Islamic issue. They were unifying 'under the whip', just as Saada Oumar said they would. The original impetus to form such an organization derived from the failure of AMUPI to do anything to support the médersa cause, and one of the Union's first acts was to write a letter to AMUPI, in August 1987 at the height of the tension, encouraging action in the same vein as the Segu letter. Although no answer was ever received to this letter, AMUPI did convene a meeting of Bamako and Segu directors in September 1987, in order to hear their grievances. Among those listed were that the government's curriculum was inappropriate and the directors wanted time to elaborate their own; that although formally designated as the intermediary between the médersas and the MEN, AMUPI was never consulted on any aspect of these matters; that the directors considered the CPLA staff to be incompetent to oversee médersa education, since only the director was literate in Arabic;[23] that they wanted the new educational establishment being set up at the *Centre Culturel Islamique* to be a lycée in order to absorb students successfully completing the second cyle of primary school.[24]

AMUPI held its Constitutive Congress in November 1987, and the published accounts of the meeting suggest that the médersa crisis was studiously kept off the agenda, which reveals how agents of *le Pouvoir* were attempting to

[21] *Manhaj al-ta'lim, al-marhala al-ibtidā'iyya* [*Programme d'enseignement, premier cycle*], 3 vols (Bamako, 1988).

[22] Interview with Thierno Hadi Thiam, 27 Sept. 1988, Bamako.

[23] The then incumbent director, Amadou Bari, had received a university degree in Arabic literature in Cairo.

[24] For some unexplained reason, the MEN insisted that this institution should offer only second cycle classes, which many médersa directors took as yet another act against their interests and 'against Islam'. It could be that this decision was taken purposefully in order to limit the prospects of médersa students, and therefore to diminish the appeal of médersa schooling, but no specific confirmation of this claim has come to light. The account of the September 1987 meeting was given in interview by Thierno Hadi Thiam, 7 Jan. 1988, Bamako.

manipulate the political forces unleashed by this situation. In his report to the meeting on AMUPI's activities, the national president, Oumar Ly, made no mention of the crisis, and he made only a few brief references to the médersas, which were in fact comments on AMUPI's own inefficacy. 'We have to recognize that we have not created a single school, médersa, or library, or constructed a single mosque.' And his remarks about the role of AMUPI in the distribution of scholarship aid were revealing of relationships with government:

One of AMUPI's objectives was to obtain scholarships in the Arab countries for our médersa students. Until now, we have not benefitted from any direct attribution for scholarships, and we had hoped, in applying Order in Council no. 112/PG/RM of 30 April 1985, which stipulated in its Article 5 that the médersas are represented by AMUPI in all relationships with the Public Powers, that the Ministry of National Education would have included us in the work of the commission which distributes the scholarships financed each year by the Arab countries to successful médersa graduates. Until now this has not been the case, which is truly unfortunate, since our presence would have allowed us to moralize [*moraliser*] the work of this commission.[25]

This reference to 'moralization' reflects the widespread opinion that 'ever since the education ministry took over the administration of scholarships, everyone knows they are for sale'! However, it is doubtful that such criticisms would have been assuaged had AMUPI been involved in the distribution of scholarships!

Ly also spoke about another failed AMUPI initiative, an effort to find financial support for the creation of an Arabic language lycée; however, so he claimed, 'the deterioration of the world economic situation, especially in the oil countries, destroyed our hopes.' One of the resolutions endorsed by the Congress referred to the pressing need for a *lycée*, and also echoed the demands of the médersa directors:

Considering that the multiplication of médersas authorized by the Government poses serious problems for the continuation of schooling into secondary school,

Congress strongly requests the creation of a Franco-Arabic lycée at the *Centre Culturel Islamique* to respond to the drop in school enrolments at this level.[26]

The Congress also passed a curiously worded resolution which might be interpreted as a reference to the médersa crisis, although it was so constructed as to avoid clear comprehension of its intent: 'Congress praises the initiative designed to explore the problems surrounding Islamic studies in order to consider recommended approaches [to resolving this question?]'[27] Was this meant to be a reference to the initiative of the Union of Arabo-Islamic Médersas, who had now decided to develop a revised curriculum to present to the MEN as a possible basis for negotiations?

[25] 'Rapport d'activité', Président National, 'Program et textes de base, Congrés Constitutif, AMUPI, Nov. 1987, Bamako.

[26] 'Résolution générale', *ibid.*

[27] The original French reads: 'Le Congrès loue l'initiative qui consiste à situer la problématique des études islamiques pour envisager les méthodes d'approche préconisés.'

Given his strong views on these matters, it is not surprising that Saada Oumar Touré was enraged by the proceedings of this meeting, although he himself had not attended. 'Oumar Ly has won out', he said with considerable anger, but without much surprise. In his view, neither Ly nor AMUPI were doing anything for Islam. 'When the government instituted their reform without consultation, they did nothing; when they said the médersa students should sit the exams, they did nothing.' But now, he continued, directors in Bamako had joined those in Segu in rejecting the government intervention, and they had set up groups to develop a revised curriculum.[28]

It would not be until September 1988, that certain directors and representatives from CPLA would sit down to consider a revised curriculum, by which time they were under direct instructions from the minister of education to find a compromise solution. During the interim, and even at the time of these meetings, little had happened to lessen tensions, although it would seem that various political forces were at work in order to undermine the momentum of médersa resistance by co-opting some of its leadership. Thierno Hadi Thiam, director of a small médersa in Bamako and one of the active founders of the Union of Arabo-Islamic Médersas, was elected Secretary for Education and Culture at the AMUPI Congress in November 1987. Shortly thereafter, he was charged by the AMUPI national executive to organize an association of médersas on the national, regional and local levels as a structure for coordinating relations between AMUPI and the médersas.

At the time Thiam seemed fairly enthusiastic about this plan, although presumably the new association would replace, or render redundant, the role of the independent Union of Arabo-Islamic Médersas. He felt he had been selected for this position so that he could speak on behalf of médersa interests in various public and semi-official contexts, and he was hopeful that with several médersa directors on the recently elected national executive, AMUPI might take a more active and effective role. Within a few months, however, he changed his tune; AMUPI was 'aligned with the government', he observed somewhat bitterly, as evidenced by the attitude of its national president toward the médersas, which was simply to advise the directors 'to obey the law'. Officials at the education ministry were either rude and dismissive or repeatedly cancelled meetings with him and other representatives of AMUPI, and he was becoming increasingly convinced that the government wanted to eliminate Islamic studies from the médersas. Later in 1988 Thiam was appointed to the National Committee for Cultural Affairs of the Central Executive of the UDPM. Here, 'among politicians', he said he felt completely out of his element and very much exposed. He felt that if he spoke about Islam he would draw an angry reaction from those who would accuse him of wanting to 'Islamize' the country, whereas what he wanted was to find a way forward for the médersas to develop, to allow the directors to fulfil what they saw as their own role.[29]

[28] Interviews with Saada Oumar Touré, 30 and 31 Dec. 1987, Segu.

[29] The preceding discussion is based on several interviews with Thierno Hadi Thiam, 7

Perhaps Thierno Hadi Thiam's experience was the product of his own hopes, ambitions and naïveté combined with the inherent processes which operate in a clientelist system, and not of some explicit and conscious plan by members of AMUPI and the UDPM to undermine médersa resistance. Whatever the facts of the matter, this episode illustrates the role which 'Islam', or representations of Islam, could play in the dynamics of power relations; government intervention in the médersas, whatever its official objectives, also allowed members of the state bureaucracy and representatives of *le Pouvoir* to identify and to assert their domination over new subjects, in this case 'Muslims'. Thiam's feelings of marginalization derived from the treatment he received as a Muslim; they were induced by officials who refused to see him or who often abused him when they did, and were further deepened by the atmosphere which prevailed in public forums which inhibited one to speak as a Muslim. His anxieties about the possible reaction he might receive in the UDPM Committee for Cultural Affairs were unpleasantly confirmed in 1989, when he proposed in a session of the *Etats Généraux sur l'Education* the establishment of a *Direction Nationale de l'Enseignement Islamique*; he was shouted down as a 'fanatic'. The *Direction Nationale de l'Enseignement Catholique*, which had existed for years, had never been similarly challenged, nor was it on this occasion.

In fact, Thierno Hadi Thiam's doubts about the government's intentions only deepened as the months and years progressed..Even after a compromise curriculum had been agreed, and official hostility toward the médersas seemed to diminish, he remained convinced that the government meant either to allow the médersas to die a natural death from lack of economic support, or to squash them. In his view, government was interested in the Arabic language only to the extent that it could be used effectively to teach secular subjects, and they remained opposed to religious studies: 'They want to control the médersas so that they can turn our sacred language into a language which will Europeanize our children.'[30]

Thierno Hadi Thiam's experience was not unique; his feelings of marginalization were shared by many others, and they were reinforced in numerous ways. What was at issue was not simply personal opinions or attitudes about religion or Islam. A much more subtle and complex process of power relations was at work, which was also reflected in the public discourse. Islam was in fact the focus of constant contestation. Secularist policies decreed that matters Islamic should remain officially invisible, that is, excluded from the public domain unless they threatened public order; however, when Muslim affairs were no longer invisible, Muslims and 'Islam' became objects through which many sought to express their pretensions to superiority and domination.

Jan., 9 and 22 Sept. 1988, Bamako.
[30] Interview with Thierno Hadi Thiam, 15 Dec. 1990.

Of course, the equation of power relations as conceptualized by Foucault includes at least two constituent forces: a will to dominate and a refusal to submit. Many Muslims were quite content for Islam to remain officially 'invisible'; for them, Islam stood outside, and indeed above, the political fray. If some Muslims privately longed for the establishment of an Islamic state, they never advocated such a position publicly; it was generally accepted that Mali was a secular state and was likely to remain so. However, official secularism provided the space in which Muslims could produce a moralizing discourse which presented Islam as a phenomenon quite separate from, and unblemished by, the 'politics of the politicians'. For many, Islam was also a refuge from the unpalatable and threatening effects of social change; as Thierno Hadi Thiam said, and many parents implied, the médersas did not threaten to 'Europeanize' their children because they were Muslim institutions. And finally, Islam was often represented as inviolable, based as it was on divine principles transmitted through the Holy Qur'an. On the other hand, Muslim spokespersons had no compunctions about commenting upon, and placing an Islamic gloss on, any and all social and political issues.

The invisibility of the médersas: discursive patterns in the public arena

The preceding discussion of attempts to domesticate the médersas, and of various resistances to this process, reveals significant aspects of power relations in the Mali of the 1980s, particularly with regard to Muslim constituencies. The many contradictions that attended this process can be illustrated by further exploring the public discourse which provided the backdrop to these political actions.

Let us begin with the official discourse. We have already alluded above to the final report of the 1983 official study of médersas that presented their prospects in vividly dualistic terms. Either the médersas would come under government control, thereby allegedly assuring that competent and well-trained 'teachers and founders of schools' would provide a 'valid education' for students who would become 'effective producers and agents of national development'; or, the médersas could remain independent of government control and continue to be run by 'incompetents and swindlers' whose students would become 'blind and dangerously fanaticized masses … susceptible to exploitation'.[31]

The reports from regional inspectors of education which provided the basic input into the 1983 study of médersas varied in their assessments of the médersas (and Qur'anic schools), and they rarely expressed their conclusions in terms as stark as those found in the final report. But they all tended to agree that control of the médersas was necessary, although occasionally for quite contradictory reasons. For example, the report from Kati argued that the proliferation of médersas (and Qur'anic schools) drew prospective

---

[31] 'Médersa au Mali', III, 54; see note 11 above.

students away from the state schools and thereby endangered their effective operation. This inspector went on to argue that médersas should be rigorously controlled and permitted to operate only where enrolment in state schools was not jeopardized.[32] On the other hand, one report from Segu argued that both Qur'anic schools and médersas could absorb children not otherwise in school and also help to decongest overcrowded schools.[33] However, observations of this kind were rarely made without accompanying comments about the fact that médersas are Muslim schools. Thus, reports from Bamako argued that médersa schooling could help to 'demystify' the population: 'Well structured and regulated, the médersas will certainly help to resolve the educational problem, especially in fanatical milieux.'[34]

Of course, there were also many criticisms of the médersas as educational institutions: that teachers were often poorly trained (or not trained at all), that the pedagogy employed was unlikely to result in quality instruction, that the material condition of many médersas was inadequate and not conducive to learning, that teaching materials were often insufficient or even non-existent, etc. In spite of these kinds of observations, the predominant and ultimately prevailing view among all participants in this exercise was that if properly regulated the médersas could contribute significantly to the education of Mali's children. The unstated assumption informing this conclusion was that the MEN was capable of ensuring both the control and improvement of educational standards in the médersas, a highly dubious assumption judging from the ministry's management of the state schools.

For example, it seems quite clear that no matter what formal decisions had been taken by government ministers about the control and administration of the médersas, these had not been effectively communicated to the schools inspectorate, which continued basically to ignore the médersas. In 1985 the same year that the decree was promulgated which integrated the médersas into the MEN, a national assessment of development needs and prospects was taking place.[35] The basic factual input into this exercise was collected in regional reports called *Diagnostics*, each of which contained a section assessing the current state of educational provision. Of six regional *Diagnostics* consulted, none contained a systematic presentation, never mind analysis, of médersa schooling.[36] Indeed, médersas are mentioned only in the reports on Mopti and Gao, where médersas were much less significant than elsewhere, and then only in passing in order to point out that many parents in these regions preferred sending their childen to médersas rather than to state schools. In other words, these reports on education, presumably prepared by many of the

[32] *Ibid.*, II, 8-10.
[33] *Ibid.*, II, 11-13.
[34] *Ibid.*, II, 26-30.
[35] See the 'Deuxième conférence internationale des bailleurs de fonds. Rapport principal', Bamako: Ministère du Plan, 1985.
[36] Kayes, Koulikoro, Segou, Mopti, Tombouctou and Gao; none was located for Sikasso or the District of Bamako.

same persons who had contributed not long before to the 1983 study of the médersas, included virtually no mention of médersa schooling in Mali, despite the fact that their potential contribution to the education of Malian children had been recently assessed and formally recognized.

Whether the médersas were purposefully eliminated from consideration in this exercise, or whether their omission was yet another lapse in bureaucratic thinking, is uncertain. However, the *Diagnostics* all seem to have been written in a similar format, presumably in response to a list of specific questions. The content of the reports suggests that the guidelines for compiling them requested respondents to comment on the factors they felt were undermining the development of education, including the causes for hostile attitudes toward state schooling, for decreasing enrolments and falling levels and standards of achievement, and to assess the observed social effects of these circumstances. Absence of comments about the médersas suggests that no specific questions were posed about them, and perhaps more significantly that they were not perceived by most educationists as contributing to educational 'development', although by now the médersas had for some time been the focus of considerable reflection and the decision had already been taken (though not officially promulgated) to integrate them into the national education program.

The *Diagnostics* are extremely candid and critical documents, occasionally slightly defensive in tone when seeking to give recognition to the efforts of educators to overcome the numerous obstacles that confronted them. Different reports focus on different aspects of the problems they assess, but they are unanimous in deploring the conditions of the schools and the instruction given in them. The following excerpt from the Koulikoro report is representative:

Even if the curricula are more or less adapted to the needs of the country, educational materials are so cruelly lacking that at times one begins to question the future of the *école fondamentale*. Everything is in short supply, even to the most basic equipment, like a blackboard. Teaching manuals are unknown in most classes. And as for school supplies, the pupils possess hardly any at all. Classes are constantly disturbed by the comings and goings of pupils borrowing rulers, pencils, erasers, and so forth from their comrades. It is not unusual to see first, second, third or even fourth-year pupils sitting on the ground with their notebooks on their knees. [...]

Most public schools are in such a disgraceful state that neither teachers nor pupils feel any desire to work there.

Example: openings in the buildings have neither doors nor windows installed in them, and the ceilings, if there are any, are riddled with pock-marks.

In addition, one must not forget that many classrooms do not conform with dimensional standards. Constructed with whatever materials are available, and not properly maintained, the classrooms are like filthy hovels and are not conducive to rewarding work. In most establishments, certain fundamental elements are missing, like windows and doors, an enclosure wall, and sanitary facilities. The absence of a surrounding wall means that the courtyard is a public place where people and animals move about at any time. The absence or insufficiency of sanitary facilities is the cause for many classes being missed by both pupils and teachers. Without the teacher, there is no school work. Thus, the teacher is the basic element of instruction. Before independence, the best students were destined for a teaching career. Nowadays, it is quite different, despite the practice of sending those with the DEF to the IPEGs [*Instituts Pédagogiques d'Enseignement Général*, which train primary school teachers]. But the output of these institutions is largely mediocre. Today, people become teachers by the force of circumstances, and the teaching corps, which is very young and without vocation, is constantly moving about seeking to provide for their material well-being; a large number of them leave teaching or simply emigrate. [...]

   If there has been a notable improvement in enrolments, the level of instruction is regressing. [...] The causes for the fall in level of pupil achievement are diverse and complex: the hostile attitude of certain parents toward the school, instruction often poorly adapted to needs, the lack of qualified teachers, the general work conditions, ... poor school attendance, inadequate number of teachers, lack of authority of the teacher etc.[37]

The point of quoting this text at such length is to demonstrate that the material and pedagogical conditions which prevailed in the state schools were no better, and in some cases considerably worse, than those in some médersas, which reinforces the question raised above about the capacity of the MEN effectively to improve médersa education. Indeed, these observations serve to clarify in part why the process of integrating the médersas into the national school system took the form of 'domestication'. Neither the government nor the ministry had anything to offer the médersas, and indeed they offered nothing; the principal result of the entire exercise, at least in its early stages, was to force the médersa constituencies to submit to the state bureaucratic order.

   But the *Diagnostics* highlight yet another contradiction in the public discourse of this period. According to many reports, poor and inadequate provision of schooling was producing numerous socially corrosive problems, including juvenile delinquency, rising rates of unemployment, rural migration toward urban centres, emigration to other countries, and the deepening hostility of parents toward the public school. One might be excused when reading through these reports for suspecting that the state schools were fully responsible for virtually all the social problems which Mali was experiencing at the time, which again raises the question of how officials came to the conclusion that integration of the médersas into such an ineffective and socially dysfunctional school system could possibly improve them.

   Among all the deleterious social effects allegedly produced by poor schools, juvenile delinquency took pride of place, having been mentioned more often than any other category of problem. This allegation is particularly interesting since Qur'anic schooling was also widely accused of contributing to the rise

---

[37] 'Diagnostic de la Région de Koulikoro': Région de Koulikoro, Comité Régional de Développement (Bamako: Ministère du Plan, 1985), pp. 231-2.

of juvenile delinquency, a theme that is evident in 'Médersa au Mali'. For example, one educational inspector asserted that most of those leaving Qur'anic schools end up in the street where, having learned no trade, they 'become lazy, and turn to juvenile delinquency, banditry, vandalism, and everything else which degrades Malian society'.[38] Charges of the drift into delinquency were also linked with the practice of begging by the students of Qur'anic schools, described in one report as 'centers for the training of beggars, bandits and parasites. [...] What was formerly done for the love of God is now done for the love of money.' The "*garibous*" [Qur'anic students] who are often adolescents, are severely exploited and subjected to the necessity to beg, which is one of the sources of the [social] decay and juvenile delinquency which is growing every day.'[39]

Interestingly, the médersas were only rarely charged with contributing to juvenile delinquency; quite the contrary, they might be praised for reinforcing Islamic faith and morals (as indeed were the Qur'anic schools by some sympathetic observers), and we have seen that many parents opted for the médersas in the hope of protecting their children from the allegedly deleterious social influences which they associated with attendance in state schools. This evidence might suggest that the médersas were managing to capture some of the moral high ground in some quarters, but it also further illustrates the patterns of contradictions which pervaded comparisons between the médersas with the state schools.

Another example of these patterns can be found in a report on private education prepared in 1990 by AMRAD, the *Association Malienne de Recherche-Action pour le Développement*, a Malian non-government organization.[40] This study was undertaken at the request of the *Bureau des Projets Education*, which was located in the MEN and which coordinated various aid projects, the most important of which at this time was the *4ème Projet Education*, which will be discussed in further detail below. As mentioned above, one of the major initiatives in this project was to increase the enrolments of primary school children through the establishment of private, fee-paying schools, referred to in the *4ème Projet* as *écoles de base*. This study is of interest to the present discussion because of the ambivalent stance adopted in it towards the médersas. On the one hand, the very first paragraph of the report explicitly states that the médersas will be excluded from consideration. The paragraph opens with the claim that there are two kinds of private schools in Mali:

Formal private schooling consists of all those schools that follow the same curriculum and lead to the same results as the public schools. Non-conventional private schooling includes all those institutions, confessional or not, which attempt to transmit

---

[38] Médersa au Mali, II, 20.

[39] *Ibid.*, 14 and 12.

[40] 'Le Développement de l'Enseignement Privé au Mali' (study conducted by the District of Bamako and the Communes of Ségou and Sikasso). final, report compiled by the Association Malienne de Recherche-Action pour le Développement, Bamako, 1990.

knowledge [*savoir*] to the populations (catechist schools, Qur'anic schools, for a long time the médersas etc.). Our study will focus on the first type of private schooling which, following the model of public schooling, enables not only the acquisition of knowledge but also social mobility.[41]

Of course, by 1990 all médersas which had been 'recognized' by the MEN were meant to be following a curriculum which conformed to those of the state schools, in addition to the program of Islamic studies which they also offered. The distinction being drawn in the AMRAD report was therefore incorrect, since the programs of at least some médersas had by now been formally accepted by the ministry. However, later in the report, the author suddenly, and without any explanation or justification, included the médersas in his discussion of the *écoles de base*, which were proclaimed to constitute the 'future for the development of private schooling'.

By *école de base* we understand a primary school created by an individual, a group of individuals or a collectivity. It is profitable in the sense that it generates revenue but it is adapted to the particular circumstances of the locality where it is established. Over time, it can develop and extend to other school cycles and become a competitive commercial educational enterprise. We do not give it a communal content even if in certain neighbourhoods or villages the local inhabitants assign it such content. And we refuse to label it 'schooling for the poor', which connotes schooling on the cheap and a sense of neglect for those who attend these schools.[42]

This reference to 'schooling for the poor' refers to a comment which appears in the section of the report on Segu, where the data-gathering and analysis for this study was based on interviews with only eight school administrators, seven from the state system plus the single individual who had set up a private secular primary school in Segu under the auspices of the *4ème Projet*. In the paraphrased view of this unrepresentative group, the médersas were '*écoles de pauvreté*' to which no parent would send a child in the expectation that he or she might become an 'important employee of the state (*grand commis de l'Etat*)'. These respondents thought the médersas might be effective in dispensing primary education to the 'masses', but they could not be counted on to provide 'instruction of quality'.[43] They went on to opine that, given 'the level of socio-economic development of the region', it was unlikely that parents would pay money to send their children to school.

All eight of these persons were sending their own children to the only Catholic private school in Segu, which provides an incisive insight into their social background and their social aspirations! But their comments also completely ignore the fact that thousands of families in the city of Segu were in fact paying money to send their children to the médersas. Clearly some people were prepared to pay for educating their children, including themselves! And what is remarkable about the AMRAD study is that no

41 *Ibid.*, p. 3.
42 *Ibid.*, 30-1.
43 *Ibid.*, 23.

effort whatsoever was made to determine precisely why parents were willing to pay to send their children to médersas, although their enrolments far exceeded any other form of private schooling in Mali at the time.

Clearly the AMRAD report is not a very sophisticated document, and the only reason to devote so much space to it is to illustrate the confused and contradictory pattern of attitudes towards the médersas that prevailed at the time. However, as in the case of the regional *Diagnostics* discussed above, it is unclear why the compilers of this report excluded from their study any direct exploration of the médersas as 'commercial enterprises'. In addition to an evident lack of research competence, one suspects the existence of a profound resistance to accepting the médersa as an 'educational establishment', an attitude which was by no means limited to the researchers of AMRAD.

We find similar attitudes expressed in the official documentation of CPLA whose remit explicitly charged them with the regulation and 'animation' of the médersas. In a brief document of only nine pages on the subject of 'Arabo-Islamic schooling' produced by CPLA in 1991, one reads 'that the evolution of the médersas began when they were taken over by the Department of Education [sic] in 1987.'[44] What was meant by this statement, as subsequently elaborated, was that it was only with the introduction of the new officially approved curriculum and of standardized examinations that the médersas became educational establishments. This statement is reminiscent of the extraordinary claim made in another ministry document, cited above,[45] that the institutional development of the médersas should be credited to government and party initiatives!

The preceding discussion illustrates that there was virtually no official interest in the médersas as a social institution nor as a popular social movement. There was a sense that the médersas could be 'captured' and placed into the service of state policies for primary schooling, but there was no interest whatsoever in the social energies that had produced them, nor even in the motives of the parents who sent their children to them. The médersas, and the social constituencies associated with them, were treated as objects of administrative and political action. Furthermore, the knowledge of médersas that circulated in official circles was based largely on received notions and preconceived assumptions; virtually none of the official documents produced about the médersas ever cited, quoted or even referred indirectly to the views and expertise of their founders and directors. So, while school inspectors and other officials might criticize conditions in state schools and decry the falling

---

[44] 'L'enseignement arabo-islamique dans le système éducatif du Mali', Division du Contrôle et de l'Animation du Système des Médersas (DCASM), 1991. By this date, CPLA had been officially renamed DCASM, in order better to reflect the nature of its supervisory role with respect to the médersas, although most people continued to refer to the department as CPLA, as we will do in this discussion.

[45] 'L'Enseignement en République du Mali. Administration, Organisation, Missions' (Bamako: Ministère de l'Education Nationale, 1985).

level of enrolments, they were also fully aware that médersa enrolments were increasing, although no sustained efforts were made to discover why. And certainly no one viewed the phenomenon of médersa success as an example of 'development'. Such was the context in which the *4ème Projet Education* was launched; designed to expand the provision of primary schooling through private education, this project would also virtually ignore the médersas.

The exclusion of the médersas: the 4ème Projet Education

The *4ème Projet Education* was integral to the structural adjustment programs which had been introduced in Mali in the late 1970s. It was a vast and ambitious project supported by a consortium of international donors and aid organizations, including the World Bank, the United States Agency for International Development (USAID), the French *Fonds d'aide et de coopération*, the Canadian International Development Agency, and the United Nations (United Nations Development Program – UNDP), among others. Among the more important objectives of this major international intervention in Mali's educational system were to improve the efficacy and to increase the availability of the provision of basic education (basic literacy and numeracy) among Malian children, to increase the enrolment of girls in schools, and to encourage the provision of private primary school education. There were also plans to control the flow of students into secondary and higher education and to orient them more toward technical and professional training. And fundamental to the entire plan was a proposed financial restructuring which included reducing the number of personnel employed by the MEN and reducing the excessively high proportion of funds expended on secondary and higher education in favor of elementary schooling; the provision of private elementary schooling was a central element in this financial restructuring.[46]

Although preliminary studies for the project recognized the médersas as providers of basic education, they were in effect excluded from virtually all of the programs which were set in place at the time of the project's inception. More significantly, perhaps, in their formulation and implementation of a program to establish a network of private non-confessional schools, neither government nor aid agencies ever systematically explored the possible lessons to be learned from the forty years of experience in the development and management of private schools which existed within the médersa constituencies. In the context of these actions and deliberations it was as if the médersas did

---

[46] The overall project is described in 'Projet de Consolidation', IDA-USAID, 19 Nov. 1 Dec. 1989. The budgetary imbalances were profound: in 1989, the first cycle of primary schooling constituted 81 per cent of school enrolments and was accorded only 35 per cent of the budget; the second primary cycle and secondary schools acounted for 17 per cent of enrolments and received 38 per cent of the budget; higher education accounted for 2 per cent of enrolments and received 19 per cent of the budget.

not exist, although the decision to integrate them into the national educational system was certainly taken in anticipation of the implementation of the *4ème Projet* and they were providing schooling for a significant percentage of Malian children.

After the removal of the régime of Moussa Traoré in 1991, the médersa constituencies were given a fuller voice in the subsequent debates about educational policy.[47] And in 1992, UNICEF launched a project to support médersa education, so that eventually the médersas would be integrated into the programs of the *4ème Projet*.[48] The fact that this initiative to address the médersas came from agencies associated with the United Nations is worthy of note, since such bodies have consistently been more prepared than most national and international aid agencies to offer support and assistance to Muslim institutions like schools.

However, the focus of the present discussion is on the late 1980s and early 1990s when the UDPM was still in place and official attitudes toward the médersas were still very much as described in the preceding section. The question that arose during field research, as it gradually became evident that the médersas were being excluded from the programs of the *4ème Projet*, was whether this exclusion was the result of 'accident' or of deliberate policy decisions. The local political marginalization of Islam and of the médersas was certainly no 'accident', but the result both of long-existing secularist policies and of the dynamics of power relations in postcolonial Mali. Furthermore, the directors of not a few médersas preferred to remain 'invisible' thus avoiding the attentions of government and administration. However, the actions which preceded the launching of the *4ème Projet* heralded a profound turning point for the médersas; their recognition as 'educational establishments' was intended to incorporate them into the national educational system, and at least by implication to make them eligible to benefit from the programs of the project. The preliminary planning and associated studies for the project suggested that the médersas would be included, and their exclusion therefore came as something of a surprise, and not only to this researcher.

What follows is a personalized account, paraphrased from my daily journal, of how I became aware of this situation and of my attempts to resolve the questions which arose from it. It is thus a stylistic departure from the form of exposition and analysis thus far employed in this book, but it has the advantage of illustrating in some detail the complex manner in which representations of Islam and development interacted in the evolution of a specific development project.

[47] See the documentation on the Débat National sur l'Education, held in Bamako in September 1991.
[48] UNICEF produced a project plan in 1992 entitled, 'Projet: Promotion de l'enseignement dans les médersas'. UNICEF, in coooperation with the Ministry of National Education, organized a seminar on 'Les tendances et les enjeux futurs des écoles médersas au Mali' in April 1992.

This process began for me in December 1990 at the beginning of one of my field trips, in the compound of the MEN where I had gone to pay a call on the then director of CPLA, AB.[49] My notes record that AB spent much of the first part of our conversation complaining about the dire economic plight of Mali, not only generally but with reference to his own work. Not only was it impossible to build proper médersas, but his own work as inspector of Arabic education was hindered since he had virtually no funds available to him. It was in this context that I asked whether it would not be possible for médersa directors to benefit from the *4ème Projet*. AB's response to my query implied to me that he had never heard of this project; he seemed to be trying to hide this fact by saying that in any case it was easier for médersa directors to obtain money from Arab countries such as Saudi Arabia, Iraq and Kuwait than through local ministerial channels.

The aspect of the *4ème Projet* to which I was referring was a program entitled FAEF (*Fonds d'appui à l'enseignement fondamental*) which made funds (granted by the World Bank) available for the construction or improvement of physical school facilities (on a 50 per cent matching basis) and for the purchase of school equipment and books (in the form of a full-cost grant). There is no need here to describe the features of this program in detail, except to say that requests for funding were intended to originate with local 'development committees' or parent associations (*Associations des Parents d'Elèves* or APEs); in other words, access to these funds was available through a procedure which was intended to encourage local initiatives in the improvement of schooling provision. Although most médersas did not have parent associations, it was nonetheless possible in theory for directors of officially recognized médersas (those which had adopted the new official curriculum) to apply for funds. There was also provision for the President of AMUPI to represent the médersas in meetings of the executive committee of FAEF.[50]

By the following day AB had apparently done a bit of homework, and he now claimed that médersa directors were uninterested in FAEF because the procedures for applying for funding were too complex and restrictive. However, it just happened that one of AB's deputies, MY, was present during this interview and he contradicted this assertion by pointing out that following a public radio announcement about the program, a number of médersa directors had expressed interest in it. It was indeed true that submitting an application was a somewhat convoluted bureaucratic process, but at this stage it seems unlikely that many médersa directors were aware of such complications, and certainly no one in CPLA even possessed any documentation on the program.

[49] Unless otherwise indicated, the information that informs this discussion is taken from my journals and field research notes, and interviews will not be cited individually.

[50] 'Comment faire appel au Fonds d'Appui à l'Enseignement Fondamental. Guide pratique pour les APE', Bureau des Projets Education, MEN, June 1989.

This episode with AB may illustrate little more than his own incompetence, and certainly cannot be said to illustrate any purposeful exclusion of the médersas from the *4ème Projet*. However, a visit on the same day to the *Bureau des Projets* that administered the FAEF program shed a different light on the situation. Here the French *conseiller technique* responsible for the program alleged that in fact there was very little money available to FAEF, and he added that he certainly had no intention of going around encouraging médersa directors to apply for it, although to date he had received one application for funding from a médersa. More to the point, he did not seem to know about the existence of CPLA, and he was surprised to learn that médersa directors were enquiring there about how to apply for FAEF funding.

The *Bureau des Projets* and the CPLA offices were located only a few yards from one another across the courtyard of the MEN, although no lines of communication apparently existed between them. When I subsequently spoke with MY, the deputy who had been present during my second interview with AB, he described CPLA's lack of information about the *4ème Projet* as 'pathetic' (*écœurante*) and further expressed his anger about the fact that a 'visitor' like myself should know more about FAEF than he, who had heard about it only on the radio.

Following these conversations I decided to explore the workings of the *4ème Projet* more systematically and my attention turned in the first instance to USAID, the agency responsible for much of the 'qualitative' content of the project, such as curriculum reform and the retraining of teachers, programs which made no provision for the médersas at all. Virtually every USAID employee consulted was aware that although early documentation on the project included references to the médersas, they had suddenly disappeared from the project during the course of its implementation. One of the first persons contacted, YM, an American attached to the *Institut Pédagogique National* (IPN), had herself been trying unsuccessfully to learn how and why this had come about. She claimed that the médersas were simply never mentioned in meetings or other conversations related to the project. It was with reference to her own efforts to understand how the project worked (she had been in the project only a few months) that she alluded to the 'culture of secrecy' which prevailed in government offices which inhibited the circulation of information. She spoke of her difficulty in obtaining even the most basic statistics about FAEF operations from the *Bureau des Projets,* and of the outright suppression of information in some instances, for example of a highly critical report on the state schools commissioned by IPN which highlighted cases of extreme brutality on the part of some teachers.[51] Her own work in the regions of Segu and Sikasso revealed that members of the local 'development committees' which were integral to FAEF operations were in fact pocketing the

---

[51] Despite repeated efforts on my part, authorization to consult this report was never obtained.

local 'development taxes' which were intended to finance schools and other local development projects.

These conversations revealed further instances of bureaucratic confusion and inefficiency, but not very much on why the médersas were not part of the project. By now I had also met BG, the USAID director of the curriculum development and teacher training program. Unlike YM, who was at the beginning of her career in development work, BG was an old hand nearing the end of a long career during which he had spent many years in Africa. He had written the curriculum development and retraining programs of the *4ème Projet* for the World Bank and had subseqùently been persuaded to come to Mali to direct it.

BG was extremely critical of Malian schooling, and claimed that it was the worst he had ever encountered anywhere. He rehearsed the usual statistics of drop-out rates and economic and human waste, and he emphasized the low morale of teachers, most of whom had received no pedagogical training at all. He said that common practice in the education ministry had been simply to distribute the curriculum to teachers and let them get on with it. (It will be recalled that these criticisms are similar to those made about the médersas when justifying their integration into the national education system.)

BG's curriculum revisions were based on what he called 'operational teaching objectives', which were designed to inject clarity and specificity into the teaching and learning processes. BG's program broke the curriculum down into lesson plans which stated specifically what children should be able to do at the end of each lesson. Each lesson was meant be congruent with overall pedagogical objectives and to present the material upon which the children would be examined. By the time I met BG, the new curriculum had been drawn up and training in its use of inspectors, principals and teachers was well underway. What was impressive about BG's approach to his job, beyond his expertise, experience and deep commitment, was his insistence that the primary aim of this project was to ensure that the children should be literate and numerate when they completed primary school. And he was completely culturally neutral; in his view 'operational teaching objectives' could be applied in any school context in any language.

When I first posed the 'médersa question' to him, BG said the médersas had never been included in the AID project remit, although he did not know why; subsequently, he claimed that the médersas had been excluded because of budgetary limitations. Perhaps this explanation was technically accurate, but it was not convincing at the time, not because there was any specific evidence to the contrary, but because of the kinds of attitudes one encountered among many AID employees at all levels of the organizational hierarchy. I had the impression, perhaps without justification, that many of them were suspicious, if not hostile, toward 'things Islamic'; many were certainly shockingly ill-informed about Islam and Muslim society and institutions in Mali. For example, AID's Women in Development project in Mali contributed to the *4ème Projet* with programs aimed at increasing and maintaining the enrolment of rural girls in the first cycle of primary school. One of the persons with whom I spoke in the Women in Development office naively associated médersas with all the popular negative stereotypes about Islam which were circulating at the time in Europe and North America. According to her, the AID program should not be applied in the médersas because Muslim women were known to be oppressed and Muslim parents were not interested in sending their daughters to school; she also associated the médersas with militant Islam ('We don't want to get mixed up with Ghaddafi'). This person was completely unaware of the fact that the médersas had actually increased school enrolments of girls in primary schools, and that many rural parents were more inclined to send their daughters to médersas than to state schools.

Albeit extreme in its mode of expression, this was not an isolated example of the misinformation and anti-Muslim attitudes which were in circulation. At times I suspected that there might actually be some sort of tacit 'Muslim policy' operating within AID designed to insure that the agency did not directly support Muslim institutions. For example, in 1991 the new transitional government asked AID to expand their project to include the médersas. At this time, there was at least one voice within AID which endorsed this idea and advocated a policy which would have placed primary emphasis on developing médersas in the rural areas, the argument being that most peasant families did not want the kinds of secular schooling offered by the state schools. However, this minority view did not prevail, and AID refused the MEN's request, using their ignorance of the médersas as an excuse. One high-ranking AID official explained to me: 'We don't even know what a médersa is.'

This disclaimer was true enough; few in the aid community had any detailed knowledge about the médersas, and any intervention in them must have appeared to pose very great problems, indeed, especially for persons whose expertise and commitment was to what they considered 'universal' forms of pedagogy and schooling. But if this fact helps to explain their reticence, it also illustrates a fundamental structural problem that confronts all forms of development intervention when introducing external programs into local contexts. Because in this case the local culture was Islamic, such structural problems became embroiled with political questions, or so I suspected.

My own suspicions about AID policies were certainly deepened by comments made to me by various Malians who were convinced that some Americans, and more especially certain French, were 'anti-Muslim'; similar accusations were also made about secularist Malians who held influential positions in the education ministry. And if the Malians themselves (many of whom were not convinced it was a good or workable plan) were having difficulty integrating médersa with secular schooling, there is no reason to expect the international aid community to have been able to resolve such a complex issue.

On the other hand, it was also clear that the evolution of these programs and events often depended on political will, or the lack of it. BG didn't know much about médersas either, but this did not hinder him from trying to learn and to see how his programs might be extended to include them; in his view, the *4ème Projet* could not ignore the médersas. Suddenly, my own status as 'objective' researcher was compromised when BG asked me to arrange a meeting between himself and THT, president of the association of médersa directors, in order to explore the possibility of integrating the médersas into the programs BG directed. The long and complex series of maneuvers that ensued came to nothing in the end, but they are worth outlining here because of the further light they cast on this entire episode. BG's strategy was designed to bring together the three major players who would have to cooperate if the médersas were to benefit from the curriculum reform and training programs: AID, the MEN, and the médersa directors. Although the médersas were not formally included in the AID project, BG claimed AID might be persuaded to cooperate if other aspects of his plan were in place. The ministry, he explained, was staffed for the most part by non-educators, often military personnel; in his view, they simply did not know what to do about the médersas, like so many other issues they faced, and were usually willing to adopt a specific proposal if the necessary funds were available. (He did not take into account the allegation that many of these persons were 'anti-Muslim'.) But the key to the plan rested with the médersa directors themselves, who would need to play a central role in getting this initiative off the ground, which is precisely where the strategy faltered, because the directors never managed to do what was recommended.

BG proposed to THT that the essential starting point for his plan would be a statement of basic pedagogical aims drawn up by the médersa directors. This statement would then be sent to the MEN, via CPLA, with a formal letter requesting endorsement of the program by the ministry and a commitment to seek financial assistance to implement it. BG predicted, with his characteristic optimism, that funding could usually be found for projects that promised practical results. He also explained that the pedagogical aims of the médersas could subsequently be translated into a curriculum structured in conformity with the 'operational teaching objectives' now being introduced in the state schools. BG responded to all of THT's queries and doubts about this proposal with enthusiastic confidence. The fact that the primary aim of the médersas was religious schooling was not a problem; the 'operational objectives' were universal in their application. The curriculum and teaching manuals could be translated into Arabic; teachers could be trained in Arabic or any of the national languages, as well as French. BG offered to assist THT in the formulation of the statement he was being asked to write, and he began to lay the groundwork for its receipt in the ministry and in AID.

However, the médersa directors never drew up such a statement, nor was any letter ever transmitted to the ministry, perhaps because of disagreements among the directors themselves about their pedagogical aims, or indeed about the wisdom of seeking assistance from non-Muslims. At issue were such matters as the balance between religious and non-religious subjects in the curriculum, whether scientific subjects could be effectively taught in Arabic, and indeed, the extent of French-language teaching in the curriculum. BG's initiative languished until the change of government in 1991, after which the médersas were no longer marginalized from the national educational and development debate.

There is no intention to extend this discussion into the post-1991 period, but it is worth noting how dramatically official attitudes toward the médersas changed with the demise of the single party state. The médersas were much in discussion during the national reassessment of the Malian educational system in September 1991,[52] which recommended that their number be expanded and their conditions, both material and pedagogical, be improved. In August 1992 the MEN held a special seminar which focused specifically on the médersas,[53] and in the same year, UNICEF announced a four-year program of assistance to the médersas which included curriculum development and the training of 500 teachers in each of three areas: 'active pedagogy', technical and professional subjects, and the teaching of French language. Financial assistance was also made available for the purchase of teaching materials on a matching of funds basis. The UNICEF project placed great emphasis on the schooling of girls, and aimed to achieve 50 per cent enrolment of girls in the médersas which they assisted; interestingly, their project paper noted that female attendance in the médersas was 'relatively high', and that 'the médersas have sometimes been perceived as the vehicle of social mobility for women and for the children of less privileged families'![54] Almost in spite of themselves, the médersas were being recognized by both government and the international aid community as legitimate educational institutions! However, as we have seen, such recognition can have ambiguous implications, because with recognition comes control!

'Governing men as things': development as a resource of extraversion

Indeed, ambiguity effectively characterizes the thematic core of this chapter. The history of the médersa movement that has been documented in this book can justifiably be described as the development of modernized Muslim schooling in Mali, although the founders and directors of these schools did not reflect on their project as a 'development program'. This history was a complex process of amassing social, material and intellectual resources, constructing buildings, administering schools, negotiating with parents, and mediating social change, all of which directly affected tens of thousands of people, both adults and children. By contrast, according to official discourse, the contribution of the médersas to 'national development' only came into

[52] Débat National sur l'Education, Bamako, 16-21 Sept. 1991.
[53] 'Les tendances et les enjeux futurs des écoles médersas au Mali', 4-6 Aug. 1992.
[54] UNICEF. 'Projet: Promotion de l'enseignement dans les médersas', 1992.

existence with their official recognition by government as 'educational establishments', the implication being that participation in 'national development' could only occur through official channels. However, the immediate result of this recognition was the systematic subjugation of the médersas to the control and regulations of the state bureaucracy, in exchange for which was offered no support or assistance whatsoever, and they were ultimately excluded from the programs of the *4ème Projet*, Mali's most ambitious educational 'development' project to date.

The results of investigations into the causes of this exclusion were similarly ambiguous. Regardless of public pronouncements to the contrary, the médersas were still being ignored in official reports and reflections on educational policy in the late 1980s. In part this situation was the result of the secularist legacy which had prevailed for many years in educational circles which, simply put, did not consider Muslim schools, either Qur'anic or médersas, to be schools; in part it was the work of persons in positions of responsibility who were themselves committed secularists, or perhaps 'anti-Muslim' as was alleged. In any case, for many in the médersa constituencies, being a secularist was equivalent to being 'anti-Muslim'. It might have been difficult, if not impossible, for the aid agencies to transcend this situation and incorporate the médersas in their projects; one suspects that the officials in the MEN did not encourage them to do so. It is also arguable that the aid agencies felt it too daunting a task to introduce their programs into what were, in effect, two quite different school systems; or perhaps this was a convenient excuse for avoiding association with Muslim institutions. Available evidence does not allow a conclusion on this question, but the assistance which was made available to the médersas shortly after the change in government in 1991, and the fact that aid for the médersas came from UN agenices leaves one with lingering suspicions about the existence of 'Islamic policies' within certain national aid agencies.

The three salient forces at work in this context were the operatives of the clientelist single-party state, the employees of the development industry, which was constrained by its own inherent structures, and the complex array of representations surrounding 'Islam', both those of the médersa constitutuencies themselves and those of the secularists, and indeed of the so-called 'anti-Muslims'. There is much material here which supports the views of those whom Frederick Cooper and Randall Packard have described as the 'postmodernist' critics of development, who see the 'development discourse as nothing more than an apparatus of control and surveillance'.[55] According to Cooper and Packard, these 'postmodernist' critics view the development discourse as an expression of European universalist and hegemonic pretensions which originated in the Enlightenment. Such hegemonic tendencies

[55] F. Cooper and R. Packard (eds), *International Development and the Social Sciences: Essays on the History and Politics of Knowledge* (Berkeley: University of California Press, 1997), 'Introduction', p. 3.

were definitely evident in the conceptualization and execution of the programs of the *4ème Projet*, and they cannot be eliminated from any assessment of its implementation and impact. But the preceding analysis has also focused on how an ideology of 'development' was employed by Malians within Mali to divert to their own advantage the 'resources of extraversion' made available by development interventions. Both internal and external factors have been in play in this process.

Some critics have asserted that 'development' has served to sustain the dominance of certain political classes who have in effect handed over the formulation and implementation of social and economic policy to foreign 'experts'. In a controversial book, Axelle Kabou has argued that despite all the rhetoric that suggests otherwise many African leaders do not really wish 'to develop'. She explores the causes for this alleged refusal and advocates that African states should take control of their own development rather than willingly placing their 'destiny in the hands of foreigners'.

The myth of the African will to develop seems to fill three essential functions: to exonerate in advance the political class from any suspicion of incompetence by diverting people's attention to a continuing international conspiracy [to keep Africa underdeveloped], because so long as that persists, the more reason one has to remain in power; to confine the African peoples indefinitely within single parties which are supposed to channel more effectively their energies toward achieving various developmental objectives, which in fact are never clearly defined; and to fatten the multitude of experts who are engaged in endless missions and studies of which the utility, judging by the continued deepening of underdevelopment, is never subjected to any assessment.[56]

Kabou argued that many Africans were avoiding taking responsibility for the state of affairs in which they found themselves by taking refuge in a 'cultural inebriation' with a mythical past, which she described as 'Africa-this-marvel-ous-continent-which-constituted-a-harmonious-whole-before-colonial-penetration.'[57] Perhaps some of the parental views discussed in the previous chapter represent a variety of this form of 'culturalism': the hope that one might escape the pain of social change by taking comfort in the moral certitudes of Islam. And the rhetoric of 'development' was certainly employed in Mali for various political objectives. But it is not true that all Malians 'refused development', witness the growth of the network of médersas; this was not a case of 'refusal of development', but a refusal by both government and aid agencies to consider the médersa movement to be an example of 'development'. It is precisely in this fact that the political dimensions of this situation are most evident: the government in effect insisted that 'development' could not take place without its authorization and participation.

A comparable case is analyzed in a perceptive and critical book by Adrian Adams, written following years of residence in eastern Senegal. Adams

---

[56] Axelle Kabou, *Et si l'Afrique refusait le développement?* (Paris: L'Harmattan, 1991), p. 18.
[57] *Ibid.*, p. 108.

describes in careful detail, largely through the words of the persons involved, how local initiatives to increase agricultural productivity were crushed by the intervention of both the Senegalese state and international aid agencies. According to Jabe So, the chief organizer of the local agricultural initiative which is the subject of Adams' book:

When we organized ourselves at the beginning, some people said to me, 'So, if we take on this work, the administration is going to come and mess us about'. I said, 'No, when a country is developing, the government is happy; we only need to do our work.' I struggled, struggled, until we organized ourselves for this work. And then they came, and they ruined the work.[58]

'They ruined the work' through a long series of actions that were designed primarily to control and dominate the local farmers, whose persistent requests that they be left alone and allowed to organize themselves were condemned as 'against the government'. At one point, they were told by a member of an official delegation that 'no development could take place without the administration.'[59] This statement resonates of the CPLA assertion that 'the evolution of the médersas began when they were taken over by the Department of Education.'

The justification given for administrative intervention in Jabe So's intitiative was an ambitious government program for the agricultural development of the Senegal River valley, the official objective of which was 'to procure for the populations of the Senegal River valley an adequate basic food supply and a growing cash income which will allow them to move beyond the uncertain subsistence economy in which they live and to enter into a modern consumer economy.'[60] In fact, the real effects of the project would be to dispossess the populations of their land and transform them into a salaried rural labor force. Nonetheless, the government decision had been taken, to which the local farmers were meant to submit even though they had not been party to any discussions or consultations about the program.

But if the objective of the administration was to ensure that the local farmers submit to their decisions and their authority, the prevailing attitude communicated by the 'developers' was that the local populations did not even exist, or that the success of their interventions would be more certain if they did not exist! According to Jabe So 'They don't know that there are living people here'.[61] And this is also Adrian Adams' most trenchant criticism of the 'development expert', whose role in her opinion remains the same no matter at what level he or she operates:

What one wants from the expert is not simply competence, or knowledge; there would be less expensive and more effective ways to obtain that. What really counts

[58] Adrian Adams, *La Terre et les gens du fleuve* (Paris: L'Harmattan, 1985), p. 195.

[59] *Ibid.*, p. 130.

[60] The program was administered by OMVERS, *Organisation pour la Mise en Valeur des Riverains du Sénégal, ibid.*, p. 119.

[61] *Ibid.*, p. 195.

is the prestige of impartiality with which the expert's presumed knowledge imbues him, which allows him to neutralize confrontations – between governments, between governors and governed – and for a time to disguise political conflicts as technical problems. An expert serves to disguise the governing of men as the administration of things, in order that men can be governed as things.

What creates and perpetuates the function of the expert is in fact the idea of development as a unique, indivisible and universal process; as modernization, if you wish. This idea implies that the peoples of Africa, Asia, South America … are in a state of need [*manque*], in a negative condition (under-development, lagging behind) that can be corrected by the provision of techniques and states of mind that have permitted the developed countries to attain their present happy state. This idea creates the role of expert, because it is through the mediation of the expert that this transformation is supposed to take place. That he is a European – in the broad 'African' sense of the term – guarantees his expertise; and his expertise justifies his presence as an expatriate. Being an expatriate is not a handicap; on the contrary, no one is an expert in his own country. Development takes place on a blank page; lack of responsibility for, and ignorance of, everything which takes place beyond one's narrow field of competence assists one not to see anything which might be distracting; nothing but the 'traditional', which is to be swept away with the same movement which installs modernity.

[…] If you consider the Europeans who have figured as experts in the experience of the people here, you will see that what they have in common is that they do not recognize in the people of the River [*les gens du Fleuve*] a present existence, rooted in the past and opening onto a future; they don't recognize them as contemporaries. That the people here should develop their region, as Jabe So wanted to do, is a notion which is void of meaning to them. What there is already belongs to the past; and the future will come from someplace else.[62]

There is much in this statement which echoes of the relationships between the médersa constituencies and the *4ème Projet*. The project was conceptualized from a technocratic perspective that largely ignored the political implications of schooling provision in the country, particularly with respect to the médersas. For many aid workers in the project, the médersas simply fell outside their remit and were considered a distraction about which they had no need to learn ('We don't even know what a médersa is'.) Perhaps some of them saw the médersas as part of the 'tradition' which Adrian Adams says is to be swept away by 'modernization'. Certainly there was little valuation placed on the relevance of the historical heritage of the communities in which the *4ème Projet* was operating. It was not that the 'experts' who worked in this project were insensitive or without concern for the Malian people with and for whom they worked, but as Adrian Adams observed, they could not avoid assuming the structural roles imposed on them as 'development experts'. The ethos of the project, although not necessarily endorsed by every participating 'expert', envisaged educational development as an indivisible and universal whole, the substance of which was to be imported 'from someplace else'.

[62] *Ibid.*, p. 203.

But a great deal of the responsibility for these attitudes rests with the local political situation. Official discourse within government and ministries provided a conceptual framework for understanding local conditions and an operational framework within which one was expected to work and which most foreign aid workers found difficult to transcend. In the *4ème Projet*, as in many development projects, only a small minority of aid workers actually worked side by side on the ground with the populations affected by their projects, sharing directly their problems and hopes.[63] Project directors and managers were even further removed from the 'grassroots'. Exceptions have been noted; there were a few persons, but usually very few, who did manage to transcend these many obstacles and who developed relatively unencumbered relationships with the people among whom they were meant to be working. But such relationships might threaten the 'objectivity' of the expertise of 'development experts' and therefore can never be the primary objective of a development project; it is in this sense that the development process contributes to the 'governance of men as things'.

Although the agents of the *4ème Projet* were for the most part completely uninterested in the médersas, the project nonetheless deeply affected these schools, not educationally so much as politically. The anticipation of this major educational intervention precipitated the official recognition of the médersas as educational institutions, with their consequent subjugation to centralized controls and regulations. Paradoxically, subsequent assessments of education and schooling ignored the médersas, as did the programs of the *4ème Projet* when they were implemented. For their part, many médersa directors would have preferred not to have been 'recognized' by government, perceiving very clearly that this act represented a shift in power relations that subjected them directly to the attentions of the state bureaucracy. And many of them did not want the Muslim 'identity' of their schools to be submerged into the curriculum of the *écoles fondamentales*.

But the dilemma faced by the médersa directors was filled with irony. In the 1980s they found themselves struggling with how to respond to government demands to integrate and/or upgrade the teaching of secular subjects in their curriculum, something the founders of the first Bamako médersa had requested and had been categorically denied by the French authorities in the 1940s. And many médersa directors agreed that the curriculum required modification in order better to respond to the ambitions of students who wanted to translate their schooling into viable jobs. But the arrogant manner in which the government approached the médersas angered many directors, and the failure to offer any assistance or support on how to merge the two bodies of subject matter pedagogically and epistemologically further alienated them.

[63] According to Jabe So, 'In the projects, they [the European technicians] never joined the peasants in their work. [...] And they are right; they come only to earn money, and then they leave', *ibid.*, pp. 194–5.

But the ambiguities, paradoxes and ironies all seem to have been inherent in the socio-political structures of power relations in postcolonial Mali. Government initiatives which were touted as contributing to 'national unity' and 'national development' (the creation of AMUPI and the recognition of the médersas as educational establishments) had resulted in a divisive confrontation which focused on competing representations of 'Islam'. Both the 'defenders of Islam' and their secularist critics conspired unwittingly to produce a discourse that gave credence to the existence of a socially and politically distinct 'Islam'. This debate about 'Islam' (a struggle to control shared meanings) was part of a larger political contest in which agents of the state bureaucracy and of *le Pouvoir* relied on a similar notion of a distinct 'Islam' in allying with the Muslim community while at the same time politically subjecting it. Whereas in the 1950s the colonial authorities exploited divisions within the Muslim community to achieve their political ends, party and government in the 1980s 'exploited' Muslim unity. Different tactics, similar motives. But there are no innocent victims in this process of shifting power relations, and one must ask if these are the kinds of forces that lead from integration to *intégrisme*.

8

REPRISE: REASSESSING THE TERMS
OF ANALYSIS

The central aim of this book has been to explore the history of Soudan
Français and Mali as a Muslim society in the twentieth century, with special
reference to the evolution of Muslim schooling. This history has been related
in considerable detail, in an effort to reveal the numerous complexities of
the process of transformation that has taken place. And it seems unlikely that
anyone who has followed the story to this point would challenge the assertion
that both Malian society and its Muslim institutions have been fundamentally
transformed during the century. But one of the aims of the book has also
been to assess the recent history of Soudan Français and Mali with reference
to the *longue durée* of Muslim societies in the region. And it would seem that
if there have been numerous dramatic breaks with the past, one can also discern some significant continuities. This concluding chapter will explore both
the breaks and the continuities by recalling and reassessing the conceptual
and analytical themes that were evoked in the Introduction. A brief overview
of certain events following the removal from power of Moussa Traoré and
the UDPM in March 1991 will provide a useful entrée into this discussion.

The fall from power of the 'old regime' produced a veritable explosion of
activities from the newly liberated 'civil society'. The first official act by the
Comité de Transition pour le Salut du Peuple (CTSP), charged with managing the
transition to democratic institutions, was to decree freedom of association.
Within months literally hundreds of new associations registered with the
Ministry of Territorial Administration, among which were quite a few organizations with specifically Muslim names and objectives (see Table 8.1). There
was a parallel explosion in the press, with numerous new newspapers appearing to join those that were already in print before March 1991. Of these, several
were Muslim in orientation: *Saniya*, which first appeared in October 1990, was
joined by *Témoignage afro-musulman* in October 1991 and the next month by the
bilingual *al-Farouq*, which included sections in Arabic and French. Over fifty
political parties were formed which hoped to contest the elections that were
to be held in 1992. However, the second decree issued by the CTSP prohibited
the formation of political parties on the basis of religion. This sudden and
uncompromising reassertion of secularism, combined with the repeal of an
existing law that had required the closure of bars and nightclubs during

Ramadan, angered certain Muslims who launched a sustained public campaign of criticism against this secularist trend.[1]

The first point to note is the extent to which the Muslim social landscape was now articulated through voluntary associations. Of course, the vast majority of Muslims did not belong to any formally constituted association, nor were the aims of all the associations political. But such organizations provided the means for persons who shared social or political objectives to join together and to speak and/or act as a Muslim interest group in the public domain. Official registration was a bureaucratic process which required each organization to provide a copy of its by-laws, to state its objectives, and to name the officers of its executive committee; all the associations thus have a president, vice-president, secretary-general, treasurer and numerous other officers charged with specific responsibilities. These positions may vary; for example, UMSPI appointed twelve *conseillers en théologie!* These bureaucratic requirements structure the manner in which interest groups present themselves in the public domain, and no doubt also influence the ways in which they conduct business among themselves.

The discursive environment also influences both the names and objectives of these associations. Terms like 'development' and 'progress' appear repeatedly; there is even an *Association Islamique Socialiste et Démocratique!* The aims of AMJM include the unification of Malian youth within Islam in order to attain 'a just and developed society'. AIDC aims 'to be an economic and financial instrument to sustain efforts for realizing the plans and programs for the national development of Mali'. Even UMSPI, whose objectives are primarily religious and very specifically Sunni (Wahhabi), express their intention to work towards the 'amelioration of the conditions of life in Malian society through the creation of work and participation in certain works of public interest'.

The most publicly visible and most politically active of these associations in 1991 were AISLAM, AIDC and Hizboullah. The president of AISLAM, a Sunni organization, was 'Abd al-Aziz Yattabary, director of the *Institut Islamique de Missira*, one of Bamako's oldest and most prestigious médersas, and its vice-president was Modibo Sangaré; the association seems to have come into formal existence early in 1991 when the opposition to Moussa Traoré was gaining momentum. The president of AIDC, which was founded after Traoré's removal from power, was Mory Sidibé, a French-educated civil servant and a Niass Tijani. However, Hizboullah was the only one of these organizations that could claim direct participation from an early date in the democratic movement to challenge Moussa Traoré. It was founded in 1989 by its president Hamidou Dramera, a Hamallist Sufi from Nioro who had received a classical Qur'anic education; he and other members of Hizboullah marched

---

[1] For a fuller exploration of these events, see Carsten Hock, 'Muslimische Reform und staatliche Autorität in der Republik Mali seit 1960. Die Ausbreitung der Wahhabiya in einer Situation der politischen Blockade gesellschaftlichen Fortschritts' (dissertation, University of Bayreuth, 1998).

Table 8.1. MUSLIM ASSOCIATIONS FORMED AFTER
MARCH 1991 (PARTIAL LIST)
(in chronological order of registration)

Hizboullah al-Islamiya (originally founded in September 1989, formally registered February 1991)
Association Islamique pour le Salut (AISLAM) (formed in February 1991 as Association des Jeunes Musulmans and renamed after the events of 26 March)
Femmes, Islam et Développement au Mali (FIDAMA) (May 1991)
Association Islamique pour le Développement et la Concorde (AIDC) (June 1991)
Association Malienne des Jeunes Musulmans (AMJM) (June 1991)
Association Malienne des Enseignants des Médersas (July 1991)
Les Témoins du Prophète (July 1991)
Association Islamique pour la Concorde et le Progrès (July 1991)
Union des Musulmans Sunnites pour le Progrès de l'Islam (UMSPI) (July 1991)
Association Culturelle Musulmane (August 1991)
Association Malienne pour le Progrès de l'Islam (August 1991)
Association des Femmes Maliennes pour le Développement de l'Islam (September 1991)
Association des Serviteurs d'Allah (March 1992)
Association Féminine pour l'Appel Islamique (AFAPI) (July 1991)
Association Islamique Socialiste et Démocratique (no date)
Association des Amis de l'ISESCO (no date)
Association des Cadres et Intellectuels Musulmans du Mali (no date)
Fondation Shaikh Ahmad Tijani Chérif (no date)

with their Qur'ans in the first mass demonstration against the Traoré régime on 30 December 1990. Some participants in the march claimed that it was Hizboullah who during the demonstration were chanting '*Allahu Akbar, vive la démocratie*'. No evidence is available to determine whether or not the Hizboullah membership formally endorsed democracy. However, Mamadou Hachim Sow, the founding editor of *Témoignage afro-musulman* and himself a member of Hizboullah, implied as much in the first issue of his newspaper:

> The task accomplished by the people on 26 March is the manifestation of a Qur'anic truth. ... It is in response to the injunction of Allah that we, Hizboullah, took an active part in the events that led to the birth of democracy. ... God has enjoined us to take the side of the oppressed and of the 'children' (students and young unemployed) who have been deprived of their rights. To take part in this revolution is to engage in 'Jihad'. Those who died are martyrs in the Qur'anic sense of the term.[2]

Sow is a French-educated researcher residing in Segu. The ideological perspective that he adopted in *Témoignage afro-musulman* is evident in the paper's name as well as in the words of his first editorial:

> Ours is a country of great civilizations. Man has forged a flourishing civilization here since earliest antiquity. ... We are the bearers of an identity that is unique in the

[2] *Témoignage afro-musulman*, 22 Oct. 1991, p. 6.

world. We are the ones who have built all the great African empires and carried civilization across Africa, and perhaps to pre-Columbian America. During this period in the life of our people, which we might call 'barbarism' because of the cultural eradication with which we are threatened, we must continually recall the adage that says 'When one forgets his roots, he ends up in difficulty'. Therefore, our aim must be to think by ourselves for ourselves in order fully to assume our identity through the lens of our Negro-Muslim heritage, while at the same time remaining open to fruitful support from outside. This newspaper is for all those who are interested in our future development. It is for everyone and it is open to everyone.[3]

Interestingly, Hamidou Dramera seemed to take a much more radical position than was expressed in the pages of *Témoignage afro-musulman*. He spoke passionately in interview about the necessity of addressing the poverty and despair of the Malian people and about how the guidance given by Qur'anic principles could assist in the social reform necessary to bring this about.[4] Although Dramera's radical social critique was not being widely disseminated in 1991, Hizboullah did continue to demonstrate publicly in order to present its demands for change in Mali. In 1991 Dramera was the only leader of any of these Muslim associations to offer a sustained critique of Malian social conditions from an Islamic or any other perspective; on the other hand, many persons were willing to talk about the political future of the state and to condemn the reassertion of secularism.

The most public challenge to the secularist ideology of the transition took place during the preparations for and the proceedings of the Conférence Nationale that was charged with formulating the political structures of the Third Republic, as post-UDPM Mali came to be known. A very vocal and insistent group of about nine participants in the conference questioned the article proposed for the new constitution that banned the formation of parties based on religious affiliation.[5] *Les Echos* interviewed Modibo Sangaré and Mory Sidibé to obtain their views on these issues in an article entitled 'The Islamists are here!'[6] Interestingly, Sangaré argued his case from a somewhat liberal position, pointing up the contradictions in the pronouncements of the CTSP who on the one hand endorsed freedom of conscience and on the other forbade the formation of religious parties, an act which in his view limited the freedom of Islamic expression. Implicit in Sangaré's argument was an endorsement of democratic principles and of their associated human rights: 'Mali cannot claim to be a country the majority of whose population is Muslim and at the same time forbid this majority the right to form a party based upon its beliefs.'

The position of the French-schooled Sidibé was much more radically *intégriste*. 'Fundamentally, a Muslim is obliged to support the Muslim state',

---

[3] *Ibid.*, p. 1.
[4] Interview with Hamidou Dramera, 22 Nov. 1991, Bamako.
[5] The article also banned the formation of parties based on ethnic, racial, regional or gender distinctions.
[6] *Les Echos*, 'Les Islamistes sont là', no. 91, p. 6.

and, according to him, all the principles required to organize the state and to govern will be found in the Qur'an and *hadith*. Nor do Sidibé's views reflect the slightest interest in democratic principles. He complained that Muslims were under-represented at the Conférence Nationale, and when someone retorted that the overwhelming majority of delegates were in fact Muslim, he denied this saying, 'None of them were Muslim, because if all the delegates were Muslim we would have declared an Islamic state right away. … The problem now is to find the ways and means to attain it in a manner that avoids trouble and division in the country.' This aim can be accomplished, according to Sidibé, by means of 'development':

AIDC wants to sensitize Muslims to the true spirit of Islam by setting up projects on the basis of Islamic principles. I said that the Islamic state is the goal of every sincere Muslim, but I also said one must move toward this goal cautiously. That means one must work through persuasion so that Muslims will be persuaded that Islam is a way of life and not a constraining force. And we think we can easily achieve this aim by focussing development projects around this question; we want to be the driving force for a way of development, a culture, based on the precepts of Islam.

Sangaré also endorsed the role of 'development' in Mali's future. 'Islam represents a social project that encompasses the economic, social, cultural, and political,' and following the failure of capitalism and communism, Mali should try the 'Islamic path of development'. Malians, he contended, should not be duped by western claims that Islam is anachronistic and has nothing to offer humanity in the twentieth century; after all, he added in a manner reminiscent of Hachim Sow, Islam contributed to building the ancient empire of Mali.

These associations and the content of the discourses produced by their members are reflections of a Muslim society whose contours contrast sharply with those that prevailed in the region on the eve of the colonial conquest. Muslim voluntary associations are a twentieth-century phenomenon, and we have traced their origins from one of the earliest to appear in Soudan Français, *Shubban al-muslimin*, the youth organization established by the founders of the first Bamako médersa and modeled on a similar organization in Egypt. However subsequent associations, like the *Union Culturelle Musulmane* (and all of those listed in on page above) were also deeply influenced by European models of voluntary associations, which during the post-war period became the most effective vehicle for organizing interest groups and broadcasting their views. The new Muslim associations were a new form of Islamic sociopolitical organization, defined in Chapter 1 as a polity or social formation that is legitimized with reference to allegedly Islamic principles. The associations were organized around Islamic aims, and the by-laws of many of them explicitly stated that their activities should be guided by the principles of Qur'an and *hadith*.

If the structure and discourses of these new associations represent a dramatic break with the local Muslim past, the innovative manner in which their founders sought to reorganize Muslim social and religious space to respond to the changing social and political context recalls the initiatives of those eighteenth- and nineteenth-century Sufis who introduced the Sufi order into West Africa with similar objectives in mind. The appearance of the Muslim voluntary association therefore illustrates underlying continuities with the Muslim past, firstly as a twentieth-century example of how Muslims have continued to experiment with various ways to organize themselves in response to the social and political conditions in which they live. Secondly and more specifically, this form of Islamic socio-political organization invokes voluntary submission to Islamic authority as the means for attracting Muslim social and religious resources, much like the Sufi orders before them.

The voluntary association has now become the preferred form of Muslim socio-political organization in Mali for those who wish to speak and act in the national political arena. Some Sufi orders in Mali enjoy a regional influence that can be very significant in certain localities, but in contrast with Senegal, they play virtually no role in the public political arena.[7] The continued political influence of the Sufi orders in Senegal can be traced to the strength of their social and economic base in the late nineteenth and early twentieth centuries, and their relationships with both colonial and post-colonial governments. Their continued strength can also be attributed to their capacity for innovative change, especially among the Mourides and the Niass Tijanis. The Malian Sufi orders never enjoyed such a political base, nor any influence with government. This pattern of difference is evident in the colonial period when the innovative activities of such persons as Saada Oumar Touré and Amadou Hampâté Ba were initiated outside the structures of the Sufi orders to which they belonged.

We have attempted to analyze the emergence of the new Muslim associations, and of the médersas, in the context of the changing nature of power relations in the colonial and postcolonial periods. Our understanding of power relations, following Foucault, is of a diffuse concatenation of relationships through which sets of actions affect the actions of others. The changing nature of power relations has been illustrated in the examples of the first founders of the Islamic médersas, and the founders of the new associations. The life experiences of these persons had dislodged them from prevailing local social and religious structures thus enabling them to experiment with new forms of social organization and innovative methods of schooling. The major factor affecting this 'liberation' was the colonial presence, which was also the major purveyor of new sets of power relations in which these Muslim innovators were becoming unavoidably enmeshed. Central to the new relationships between power and knowledge introduced by the French was French-language schooling, which was to be the institution most responsible for

---

[7] See Benjamin F. Soares, 'The Spiritual Economy of Nioro du Sahel' and 'A Contemporary Malian Shaykh: al-Hajj Shaykh Sidy Modibo Kane Diallo, the Religious Leader of Dilly', *ISASS*, no. 10 (1996), pp. 145-53.

forging new technologies of power and new forms of power relations. This situation led to further breaks, and continuities, with the past.

In Chapter 1 we described the characteristics of descent-based forms of Islamic socio-political organization in which Islam functioned as a kind of 'craft' in a regional political economy which was organized as a collection of hereditary occupation groups. Members of 'Muslim lineages' controlled religious and educational resources and provided religious services but were (in theory) barred from governing or ruling. Members of the ruling lineages, even if they were Muslim, were not considered 'good Muslims'; they were often unschooled (at least to any level of serious learning) and they tended to ignore even the most fundamental doctrinal tenets of Islam: they rarely prayed, and many openly drank alcohol.

Much the same pattern was reproduced in postcolonial Mali where Muslim 'secularists' who often carry their Islam very lightly have assumed the roles of governance from which the 'Muslims' are barred. The role of the 'Muslims' is limited to the provision of religious services to the community, including Muslim schooling. And as we have seen, during the transition to democracy some 'Muslims' accused 'secularists' in positions of authority of not being good Muslims, or of not being Muslims at all because they did not endorse the project of the Islamic state and because they ignored and even flouted their disregard for basic Islamic precepts by rescinding legislation which required the closing of bars and nightclubs during Ramadan.

Of course, important differences exist between these two historical situations. An 'associational ideology' of social organization is challenging the pre-colonial lineage ideology, and the technologies of power that create and maintain social difference have shifted from the skills of warfare to the knowledges acquired through French-language schooling.[8] But these differences are very much the product of an underlying and continuing social and political dynamic. The religious status of the 'Muslim lineages' evolved in response to social, political and economic conflicts in which the knowledge and practice of Islam, in the context of broadly shared Islamic values, could be mobilized to resist subjugation by warrior groups and to ensure a special 'protected' status for these lineages. These same Islamic resources could also be used to transcend this status, as in the West African *jihads* and in the formation of the Mauritanian emirates when Shaikh Sidiyya called on his tribal affiliations to mobilize social resources and evoked his religious persona as a Sufi to legitimate his authority.

Similar processes have been at play in postcolonial Mali, where the secularist policies of successive governments in effect granted a kind of implicit autonomy to the médersa constituencies, allowing them to operate in the religious field free from official interference. And when the state intervened in

[8] One might argue that the 1968 *coup d'état* and the period of military rule was a reversion to governance by a warrior class, but all the military leadership had also received French-language schooling.

médersa affairs in the 1980s, many directors tried to defend this autonomy by asserting the inviolability of 'Islam'. Similarly, in the early 1990s, some Muslims tried to appeal to shared Islamic values in their public discourse by placing an Islamic gloss on the events of March 1991, referring to them as a *jihad* or as 'the popular revolution of Ramadan'. Indeed, Mory Sidibé's accusation that those who do not endorse the project of a Muslim state are not Muslims recalls the extreme language that has been used to justify many a *jihad* in West Africa, even if, in an apparent gesture toward Mali's experiments with democracy, he was quick to add that he would strive to achieve his goals through persuasive means.

So it would seem that the underlying social and political dynamics of West African Muslim societies have changed rather less over the past two centuries than the institutions and discourses through which this dynamic is expressed. And we have seen that this process was complex, involving a rich mix of local, Middle Eastern and French influences. If many Muslims were seeking to redefine and redeploy the Islamic cultural resources available to them (including those now being discovered in the Middle East) in order to reassert their position as Muslims in the changing social environment, they inevitably did so in constant relationship with the colonial and postcolonial political orders. In other words, both the form and substance of new Muslim institutions, as well as Muslim discourses, evolved in constant dialog with the new political environment.

The discursive field also reveals breaks and continuities. The appropriation of the concepts of 'democracy' and 'development' into the Muslim discourse, as well as the claim to one's 'rights' as a Muslim, are late twentieth-century innovations. On the other hand, the Muslim discourse on ignorance and truth has persisted as the primary means through which Muslims express differences among themselves, as evidenced by the pronouncements of Mory Sidibé. Similarly, the anti-Muslim discourse has maintained a thematic coherence over time. The disparaging criticisms of the médersas by many government officials in the 1980s is reminiscent of the mutual contempt that existed in precolonial times between some 'Muslims' and 'rulers'; the role of an 'Islamic' factor in these confrontations becomes patently clear when one recalls that these same officials were fully aware of the fact that schooling offered by the state schools was often no better, and sometimes much worse, than what was available in some médersas. We have also noted how anti-Muslim attitudes have persisted throughout the century, despite an evolution in terminology from accusations of 'fanaticism' at the beginning of the century, to 'Wahhabism' in the 1950s and then to '*intégrisme*' during the 1990s. We have analyzed aspects of this discourse in terms of the construction of identities, focussing primarily on the simultaneous invention of 'Wahhabism' and 'traditionalism' in the 1950s. From the Muslim perspective, this process is an excellent example of how a discourse on ignorance and truth, in this case focussing on Salafi doctrine, can produce difference among Muslims.

Salafi doctrine itself owes nothing to the colonial situation, having been developed in quite different times and places. However, its introduction into Soudan Français in the form of 'Wahhabism' was profoundly politicized, both by the French who saw it as a threat and by its adherents who embraced it as a new form of Muslim identity. Whatever its personal appeal for individual Muslims, Salafi doctrine was also conveniently compatible with the newly emerging social and political environment: it advocated a complete break with local historical forms of Muslim expression and at the same time provided a new religious platform from which to challenge the dominant political order on its own ground. Salafi doctrine also offered a vital point of reference for reasserting Islamic values in the context of the new forms of power relations that were emerging. And we have argued that the conjuncture of shifting identities with changing structures of power relations has been the vital catalyst that has produced the new 'Muslim subjectivities' that began to appear in the latter half of the twentieth century: new forms of Muslim self-consciousness and new concepts about how and where Muslims should fit into the social and political order.

This study has focused on schooling as a key institution in the production of these new Muslim subjectivities. Schooling has not been the only factor, of course, as our analysis of the social and political complexities of postcolonial Mali have shown. But the political implications of schooling (both French-language and médersa) have been profoundly pervasive, especially in the uneven distribution of the cultural, political and economic resources that schooling represents. And it is in the evolution of médersa schooling that one can best perceive the impact of power relations on the emergence of new Muslim subjectivities.

We have argued that médersa schooling was both subjected to and contributed to the appearance of a rationalist *episteme* among Muslims. We will return to this theme below, but first let us summarize how power relations effected the 'rationalization' of médersa schooling. 'Rationalization' in this context refers to efforts to render Muslim schooling relevant to the contemporary social and political context. The impact on Muslim schooling of this process is most evident when comparing Qur'anic and médersa schooling, where everything from pedagogical methods to the socio-economic foundations of the two institutions differs, often dramatically. But the 'rationalization' of médersa schooling does not derive so much from attempts by directors to distance it from Qur'anic schooling as it does from its interactions with French schooling, principal producer of the new technologies of power based on French-language literacy.

The process can be observed from two perspectives. First, the struggles with the colonial authorities that the médersa pioneers endured forced them to organize their institutions in a manner that would conform to administrative requirements. Rather like the process that constructed Wahhabism in Soudan Français, the administrative and pedagogical structures of the first médersas were constructed in part through conflictive relations with the French authorities.

Subsequently, as the network of médersas expanded, directors increasingly felt the need to provide a course of study that would offer their students not only religious training but also opportunities to thrive economically and socially. Such practical aims were new to Muslim educators and could not be achieved except by adopting in some sense the pedagogy and institutional structures of the French schools. Consequently, after independence when the médersas enjoyed almost two decades of semi-autonomy from government intervention, many directors continued this trend toward the 'rationalization' of Muslim schooling.

Nor was the teaching of secular subjects, which eventually became *de rigueur* in virtually all médersas, the most important of these 'rationalizing' forces. More fundamental and subtle was how médersa schooling was now collaborating in the construction of the new technologies of power that were emerging in the postcolony, the most important of which Etienne Gérard would identify as the 'power of writing' and the French language. Since both these technologies, as applied to governance, are associated primarily with French-language schools, it may seem at first glance paradoxical to associate the médersas with them. However, let us explore this theme with reference to the persistent grip of clientelism in postcolonial Mali, and the forces that have opposed it.

Jean-Loup Amselle has argued that three social categories in Mali have tended to oppose clientelism: the Wahhabis (who now prefer to call themselves Sunnis), the westernized intellectuals, and the young economic entrepreneurs.[9] Our findings tend to confirm this view: Wahhabi/Sunni attacks against the Sufi hierarchies and the many complaints by young people who feel their possibilities for social and economic advancement are hindered by their exclusion from clientelist networks would support Amselle's interpretation. However, up to the early 1990s, this opposition had done little to dislodge clientelism in Mali, which had thus far managed to divert and absorb virtually all the energy of these emerging social groups. Certainly, the eruption of the democratic movement was in part an attack against clientelism and the corrupt practices associated with it, and it was led largely by individuals who fall into the social categories mentioned by Amselle, although the elimination of clientelism from the new political order is far from assured.

Structurally, the médersas have also contributed to the undermining of clientelism, primarily by the elimination of 'sacralized' deferential relationships between teacher and pupil. This change in teacher-student relationships, which removes all initiatic overtones from the process of transmitting religious knowledge, has been a crucial element in the shift to a rationalist *episteme*. The 'rationalizing' changes taking place in the médersas are not driven primarily by doctrinal arguments, although these are among the kinds of changes

[9] J.-L. Amselle, 'Fonctionnaires', p. 72, and 'La corruption', pp. 636-7.

advocated by Sunnis. In fact, most médersas in Mali are directed by Sufis who certainly have no interest in attacking the hierarchical structures of the Sufi orders. Thus it would seem that médersa schooling and the Sunnis collude in advancing 'rationalizing' forces of change, although the médersa constituencies participate in this process perhaps less consciously than do the Sunnis, who openly advocate such change through their doctrinal discourse.

On the other hand, we have seen that most parents select médersa schooling for their children for somewhat conservative reasons, which is one of the more arresting contradictions that has emerged from this study. Parents hope the médersas will instill Islam in their children as they know it and also reproduce the social order as they have lived it. But médersa schooling, for all the reasons here under discussion, contributes to the production of new understandings of Islam and new self-perceptions of what it means to be a Muslim that are more compatible with contemporary social conditions. The evidence therefore suggests, in line with the findings of Etienne Gérard, that institutionally the médersas both mediate and actively contribute to the process of social change.

This point brings us back to the theme of newly emerging Muslim subjectivities. The reader will recall that in this study 'subjectivities' are understood in the ambiguous sense employed by Foucault, as both subjective consciousness of self (how one sees oneself as a Muslim) and as being subject to the control of another. It is the latter point that is the more difficult to grasp: how do the médersas prepare Muslims to accept their position in new structures of authority and social order? To put the question another way, what are the factors that convince an individual Muslim to endorse the legitimacy of one form of Islamic authority as opposed to another? A demonstrable control of Islamic knowledge is certainly a key element, but we have seen that in spite of the undeniable significance of doctrinal argumentation, that this alone is rarely enough to convince others of the legitimacy of any particular claim. Argumentation may be an essential part of the process of power relations that convinces one of claims to legitimacy, but this process is never a 'purely' intellectual one.

And we have seen that there was a healthy skepticism about intellectuals in postcolonial Mali, in spite (and because of) the fact that the bureaucratic bourgeoisie of the country consisted almost exclusively of French-schooled 'intellectuals'. We noted the rural contempt expressed for those administrators who 'come because of a piece of paper and leave by a piece of paper'; concepts of legitimacy in this context have little to do with school learning. In the 1980s, some Muslims expressed similar contempt for the new Muslim 'intellectuals', those 'students returning from Saudi Arabia who settle in Bamako rather than go to the bush where they are needed'! These intellectuals, it was alleged, have spoiled religion and are more interested in seeking their own pleasure than in 'speaking the truth'. God has punished more than one people 'because of great intellectuals who knew the Qur'an but left their people in ignorance, which is why one must always speak the truth'. 'Islam cannot develop unless its preachers speak the truth'.[10] Further evidence of the continuing import of the Muslim discourse about ignorance and truth.

But the discourse of the new médersa-schooled intellectuals does have a positive resonance in many social contexts. Those who continue their studies to an advanced level gain an exceptional competence in Islamic knowledge and moreover often speak Arabic fluently, both of which are highly valued and respected assets in a Muslim society. These intellectuals therefore attract an increasing audience of interested Muslims in spite of continuing dissent and criticism from some quarters. And they have been largely responsible for the postcolonial emergence of 'Islam' in the public domain in Mali, through the public activism of many Sunnis, government recognition of the contribution of médersa schooling to the development of national education and more recently in the form of the Islamist initiatives discussed above.

All of these examples demonstrate how perceptions of Islam and Muslim subjectivities have been affected and produced by changing patterns of power relations. The historical itineraries of Salafi doctrine, of Wahhabism/Sunnism, and of the médersas in Mali cannot be separated from the histories of French and postcolonial government policies, of secularism, and of French schooling; both prepared the ground for the emergence of Mory Sidibé's highly politicized Islamist discourse that places Islam at the service of a developmentalist state. Significantly, Sidibé is a French-schooled Muslim whose politics are much more radical than those of the vast majority of médersa-trained scholars who seem to be much more prepared to compromise with the secular state so long as basic Muslim values are not abused. His ideas would be described by many as *intégriste*. Certainly his discourse is an example of a 'rationalized' form of Muslim expression that seeks to place contemporary technologies of power at the service of Muslim doctrine. Or arguably the reverse: to place Muslim doctrine at the service of contemporary technologies of power. In either case, we are faced with yet another paradox in the relationship of knowledge to power. But however one might like to structure this equation, its two elements have evolved in tandem with one another.

And so we return to the title of this book, *Controlling Knowledge*, and questions raised in the introduction about how 'knowledges' can act as controlling forces and when, if ever, 'knowledges' can be effectively controlled by conscious agents.

Both French colonial authorities and médersa directors can be said to have acted as conscious agents in establishing their respective kinds of schools and the curricula and pedagogical methods employed in them. They can thus be said to have controlled to a certain extent the knowledges (on the level of *connaissance*) transmitted to their pupils. But of course, none of these agents can control the uses made of knowledges acquired in school, and in

[10] These quotations are taken from undated tape recordings of preaching by Bassidy Haïdara and Ousmane Haïdara purchased in Bamako in the late 1980s.

any case this study has demonstrated that curriculum content is far from the most significant of the 'knowledges' one acquires in school. The French, for example, intended that their schools should produce 'loyal subjects', whereas in fact French schooling produced the very people who would lead the independence movement and eventually take over the reins of state power for themselves.

Schooling is primarily a process of socialization, and in the Malian context modernized forms of schooling (in contrast with Qur'anic schooling) have transmitted to their students new technologies of power and socialized them into new forms of power relations. In Gramscian terms, Mali's schools have been producing the country's contemporary 'organic intellectuals'. From this perspective, schooling is part of a highly politicized domain where different social constituencies compete for access to the limited resources associated with schooling and contest the legitimacy of different kinds of schooling and the relevance of the various knowledges they claim to transmit. This confrontation produces a discursive space (on the level of *savoir*) in which, for example, the médersa constituencies and the advocates of secular schooling debate *about* schooling. An individual might participate in this debate in the hope of influencing its shape as well as the views of others, but no single participant can control the 'knowledges' that circulate in this discursive environment. Nor, seemingly, can governments: secularist policies have never succeeded in prohibiting Muslim issues and 'knowledges' from entering the public discursive space, just as French-language schooling did not succeed in producing loyal subjects.

Foucault argued that a third level of knowledge exists, which he called the *episteme*, that determines the shape of the other two (*connaissance* and *savoir*). We have argued that a rationalist *episteme* is gradually beginning to replace the esoteric *episteme* to become the predominant controlling influence in the shaping of Muslim discourses in the public domain. The discourses of esoteric spirituality are no longer so easily projected into the public political arena as in the past. Administrative, legal and developmentalist discourses of governance in Mali are now informed by a rationalist *episteme* that contrasts sharply with the esoteric *episteme* that predominated in the past. Even when Sufis like Saada Oumar Touré or Mory Sidibé participate in national debates, they do not present themselves *as Sufis*. Amadou Hampâté Ba may have been the last public figure to have attempted to inject a Sufi discourse into the national political arena when he built his program of counter-reform around the teachings of his own Sufi master, Cerno Bokar. And the French authorities supported counter-reform precisely because they saw it as a possible barrier to the advance of a new form of politicized Islamic expression and action that they feared might successfully challenge their own hegemony. The French (and their Soudanese allies) tried to discredit Salafi doctrine and Wahhabism as alien intrusions but failed to recognize their own role in preparing the ground for this 'rationalizing' form of Muslim expression. Engagement in the national political arena of the colonial state required participation in its institutions, its bureaucracies and of course its schools, all of which functioned within and produced a discursive environment informed by a rationalist *episteme*. The French supposed that Muslims operating in this environment would become secularists; but Salafi doctrine (and the médersas) offered a Muslim alternative for initiation into the rationalist *episteme*.

It is important not to exaggerate the extent of this epistemic shift, which is both limited and uneven. It is probable that the vast majority of Malians, including many products of French schooling, still operate under the influence of the esoteric *episteme* in many aspects of their lives. It is certainly not unusual for persons to espouse rationalist formulations in public while embracing esoteric ones in private; Moussa Traoré and many of his associates are said to have retained '*marabouts*' in order to protect their interests. But the uneven and tentative nature of the epistemic shift negates neither the present hegemony of the rationalist *episteme* in the realm of national governance and its associated institutions, nor its influence in the formulation of power relations in postcolonial Mali.

A rationalist *episteme* cannot exist independently of its social roots; in Mali, it was both the product of underlying social, economic and political factors and of the experience of schooling. If a rationalist *episteme* was first introduced into Mali through the influence of the French colonial presence and the technologies of power that were at the heart of French administrative institutions and schools, Muslims also came to contribute to these 'rationalizing' influences through the Islamic *médersas* and Salafi doctrine. The irony of this development resides in the fact that while on the one hand certain Muslims have sought to distance themselves from the secularizing influences they perceive in certain French-inspired institutions, on the other hand they are unconsciously perpetuating many of these same influences: an excellent example of the paradox of being controlled by knowledges while attempting to control them! And also an illustration of what seems to be a universal human conceit: the illusion that individuals are able to possess and to control 'knowledge'.

And so we can conclude as we began this study, by reasserting the claim that whereas 'Islam' exists as an ideal toward which Muslims strive, Muslim societies are inevitably pluralistic because, like any social formation, they are the product of conflicting social and political forces. The variations of Muslim expression in postcolonial Mali therefore reflect the pluralism of Malian society itself. The content and contours of any particular form of Muslim expression is produced in relationship to a particular social context. Thus, we have argued that *intégrisme*, or so-called 'Islamic fundamentalism' or Islamism, can be understood as an effort to combine Muslim doctrine with contemporary technologies of power, most of which have their origins in European culture. It would seem that the advancing hegemony of a rationalist *episteme* makes possible the appearance of many contemporary forms of Islamism. However, many Islamists seem to be unaware of the indebtedness of some of their ideas to the very culture from which they seek to distance themselves. Similarly, most reactions to, as well as many critical analyses of, Islamist activities fail to recognize that Islamism in its present form is in some part the product of 'rationalizing' influences that have accompanied European imperial expansion in recent centuries. Rather like the situation that prevailed in Soudan Français in the 1950s, the most vocal critics of these developments are often unaware of the complicity of their own culture in them. This is yet another of the many paradoxes to have appeared in the course of this study.

BIBLIOGRAPHY

ARCHIVES CONSULTED

Archives du Ministère de l'Intérieur du Mali, Bamako (AMI)
Archives Nationales du Mali, Bamako (ANM)
Archives Nationales du Sénégal, Dakar (ANS)
Centre des Archives d'Outre-Mer, Aix-en-Provence, France (CAOM)

GOVERNMENT DOCUMENTS

DNAFLA (Direction Nationale de l'Alphabétisation Fonctionnelle et de la Linguistique Appliquée)

'Quelle éducation pour quel développement?', 1977.

'Rapport général sur le séminaire-atelier sur l'élaboration d'un system unifié de transcription du Songhoy en caractères arabes. Bamako, 9-14 mars 1987'.

'Rapport général sur le séminaire-atelier sur l'élaboration d'un système unifié de transcription du Fulfulde en caractères arabes. Bamako, 9-14 mars 1987'.

Ministère de l'Education Nationale

'Annuaire des étudiants maliens boursiers à l'étranger, 1986-7'. 1987.

'Annuaire des statistiques scolaires, 1990-1991'. 1992.

Débat National sur l'Education. Bamako, 16-21 septembre 1991.

    Commission I. Evaluation dans le système éducatif.

    Commission II. Démocratisation du système éducatif.

    Commission III. Elargissement de la base du système éducatif.

    Commission IV. Adéquation, formation, emploi.

    Commission V. Financement et gestion de l'éducation.

'Deuxième séminaire national de l'éducation, décembre 1979'. Institut Pédagogique National, 1980.

'L'enseignement arabo-islamique dans le système éducatif du Mali', Division du Contrôle et de l'Animation du Système des Médersas (DCASM), formerly CPLA, 1991.

'L'enseignement en République du Mali. Administration. Organisation. Missions', 1985.

'Etude sur la demande sociale d'éducation en milieu rural au Mali'. Réalisée par l'Institut Pédagogique National en collaboration avec l'Institut Malien de Recherches Appliquées au Développement (IMRAD). Avril 1989.

'Comment faire appel au Fonds d'Appui à l'Enseignement Fondamental: Guide pratique pour les APE', Bureau des Projets Education, June 1989.

Al-manhaj al-rasmī li 'l-madāris al-ahliyya al-'arabiyya (al-marḥala al-ibtidā'iyya) [Programme officiel pour les médersas populaires arabes (Premier Cycle)]. Centre de Promotion de la Langue Arabe, 1986.

'Médersa au Mali. Documents d'informations', 3 vols. Direction de l'Enseignement Fondamental, 1983-4.

'Projet pilote d'amélioration de l'école coranique au Mali'. No date.

'Projet: Promotion de l'enseignement dans les médersas', 1992.

'Propositions pour une politique de l'éducation en République du Mali'. Période décennale 1974-1983), MEFJS-MESSRSM, Bamako: 1974.

'Rapport final. Table Ronde Nationale sur l'éducation de Base pour Tous d'ici à l'an 2000', Bamako, 3-7 Sept. 1991.

'Rapport Général sur le Débat National sur l'Education tenu les 16, 17, 18, 19, 20 et 21 Septembre 1991', Oct. 1991.

'Rapport de Rentrée: Médersas 1991-2'. Inspection Enseignement Fondamental, Bamako, District VI.

'Rapport du Séminaire National sur l'utilisation de l'alphabet arabe dans la lutte contre l'analphabétisme en Afrique. 21-6 juillet, 1986'. Centre pour la Promotion de la Langue Arabe. 1986.

'Rapport de suivi et d'évaluation du IVème projet'. Institut Pédagogique National. IVème Projet de Développement de l'Education de Base, July 1992.

'La réforme de l'enseignement au Mali', 1965.

'Séminaire national sur les tendances et enjeux futurs des écoles fondamentales en langue arabe (médersas) au Mali. Document final', Bamako, 3-6 Aug. 1992.

Ministère du Plan

Actes du séminaire national sur les politiques de populations au Mali. 1983.

L'aide étrangère au bénéfice de la République du Mali de 1960 à 1980. 1982.

Bilan provisoire de l'aide publique extérieure accordée au Mali, 1981-1985. 1986.

Deuxième conférence internationale des bailleurs de fonds. Rapport principal. 1985.

Diagnostic de la Région de Gao. Région de Gao, Comité Régional de Développement, 1985.

Diagnostic de la Région de Kayes. Région de Kayes, Comité Régional de Développement, 1985.

Diagnostic de la Région de Koulikoro. Région de Koulikoro, Comité Régional de Développement, 1985.

Diagnostic de la Région de Mopti. Région de Mopti, Comité Régional de Développement, 1985.

Diagnostic de la Région de Ségou. Région de Ségou, Comité Régional de Développement, 1985.

Diagnostic de la Région de Tombouctou. Région de Tombouctou, Comité

Régional de Développement, 1985.

Recensement Général de la Population et de l'Habitat (du 1er au 14 avril 1987), July 1987.

Recensement Général de la Population et de l'Habitat (du 1er au 14 avril 1987). Population Urbaine (Résultats Provisoires), July 1987.

UNPUBLISHED DOCUMENTATION

AMUPI, 'Statuts'.

AMUPI. Programme et textes de base, Congrès Constitutif, novembre 1987, Bamako.

Association des Médersas du Mali. 'Intervention du délégué de l'Association des Médersas du Mali', Débat National sur l'Education. Bamako, 16-21 Sept. 1991.

Association des Médersas Islamiques du Mali. 'Manhaj al-ta'līm, al-marḥala al-ibtidā'iyya.' [Programme d'enseignement, premier cycle]. 3 vols., Bamako, 1988.

Basic Education Expansion Project, United States Agency for International Development. First amendment, 1991.

Colonna, Fanny. 'Le Kuttab-"Ecole coranique"-Prime éducation islamique et diversification du champ éducatif'. Rapport, élaboré à la demande de l'Institut international de planification de l'éducation, UNESCO. No date (1984?).

Coulibaly, Soumaila, 'L'incidence du travail sur les rapports entre les jeunes et leur environnement social: points de vue des jeunes', 1992.

Déclaration Mondiale sur l'Education Pour Tous et Cadre d'Action pour Répondre aux Besoins Educatifs Fondamentaux, adoptés par la Conférence sur l'Education Pour Tous, Jomtien, Thailand, 5-9 Mar 1990.

Dembele, Nagognimi U., 'L'insertion socio-professionnelle des jeunes en milieu rural: Etude de cas de trois communautés Mininka et deux communautés bamanan du Ciakédugu, Haut Niger'. Communication to the seminar on 'L'insertion sociale et professionnelle des jeunes', Bamako, 1989.

'Le Développement de l'Enseignement Privé au Mali'. Etude menée dans le District de Bamako et les Communes de Ségou et Sikasso. Rapport Final, établi par l'Association Malienne de Recherche-Action pour le Développement, Bamako, 1990.

Dramé, Kady. 'Al-ta'līm al-'arabī wa'l-'ulūm al-islāmiyya fī 'l-madāris al-taqlīdiyya.' Communication présentée au Colloque sur l'enseignement islamique en Afrique, Centre Islamique Africaine, Khartoum, 29 Feb. to 3 Mar. 1988.

'L'Education au Mali'. Bamako: BPF-UNESCO, 1981.

Haughton, Jonathan, 'Financement et réforme de l'éducation au Mali', World Bank, 1986.

Konaté, B., 'L'impact des facteurs familiaux sur la réussite scolaire des élèves de neuvième année fondamentale du district de Bamako', doctoral thesis

(3rd cycle), University of Strasbourg 2, 1984.

Maiga, Kader, 'Jeunes, grins et mouvements sociaux' (Le cas de Magnambougou, District de Bamako), 1992.

Maiga, Tacko dite Oumou, 'Les Jeunes face au mariage et au chomage. Cas des jeunes de Magnambougou (District de Bamako)', 1992.

Miller, David, M., 'Literature Review: Girls' Primary School Education in Mali: Benefits, Determinants and Pilot Projects', November 1990.

'Projet de Consolidation', IDA-USAID, 19 Nov. – 1 Dec. 1989.

Tolo, Hamadoun, 'Les Filles et la médersa (Cas des Instituts Naharu Djoliba et Sabil al-Hidaya de Bamako)', 1992.

Touré, Oumar S. 'Etude sur des expériences en cours d'éxecution et sur l'état actuel de l'utilisation de l'alphabet arabe dans l'enseignement formel et non-formel au Mali', report to UNESCO, 1985.

Traoré, Boukary, 'Le déferlement massif des jeunes vers les institutions islamiques (médersas), 1992.

Traoré, Mamadou Lamine, 'Jeunes et Médersa: l'Institut Yattabary de Bamako'. Communication présentée à la Conférence Internationale 'La Jeunesse en Afrique. Encadrement et Rôle dans la Société Contemporaine. Héritages, Mutations, Avenir', Paris, 6-8 Dec. 1990.

UNESCO, 'Sub-regional Seminar on the Use of the Arabic Alphabet in the Struggle against Illiteracy in Africa', Dakar, Sénégal, 11-15 Nov. 1985.

UNICEF, 'Projet: Promotion de l'enseignement dans les médersas', 1992.

United States Embassy, Bamako. 'Economic Assistance', unclassified cable to US Secretary of State, 9 Oct. 1988, US Information Agency Archives.

'Vers un plan d'action pour les systèmes éducatifs des pays du Sahel'. Document de travail préparé pour la réunion des Ministres de l'Education des pays du Sahel. Bamako, 15-18 janvier 1990. Prépared by P. Jarousse and A. Mingat of IREDU-CNRS (Université de Bourgogne).

UNPUBLISHED THESES

Balogun, I.A.B., 'A Critical Edition of *Ihyā' al-sunna wa ikhmād al-bid'a* of 'Uthman b. Fudi, popularly known as Usuman dan Fodio'. Ph.D., School of Oriental and African Studies, University of London, 1967.

Batran, A.A., 'Sidi al-Mukhtar al-Kunti and the recrudescence of Islam in the Western Sahara and the Middle Niger'. Ph.D., University of Birmingham, 1971.

Berte, Baba, 'Les implications socio-économique et culturelle de l'Islam en milieu Sénoufo (Arrondissement de Kigan, Cercle de Sikasso)', mémoire de fin d'études, ENSup, Bamako, 1985.

Bonte, Pierre, 'L'émirat de l'Adrar. Histoire et anthropologie d'une société tribale du Sahara occidental', 4 vols, thèse de doctorat d'état, Ecole des Hautes Etudes en Sciences Sociales, Paris, 1998.

Boré, Hamdoun, 'Le fonctionnaire vu par l'administré', mémoire de fin d'études, ENA, Bamako, 1989.

Bouche, D., 'L'enseignement dans les territoires français de l'Afrique occidentale de 1817 à 1920', thèse d'état, University of Paris, I, 1975.

Brown, W.A., 'The Caliphate of Hamdullahi, ca.1818-1864: A Study in African History and Tradition', Ph. D., University of Wisconsin, Madison, 1969.

Camara, Diaba, 'L'organisation judiciaire en droit musulman', mémoire de fin d'études, ENA, Bamako, 1985.

Camara, Oumar, 'Notion de propriété en droit musulman', mémoire de fin d'études, ENA, Bamako, 1985.

Camara, Seydou, 'Attitudes des parents d'élèves face à l'école malienne. Opinions sur leur autofinancement de l'école et perceptions de rôle de la formation scolaire au Mali (cas des Communes II et IV du District de Bamako)', mémoire de fin d'études, ENSup, Bamako, 1987.

Camara, Seydou, 'Les forces religieuses face à l'administration territoriale dans le cercle de Nioro', mémoire de fin d'études, ENA, Bamako, 1975.

Chamberlin, J.W., 'The Development of Islamic Education in Kano City, Nigeria, with emphasis on Legal Education in the 19th and 20th Centuries', Ph.D., Columbia University, 1975.

Cissé, Amadou Diadié, 'Le problème de la dégradation de l'image de l'école au Mali. L'attitude des élèves de la 9e année du cycle fondamental face à la crise de l'emploi (District de Bamako)', mémoire de fin d'études, ENSup, Bamako, 1988.

Cissé, Seydou, 'L'alphabétisation fonctionnelle. l'expérience malienne', thèse de doctorat (3e cycle), Université de Strasbourg, 1981.

——, 'L'Islam et l'éducation musulmane au Mali', thèse de doctorat d'état, Strasbourg, 1989.

Coulibaly, Hamadoun. 'Sociologie de la religion dans le cercle de Koulikoro', mémoire de fin d'études, ENA, Bamako, 1984.

Coulibaly, Lamine Zanga, and Assanatou Traoré, 'Statut et rôle de la femme bambara dans l'Islam tels qu'interprétés en milieu urbain de Bamako', mémoire de fin d'études, ENSup, Bamako, 1987.

Coulibaly, Soumaila, 'Les jeunes et l'école (étude de cas)', mémoire de fin d'études, ENSup, Bamako, 1990.

Coulibaly, Tiécoura, 'Roger Garaudy. Du Marxisme à l'Islam', mémoire de fin d'études, ENSup, Bamako, 1987.

Couchoud, Laurence, 'La migration sur place. Etude de la marginalité à Bamako (Mali)', mémoire de fin d'études de DEA, EHESS, Paris, 1987.

Dabo, Adama N'Faly, 'L'influence du droit musulman sur le droit malien', mémoire de fin d'études, ENA, Bamako, 1979.

Danioko, Doulaye, 'Education et développement économique et social au Mali', thèse de sciences economiques, Université de Paris I, 1974.

Dansogo, B., 'La prolifération des médersas islamiques. Est-ce une colonisation culturelle ou facteur d'épanouissement culturel indépendant du Mali', mémoire de fin d'études, ENSup, Bamako, 1985.

Daou, Souleymane, 'Mendicité et identité culturelle. Étude à Bamako', mémoire de fin d'études, ENSup, Bamako, 1986.

Dena, André, 'Perception actuelle de l'école par les parents d'élèves. Cas du District de Bamako', mémoire de fin d'études, ENSup, Bamako, 1989.

Deyoko, Abdoulaye, 'Disparités régionales en matière en politique scolaire au Mali', maîtrise, Université de Paris I, 1975.

Diaby, (Mlle) Sadio, 'L'échec scolaire à travers les méthodes d'enseignement dans le district de Bamako', mémoire de fin d'études, ENSup, Bamako, 1984.

Diakité, Alfousseyne, and Mori M. Konaté, 'L'enseignement arabo-islamique dans le district de Bamako (place, fonction, incidences scolaires et sociales)', mémoire de fin d'études, ENSup, Bamako. 1985.

Diakité, Soumaila, 'Education, the State and Class Conflict: A Study of Three Education Policies in Mali', Ph.D., Stanford University, 1985.

Diakité, Yoro, 'L'impact de la religion sur la politique socio-économique du Mali: Etude comparée des cas du Touba et Kiban à travers l'islam', mémoire de fin d'études, ENA, Bamako, 1987.

Diallo, Hamidou, 'Les successions en droit musulman, place et intérêt au Mali', mémoire de fin d'études, ENA, Bamako, 1984.

Diallo, Issoufou Sékou, 'L'adultère en droit musulman', mémoire de fin d'études, ENA, Bamako, 1985.

Diallo, Oumar, 'Etude sur les écoles coraniques à Sikasso', mémoire de fin d'études, ENSup, Bamako, 1987.

Diarah, (Mme) Bintou Sanankoua, 'Organisation politique du Macina: Dina (1818-1862)', thèse de doctorat (3e cycle), Université de Paris, 1982.

Diarra, B., 'Nécessité d'un dialogue islamo-chrétien dans le district de Bamako', mémoire de fin d'études, ENSup, Bamako, 1987.

Dicko, Ilorou, 'Le droit musulman de la famille', mémoire de fin d'études, ENA, Bamako, 1987.

Dicko, Seidna O., 'La politique musulmane de l'administration coloniale au Soudan français dan la première moitié du XXe siècle, 1912-45', mémoire de fin d'études, ENSup, Bamako. 1978.

Diop, Boubacar, 'Histoire de l'enseignement à San. Son impact sur le développement des mentalités', mémoire de fin d'études, ENSup, Bamako. 1986.

Dolo, Hadiaratou, 'Les circonstances atténuantes en matière de repression en droit musulman', mémoire de fin d'études, ENA, Bamako, 1986.

Doucouré, Mohamed El-Bechir, 'La politique musulmane de l'administration coloniale au Soudan français de 1919 à 1939', mémoire de fin d'études, ENSup, Bamako, 1985.

Doumbia, Fodé, 'La répartition géographique des établissements du culte musulman dans le district de Bamako', mémoire de fin d'études, ENSup, Bamako, 1984.

Dramé, Abdoulay, 'Déperdition scolaire et délinquance juvénile au Mali', mémoire de fin d'études, ENSup, Bamako, 1977.

Dramé, Abdoulaye, 'Les régimes matrimoniaux en droit musulman', mémoire de fin d'études, ENA, Bamako, 1984.

Gérard, Etienne, 'L'Ecole déclassé. Une étude anthropo-sociologique de la scolarisation au Mali. Cas des sociétés malinkés', thèse de doctorat (nouveau régime), Université Paul Valéry, 1992.

Guedj, P., 'L'enseignement supérieur en Afrique. Instrument de développement ou facteur de désintégration. Une étude de cas: le Mali', thèse de doctorat (nouveau régime), Université de Tours, 1986.

Haïdara, Hamadoun., 'L'esclavage. Les pratiques coutumières, l'Islam et le droit positif', mémoire de fin d'études, ENA, Bamako, 1987.

Harmon, Stephen A., 'The Expansion of Islam among the Bambara under French Rule: 1890 to 1940', Ph.D., University of California, Los Angeles, 1988.

Hock, Carsten, 'Muslimische Reform und staatliche Autorität in der Republik Mali seit 1960. Die Ausbreitung der Wahhabiya in einer Situation der politischen Blockade gesellschaftlichen Fortschritts', University of Bayreuth, 1998.

Kader, Dramane, 'Le Centre Ahmed Baba de Tombouctou. CEDRAB', mémoire de fin d'études, ENA, Bamako, 1985.

Kaïl, Bénédicte, 'L'insertion des jeunes sur le marché du travail à Bamako. Enjeux de la scolarisation et de l'insertion professionnelle selon le genre', thèse de doctorat, l'EHESS, Paris, 1998.

Kamissoko, Fadiala Sanfing, 'Les images de l'enseignement chez les élèves du second cycle de la ville de Bamako', mémoire de fin d'études, ENSup, Bamako, 1987.

Kane, Kaman, 'Le pèlerinage des Maliens aux lieux saints de l'Islam', mémoire de fin d'études, ENA, Bamako, 1978.

Kane, Ousmane., 'La confrérie Tijaniyya réformée à Kano', mémoire de fin d'études de DEA, University of Paris V, 1987.

――――, 'Les mouvements islamiques et le champ politique au nord du Nigéria: Le cas du mouvement Izâla à Kano', thèse de doctorat, Institut d'Etudes Politiques, Paris, 1993.

Kanté, Nianguiry, 'Contribution à la connaissance de la migration Soninke en France', thèse de doctorat (3e cycle), Université de Paris VIII, 1987.

Kavas, Ahmet, 'L'évolution de l'enseignement moderne arabo-islamique en Afrique francophone. Les médersas de la République du Mali (Cas de Bamako 1980-1994) (Rôle social, mode de fonctionnement et contenu d'enseignement)', thèse de doctorat, Université de Paris VII, 1996.

Keita, Arouna, 'L'Islam et ses implications socio-économiques dans le district de Bamako', mémoire de fin d'études, ENSup, Bamako, 1987.

Keita, Emile, 'Idéologies religieuses et développement dans le cercle de Tominian', mémoire de fin d'études, ENA, Bamako, 1985.

Koné, Danzeni Broulaye, 'Les aspects socio-économiques et religieux de la mendicité dans le District de Bamako', mémoire de fin d'études, ENSup, Bamako, 1989.

Kone, Florent. 'La mendicité au Mali', mémoire de fin d'études, ENA, Bamako, 1978.

Konta, Aly, 'Une approche géographique des pratiques islamiques au Mali. Une étude de cas', mémoire de fin d'études, ENSup, Bamako, 1984.

Magassa, Abdoulaye, 'Religion et développement', mémoire de fin d'études, ENSup, Bamako, 1987.

Mahamane, Alliman, 'Le mouvement wahhabite à Bamako, (origine et évolution)', mémoire de fin d'études, ENSup, Bamako, 1985.

Mahmoudi, A., 'La coopération arabo-africaine. Etat et perspectives', Mémoire de magister en sciences politiques, Institut des Sciences Politiques et de l'Information, Université d'Alger, 1982.

Maiga, Abdourahman, 'La résistance de la population rurale face à la scolarisation: Cas du cercle de Bourem', mémoire de fin d'études, ENSup, Bamako, 1987.

Maiga, Hamidou Younoussa, 'Le droit islamique et le mariage', mémoire de fin d'études, ENA, Bamako, 1974.

Maiga, Harber, 'Le Centre de Documentation et de Recherche Historique Ahmed Baba (CEDRAB) de Tombouctou et la problématique d'une pédagogie de développement pour le Mali', mémoire de fin d'études, ENSup, Bamako, 1986.

Maiga, Tacko *dite* Oumou, 'Les jeunes et l'école. Cas des adolescents scolarisés de Sogoniko (District de Bamako)', mémoire de fin d'études, ENSup, Bamako, 1990.

Malle, Yacouba, 'La résistance à la scolarisation en milieu rural: cas du village de Bamantoun (Région de Koulikoro)', mémoire de fin d'études, ENSup, Bamako, 1989.

Mété, Yacouba, 'Idéologie scolaire-idéologie populaire. Conflit de valeurs école-société comme facteur de destructuration sociale et d'échec sociale', mémoire de fin d'études, ENSup, Bamako, 1984.

Moulaye, Zeyni, 'Les relations du Mali avec les états nord Africains de 1960-1980. Contribution à l'étude des relations internationales de la République du Mali', thèse de doctorat (3e cycle), Université de Paris I, 1982.

N'Faly, Adama, 'L'influence du droit musulman sur le droit malien', mémoire de fin d'études, ENA, Bamako, 1979.

Niezen, Ronald W., 'Diverse Styles of Islamic Reform among the Songhay of Eastern Mali'., Ph.D., Cambridge University, 1987.

Ouattara, Ouda, 'Attitude et perception des ruraux du Kénédougou face à l'école. Cas de l'arrondissement central de Sikasso', mémoire de fin d'études, ENSup, Bamako, 1989.

Oula, Ousmane, 'Pouvoir et religion (cas de l'Islam au Mali)', mémoire de fin d'études, ENSup, Bamako, 1984.

Ould Cheikh, Abdel Wedoud, 'Nomadisme, islam et pouvoir politique dans la société maure précoloniale', thèse de doctorat, Université de Paris V, 1985.

Quellien, A., 'La politique musulmane dans l'Afrique Occidentale Française', thèse de doctorat, Paris, 1910.

Sall, Amadou, 'Le maître et la déperdition scolaire au premier cycle fondamental à Bamako', mémoire de fin d'études, l'ENSup, Bamako, 1982.

Samaké, M., 'Organisation politique de Bamananw. Les *Kafow* de la région de Buguni (Mali)', mémoire de DEA, EHESS, Paris, 1981.

Samaké, M., 'Pouvoir traditionnel et conscience politique paysanne: les Kafow de la région de Bougouni, Mali', 2 vols, thèse de doctorat (3e cycle), EHESS, Paris, 1984.

Samaké, Seydou. 'L'Islam comme forme d'intégration sociale', mémoire de fin d'études, ENSup, Bamako, 1987.

Sangaré, Oumar, 'Les commerçants à Bamako', mémoire de fin d'études, ENSup, Bamako, 1977.

Sanogo, Hamed, 'Le statut social de la femme en droit musulman', mémoire de fin d'études, ENA, Bamako, 1985.

Sanogo, Néguédougou, 'L'école malienne et la problématique de l'emploi', mémoire de fin d'études, ENSup, Bamako, 1984.

Sidibé, Cheick Omar, 'Education and Society: Malian School System in Transition', Ph.D., State University of New York at Buffalo, 1982.

Sidibe, Raoul E., 'La dégradation de la conscience professionnelle chez les enseignants maliens. Cas des enseignants du second cycle des écoles fondamentales', mémoire de fin d'études, ENSup, Bamako, 1988.

Sidibe, Zoumana, 'Impact des religions sur les structures juridico-politiques au Mali depuis 1960; Cas de l'islam et du Christianisme', mémoire de fin d'études, ENA, Bamako, 1987.

Soares, Benjamin F., 'The Spiritual Economy of Nioro du Sahel: Islamic Discourses and Practices in a Malian Religious Center', Ph.D., Northwestern University, 1997.

Soumeïlou, Elmahmoud, 'L'influence du droit musulman sur le code du mariage et de la tutelle en République du Mali', mémoire de fin d'études, ENA, Bamako, 1985.

Sounfountera, Ibrahima, 'Etude sur les écoles coraniques à Djenné', mémoire de fin d'études, ENSup, Bamako, 1977.

Sow, Boubacar, 'L'état et la religion au Mali', mémoire de fin d'études, ENA, Bamako, 1978.

Talfi Ag Hamma, 'Les jeunes et les médersas. Etude d'un cas: Institut Islamique Yattabary', mémoire de fin d'études, ENSup, Bamako, 1990.

Tamari, Tal, 'Les castes au Soudan occidental. Étude anthropologique et historique', thèse de doctorat, Université de Paris X – Nanterre, 1987.

Thera, Moustapha, 'Les festivités du XVe centenaire de l'hégire au Mali', mémoire de fin d'études, ENA, Bamako, 1986.

Tidiane, Cheick Amadou, 'Les jeunes et les médersas. Etude de cas: Institut Islamique Khaled Ben Abdul Aziz (District de Bamako)', mémoire de fin d'études, ENSup, Bamako, 1991.

Tolo, Hamadoun, 'Les jeunes et la médersa. Cas de l'Institut Islamique Naharu Djoliba de Bamako', mémoire de fin d'études, ENSup, Bamako, 1991.

Touré, Abdourahamane Hasseye, 'Tombouctou. Le monde culturel non-islamique', mémoire de fin d'études, ENSup, Bamako, 1985.

Touré, Youssoufi Alassane, 'Rôle de la mystique confrérique dans l'islamisation au Soudan de la première moitié du xixe siècle à 1939. Contribution à l'étude de l'Islam au Mali', mémoire de fin d'études, ENSup, Bamako, 1986.

Touré, Ibrahim Baba, 'L'Islam dans ses manifestations actuelles à Bamako', mémoire de fin d'études, ENSup, Bamako, 1989.

Traoré, Boubacar Daba, 'Le Panislamisme en Afrique noire (cas du Mali)', mémoire de fin d'études, ENSup, Bamako, 1987.

Traoré, Boukary, 'Les jeunes et les médersas: Cas de la Médersa Sabil al-Hidaya de Niarela, Bamako', mémoire de fin d'études, ENSup, Bamako, 1991.

Traoré, Cheick H., 'L'école coloniale au Soudan, 1900-1939', mémoire de fin d'études, ENSup, Bamako, 1978.

Traoré, Moussa, 'Les médersa à Bamako', mémoire de fin d'études, ENSup, Bamako, 1987.

Traoré, Soumana, 'Réflexions sur les causes psycho-pédagogiques de la baisse du niveau des élèves de l'enseignement fondamental au Mali', mémoire de fin d'études, ENSup, Bamako, 1988.

Ward, J., 'The Bambara-French Relationships, 1890-1915'. Ph.D., University of California, Los Angeles, 1976.

NEWSPAPERS AND PERIODICALS PUBLISHED IN MALI

Iqra'. Majalla shahriyya tarbawiyya thaqafiyya islamiyya. (Revue mensuelle sur l'éducation et la culture islamiques) published by the Association des Médersas arabo-islamiques du Mali. Since Jan. 1991.

Jamana. Revue culturelle malienne, Bamako.

Les Echos, Bamako.

al-Farouq, Bamako, Bimonthly, first published Nov. 1991, founding director Kady Dramé, bilingual in French and Arabic.

Témoignage afro-musulman. Segu. bimonthly, first published October 1991; founding editor Mamadou Hachim Sow.

al-Risalat al-tarbawiyya ilā 'l-mu'allmīn wa 'l-mu'allmāt fī madāris al-marhalat al-ibtidā'iyya (Message éducatif adressé aux enseignants dans les médersas du premier cycle), Bamako: Association des Médersas arabo-islamiques du Mali,1991.

Saniya, Bamako. Monthly, first published Oct. 1990, founding editor El Hadj Seydou Faganda Diarra.

Sankore, Tombouctou: Centre de Documentation et de Recherches Ahmed Baba.

PUBLISHED SOURCES

Abitbol, M., *Tombouctou et les Arma.* Paris: Maisonneuve et Larose, 1979.

Adams, Adrian, *La terre et les gens du fleuve.* Paris: L'Harmattan, 1985.

L'Afrique Française: Bulletin du Comité de l'Afrique française et du Comité du Maroc.

Ag Athaer Insar, Mohamed Ali, 'La scolarisation moderne comme stratégie de résistance', REMMM, no. 57 (1990), pp. 91-7.

Ag Foni, Eghleze, 'Récit d'un internement scolaire', REMMM, no. 57 (1990), pp. 113-21.

d'Almeida-Topor, H., C. Coquery-Vidrovitch, O. Goerg, and Fr. Guitart (eds), *Les Jeunes en Afrique*, vol. I: *Evolution et rôle (XIXe-XXe)*; vol. II: *La Politique et la ville*. Paris: L'Harmattan, 1992.

Amselle, J.-L., 'A Case of Fundamentalism in West Africa: Wahabism in Bamako', in L. Caplan (ed.), *Studies in Religious Fundamentalism*. London: Macmillan Press, 1987.

——, 'La conscience paysanne. La révolte de Oulossébougou (juin 1968, Mali)', *Revue canadienne des études africaines*, 12 (3), 1978, pp. 339-55.

——, 'La corruption et le clientélisme au Mali et en Europe de l'Est: quelques points de comparaison', *Cahiers d'Etudes Africaines*, 32 (4), 128, 1992, pp. 629-42.

——, 'Un Etat contre l'Etat. Le Keleyadugu', *Cahiers d'Etudes Africaines*, 28 (3-4), 111-12, 1988, pp. 463-83.

——, 'L'ethnicité comme volonté et comme représentation, à propos des Peul du Wasolon', *Annales ESC*, 42 (2), 1987, pp. 465-89.

——, 'Fonctionnaires et hommes d'affaires au Mali', *Politique Africaine*, 26 (1987), pp. 63-72.

——, *Logiques métisses. Anthropologie de l'identité en Afrique et ailleurs*. Paris: Payot, 1990.

——, *Les négociants de la savane. Histoire et organisation sociale des Kooroko (Mali)*. Paris: Anthropos, 1977.

——, 'La politique de la Banque Mondiale en Afrique au Sud du Sahara', *Politique Africaine*, no. 10 (1983), pp. 113-18.

—— (ed.), *Le sauvage à la mode*. Paris: Le Sycomore, 1979.

——, 'Socialisme, capitalisme et précapitalisme au Mali (1960-1982)', in H. Bernstein and B. Campbell (eds), *Contradictions of Accumulation in Africa*. Beverly Hills: Sage, 1985, pp. 249-66.

—— 'Le Wahabisme à Bamako (1945-1985)', *Canadian Journal of African Studies*, XIX, no. 2 (1985), pp. 345-57.

——, and E. Grégoire. 'Complicités et conflits entre bourgeoisie d'état et bourgeoisie d'affaires: au Mali et au Niger'. in E. Terray (ed), *L'Etat contemporain en Afrique*. Paris: Editions L'Harmattan, 1987.

Amselle, J.-L. et E. M'Bokolo. *Au coeur de l'ethnie: Ethnies, tribalisme et Etat en Afrique*. Paris: La Découverte, 1985.

Bâ, A.H., *Vie et enseignement de Tierno Bokar, le sage de Bandiagara*. Paris: Editions du Seuil, 1980.

——, *Amkullel, l'enfant peul*. Paris: Actes Sud, 1991.

——, *Oui mon commandant! Mémoires II*. Paris: Actes Sud, 1994.

——, and Marcel Cardaire, *Tierno Bokar, le sage de Bandiagara*. Paris, 1957.

—— and J. Daget, *L'empire peul du Macina (1818-1853)*. Abidjan: Nouvelles Editions Africaines, 1984.

Bah, Abu Bakr Khalid, 'Risālat al-Islām wa dauruhā fī 'l-thaqāfat al-ifrīqiyya', in *Ifrīqiyya wa'l-thaqāfat al-'arabiyyat al-islāmiyya* (Africa and Arabo-Islamic Culture), Rabat: ISESCO, 1987.

Bagayogo, Shaka, 'Les jeunes et l'état au Mali ou les revers d'une désarticulation', *Jamana* (Bamako), no. 35 (Mar. 1994), pp. 16-25.

——, 'L'Etat au Mali. Représentation, autonomie et mode de fonctionnement' in E. Terray (ed.), *L'Etat contemporain en Afrique*. Paris: L'Harmattan, 1987.

Bastien, Christine, *Folies, mythes et magies d'Afrique Noire. Propos de guérisseurs du Mali*. Paris: L'Harmattan, 1988.

Batran, A.A., 'An introductory note on the impact of Sidi al-Mukhtar al-Kunti (1729-1811) on West African Islam in the 18th and 19th centuries', *Journal of the Historical Society of Nigeria*, VI, 4 (1973), pp. 347-52.

Bayart, Jean-François, *L'Etat en Afrique. La politique du ventre*. Paris: Fayard, 1989; published in English as *The State in Africa : The Politics of the Belly*, tr. by Mary Harper, Christopher and Elizabeth Harrison. Moscow and New York: Longman, 1993.

——, A. Mbembe, C. Toulabor, *Le politique par le bas en Afrique noire*. Paris: Karthala, 1992.

——, 'Le politique par le bas en Afrique noire. Questions de méthode', *Politique Africaine*, no. 1, (1981), pp. 53-82.

Behrman, Lucy C., *Muslim Brotherhoods and Politics in Senegal*. Cambridge, MA: Harvard University Press, 1970.

Benoist, Joseph-Roger de, *Eglise et pouvoir colonial au Soudan Français. Les relations entre les administrateurs et les missionnaires catholiques dans la Boucle du Niger, de 1885 à 1945*. Paris: Karthala, 1987.

Benoist, Joseph-Roger de, *Le Mali*, Paris: L'Harmattan, 1989.

Binger, L.-G., *Le péril de l'Islam*, Paris: 1906.

Bledsoe, C.H., and K.M. Robey, 'Arabic literacy and secrecy among the Mende of Sierra Leone', *Man*, 21 (1986), pp. 202-26.

Bonte, Pierre, 'Égalité et hiérarchie dans une tribu maure: Les Awlâd Qaylân de l'Adrar mauritanien, in P. Bonte et al, *Al-Ansâb. La Quête des origines. Anthropologie historique de la société arabe*. Paris: Editions de la Maison des Sciences de l'Homme, 1991. Pp. 145-99.

Bouche, D., 'Les écoles françaises au Soudan à l'époque de la conquête (1884-1890)', *Cahiers d'Etudes Africaines*, VI (1966), pp. 228-67.

Bourdieu, P. *Choses Dites*. Paris: Editions de Minuit, 1987.

——, *The Field of Cultural Production: Essays on Art and Literature*. Cambridge: Polity Press, 1993.

——, 'Genèse et structure du champ religieux', *Revue française sociologique*, XII (1971), pp. 295-334.

——, *Outline of a Theory of Practice*. Cambridge University Press, 1977.

—— and J.C. Passeron, *Reproduction in Education, Society and Culture*. London: Sage, 1977.

Bowen, John R., *Muslims through Discourse: Religion and Ritual in Gayo Society*.

Princeton University Press, 1993.

Brenner, L., 'Amadou Hampâté Bâ, Tijani francophone' in J.-L. Triaud and D. Robinson (eds), *L'ascension d'une confrérie musulmane. La Tijaniyya en Afrique de l'Ouest et du Nord (XIXe-XXe siècles)*, forthcoming.

——, 'Becoming Muslim in Soudan Français' in D. Robinson and J.-L. Triaud (eds), *Le temps des marabouts*, pp. 467-92.

——, 'Concepts of Tariqa in West Africa: the Case of the Qadiriyya' in D. Cruise O'Brien and C. Coulon (eds). *Charisma and Brotherhood in African Islam*. Oxford: Clarendon Press, 1988.

——, (ed.). *Muslim Identity and Social Change in Sub-Saharan Africa*. London: Hurst; Bloomington: Indiana University Press, 1993.

——, 'Constructing Muslim Identities in Mali' in L. Brenner (ed.), *Muslim Identity and Social Change in Sub-Saharan Africa*, pp. 59-78.

——, 'La culture arabo-islamique au Mali' in René Otayek (ed.), *Le radicalisme islamique en Afrique subsaharienne. Da'wa, arabisation et critique de l'Occident*. Paris: Karthala, 1993, pp. 161-95.

——, 'The Esoteric Sciences in West African Islam' in B.M. Du Toit and I. Abdalla (eds), *African Healing Strategies*. Buffalo, NY: Trado-Medic Books, 1985.

——, 'Essai socio-historique sur l'enseignement islamique au Mali' in Sanankoua and Brenner, *L'enseignement islamique au Mali*. Bamako: Editions Jamana, 1991, pp. 1-23.

——, 'Al-Hajj Saada Oumar Touré and Islamic Educational Reform in Mali' in E. Breitinger and R. Sander (eds), *Language and Education in Africa*, Bayreuth African Studies series, no. 5, 1986.

——, 'The Jihad Debate between Sokoto and Borno: an Historical Analysis of Islamic Political Discourse in Nigeria' in J.F. Ade Ajayi and J.D.Y. Peel (eds), *Peoples and Empires in African History*. London: Longman, 1992.

——, 'Médersas au Mali. Transformation d'une institution islamique', in Sanankoua et Brenner, *L'enseignement islamique au Mali*. Bamako: Editions Jamana, 1991, pp. 63-85.

——, 'Muslim Thought in Eighteenth-Century West Africa: The Case of Shaikh 'Uthman b. Fudi' in N. Levtzion and J. Voll (eds), *Eighteenth Century Renewal and Reform Movements in Islam*. Syracuse University Press, 1987.

——, *Réflexions sur le savoir islamique en Afrique de l'Ouest*. Centre d'Etude d'Afrique Noire, University of Bordeaux I, 1985.

——, 'Representations of Power and Powerlessness in West African Islam'. in J.-P. Chrétien *et al.* (eds), *L'invention religieuse en Afrique. Histoire et religion en Afrique noire*. Paris: Karthala, 1993, pp. 213-34.

——, 'Sufism in Africa' in J. Olupona (ed.), *African Spirituality*. New York: Crossroad Press, forthcoming.

——, 'Three Fulbe Scholars in Borno', *Maghreb Review*, X, no. 4-6 (1985), pp. 107-17.

——, 'Two Paradigms of Islamic Schooling in West Africa' in H. Elboudrari (ed.), *Modes de transmission de la culture religieuse en Islam*. Cairo: Institut Français d'Archéologie Orientale, 1993, pp. 159-80.

——, *West African Sufi: The Religious Heritage and Spiritual Search of Cerno Bokar Saalif Taal*. London: Hurst; Los Angeles: University of California Press, 1984.

——, 'Youth as Political Actors in Mali' in Pearl T. Robinson, Catherine Newbury, and Mamadou Diouf (eds), *Transitions in Africa: Expanding Political Space*, forthcoming.

—— and M. Last, 'The Role of Language in West African Islam', *Africa*, 55 (4), 1985, pp. 432-46.

Brevié, J., *Islamisme contre 'Naturisme' au Soudan Français*. Paris: Leroux, 1923.

Brown, G.N., and M. Hiskett (eds), *Conflict and Harmony in Education in Tropical Africa*. London: Geo. Allen & Unwin, 1975.

Caillié, R., *Voyage à Tombouctou*. Paris: François Maspéro/La Découverte, 1982.

Campmas, P., *L'Union Soudanaise R.D.A. L'histoire d'un grand parti politique africain*, vol. I: *1946-1960*. Libreville: Editions Communication Intercontinentale, no date.

Cardaire, M., *Contribution à l'étude de l'islam noir*. Cameroun: IFAN, 1949.

——, *L'Islam et le terroir africain*. Koulouba: Imprimerie du Gouvernement, 1954.

——, 'Islam et la cellule sociale africaine', *Afrique et l'Asie*, no. 29 (1955), pp. 22-8.

Chailley, M., 'Aspects de l'Islam au Mali' in M. Chailley *et al.*, *Notes et études sur l'Islam en Afrique Noire*, Collection du CHEAM, Paris: Peyronet, 1962.

Cissé, Bokar., *Historique de l'enseignement au Soudan français*. Bamako, no date.

——, *La scolarisation des jeunes filles dans les écoles du Soudan français*. Bamako, 1986.

Cissé, Issa, 'Les médersas au Burkina. L'aide arabe et la croissance d'un système d'enseignement arabo-islamique', *ISASS*, no. 4 (1990), pp. 57-72.

Cissé, Mahamoudou,. 'Etre jeune aujourd'hui. Etude psycho-sociologique sur la jeunesse malienne', *Etudes maliennes*, spécial nos 35-36, 1985.

Cissé, Seydou, 'L'éducation islamique' in *Culture et Civilisation Islamiques. Le Mali*. Rabat: ISESCO, 1988, pp. 287-9.

——, *L'enseignement islamique en Afrique noire*. Paris: L'Harmattan, 1992.

——, 'Les médersas de Ségou' in *Culture et Civilisation Islamiques. Le Mali*, (Rabat: ISESCO, 1988), pp. 149-50.

Cissoko, Sekéné Mody, *Tombouctou et l'Empire Songhay*. Abidjan: Nouvelles Editions Africaines, 1975.

Comité Sahel, *Qui se nourrit de la famine en Afrique?* Paris: Maspéro, 1975.

Combelles, Henri, 'La scolarisation et les écoles nomades au Mali' in E. Bernus *et al.* (eds), *Nomades et commandants. Administration et sociétés nomades dans l'ancienne A.O.F.* Paris: Karthala, 1993, pp. 133-8.

Conklin, Alice L., *A Mission to Civilize: The Republican Idea of Empire in France and West Africa, 1895-1930*. Stanford University Press, 1997.

Cooper, Frederick, and Randall Packard (eds). *International Development and the Social Sciences: Essays on the History and Politics of Knowledge*. Berkeley: University of California Press, 1997.

Coulon, Christian, *Le marabout et le prince: Islam et pouvoir au Sénégal*. Paris: A. Pedone, 1981.

——, *Les musulmans et le pouvoir en Afrique noire*. Paris: Karthala, 1983.

——, 'Le réseau islamique', *Politique Africaine*, no. 9 (1983), pp. 68-83.

Cruise O'Brien, Donal, *The Mourides of Senegal: The Political and Economic Organization of an Islamic Brotherhood*. Oxford: Clarendon Press, 1971.

Cuoq, Joseph-Marie, *Recueil des sources arabes concernant l'Afrique Occidentale du VIII au XVIème siècle*. Paris: CNRS, 1975.

Culture et Civilisation Islamiques. *Le Mali*. Rabat: ISESCO, 1988.

Decraene, Philippe, *Le Mali*. Paris: Presses Universitaires de France, 1980.

Delafosse, M., 'L'animisme nègre et sa résistance à l'islamisation en Afrique occidentale', *Revue du Monde Musulman*, XLIX (Mar. 1922), pp. 121-63.

——, 'L'Islam et les sociétés noires de l'Afrique', *L'Afrique Française: Bulletin du Comité de l'Afrique française et du Comité du Maroc*, pp. 321-333.

Devey, Muriel., *Hampâté Bâ. L'homme de la tradition*. Dakar: NEA Sénégal, 1993.

Diaby, S.M.C., *Les textes fondamentaux de la IIIe République du Mali*. Bamako, 1992.

Diakité, Drissa, 'Les fondements historiques de l'enseignement islamique au Mali' in Sanankoua and Brenner (eds), *L'enseignement islamique au Mali*. Bamako: Editions Jamana, 1991, pp. 25-44.

Diané, Djiba. 'Cheikh Fanta Madi Cherif, grand marabout de Haute-Guinée', *ISASS*, no. 2 (1988), pp. 107-13.

Diané, al-Hajj Kabiné, *Recueil des cinq piliers de l'Islam*, 2 vols. Algiers: Imprimerie P. Guiauchain, 1956.

——, *Le Coran. Lumière du Créateur*, 2 vols, 8th edn. Algiers: Imprimerie P. Guiauchain, 1956.

Diarrah, Cheick Oumar, *Le Mali de Modibo Keita*. Paris: L'Harmattan, 1986.

——, *Mali. Bilan d'une Gestion Désastreuse*. Paris: L'Harmattan, 1990.

——, *Vers la IIIe République du Mali*. Paris: L'Harmattan, 1991.

Diawara, M., *La graine de la parole*. Stuttgart: Franz Steiner Verlag, 1990.

Doumbia, Fodé, 'Les mosquées à Bamako', *Jamana*, no. 13 (May-June 1987), pp. 31-5.

Dreyfus, H.L., and P. Rabinow, *Michel Foucault : Beyond Structuralism and Hermeneutics*. London: Harvester Wheatsheaf, 1982.

Dumestre, G., *La geste de Ségou (racontée par des griots Bambara)*. Paris: Armand Colin, 1979.

Dumont, F., *L'Anti-sultan ou Al-Hajj Omar Tal du Fouta, Commbattant de la Foi*. Dakar, Abidjan: Nouvelles Editions Africaines, 1974.

Eickelman, Dale F., *Knowledge and Power in Morocco : The Education of a Twentieth-Century Notable*. Princeton University Press, 1985.

El Ghassem, Ould Ahmedou, *Enseignement traditionnel en Mauritanie. La mahadra ou l'école 'à dos de chameau'*. Paris: L'Harmattan, 1997.

Elleli Ag Ahar, 'L'Initiation d'un *ashamur*', *REMMM*, no. 57 (1990), *Touaregs, exil et résistance*, pp. 141-52.

'L'Enseignement en République du Mali (Dix ans après la réforme de 1962)', Contact Spécial, *Bulletin Pédagogique*, no. 4. 1973.

Erny, P., 'Ecoles d'églises en Afrique noire. Poids du passé et perspectives d'avenir', *Nouvelles revue de science missionaire*, 1982.

Facheux, François, 'Rôle de l'école dans la structuration sociale du Mali', *Cahiers Internationaux de Sociologie*, LXIII (1977), pp. 315-40.

Fay, Claude. 'La démocratie au Mali, ou le pouvoir en pâture', *Cahiers d'Études africaines*, 137, XXXV-1, (1995), pp. 19-53.

Feierman, Steven, *Peasant Intellectuals: Anthropology and History in Tanzania*. Madison: University of Wisconsin Press, 1990.

——, 'Struggles for Control: The Social Roots of Health and Healing in Modern Africa', *African Studies Review*, vol. 28, no. 2/3, 1985, pp. 73-147.

Foltz, William, J., *From French West Africa to the Mali Federation*. New Haven, CT: Yale University Press, 1965.

François, Pierre, 'Class Struggles in Mali', *Review of African Political Economy*, no. 24 (1982), pp. 22-38.

Froelich, Jean-Claude, *Les musulmans d'Afrique noire*. Paris: Editions de l'Orante, 1962.

——, 'Le réformisme de l'Islam en Afrique noire de l'Ouest', *Revue de Défense Nationale* (Paris), Jan. 1961, pp. 77-91.

Foucault, Michel., *The Archaeology of Knowledge*. Translated from the French by A.M. Sheridan Smith, London: Tavistock, 1986.

——, *Discipline and Punish: The Birth of the Prison*. London: Penguin Books, 1991.

Garcia, Sylvianne, 'Al-Hajj Seydou Nourou Tall, 'grand marabout' tijani: l'histoire d'une carrière (v. 1880-1980)' in D. Robinson and J.-L. Triaud (eds), *Le temps des marabouts*, pp. 247-75.

Gardinier, David E., 'The French Impact on Education in Africa, 1817-1960' in G. Wesley Johnson (ed.), *Double Impact: France and Africa in the Age of Imperialism*. Westport, CT: Greenwood Press, 1985, pp. 333-44.

Gast, Marceau, 'L'école nomade au Hoggar. Une drôle histoire', REMMM, no. 57 (1990), pp. 99-111.

Geertz, C., *Local Knowledge: Further Essays in Interpretive Anthropology*. New York: Basic Books, 1983.

Gérard, Etienne, 'Entre Etat et populations. L'école et l'éducation en devenir', *Politique Africaine*, no. 47 (Oct. 1992), pp. 59-69.

——, *La tentation du savoir en Afrique. Politiques, mythes et stratégies d'éducation au Mali*. Paris: Karthala/ORSTOM, 1997.

Gomez-Perez, Muriel, 'Associations islamiques à Dakar', *ISASS*, no. 5 (1991), pp. 5-19.

Graham, W.A., 'Qur'an as Spoken Word: An Islamic Contribution to the Understanding of Scripture' in R.C. Martin (ed.), *Approaches to Islam in Religious*

Studies. Tucson: University of Arizona Press, 1985.

Gresh, A., 'L'Arabie saoudite en Afrique non-arabe', *Politique Africaine*, no. 10 (1983), pp. 55-74.

Griaule, Marcel., *Conversations with Ogotemmêli: An Introduction to Dogon Religious Ideas.* Oxford University Press, 1965.

Guedj, Pierre, 'Lè système éducatif malien. Sa structure et ses principes de base à travers l'analyse de la réforme de l'éducation et de ses prolongements', *Etudes et Documents* (Ecole Nationale d'Administration, Bamako), no. 4, April 1986, pp. 1-17.

Hamès, Constant, 'Deux aspects du fondamentalisme islamique. Sa significa-tion au Mali actuel et chez Ibn Taimîya', *Archives en Sciences Sociales des Religions*, 50/2 (Oct.-Dec. 1980), pp. 177-90.

——, 'L'enseignement islamique en Afrique de l'ouest (Mauritanie)' in N. Grandin and M. Gaborieau (eds), *Madrasa. La transmission du savoir dans le monde musulman.* Paris: Editions Arguments, 1997, pp. 219-28.

Harrison, Christopher, *France and Islam in West Africa, 1860-1960.* Cambridge University Press, 1988.

Hawad, 'La *teshumara* antidote de l'Etat', *REMMM*, no. 57 (1990), *Touaregs, exil et résistance*, pp. 123-38.

Hiskett, M., 'The "Community of Grace" and its opponents, the "Rejecters": A Debate about Theology and Mysticism in Muslim West Africa with spe-cial Reference to its Hausa Expression', *African Language Studies* (London), XVII, 1980, pp. 99-140.

——, 'Problems of Religious Education in Muslim Communities in Africa', *Oversea Education*, 32, no. 3 (1960), pp. 117-26.

Hodgkin, Elizabeth. 'Islamism and Islamic Research in Africa', *ISASS*, no. 4 (1990), pp. 73-130.

Hodgkin, T., and R.S. Morgenthau, 'Mali' in J.S. Coleman and C.G. Rosberg (eds), *Political Parties and National Integration in Tropical Africa.* Berkeley: University of California Press, 1964.

Hopkins, Nicholas S., *Popular Government in an African Town: Kita, Mali.* Uni-versity of Chicago Press, 1972.

Hountondji, P.J., *African Philosophy: Myth and Reality.* London: Hutchinson, 1983.

——, *Les Savoirs endogènes. Pistes pour une recherche.* Dakar: CODESRIA, 1994.

Hunwick, J.O. 'Secular Power and Religious Authority in Muslim Society: The Case of Songhay', *Journal of African History*, 37 (1996), pp. 175-94.

Hyden, Göran, *No Shortcuts to Progress: African Development Management in Per-spective.* London: Heinemann, 1983.

ISESCO. *Ifrīqiyya wa'l-thaqāfat al-'arabiyyat al-islāmiyya* (Africa and Arabo-Islamic Culture). Rabat: ISESCO, 1987.

Jah, Dauda Muhammad al-Amin, *Hayāt al-Ḥājj Saiku 'Umar Bachīlī 1928-1981.* Bamako, issued privately, no date.

Joly, Vincent, 'Sources concernant l'Islam et la politique musulmane au Mali',

ISASS, no. 2 (1988), pp. 193-202.

Kaba, L., 'Cheikh Mouhammad Chérif de Kankan. Le devoir d'obéissance et la colonisation (1923-1955)' in D. Robinson and J.L. Triaud (eds), *Le temps des marabouts*, pp. 277-97.

——, 'The Politics of Quranic Education among Muslim Traders in the Western Sudan, the Subbanu Experience', *Canadian Journal of African Studies*, X, no. 3 (1976), pp. 409-21.

——, *The Wahhabiya. Islamic Reform and Politics in French West Africa*. Evanston, IL: Northwestern University Press, 1974.

Kabou, Axelle, *Et si l'Afrique refusait le développement?* Paris: L'Harmattan, 1991.

Kane, Mouhamed Moustapha. 'La vie et l'oeuvre d'el-Hadjj Mahmoud Ba Diowol (1905-1978). Du pâtre au patron de la 'Révolution al-Falah" in D. Robinson and J.-L. Triaud (eds), *Le temps des marabouts*, pp. 431-65.

Kane, Oumar., 'L'enseignement islamique dans les médersas du Mali' in Sanankoua and Brenner (eds), *L'enseignement islamique au Mali*, Bamako: Editions Jamana, 1991, pp. 87-104.

Kane, Ousmane, 'Muslim Missionaries and African States' in S.H. Rudolph and J. Piscatori (eds), *Transnational Religion and Fading States*. Boulder, CO: Westview Press, 1997.

Kassibo, Bréhima, 'La géomancie ouest-africaine. Formes endogènes et emprunts extérieurs', *Cahiers d'études africaines*, XXXII (4), no. 128 (1992), pp. 541-96.

Khayar, I.H., *Le refus de l'école. Contribution à l'étude des problèmes de l'éducation chez les musulmans du Ouaddaï (Tchad)*. Paris: Maisonneuve et Larose, 1976.

Konaré, Alpha Oumar, *Les Constitutions du Mali*. Bamako, no date (1985?).

Konaté, Moussa, *Mali. Ils ont assassiné l'espoir*. Paris: L'Harmattan, 1990.

Laitin, David D., *Hegemony and Culture: Politics and Religious Change among the Yoruba*. University of Chicago Press, 1986.

Last, Murray, 'The Power of Youth, Youth of Power: notes on the religions of the young in northern Nigeria' in H. d'Almeida-Topor *et al.* (eds), *Les Jeunes en Afrique*, II, pp. 375-99.

Launay, Robert, *Beyond the Stream: Islam and Society in a West African Town*. Berkeley: University of California Press, 1992.

——, *Traders without Trade: Responses to Change in two Dyula Communities*. Cambridge University Press, 1982.

Le Chatelier, A., *L'Islam dans l'Afrique occidentale*. Paris: G. Steinheil, 1899.

Lavers, J.E., 'Diversions on a Journey, or the Travels of Shaykh Ahmad al-Yamani (1630-1712) from Halfaya to Fez' in Y.F. Hasan and P. Doornbos (eds), *The Central Bilad al-Sudan, Tradition and Adaptation*. Khartoum, no date.

Levtzion, N., *Muslims and Chiefs in West Africa*. Oxford: Clarendon Press, 1968.

——, 'Islam in West African Politics: Accommodation and Tension between the *'ulamâ* and the Political Authorities', *Cahiers d'Etudes Africaines*, 71, XVIII, 3, 1979.

—— and J. Voll (eds), *Eighteenth Century Renewal and Reform Movements in Islam.* Syracuse University Press, 1987.

Loimeier, Roman, *Islamic Reform and Political Change in Northern Nigeria.* Evanston, IL: Northwestern University Press, 1997.

Loum, Souleymane. 'Radioscopie d'un enseignement importé et mal adapté', *PopSahel,* Bulletin du CERPOD, Bamako, no. 15 (Dec. 1990), pp. 10-14.

Ly, Oumar T., 'La structuration du concept de "jeunesse" dans le discours de l'Union Soudanaise du RDA (1947-1962)' in H. d'Almeida-Topor *et al.* (eds), *Les Jeunes en Afrique,* II, pp. 85-99.

Ly-Tall, Madina., *Un Islam militant en Afrique de l'ouest au XIX siècle. La Tijaniyya de Saïku Umar Futiyu contre les Pouvoirs traditionnels et la Puissance coloniale.* Paris: L'Harmattan, 1991.

Mahibou, S.M, and J.-L. Triaud, *Voilà ce qui est arrivé. Bayân mâ waqa'a d'al-Hâgg 'Umar al-Fûtî. Plaidoyer pour une guerre sainte en Afrique de l'Ouest.* Paris: CNRS, 1983.

Mallé, Boubacar N., *Les Gouvernements de la République du Mali, de l'indépendance à nos jours.* Bamako: Editions Imprimerie du Mali, 1992.

Mama, Baba, 'La médersa de Tombouctou' in *Culture et Civilisation Islamiques, Le Mali.* Rabat: ISESCO, 1988, pp. 146-8.

Manley, Andrew, 'The Sosso and the Haidara: Two Muslim lineages in Soudan français, 1890-1960' in D. Robinson and J.-L. Triaud (eds), *Le temps des marabouts,* pp. 319-36.

Marty, Paul, *Etudes sur l'Islam au Sénégal.* Paris: Ernest Leroux, 1917.

——, *Etudes sur l'Islam et les tribus du Soudan,* vol. I: *Les Kounta de l'Est-les Berabichles Iguellad.* Paris: E. Leroux, 1920.

Mauny, R., 'Notes archéologiques au sujet de Gao', *Bulletin d'IFAN,* series B, XIII (no. 3, July 1951), pp. 839–52.

Mbembe, Achille, *Afriques indociles. Christianisme, pouvoir et Etat en société postcoloniale.* Paris: Karthala, 1988.

——, 'Provisional Notes on the Postcolony', *Africa,* 62 (1), 1992, pp. 3-37.

Mbembe, J.A., *Les jeunes et l'ordre politique en Afrique noire.* Paris: L'Harmattan, 1985.

Meillassoux, C., *Urbanization of an African Community: Voluntary Associations in Bamako.* Seattle: University of Washington Press, 1968.

——, 'A class analysis of the bureaucratic process in Mali', *Journal of Development Studies,* VI, 2 (1970), pp. 97-110.

Mommersteeg, G., 'L'éducation coranique au Mali: le pouvoir des mots sacrés', in Sanankoua et Brenner (eds), *L'enseignement islamique au Mali.* Bamako: Editions Jamana, 1991, pp. 45-61.

——, '"He has smitten her to the heart with love": The Fabrication of an Islamic Love-amulet in West Africa', *Anthropos,* 83 no. 4/6 (1988), pp. 501-10.

Monteil, Ch., *Les Bambara du Ségou et du Kaarta.* Paris: Maisonneuve et Larose, 1977.

Monteil, Vincent, *L'Islam noir,* 3rd edn. Paris: Editions du Seuil, 1980.

Morgenthau, Ruth, *Political Parties in French-Speaking West Africa.* Oxford: Clarendon Press, 1964.

Mudimbe, V.Y., *The Idea of Africa.* Bloomington: Indiana University Press, 1994.

——, *The Invention of Africa: Gnosis, Philosophy, and the Order of Knowledge.* Bloomington: Indiana University Press, 1988.

Mulder, D.C., 'The Ritual of the Recitation of the Qur'an', *Nederlands Theologisch Tijdschrift*, 37, no. 2 (1983).

N'Diaye, Bokar, *Les castes au Mali.* Bamako: Editions Populaires, 1970.

N'Diaye, Issa. 'Etre bamanan et musulman', *Jamana*, no. 27 (July-Dec. 1990), pp. 27-30.

Ndiaye, Mamadou, *L'enseignement arabo-islamique au Sénégal.* Istanbul: Centre de Recherches sur l'Histoire, l'Art et la Culture Islamiques, 1985.

Nicolas, Guy, *Dynamique de l'islam au sud du Sahara.* Paris: Publications Orientalistes de France, 1981.

Niezen, Ronald W., 'The "Community of Helpers of the Sunna": Islamic Reform among the Songhay of Gao (Mali)', *Africa*, 60 (3), 1990, pp. 399-423.

——, 'Hot Literacy in Cold Societies: A Comparative Study of the Sacred Value of Writing', *Comparative Studies in Society and History*, vol. 33, no. 2 (April 1991), pp. 225-54.

Niang, Mody, 'L'état doit organiser l'effort national en faveur de l'éducation', *PopSahel*, Bulletin du CERPOD, Bamako, no. 15 (Dec. 1990), pp. 15-20.

Norris, H.T., *Sufi Mystics of the Niger Desert: Sidi Mahmud and the Hermits of Air.* Oxford: Clarendon Press, 1990.

Olivier de Sardan, Jean-Pierre, *Les sociétés songhay-zarma (Niger-Mali). Chefs, guerriers, esclaves, paysans...* Paris: Karthala, 1984.

Otayek, René, *Le radicalisme islamique au sud du Sahara: Da'wa, arabisation et critique de l'Occident.* Paris: Karthala, 1993.

Ould Cheikh, Abdel Wedoud, 'La tribu comme volonté et comme représentation. Le facteur religieux dans l'organisation d'une tribu maure, les Awlâd Abyayri' in P. Bonte *et al.*, *Al-Ansâb. La Quête des origines. Anthropologie historique de la société arabe.* Paris: Editions de la Maison des Sciences de l'Homme, 1991, pp. 201-38.

——, 'La tribu dans tous ses états', *al-Wasit* (Nouakchott), no. 1 (1987), pp. 89-98.

——, *Éléments d'histoire de la Mauritanie.* Nouakchott: Institut Mauritanien de la Recherche Scientifique et le Centre Culturel Français, 1988.

Person, Yves, *Samori. Une révolution Dyula*, vols 1-3, Dakar: IFAN, 1968-75.

Ranger, T.O., 'The Invention of Tradition in Colonial Africa' in E. Hobsbawm and T. Ranger (eds), *The Invention of Tradition.* Cambridge University Press, 1983).

Reichmuth, Stefan, 'Education and the Growth of Religious Associations among Yoruba Muslims – the Ansar-Ud-Deen Society of Nigeria', *Journal of Religion in Africa*, XXVI, 4 (Nov. 1996), pp. 365-405.

——, 'A Regional Centre of Islamic Learning in Nigeria: Ilorin and its Influence on Yoruba Islam' in N. Grandin and M. Gaborieau (eds), *Madrasa. La transmission du savoir dans le monde musulman*. Paris: Editions Arguments, 1997, pp. 229-45.

——, *Islamische Bildung und soziale Integration in Ilorin (Nigeria) seit ca. 1800*. Münster: LIT Verlag, 1998.

Robinson, David, *Chiefs and Clerics: The History of Abdul Bokar Kan and Futa Toro, 1853-1891*. Oxford: Clarendon Press, 1975.

——, *The Holy War of Umar Tal: The Western Sudan in the Mid-Nineteenth Century*. Oxford: Clarendon Press, 1985.

Robinson, David, and J.-L. Triaud (eds), *Le temps des marabouts. Itinéraires et stratégies islamiques en Afrique Occidentale Française, ca. 1880-1960*. Paris: Karthala, 1997.

Ryan, Patrick, *Imale: Yoruba Participation in the Muslim Tradition: A Study of Clerical Piety*. Missoula, Mont: Scholars Press, 1978.

Saad, Elias N., *Social History of Timbuktu: the Role of Muslim Scholars and Notables, 1400-1900*. Cambridge University Press, 1983.

Salvaing, Bernard., 'Les jeunes et le développement des médersas au Fouta-Djalon face à la culture traditionnelle' in H. d'Almeida-Topor *et al.* (eds), *Les Jeunes en Afrique*, II, pp. 430-42.

Sanankoua, Bintou, 'Les associations féminines musulmanes à Bamako' in Sanankoua et Brenner (eds), *L'enseignement islamique au Mali*. Bamako: Editions Jamana, 1991. 105-25.

——, 'Les Ecoles "coraniques" au Mali. Problèmes actuels', *Canadian Journal of African Studies*, XIX, no. 2, (1985), pp. 359-67.

——, *Un empire peul au xixe siècle. La Diina du Maasina*. Paris, Karthala, 1990.

——, 'L'enseignement islamique à la radio et à la télévision au Mali' in Sanankoua et Brenner (eds), *L'enseignement islamique au Mali*. Bamako: Editions Jamana, 1991, pp. 127-41.

—— and Louis Brenner (eds). *L'enseignement islamique au Mali*. Bamako: Editions Jamana, 1991.

Sanneh, Lamin, 'The Islamic Education of an African Child: Stresses and Tensions' in G.N. Brown and M. Hiskett (eds), *Conflict and Harmony in Education in Tropical Africa*, London: Geo. Allen & Unwin, 1975.

——, *The Crown and the Turban: Muslims and West African Pluralism*. Boulder, CO: Westview Press, 1997.

——, *The Jakhanke Muslim Clerics: A Religious and Historical Study of Islam in Senegambia*, University Press of America, 1989.

Santerre, R., *Pédagogie musulmane d'Afrique noire*. Montréal: Les Presses de l'Université de Montréal, 1973.

——, (ed.), *La quête du savoir. Essais pour une anthropologie de l'éducation camerounaise*. Montréal: Les Presses de l'Université de Montréal, 1982.

Saul, M., 'The Quranic School Farm and Child Labour in Upper Volta', *Africa*, 54, no. 2 (1984), pp. 71-87.

Schmitz, Jean., 'Autour d'al-Hajj Umar Taal, Guerre sainte et Tijaniyya en Afrique de l'Ouest', *Cahiers d'Etudes Africaines*, 100, XXV-4, (1985), pp. 555-65.

——, 'L'Etat géomètre. Les *leydi* des Peul du Fuuta Tooro (Sénégal) et du Maasina (Mali)', *Cahiers d'Etudes Africaines*, 103, XXVI-3, (1986), pp. 349-94.

——, 'Un politologue chez les marabouts', *Cahiers d'Etudes Africaines*, 91, XXIII-3, (1983), pp. 329-51.

Skinner, D.E., 'Islam and education in the colony and hinterland of Sierra Leone (1750-1914)', *Canadian Journal of African Studies*, X, no. 3 (1976), pp. 499-520.

Snyder, F.G., *One-Party Government in Mali*. New Haven, CT: Yale University Press, 1965.

Soares, Benjamin F., 'A Contemporary Malian Shaykh: al-Hajj Shaykh Sidy Modibo Kane Diallo, the Religious Leader of Dilly', *ISASS*, no. 10 (1996), pp. 145-53.

Sow, I., 'L'apprentissage de la numération chez les Malinké de la région de Kita', *Jamana. Revue culturelle malienne*, no. 12 (March-April 1987), pp. 38-41.

Stewart, C.C., with E.K. Stewart, *Islam and Social Order in Mauritania: A Case Study from the Nineteenth Century*. Oxford: Clarendon Press, 1968.

Stoler, Laura Ann, *Race and the Education of Desire*. Durham, NC: Duke University Press, 1995.

——, 'Rethinking colonial categories', *Comparative Studies in Society and History*, 31 (1989), pp. 134-61.

Sylla, 'Abd al-Qadir, *Al-Muslimūn fī 'l-Sinighāl, ma'ālim al-hādir wa āfāq al-mustaqbal* (The Muslims of Senegal, contemporary characteristics and future horizons). Qatar: al-Wahda, 1986.

Tamari, Tal, *Les castes de l'Afrique occidentale. Artisans et musiciens endogames*. Nanterre: Société d'Ethnologie, 1997.

Tamari, Tal. 'The Development of Caste Systems in West Africa', *Journal of African History*, 32 (1991), pp. 221-50.

Tempels, P., *Bantu Philosophy*. Paris: Présence Africaine, 1969.

Tounkara, Bréhima, 'L'offre d'éducation perturbée par les variables démographiques', *PopSahel*, Bulletin du CERPOD, Bamako, no. 15 (Dec. 1990), pp. 29-34.

Touré, Cheikh, *Afin que tu deviennes un croyant*. Dakar: Imprimerie Diop, 1957.

Touré, Saada Oumar, *al-Adwā' al-sāfiyya 'alā al-awrād al-Tijāniyya*. Tunis, 1997.

——, *Ahkām al-salāt wa'l-tahāra 'alā madhhab al-sāda al-Mālikiyya*, with French translation: *La prière musulmane, rite malékite*. Tunis, 1972.

——, *Ahkām saum shahr Ramadān 'alā madhhab al-sāda al-Mālikiyya*, with French translation: *Règlements religieux du jeûne du mois de Ramadhan (Rite Malékite)*. Tunis, 1961.

——, *Dhikr Allāh ta'ālā*, with French translation: *Les invocations*. Tunis, no date.

——, *al-Durūs al-nahwiyya li'l-madāris al-ibtidā'iyya*. 2 parts, Tunis, no date.

——, *L'église actuelle, est-elle chrétienne ou Paulinienne?* No publisher, 1981.

——, *Ḥaqīqat al-muḥdathāt wa'l-bida' wa-mā laysa minhā fī'l-shar'*. Tunis, 1988.

——, *'L'Islam et ses détracteurs'*, unpubl. ms., completed 6 Dec. 1965.

——, *al-La'ālī wa'l-durar fī'l-ādāb wa'l-maḥāsin al-ghurar*, with French translation: *Perles précieuses de l'éducation islamique*. Tunis, no date.

—— *al-Mabādi' al-ṣarfiyya li'l-madāris al-ibtidā'iyya*, 2 parts. Tunis, 1974.

——, *Mahomet – sa mission*. Bamako, no date.

——, *Sauvegarde des élèves des medersahs des étudiants et toute notre jeunesse musulmane contre les tentatives de dévoiement des hommes des églises chrétiennes*. Casablanca, 1993.

——, *al-Tawḍīḥāt al-basīṭa 'alā 'l-manẓūma al-Bayqūniyya*. Casablanca, 1989.

——, *al-Tuḥfa bi-mā yajūzu wa-yaḥrumu min at-tadāwī wa'l-ta'awwudh wa'l-ruqya* (The Gift about what is lawful and unlawful as regards medication, talismans and charms). Tunis, 1987.

Traoré, Alioune, *Cheikh Hamahoullah, homme de foi et résistant*. Paris: Maisonneuve et Larose, 1983.

Triaud, Jean-Louis, 'Abd al-Rahman l'Africain (1908-1957), pionnier et précurseur du wahhabisme au Mali' in O. Carré et P. Dumont (eds), *Radicalismes islamiques*, vol. II. Paris: L'Harmattan, 1986.

—— after Fodé Doumbia, 'Bamako, la ville aux deux cents mosquées, ou la victoire du 'secteur informel' islamique', *ISASS*, no. 2 (1988), pp. 166-77.

——, 'Le Crépuscule des "Affaires Musulmanes" en A.O.F. (1950-1956)' in D. Robinson and J.-L. Triaud (eds), *Le temps des marabouts*, pp. 493-519.

——, 'L'Islam en Afrique de L'Ouest: Problèmes de lecture historique', communication to the Colloque de la Société pour l'Avancement des Etudes Islamiques, Collège de France, 27-28 Mar. 1981.

——, 'Le mouvement réformiste en Afrique de l'Ouest dans les années 50', in *Sociétés africaines, monde arabe et culture islamique. Mémoires du CERMAA*, no. 1, 1981, pp. 207-24.

Tripp, Charles, 'Islam and the Secular Logic of the State in the Middle East' in A.S. Sidahmed and A. Ehteshami (eds), *Islamic Fundamentalism*. Boulder, CO: Westview Press, 1996. Pp. 51-69.

'Umar b. Sa'īd al-Fūtī, *Rimāḥ al-raḥīm 'alā nuḥūr ḥizb al-rajīm*, published in the margins of 'Alī Harāzim, *Jawāhir al-Ma'ānī*. Beirut, no date.

Vansina, Jan., *Paths in the Rainforest: Toward a History of Political Tradition in Equatorial Africa*. Madison: University of Wisconsin Press, 1990.

Villalon, Leonardo A., *Islamic Society and State Power in Senegal: Disciples and Citizens in Fatick*. Cambridge University Press, 1995.

Vuarin, Robert, 'L'enjeu de la misère pour l'Islam sénégalais', *Revue Tiers Monde*, XXXI, no. 123, July-Sept. 1990, pp. 601-21.

Wagner, D.A., 'Islamic Education: Traditional Pedagogy and Contemporary Aspects' in T. Husen and T. Neville Postlethwaite (eds), *International Encyclopedia of Education*, vol. 5. Oxford: Pergamon Press, 1985.

Warms, Richard L., 'Merchants, Muslims, and the Wahhabiyya: The Elaboration of Islamic Identity in Sikasso, Mali', *Canadian Journal of African Studies*, 26 (3), 1991, pp. 485-507.

Westerlund, David, and Eva Evers Rosander (eds), *African Islam and Islam in Africa: Encounters between Sufis and Islamists*. London: Hurst, 1997.

Wilks, I., 'The Transmission of Islamic Learning in the Western Sudan' in J. Goody (ed.), *Literacy in Traditional Societies*. Cambridge University Press, 1968, pp. 162-97.

Willis, J.R., 'Reflections on the Diffusion of Islam in West Africa' in J.R. Willis (ed.), *Studies in West African Islamic History*, vol 1: *The Cultivators of Islam*. London: Frank Cass 1979.

Yansané, A.Y., 'The Impact of France on Education in West Africa' in G. Wesley Johnson (ed.), *Double Impact: France and Africa in the Age of Imperialism*. Westport, CT: Greenwood Press, 1985, pp. 345-62.

Yusif al-Khalifa Abu Bakr, 'The Development of Islamic Education in Africa', *Bulletin on Islam and Christian-Muslim Relations in Africa*, vol. 6, no. 4 (Oct. 1988), pp. 12-18.

Zouber, M.A., *Ahmad Baba de Tombouctou (1556-1627). Sa vie et son oeuvre*. Paris: Maisonneuve et Larose, 1977.

INDEX

333